Philosophy of Meaning

Volume I

Translated from French by DeepL, reviewed by the author

Cover image:
Walker Evans (American, 1903-1975)
Roadside Store Between Tuscaloosa and Greensboro, Alabama
1936
Gelatin silver print
19.4 x 24.4 cm
Getty Museum Collection
Digital image courtesy of Getty's Open Content Program
Public Domain

Philosophy of Meaning

Volume I

To live without philosophizing is in truth the same as keeping the eyes closed without attempting to open them.

René Descartes, *Principles of Philosophy*, letter-preface, 1644

Life without music is simply a mistake, a tiresome task, an exile.

Friedrich Nietzsche, *Letter to Peter Gast*, 15 January

Introduction

PHILOSOPHY IS AN ANTI-RELATIVISM — From the origins of human thought to the current crisis of rationality, the question of truth has been the central problem of philosophy and its regulating idea. From Greek antiquity onwards, philosophy has been built on the fundamental presupposition that the human mind is not only capable of progressively expanding its knowledge of natural phenomena, but also of deepening its understanding of the principles that make this knowledge possible. Sceptical and relativistic objections, although frequently used as a spur to philosophical thought — from Socrates '*I know that I know nothing*' to Cartesian doubt — were not then established as paradigms. Despite the sometimes-heated controversies, the history of thought, up until the Enlightenment, offered a broad picture of a progression of ideas towards greater precision and clarity. While it is true that powers and claims of reason were challenged, sometimes radically, in a number of philosophical disputes, until the turn of the nineteenth century this challenge appeared to be a minority, not to say anecdotal. The nineteenth century, which was the century of many contradictions, beginning with Chateaubriand and ending at the dawn of the brutal outburst of the Great War, was also the century which, in the wake of the theoretical successes of the late eighteenth century, made the practical successes of science visible. The second industrial revolution, which established the new civilisation of rail, iron and then steel, brought profound and lasting changes to Western societies, creating new ways of life and overturning the balance of power. Carried along by the pragmatic ideas of modern science, the spirit of progress blew with such intensity that it ended up undermining the theoretical framework from which it had emerged: the old philosophy was consigned to the archives of history alongside theology and metaphysics, so that philosophers ended up saying, as if to absolve themselves of a burden that had ended up weighing too heavily on their shoulders: "the rest of us have nothing more to do with the idea of *truth*". And how, indeed, in the atmosphere of the late nineteenth century, saturated with the fumes of industry and progress, could one survive as a philosopher? Did you have to be so naive as to believe that you could still claim to be searching for the Beautiful, the Good, the True? Didn't the disillusioned philosopher have to show that he was taking note of the advances in science and immediately renouncing all his old fantasies?

From the middle of the nineteenth century until the 1930s, a large part of philosophy was involved in a movement to align itself with the epistemic model of science. Scientism, positivism, historical materialism, radical materialism, physicalism, structuralism and reductionism were all attempts to bring philosophical reflection into line with the methodological imperatives and validation methods of the sciences. From then on, the philosopher's claim to unveil the inner workings of things and to grasp their ultimate causes was delegitimised: his task was reduced to analysing the structures, regularities and formal conditions of knowledge, from a perspective in which the quest for a founding principle gave way to the immanent explanation of phenomena. At most, like the scientist, he was left with the possibility of extracting a few islands of truth — these second truths that we cautiously call 'results'. But the primary question, the one that conditions all philosophical endeavour, namely the very possibility of understanding and expressing the world, had itself dissolved, as if struck down by obsolescence. The disappearance of the horizon of truth profoundly transformed the philosopher. What could he expect from a world the knife of evidence? Caught between the scientist, the ideologue and the simpleton, and forced to choose between the chronicle of deconstruction and ideological trans-mutation, the philosopher experienced the inexorable thinning of his field, so that he soon found himself faced with a terrible question for any man who aspires to the search for truth: is philosophy dead

If the question of the death of philosophy was correlated with the inexorable advance the pragmatic spirit that animated modern science, it was also contemporary with an internal debate within philosophy that was largely provoked by the reception of Nietzsche's work in Europe at the end of the nineteenth and beginning of the twentieth centuries. By putting the old idea of truth on trial[1], Nietzsche's philosophy was in effect the starting point for a new branch of continental European philosophy which, turning for the most part against the spirit of the Enlightenment and Kant's philosophy, would end up annexing the problem of truth to the question of values

---

[1] On this subject, see Éric Blondel, *Les guillemets de Nietzsche : philologie et généalogie in Nietzsche aujourd'hui ?*

(truth becoming a "value like any other[2]"). Whereas Nietzsche had been the architect of the dynamiting of the theological roots of philosophy, he paradoxically became the inspirer of a new theology without roots that animated much of twentieth-century Western philosophy. The destruction of the rationalist tradition and the radical questioning of the idea of truth were taken "literally", so to speak, by many of Nietzsche's successors, who thought of history as written. In short, Nietzsche's anti-idealistic prophecy had the value of a decree: the thread of the philosophical tradition had been broken, and this had to be acknowledged, but was Nietzsche right in announcing the destruction of the old philosophy of knowledge.

In reality, the question of truth was not settled by Nietzsche or his heirs, firstly because a negative settlement of the question could only be achieved at the price of a logical reversal that Nietzsche always refused to consider — the assertion that there is no such thing as truth, if it claims to be valid, contradicts itself insofar as it creates a particular truth while denying the general possibility of truth[3] — then because Nietzsche was careful not to confront rational philosophy with the arguments of rationalism, often preferring the accommodating polysemy of the aphorism to the

---

[2] See Geoffroy de Clisson, *Les Anti-humanistes ou l'avènement des Contre-Lumières*.

[3] What are we to make of Nietzsche's assertion that "there is no truth"? Either it is true and contradicts itself, since there is at least one true assertion (the one asserting that there is no truth), or it is false and truth exists.

rigour of logical demonstration[4]. This is why we, who are Nietzsche's successors, are not his trustees (we are not bound by any inheritance). It is therefore up to us to ask ourselves the questions that run through his work, and not to consider them irrevocably settled until we have revisited the difficulties and reassessed the promises. What is a thing? What is being? What can I say about the world? The philosopher is like the child, never completely satisfied with a provisional answer. By endlessly repeating "why?", they seek to get as close as possible to things, to understand their workings and connections. But how precisely can we grasp and say something about the world? How can we find the *harmony* between our discourse on things and the things themselves? On the survival of this question undoubtedly depends the survival of philosophy and probably also that of science itself.

When the vast majority of modern scientists adopted the materialist point of view as a method and then as a doctrine, thought they had rid themselves of epistemological questions. But it was the emergence of a new *anti-materialist* paradigm that finally detached science from the fundamental questions it had traditionally set out to answer. It was in October 1927, at the famous Solvay annual congress attended by twenty-nine leading scientists — seventeen of whom were or were to become Nobel Prize winners in physics — that the major ideological turning point in the epistemology of science in the twentieth century took place. The representatives of the Copenhagen school

---

[4] "What needs to be demonstrated in order to be believed is not worth much", wrote Nietzsche in *Twilight of the Idols*.

(Niels Bohr and Werner Heisenberg in particular), advocates of a probabilistic quantum mechanics that made a profound break with the principles of classical physics, opposed the supporters of the deterministic theory to which Albert Einstein, Erwin Schrödinger, Louis de Broglie and Paul Dirac in particular continued to adhere. A long controversy ensued between Niels Bohr and Albert Einstein which, despite the theoretical successes that vindicated Bohr on the non-local nature of quantum mechanics, has still not been definitively resolved. The principle of complementarity that Niels Bohr set out publicly for the first time at the International Congress of Physics held in Como on 16 September 1927 — just a few weeks before the Solvay Congress — was at the origin of a separation of modern physics into two branches made up, on the one hand, of those who, with Einstein, On the other hand, there were those who, in the wake of Bohr, considered that the theoretical impasses of quantum mechanics could not be overcome within the epistemological framework of classical physics. In the 1920s and 1930s in particular, Nils Bohr's principle of complementarity was the subject of numerous developments, deepenings and extensions, both from the point of view of understanding science and from the perspective of the philosophy of knowledge that Bohr attempted to sketch out from his initial idea[5]. Nils Bohr originally came up with the idea of complementarity in an attempt to provide an answer to the seemingly insurmountable contradictions raised by the early

---

[5] See Bernadette Bensaude-Vincent, *L'évolution du principe de complémentarité dans les textes de Bohr (1927-1939)*, in *Revue d'histoire des sciences*, 1985, pp. 231-250.

developments of quantum theory. The apparently dual nature of matter, both wave and particle, and the problem of indeterminacy, whereby it is impossible to know simultaneously the position and the momentum of a single particle — which Heisenberg theorised under the name of the "uncertainty principle" — plunged physicists into epistemological questions that seemed inextricable. Rather than give in to the idea, defended in particular by Einstein, that quantum mechanics did not offer a complete description of reality, Nils Bohr argued that there had to be several necessary descriptions of the same phenomenon, that pairs of mutually exclusive descriptions could be applied simultaneously, without any of the isolated descriptions being sufficient to give an exhaustive description of the phenomenon in question (an exhaustive description in the classical sense being, therefore, impossible). The idea of complementarity was a response to this threefold observation: the quantum description of a phenomenon, although contradictory to the classical description, was in fact "irreducibly" complementary to it. The quantum description of the phenomenon was no longer in direct contradiction with classical physics, and the change of scale justified the paradigm shift. In Bohr's approach, however, we must not overlook the significance of the problem of indeterminacy, which is itself closely linked to the more fundamental problem of measurement. Whereas, in classical physics, the question of measurement remained secondary, on the atomic scale it became of decisive importance. Since the measurement of any phenomenon can only be envisaged in terms of its interaction with that phenomenon, it was only to be expected that the observer would have to play a gradually disruptive role as he approached the atomic scale. Whereas in classical physics the experimenter was always dealing with the measurement of an organised system, on the quantum mechanical scale the physicist was confronted with the individuality[6] of atomic phenomena, an individuality inevitably disturbed by the duality introduced by the very idea of measurement. It was therefore necessary to give up the Sirius point of view that the classical physicist thought he could have on things and to integrate the observer (the measuring instrument) into the very heart of quantum theory. In short, on the scale of atomic observation, the old philosophical problem of the separation between subject and object, and the question of their respective delimitation in the definition and description of phenomena, reappeared. At the atomic level, however, the separation was no longer a problem for theorists but called into question the very idea of experiment and experimentation. Bohr's solution was to reconcile two irreconcilable descriptions of reality in a modular and pragmatic approach to physical phenomena: at the level of organised systems of particles, classical epistemological principles continued to apply, whereas the description of quantum phenomena could rightly claim — in the name of complementarity — to be free from the space-time principles and causality that dominated classical physics (causality that the observer could no longer observe himself, his position as a disrupter condemning

---

[6] A notion that Bohr himself put forward in explaining his principle of complementarity.

him to become the decoder-interpreter of his own experiments[7].

Although Bohr continued to reflect on the relationship between classical epistemology and quantum physics for most of his life, it was mainly the pragmatic dimension of his approach that was adopted by the followers of the Copenhagen school. Following Bohr's remarks, scientists generally ended up turning away from epistemological questions and devoting themselves to developing descriptive theoretical models whose ambition was no longer to explain reality in the terms of classical physics[8]. From the 1940s onwards,

---

[7] The closer the physicist gets to the quantum scale, the more the results are deduced rather than observed. This deductive and interpretative approach becomes inevitable at the particle scale.

[8] In this they probably betrayed the ambition of Nils Bohr, who wrote in 1949: " The new progress in atomic physics was commented upon from various sides at the International Physical Congress held in September 1927, at Como in commemoration of Volta. In a lecture on that occasion, I advocated a point of view conveniently termed "complementarity," suited to embrace the characteristic features of individuality of quantum phenomena, and at the same time to clarify the peculiar aspects of the observational problem in this field of experience. For this purpose, it is decisive to recognise that, *however far the phenomena transcend the scope of classical physical explanation, the account of all evidence must be expressed in classical terms.* The argument is simply that by the word "experiment" we refer to a situation where we can tell others what we have done and what we have learned and that, therefore, the account of the experimental arrangement and of the results of the observations must be expressed in

quantum mechanics was increasingly seen as a theoretical formalism and less and less as an attempt to provide a rational explanation of phenomena. "If you think you understand quantum mechanics, you don't understand it", the physicist Richard Feynman, who was awarded the Nobel Prize for Physics in 1965, used to say in his university lectures: the modern theories of quantum physics were not intended to explain the world, but simply to make it work. The major difficulties caused by the unresolved contra-dictions between the theory of general relativity developed by Einstein — valid at the level of large ensembles, but inoperative at the atomic and subatomic levels — still bear witness to the epistemological rifts that opened up in the 1920s and never really closed. Modern science, no doubt carried away by the flow of its practical-theoretical development, increasingly neglected the study of its epistemological foundations: materialism itself had ended up in the epistemological dead ends of quantum indeterminism.

While many physicists were careful not to take a position on the question of the general coherence of quantum mechanics and its completeness — the majority leaning towards the completeness hypothesis — this was not entirely the case with biologists and neuroscientists, most of whom remained committed to the classical ideas of materialism (ideas that remained valid on their own scale). Here too, however, the problem of complementarity arose, albeit in very

---

unambiguous language with suitable application of the terminology of classical physics. in *Discussions with Einstein on Epistemological Problems in Atomic Physics*.

different terms. Already in the 1930s, Nils Bohr, reviving the positions taken by his father Christian Bohr, professor of physiology at the University of Copenhagen, saw in the debate between mechanism and finalism[9] a possible extension of his principle of complementarity. In Bohr's view, mechanism and finalism, fruitful though mutually exclusive scientific theories, could be seen as complementary. In biology, as in psychology, Bohr insisted on the limits of the purely mechanistic approach which, in attempting to reduce psychic or physical processes to the individuality of isolated particles, overlooked the individuality and integrity of the whole organism. In an interview he gave on 17 November 1962[10], shortly before his death, Bohr

---

[9] In biology, mechanism and finalism are two opposing explanatory frameworks. Mechanism considers that biological phenomena result solely from material and efficient causes, without intention or purpose. It is part of a physico-chemical approach in which organisms are analysed as systems governed by blind causal interactions (e.g. natural selection explains evolution without any underlying intention). Finalism, on the other hand, postulates that biological structures and functions tend towards an intrinsic finality, as if they were oriented towards a goal (e.g. the eye seems designed to see). In modern biology, finalism is generally rejected as a causal explanation, but certain concepts, such as teleonomy, make it possible to talk about apparent finality without resorting to an intentional principle.
[10] On 17 November 1962, shortly before his death, Niels Bohr gave an interview to Thomas S. Kuhn, Leon Rosenfeld, Aage Petersen and Erik Rudinger. This discussion was part of a series of interviews conducted between 31 October and 17 November 1962, as part of the *Archives for the History of*

revealed that the application of the principle of complementarity to psychology had been inspired by his reading, around 1905, of *The Principles of Psychology* by the pragmatist William James, in which James showed that it is impossible to break down consciousness into its component parts[11]. In the contemporary debate within the neurosciences, this problem of complementarity — or, at any rate, of the juxtaposition of two fertile positions that seem mutually irreconcilable — arose again through the questions linked to the emergence of consciousness: how, in short, can a mass of matter think, feel, speak... and claim to say something about the world? Neuroscientists assure us that this problem of emergence will soon be solved, so that materialism can find its ultimate justification in developments in the life sciences. But can we be sure of this? By promising us a solution in the near future to a problem that is thousands of years old[12], will neuroscientists not also believe — as philosophers once did — in the possibility of leaping over their own shadow? Will they not find, at the end of the road, the great questions that have driven philosophy since the origins of thought? And what will happen when, after so much wandering and trial and error, they think they have found that ultimate,

---

Quantum Physics. These interviews took place in Bohr's office at Carlsberg, Copenhagen, Denmark.

[11] *The Principles of Psychology*, "The stream of thougts", William James, 1896, quoted by Bernadette Bensaude-Vincent, *L'évolution du principe de complémentarité dans les textes de Bohr (1927-1939)*, in *Revue d'histoire des sciences*, 1985, p. 248.

[12] See in particular Stanislas Dehaene, *Consciousness and the Brain: Deciphering How the Brain Codes Our Thoughts*

foundational 'truth' whose possibility they began by denying[13]?

For man, the question of truth is neither a technical issue nor an appendix to philosophy. In fact, it goes far beyond the issue of the future of philosophy: it determines the way we relate to the world, the way we understand it and the way we act in it. It is a compass, a thread of Ariadne, for every man who asks questions about things, a thread that he strives to feel and follow through the specious twists and turns of ideologies, integral relativism, anti-rationalism and anti-science. Throughout the twentieth century, the century of modern wars, general violence and suspicion, the idea gradually took hold that the compass had been lost, that the thread had broken. We had to admit that "all points of view are equal", and that truth was a chimera. "*Let's leave it at that*", declared Jean-Luc Nancy in a lecture he gave at the Zurich University of Applied Sciences in 1980[14]. The *credo* of the twentieth century was that we should no longer bother ourselves with a question that

---

[13] The idea of materialism (a monistic system) by definition denies the idea of an absolute truth, as we shall see later.

[14] Jean-Luc Nancy, *Notre Probité* in *L'Impératif catégorique*, lecture given in January 1980 at the *Philosophische Fakultät* in Zurich: "We know that it is easy to try to 'nail' Nietzsche, who would only speak in the name of one more adequate truth, or rather of the always identical adequate truth.

We also know, as Heidegger has shown, that anyone who thinks he is telling the truth about Nietzsche in this way - in order to denounce him - is himself claiming the truth of his discourse on Nietzsche. Now, if he wants to take Nietzsche to task in the name of the proposition that truth is illusion, he in falls under the accusation, etc. So let's leave it at that.

belonged to the past, and that we should dig the bewitching furrow of irrationalism. It was thought at the time that the disaffection with the question of truth was the result of a long and irreversible evolutionary process, and that the entire history of philosophy tended towards this conclusion. Nothing could be further from the truth. Distrust of the idea of truth is not the result of a linear progression in the history of ideas. Doubt, struggle and confrontation have always existed and marked the cleavages in the history of thought. Plato against the Sophists, the Humanists against Scholasticism, the Enlightenment against the Anti-Enlightenment... Throughout history, ideas have always given rise to their own contradictions. In the field of thought, as elsewhere, we must be wary of the myth of linear progress.

Preliminary Note

In this book, I endeavour to show that the question of truth has not been definitively settled by the advent of modern science and materialist methodology — of which Darwinism was one of the manifestations and one of the resounding successes — that it cannot have been, and that it remains a central issue. It seems to me, however, that the proposition of putting the question of truth back on the table can only be admissible under certain conditions. First of all, I believe that any philosopher who claims to be doing serious work on the question of truth and the foundations of knowledge must not only have a good knowledge of the history of philosophy, but also, and perhaps above all, must have taken a close interest in the great scientific revolutions of the modern era, and especially in those that have revolutionised the twentieth century: the theory of relativity and quantum mechanics (which does not exclude the more recent discoveries and theories that are often linked to or derived from them). Of course, I don't claim to have covered all these issues (who could?), but at least I feel that I have grasped their main methodological and epistemological foundations. So, I have tried to provide some answers, or at least some contradiction. Secondly, it seemed to me that a 'new' form should be sought. Thus, I opted for a 'schematic' and 'visual' presentation of my ideas rather than a work that would have placed greater emphasis on logical argumentative sequences (although these sequences remain in the present work). I have favoured short paragraphs and aphorisms where I felt this was appropriate, and tried to put my thoughts into images where I felt this was relevant. This form seems to me to be in keeping with the basic idea that I want to defend here: truth is always conceived in the mode of *harmony*, agreement, correspondence and parallelism, and the deductive method of logic is merely a means of 'showing' it. Truth, as I shall try to show, is not grasped solely by the dryness of rational argument but manifests itself through several modes of relation to the object (visual, auditory, imaginative, sentimental...). Moreover, it seems to me that an overly mechanistic conception of reason has been the source of many misunderstandings throughout the history of philosophy. The form I am proposing here also argues, by way of parallelism, for a broadening of rationalism. I don't always intend to win people over with an argument that seeks to persuade, but rather to explain, to show, to make them feel where possible, without giving in to the facilities of didacticism. Finally, it seemed to me that the criticisms of materialism, including the most recent materialism (I'm thinking in particular of physicalism) which radicalises the positions of classical materialism with regard to the idea of truth, should be taken seriously. This is why the beginning of this book was conceived as a response to materialists, and in particular to physicalists and neo-Darwinists. The two fundamental criticisms that sceptical materialism makes of classical philosophy are, in my view, the following: firstly, there is nothing to indicate that there is anything other than matter, forces and particles that organise and structure reality. The idea of individuality therefore needs to be rethought in the light of the fact that the individual is merely an organisational unit made up of matter. Consequently, what we call will, freedom, ideas and truth are in turn nothing more than particular manifestations of an organisation of matter, this organisation being the result of a long evolutionary process governed by chance. Thus, where we think we see 'truths', there are in reality only chemical and mental processes which, through an exchange of matter, give us the illusion of absolute agreement, when in fact there are only chain reactions which mean nothing in and of themselves (circularity argument). The corollary of this argument is the idea that, secondly, man cannot claim to transcend the matter of which he is made (argument from finitude), insofar as, like any organism, animate or inanimate, he is totally reduced to it and cannot extricate himself from it to adopt a position of superiority. As Protagoras asserted more than two thousand years ago, it is itself the standard of what it claims to measure: "the measure of all things". While these criticisms are not entirely new in substance, they have the advantage of being radical (which sometimes brings a form of clarity). So, it seemed to me essential to consider them in all their depth and in all their implications. In a universe where there is nothing to indicate that it is not made up entirely of finite matter, how can we claim to be free from the circularity of our reasoning, our desires and our feelings? How can we even attach any meaning to the idea of truth and all the other ideas produced by our reason? If man is the measure of all things, then in order to answer these questions we must undoubtedly go back to the unit of organised matter we call man. In this attempt to return to the human being, we will look at what, since the origins of humanity, has perhaps been one of the keys to understanding man, as well as a fundamental question for philosophy and science: music. Although it may seem surprising to link the fate of truth to that of music, it was through music that the question of truth first came to mind. At first glance, music does not seem to be the most obvious route to the question of truth: it is non-figurative, designates or signifies nothing, corresponds to nothing and seems intimately linked to subjectivity, feeling and imagination. So, there is nothing here that would dispose me to pose the question of truth in a new way, all the more so since it was not my intention to recycle the old Nietzschean idea of aesthetic truth, freed from the concept of adequacy. Yet the study of music, of its mechanisms, without being reduced to the study of the physical laws that drive the universe, is similar in many respects. Although it does not possess the explanatory power of physical law, music exposes a raw logical reality, that of the numerical essence of the world, at the same time as it refers us, without being totally reduced to it, to our own subjectivity, to what makes us react, think, feel — in short, that we are human beings.

BOOK I

WHAT DO WE MEAN BY KNOWLEDGE ?

WHY MATERIALISM IS A LOGICAL DEAD END

> Please don't forget that materialism is also a metaphysical hypothesis, a hypothesis that has certainly proved very fruitful in the natural sciences, but which remains a hypothesis nonetheless. However, if we forget that this is its nature, it becomes a dogma which, like other dogmas, can hinder the progress of science and lead to intolerant passion.
>
> Herman Helmholtz, *On thought in medicine*, 1877

THE LOGICAL IMPASSES OF REDUCTIONIST PHYSICALISM AND NEO-DARWINISM

1.

WHAT IS DARWINISM FROM THE STANDPOINT OF THE EPISTEMOLOGY OF SCIENCE? — Darwinism, as a rigorous application of the old materialist principle to biology, is based on the idea that matter is without intention. Subjected to the play of chance, it ends up self-organising in the image of the cellular figures that appear in John Horton Conway's famous mathematical simulation entitled "The Game of Life". This so-called "zero-player" game — since it requires no intervention from outside players — has very simple rules designed to mimic the appearance of the first forms of life. The game is played on a two-dimensional grid that resembles a game of go. The squares of the game, called "cells", can only be in one of two states: alive or dead. At each iteration of the game, the inert cells that are in the immediate vicinity of exactly three living cells in turn become alive: they are born. Cells in close proximity to two or three living cells remain alive, otherwise they die. Each cell is in direct contact with eight other cells. Living cells are coloured on the grid. Dead cells are colourless. The main attraction of this game lies in the fact that relatively simple starting rules can be used to generate complex figures, such as the glider that shifts diagonally every four generations, or cannons that themselves generate a flow of gliders. Stable, unstable or periodic structures emerge as the game evolves towards increasing complexity.

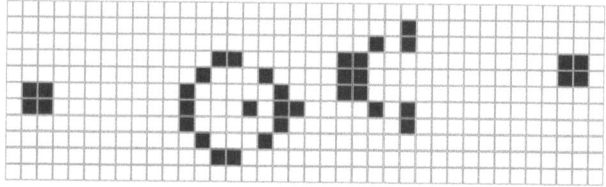

Gosper gun gliders

The figure reproduced above is a cannon glider. Cannons are figures that release debris. They are themselves capable of producing gliders at a variable rate (the first glider to be discovered, for example, was formed every thirty generations). The game is a good illustration of the principles of Darwinist evolution. It shows that it is possible, with very simple starting rules, to dispense with the hypothesis of the intentionality of

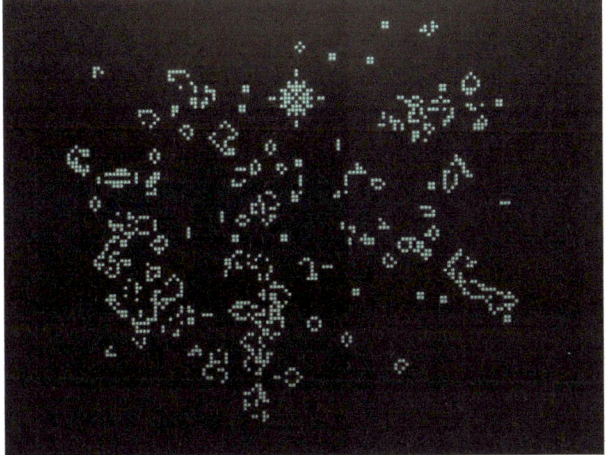

(Ctrl + Click on the image for online version)

 matter. The disorderly chance of the starting conditions ends up producing organised figures that emerge and dominate the game. In short, the game of life illustrates the principle of sufficient reason defended by Darwinism: if it is not necessary to appeal to a set of reasons to explain a phenomenon, then we must stick to sufficient reason. In this case, the aim is to demonstrate that matter needs nothing other than

itself to organise and animate itself[15]. Attempts to unify science derive from this principle of sufficient reason: we must always try to find the simple unitary mechanism behind the complexity of a phenomenon. If a complex phenomenon can be explained using a simple rule, then, in the language of mathematicians, the demonstration is "elegant". These simple rules that thought must apply to itself — avoid contradiction, achieve a greater degree of unity by synthesising experience into fruitful unifying principles — come from philosophy (the principle of sufficient reason was formulated by Leibniz in the seventeenth century, intuitions can be found as far back as Antiquity, the principle of non-contradiction was already defined by Aristotle); there is no reason why philosophy should not continue to adhere to them.

2.

IS PHYSICALIST MONISM LOGICALLY TENABLE? — Contemporary neuroscientists[16], working within the methodological frameworks of Darwinism and materialism, have predominantly adopted the postulate that the meaning of mental processes can be assimilated to their material substratum (psycho-

---

[15] See

[16] I'm thinking in particular of Jean-Pierre Changeux, Stanislas Dehaene, António Damásio and Daniel C. Dennett, although he is a philosopher of science rather than a neuroscientist.

logism). For the most part, however, they dispensed with any attempt at demonstration or critical substantiation, establishing as an unquestioned principle what was originally no more than a working hypothesis. For the majority of neuroscientists and philosophers of consciousness, the ability to account for the phenomenon of the emergence of life — or, more precisely, the self-organisation of matter — without resorting to an explanatory principle that went beyond matter, seemed to constitute sufficient proof for the assertion that 'everything is matter'.

Following in the footsteps of cybernetics, neuroscientists reduced information to an exclusively material reality, its physical properties alone being considered sufficient to explain its signifying power (including, by extension, the information that 'everything is matter', which, as we shall see later, raises questions about the status of this assertion in relation to the general problem of truth). Prior to the emergence of neuroscience, modern science had already begun its epistemological transformation in the 1940s, by adopting a new approach to the problem of meaning, centred on the reduction of information to the question of its practical modelling. It was in this context that cybernetics, formulated by Norbert Wiener in the 1940s and 1950s, conceptualised information as an intrinsically material process, inherent in the exchange and processing of physical signals within given systems. Wiener's cybernetics, which aimed to understand the control and communication systems in machines and living organisms, shared with the emerging neurosciences an interest in the processes of information, regulation and adaptation. Thus, from the 1950s and 1960s onwards, neuroscientists integrated most of the key concepts of cybernetics, in particular the central idea that the brain and nervous system operated as dynamic systems for exchanging and processing information. Although neuroscience historically emerged as a discipline from biology and medicine, imbued with the scientism of the nineteenth century and based on the postulate of the absence of any endogenous (self-generated) cause in the explanation of human behaviour, it was cybernetics which, by introducing a systemic and physical vision of information processing, completed the conceptual framework of the brain sciences. It was within this renewed conceptual framework that neuroscientists, in the second half of the twentieth century, set about tackling the problem of the 'emergence' of consciousness. The problem of consciousness, which arose directly from the question of the physical modelling of information flows, was in fact essentially relegated to the status of a 'residual' problem, emerging as a peripheral difficulty within an explanatory framework mainly oriented towards the materiality of processes.

One way of minimising the importance of the problem of consciousness was to try to show that it was not an important factor in the functioning of living organisms and that most decision-making processes could take place outside its field. In 1983, Benjamin Libet, an American neurobiologist and neurologist, conducted an experiment in which he asked participants, whose brain activity was recorded by an electroencephalogram (EEG) and muscle activity by an electromyogram, to stare at the centre of a clock. The clock had a dial divided into sixty demarcations corresponding to intervals of 43 milliseconds, for a total revolution time of 2.56 seconds[17]. A point of light moved around the dial. Participants were invited to spontaneously let emerge an intention or a need to perform a simple flexion of the index finger or wrist, without planning or concentrating on a precise moment to act. At the end of each trial, they were asked to indicate the position of the point of light on the dial at the moment when they became aware of their decision to act. The results of the study showed that the "motor preparation potential" located in the supplementary motor area (a region of the cerebral cortex located in the frontal lobe, on the medial side of each hemisphere) was activated 550 milliseconds *before* the start of the motor act and, most remarkably, 350 to 400 milliseconds *before* the moment of conscious decision making reported by the subjects in the experiment.

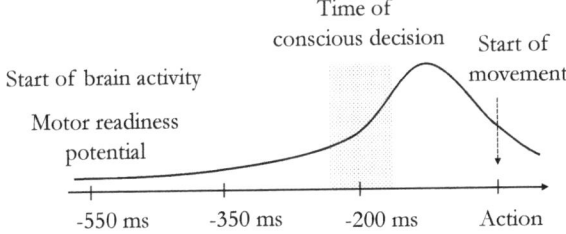

This discrepancy between awareness of the decision and the act itself (the act preceding, in short, the conscious decision to act) led most neuroscientists to assert that the intentions to act could not be at the

---

[17] We are referring here to the experiment as described by Krystèle Appourchaux in her essay, *Un nouveau libre arbitre*, Ch. III, *Les expériences de Benjamin Libet et leurs critiques*.

origin of the action (since awareness of the desire to act was, according to Libet's interpretation of the experiment, posterior to the preparation of the act itself). By confining the problem of intentionality to that of the conscious perception of the act, and by reducing the subject of the decision to its material realisation, the commentators on Libet's experiment[18] were in fact adopting a very restrictive view of the determination of our behaviour. Basing their argument on the temporal primacy of unconscious processes over the conscious act, the neuroscientists were in fact directing their criticism against a dated philosophical conception of freedom. In fact, the concept of freedom that the neuroscientists were attacking came close to the idea of a 'free will', a capacity for total determination on the part of the subject that would hover above any physical or natural mechanism. Although the notion of free will was first formulated in Greek antiquity (by Socrates, Plato and Aristotle in particular), it was of particular concern to the Christian philosophers of the Middle Ages (from Saint Augustine to Thomas Aquinas), who considered the problem in terms of the determinants of human action and man's moral responsibility to God. Theological discussions on free

---

[18] These include Daniel Wegner, *The Illusion of Conscious Will* (2002), Sam Harris *Free Will* (2012), Patrick Haggard, Thomas Metzinger, John-Dylan Haynes (who showed that intentions to act could be predicted up to 7 seconds before they became conscious,), Peter Carruthers (a philosopher of psychology who uses Libet's experiment to combat the idea of free will) and, in France, Stanislas Dehaene, who takes up more or less the same theses in *Consciousness and the Brain* (2013), based on Libet's experiment.

will were thus mainly part of controversies on the definition of sin or the nature of divine intervention (for example, the theological debates on efficacious grace and sufficient grace[19]). It should also be pointed out that most of the defenders of the doctrine of free will took note of the problem of the material determinants of action, with divine intervention constituting for them the third term that would in some way make it possible to overcome the contradictions of the doctrine of sin (if men are determined to commit sin and God is the creator of men, does that necessarily mean that God wills them to sin?) Apart from the fact that the objections formulated by neuroscientists against the classical conception of free will did not fully grasp the conceptual richness and nuances developed by medieval Christian philosophy — reducing this doctrine in particular to an alleged human capacity to act "in the image of God", without taking account of material determinations — the criticisms of neuroscientists also appear to be misguided. They overlooked a fundamental issue: the hierarchy of intentions, which is the nodal point of any reflection on freedom and conscience. In commenting on the conclusions of Libet's experiment, for example, the neuroscientists systematically failed to mention that,

---

[19] The Jesuits, adopting the positions of Luis de Molina, who tried to reconcile divine omnipotence with human free will, while the Jansenists, aligning themselves with the theology of Jansenius, who himself returned to a strict interpretation of Augustinian thought, defended the idea that human beings were marked by original sin and that only God's "sufficient" and irresistible grace could free them from their material determinisms (bottom).

for the subject of the experiment, the decision to press the button at random was only made possible by what Kant called an 'metadecision' (the overall framework of the decision to press — in other words, the rule of behaviour that I set for myself before the event and that will determine my decision when it occurs), this metadecision being the primary condition of the decision, for the subject of the experiment, to press the button. So, if the subject of the experiment had the undoubtedly erroneous feeling that he was aware of the moment when the decision was made before the actual decision was made, he was not mistaken in thinking that he was the only one to decide on the very *possibility of* pressing the button (if this action had been likely to result in the subject's death, for example, we can easily imagine that he would have dismissed the idea, in his arch-decision, of pressing the button at any time).

Using the example of this famous experiment, we can see how a subtle but significant shift took place among neuroscientists: what was initially just a methodological framework with no specific ontological claim (methodological materialism) was transformed into a philosophical-scientific assertion that transmuted methodology into ontology (onto-logical materialism). This ontological materialism, often claimed by neuroscientists whom we conveniently refer to as 'neo-Darwinists', was in fact based on the misuse of the principle of sufficient reason and its application to problems that went beyond the strict domain of physics (which, paradoxically, led neuroscientists to adopt metaphysical positions, i.e. positions *that could not be demonstrated* within physics or biology). In the context of biology, this principle of unification supported

Darwin's theory of evolution: with the (biologically supportable) hypothesis of integral materialism, there was no need to postulate the intentionality of matter to explain the emergence of life. However, what was merely a heuristic tool in Darwin's case was sliding, in the case of certain radical neo-Darwinists, towards an ontology that supported the "all-material" thesis. The methodological principle of the rational unification of causes and effects (sufficient reason) was thus transformed into a specific philosophical thesis, according to which the world was entirely reducible to its material unity. This methodological-ontological shift represented a dangerous confusion between an explanatory method and a global vision of reality. What was originally a locally effective hypothesis was transformed into a general law. Thus, the hypothetical assertion that the appearance of living organisms and their evolution could be fully explained by the evolution of material combinations (according to the principle of sufficient reason) was transformed into a metaphysical proposition: "everything is matter" — This proposition could in turn be reduced to the unprovable statement that "there is nothing that is not matter". In the context of language theory, the ontological-materialist paradigm led to the assertion of an equally unprovable equivalence — between the physical support of information (the neuronal substrate) and information itself. Neuroscience was in fact attempting to remove the boundary between the meaning of a word and its physical properties. Words such as 'cat', 'table' or 'tree', for example, were reduced to their neurobiological correlates or to the mental *stimuli* from which they originated (the mentally induced representation of a cat, a table or a tree). Such an approach effectively abolished the fundamental distinction between signifier and signified, reducing the intentional and conceptual complexity of language to the mechanics of material interactions. This shift from an empirical method to a reductionist ontology revealed a profound discrepancy between scientific observations and the metaphysical conclusions purportedly drawn from them.

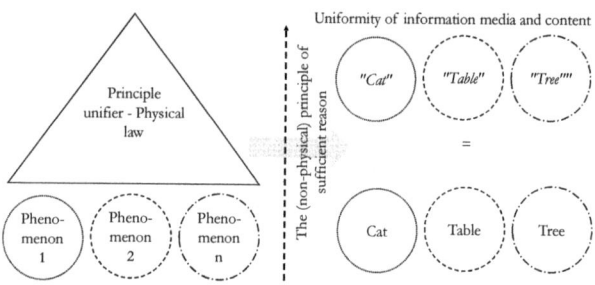

The diagram above illustrates the idea that modern science, based on the principle of sufficient reason (which we also support), naturally tends towards a form of unification (left-hand side of diagram). This unification stems from the idea that several phenomena linked together by the same cause can be included in a unifying explanatory model or theory. However, the problem with ontological materialism arises from the application of this principle to entities that are not necessarily reducible to pure materiality (right-hand side of the diagram). As we shall see later, the unifying rule, for example, cannot itself be said to be "material". Meaning is not necessarily reduced to its physical supports. The extension of the principle of sufficient reason led neuroscientists to straddle the whole issue of meaning by assimilating it, in a coup de force, to the issue of matter. In doing so, they decreed an unproven equivalence between the material support of phenomena and their meaning. For the neuroscientist, the neuro-cerebral support of the word "cat"

(what happens in my brain when I see a cat or think of a cat) was strictly equivalent to my feeling and experience of the word "cat". Information is equal to its manifestation (its physical medium). In other words, "cat" (the material observation of the effect of perceiving or thinking about a cat in my brain) = cat (the general idea I have of the cat), which is an unfounded psychologistic position, as we shall show later.

In their analysis of language, neuroscientists effectively abolished any distinction between meaning and its material substratum. This reduction led to the assimilation of thought, in its entirety, to a simple physical process: the mental and psychic were reinterpreted entirely through the categories of physics. This rejection of any form of dualism — rooted in a generalised application of the principle of sufficient reason — led to a conception of reality that was intrinsically monolithic, monistic and flat. In this, materialist radicalism perhaps betrayed a deeper misunderstanding of the very notion of 'idea'. Indeed, many neuroscientists seemed to have stuck to a literal interpretation of the allegory of the cave, no doubt imagining the 'world of ideas' as a separate, unreal universe, where the winged chariot of the soul collided with an imaginary vault of heaven. And yet, by attributing a physical content to a model initially conceived based on a principle devoid of any phenomenal or empirical reference, neuroscientists, without probably being fully aware of it, were indeed taking a properly metaphysical approach, in contradiction with their own methodological requirements. This tension revealed the fundamental aporia of a discourse which, while claiming to exclude metaphysics, could not help resorting to it when it claimed to account for reality in its entirety.

3.

MATERIALISM IS BASED ON A PETITION OF PRINCIPLES — Reductionist materialism proceeds in the same way as the structuralism of the 1960s: the initially agnostic method (the working hypothesis) moves away from its strictly utilitarian purpose to become a fallacious theory of the whole, which mistakes its premises for its conclusions.

The materialist model of the evolution of living things (the theory of evolution), based on the principle of sufficient reason (while omitting to examine the meaning of the principle of sufficient reason: is it itself material, and if so, what is its physical equivalent?), excludes in principle any other reason for evolution. From this, neo-Darwinists conclude that everything is matter, a proposition that can only be supported by a tautological demonstration and is therefore unscientific.

4.

PHYSICALIST TAUTOLOGIES AND THE DEAD-ENDS OF MONIST THEORIES — To prove that everything is matter, it would be necessary to show that there is nothing that is not matter, but if the statement postulates precisely that everything is matter, we will soon be asserting that what is not matter is also matter, In other words, "everything is matter" is tantamount to saying "all the entities in the universe are matter" or "everything that exists is matter", which is tantamount to saying that matter is everything, including the assertions that "everything is matter" and "everything is not matter". The statement "everything is matter" is therefore purely tautological and self-fulfilling, in that it is strictly equivalent to the proposition "matter is everything", which ultimately amounts to saying that "matter is matter".

"Everything is matter."

"If there is something non-material, then it is matter."

"Matter is everything."

"Not everything is matter is itself matter."

"There is nothing that exists that cannot be matter."

In its meaning, the statement "everything is matter" is strictly equivalent to the statement "nothing is matter". The statements "everything is" or "nothing is" fall under the same criticisms of inconsistency and indeterminacy.

At the extremes, absolute idealism and radical materialism are therefore strictly equivalent as monistic, tautological theories. The most enthusiastic idealists were delighted in the 1920s and 1930s when matter was gradually observed to dissolve in the interplay of forces (gravitational interaction, electro-magnetic interaction, weak interaction and, in the 1970s, strong interaction). We were then quick to assert that nothing existed other than the law, that nothing was matter, that everything was an idea. In absolute idealism, as in radical materialism, the monist theory is tautological, signifying nothing and having no concrete content.

5.

Neo-Darwinists are generally not short of tautological assertions, one of which is that language is only the result of the development of the structures that enable language. We couldn't agree more.

6.

"MY BRAIN SAID THAT" — A few years ago, when I was reading *L'homme neuronal*[20] by Jean-Pierre Changeux, my daughter, who must have been four or five at the time, was very intrigued by the diagrams and graphics in the book. To answer her questions, I briefly explained to her, as best I could, the general subject of the book: how the brain and neurons work. A few days later, when she had just let slip a little insolence (which she is wont to do), she told me: "It wasn't me, it was my brain that said that".

---

[20] *The Neuronal Man*

THE QUESTION OF THE EMERGENCE OF CONSCIOUSNESS

7.

HOW DOES MATTER THINK? DOES MATTER MAKE HYPOTHESES ABOUT ITSELF? — Until we can explain the miracle by which matter happens to think, we cannot seriously support the thesis of absolute materialism. Even if we were to admit that, by some miracle, self-engendered matter, by following pre-existing rules (which it is simply replaying blindly), has ended up organising itself with a certain degree of complexity or astonishing regularity (think, for example, of the molecular structure of crystals), we would still be no better placed to explain the qualitative leap from inert matter to living matter. How can matter become a living organism whose mode of interaction with the world differs radically from the most complex inert forms? How does living matter emerge from inert matter? How do living organisms become conscious? How do living beings become self-aware? How do living things become rational? These are the questions that radical materialism and physicalism systematically stumble over. At each stage of the emergence of the living being, there is the same qualitative leap, the same blind spot. From the strict point of view of reductionist physicalism, the only solution to the problem is to deny the problem (i.e. to remain within the tautological dialectic we detailed earlier): matter does not emerge from the inert, it is moved by forces, the living does not become conscious, consciousness is an illusion, a philosopher's concept that we will get round, identity does not exist, there is no self-awareness and, insofar as ideas do not exist, rationality is nothing. In short, everything is matter and matter is everything. But as soon as the physicalist has completed his profession of faith (a metaphysical one, as we pointed out earlier), he is quick to fall into the traps he has set for himself.

The epistemological difficulties raised by the ontological materialism generally adopted by neuroscientists are particularly striking in a book published in 1998, the result of a dialogue between the philosopher Paul Ricœur and the neurobiologist Jean-Pierre Changeux, entitled *Ce qui nous fait penser, la nature et la règle*[21]. While Jean-Pierre Changeux defended the idea that thought is identified with cerebral activity (thought as a manifestation of neuronal interactions, modulated by evolutionary and genetic mechanisms), Paul Ricœur pointed out to Changeux that he was confusing two distinct meanings of the word 'origin': origin in the Darwinian sense (biological and historical origin), and origin in the sense of *motive*, of justification (in the sense that we might speak of the origin of a behaviour for example: the foundation, the legitimacy, but also, in a sense the finality, the motive and the objective of the behaviour). However, understanding between the two speakers is difficult insofar as the second meaning of the word "origin" does not exist for Jean-Pierre Changeux. Since the biological evolution of matter is the sole criterion for explaining the world, the origin of our behaviour, the motive for an action, etc., always ultimately relates to the historical, biological origin, i.e. the physical cause that triggers the action. As soon as Jean-Pierre Changeux denies the existence or relevance

---

[21] *What Makes Us Think: Nature and Rule*

of the second meaning of the word 'origin', we find ourselves in a stalemate, with neither side willing to start from the other's axiomatic foundations. This mutual rejection cannot be fruitful: by depriving the two protagonists of a common foundation, it prevents the dialogue from progressing (the dialogue deepens its circularity). If we want to get out of the aporias of the discussion between Changeux and Ricœur, we have no choice but to accept the axiomatic foundations of one of the two theses and then try to observe where these foundations lead us. In the case of two mutually exclusive propositions, in principle it will suffice to show the contradiction of one in order to give credence to the other (the principle of the excluded third[22]). However, if we choose to remain within the logic of the reductionist physicalist[23] and approach the problem of *origin* by means of biological determinism, we immediately see that the question of biological origin is in fact deeply intertwined with that of finality. For Darwin, the biological world also tends towards an end, that of the best possible adaptation of an organism to its environment. Darwinism is indeed a theory of the *adaptive* evolution of living organisms to their environment. As such, it too *has its* truth, and it too thinks in terms of suitability, with the random combinations of life groping their way through a multitude of combinations towards the form of life that

---

[22] We know that the principle of excluded thirds has also been called into question, notably in the intuitionism of L.E.J. Brouwer.

[23] Jean-Pierre Changeux denies that he is, but I have to admit that the difference between his theory and reductionism did not seem obvious to me.

is *best suited to a given environment.* If the environment evolves, the formula for suitability will tend to evolve with it. In this respect, Darwinism is already, in a sense, a dualism (a confrontation between an organism and a given reality). We cannot therefore assert, as Changeux does and as the Darwinian tradition would have it, that matter is devoid of intentionality. If there is a finality to matter (organised matter tends towards an objective, that of its survival, as a function of a given reality), there is also a form of intentionality to organised matter (intention of conservation, survival and reproduction *a minima*). We must not be too quick to equate inert matter with living, organised matter. If, in fact, we deprive organised living matter of intentionality, we also deprive ourselves of the criterion for differentiating inert matter from living matter (what is inert matter if not matter devoid of intention?). From the moment that matter becomes a body (matter comes together, forms part of a general, organic organisation), it acquires a direction and a purpose, in other words, an intention. Just because unitary matter lacks such an intention (what is the intention of a protein?) does not mean that the living organism (made of matter) lacks one. Once again, this assimilation of one proposition to another goes beyond the strict framework of methodological materialism. But the story does not end there. In the most advanced forms of life the adaptation of species to their environment led to the emergence of rational forms of intelligence, one of the key moments in this emergence being the appearance in humans of the ability to designate and name things. By enabling him to objectify the world, language led man (a "superiorly organised" form of matter) to gradually understand himself as a being separate from his environment, capable of using his industry to tame nature, of which he made himself "the master and possessor[24]". With the emergence of language, the intention of matter was no longer merely effective (observed); it also became codified, formalised in an objective language: matter was now capable of thinking and communicating its thoughts. If we adopt the strict Darwinian point of view (a biological and physical approach to the question of the *origin of* our behaviour), we can see how we are led to limit from the outset the explanatory power of radical materialism. Starting from the idea of random and blind combinations and recombinations of matter, we have in fact been led to

---

[24] René Descartes, *Discourse on The Method*, text compiled by Victor Cousin, Levrault, 1824, volume I, part six. This well-known quotation has been commented on and caricatured so much that we reproduce it *in full* below. In my opinion, it fits perfectly into the context we are describing here:

"But, as soon as I had acquired some general notions concerning physics, and as I began to test them in various particular difficulties, I noticed how far they could lead, and how much they differed from the principles which had been used up to now, I thought that I could not keep them hidden without sinning greatly against the law which obliges us to procure as much as is in us the general good of all men: for they have shown me that it is possible to arrive at knowledge that is very useful to life; and that instead of this speculative philosophy taught in schools, we can find a practical one, by which, knowing the force and actions of fire, water, air, the stars, the heavens, and all the other bodies that surround us, as distinctly as we know the various trades of our craftsmen, we could use them in the same way for all the uses to which they are suited, and thus make ourselves as masters and possessors of nature. "

evoke (i) the qualitative leap from inert matter to organic matter (ii) the problem of the adaptation of organisms, (iii) the question of the intentionality of organic matter, the living organism seeking survival, growth and reproduction, and finally (iv) the question of the formalisation of matter by matter — what we call thought — in an organised language. We also note that the strict theoretical framework of integral materialism proves incapable of offering a unified and coherent description of these phenomena (insofar as materialism remains within a monistic framework that rejects any theory of intentionality, intention itself being inevitably reduced to matter, which again poses the problems we have just mentioned). The problem of the intentionality of matter arises with even greater intensity when we consider human behaviour (behaviour that is itself partly determined by language, which is in turn a manifestation of the intentionality that materialism tries to reduce). Contrary to what we might say about simple organisms, we cannot seriously maintain that man simply gropes his way through millennia of 'haphazard luck' to find the most satisfactory formula for adapting to his environment (we could no doubt make the same point about most animal species, and no doubt plant species too). If man, for example, finds himself in a cold environment, he will take refuge in a cave or build a shelter (or light a fire if he has already reached the fire age): he will not wait for evolution to give him long hair or a seal skin. Adaptation here is "immediate", the fruit of the subject itself and not of an infinitely slow process of evolution: man (like most animals) can interact with his environment, modify it and modify himself without this being the result of a long selective process of an evolutionary nature (combinations tested at random).

In the same way, faced with the emergence of a new disease, the human species will no longer wait to be decimated and to develop, through selection of the most robust organisms, resistances acquired over several generations, but will develop a vaccine whose almost immediate action will have a protective effect on the species. To this, neo-Darwinists are quick to reply that human behaviour is in itself evolutionary in nature. In other words, they will argue, it is because evolution has given us situational intelligence that we instinctively seek refuge in a cellar, build a hut or make a vaccine (here again we see the mark of regressive and tautological reasoning). In so doing, neo-Darwinists once again miss the difference in nature between the material process that leads to the emergence of organised forms of life (an undoubtedly random and combinatorial process) and the phenomenon of the *emergence* of life itself, i.e. the generation of autonomous matter (which has its own rules, which acts according to its own interests, i.e. which is *endowed with* intentionality). What neo-Darwinists almost universally treat as a residual problem (the problem of emergence) is in fact the central problem of any reflection on the foundations of science and philosophy. Let us point out that in the case of the creation of a new vaccine, not only will the "natural" selective mechanism no longer operate (in the face of a given aggression, the most fragile are protected in the same way as the most robust), but it can no longer be asserted that matter acts here at random and without intention[25]. In our

---

[25] Murray Gell-Mann, the American physicist who won the Nobel Prize in Physics for his work on the theory of quarks,

wrote in *The Quark and the Jaguar: Adventures in the Simple and the Complex* (1994): "[The kind of learning that bacteria do] differs in an interesting way from the kind that takes place through the use of a brain. We have emphasized that mutant forms of a bacterium exhibiting resistance to an antibiotic may easily be present by chance when the drug is introduced and that in any case those norms have existed from time to time in the past. Ideas, however, more often arise in response to a challenge rather than being available when the challenge is presented". Op. cit., p. 69, W.H. Freeman and Company, New York, 1960,2002. Here, Gell-Mann is expressing an idea more or less similar to our own: the difference between the adaptation of a bacterium to an antibiotic and the birth of the idea of a vaccine. These two types of response cannot be equated with each other: "There is," says Gell-Mann, "some slight evidence for genetic mutation in biology occasionally arising in response to a need, but if the phenomenon really exists, it is comparatively insignificant compared to chance mutation". Curiously, Murray Gell-Mann later seems to try to equate the evolution of scientific theories with biological evolution. We are not opposed in principle to this view, but it should be pointed out that the process of selecting theories depends on their effectiveness (their correspondence with the facts, their ability to explain them). It is the effectiveness of the theory, like the adaptation of the organism, that explains its survival. But (i) the normative criterion of effectiveness precedes the theory (and the survival of the most appropriate organism): it is because the organism or the theory corresponds to a norm imposed by reality, by the biological environment, that it is correct or adapted, and not the other way round: (i) the rule precedes existence and (ii) the human brain, through its ability to grasp the rule, to grasp the idea that precedes its effective realisation, is not subject to the same biological mechanism as bacteria that grope randomly to resist antibiotics, the groping being the result of

example, the "superiorly organised" matter (man) has developed defences that are not acquired through an evolutionary process (the rational faculty is acquired, of course, but the response to aggression from a new virus is not — this is the difference between a vaccine and acquired resistance). Starting from the theory that matter organises itself by chance and without intentionality in a pre-existing world, we arrive at the opposite conclusion: matter ends up developing intentional mechanisms, i.e. mechanisms that are not random. If, then, I define matter as an organisation without intentionality, determined by an interplay of blind forces, I inevitably arrive at a paradox: either intentionality is historically added to matter, and it then becomes something other than simple matter (the problem of emergence), or matter is, from the outset, endowed with intentionality, (since the definition of matter endowed with intentionality is contradictory to our initial theory, according to which matter is precisely that which is not endowed with intentionality, but which is driven by a play of random forces that forces it to slowly adapt to a given environment). Reducing everything to matter is therefore tantamount to endowing manner with intentionality, i.e. something other than matter, which is contradictory.

---

a selective process involving the death of non-resistant bacteria: nothing of the kind in the functioning of the brain that formulates an idea (the cells that do not contribute to forming the appropriate idea are not punished by death!). Despite his comments against reductionism, Gell-Mann often seems trapped by the reductionist presuppositions of modern neurobiology ("virtually all of us are, in this sense, reductionists", he declares, p. 116).

Theory	Facts	Conclusion
1. Matter is everything 2. The material does not have intentions, it is solely driven by blind forces 3. The material offers combinations *randomly*, with only the winning combinations retained ("*selection of the fittest*")	Organising matter no longer offers combinations blind. These are targeted, non-random combinations (scientific experiments).	1. Matter is not everything 2. Matter can be endowed with intention, so it is not just matter. 3. The material offers non-random combinations

Counter-argument: Science itself is the product of a hazardous evolutionary process.

Answer: Scientists do not grope around randomly. Even if we were to accept the purely experimental model (science as a series of random tests), we could not seriously assert that the correction of the first hypothesis would be evolutionary (random) in nature. The scientist will not test all the combinations in order to arrive at an experimentally confirmed hypothesis, like randomly testing the combinations in a safe. He is always driven by an idea, an intuition (a projection of the imagination) that he tests. If it were otherwise, there would be no scientists, only hypothesis testers groping their way through an infinite number of possibilities. This is why the development of science is exponential in nature, which is not the case with the evolutionary processes described by Darwin (despite nature's ability to test being infinitely superior to that of the scientist). On this subject, Einstein noted that the idea that scientists do not make hypotheses, an idea that has been the *credo of* leading scientists, is in fact not seriously tenable: "We now see clearly how mistaken are the theorists of knowledge who believe that theory comes by induction from experience. Even the great Newton could not free himself from this error (*Hypotheses non fingo*)[26]."

8.

— In an attempt to find a way out of the logical impasses of reductionist physicalism, Thomas Nagel[27] put forward the idea of a universe that was 'fertilised' from its very beginning, and which would eventually give rise to a multitude of consciousnesses potentially contained within the original elements of the universe. The merit of this metaphorical theory is that it pushes the paradox of physicalism to its logical conclusion: the original problem of fecundity, and therefore of the intentionality of matter. On the other hand, it only scratches the surface of what we consider to be a more fundamental problem: that of the law that governs our universe and makes its fecundity possible.

---

[26] Albert Einstein, *Physics and Reality*, 1936, p. 301, from the Journal of the Franklin Institute, Vol. 221, No. 3, 3 March 1936

[27] Thomas Nagel, an analytical philosopher born in 1937, is of Yugoslav origin and is a naturalised American. He is Professor of Philosophy and Law at New York University. He opposed the reductionist physicalist thesis that identifies mental states with neurobiological processes, notably in a famous article published in 1974 entitled "*What is like to be a bat*".

9.

THE PROBLEM OF THE EMERGENCE OF CONSCIOUSNESS WITHIN THE FRAMEWORK OF A MONISTIC EPISTEMOLOGY — There is, strictly speaking, no "problem of the emergence of consciousness" that we could pose in the terms of reductionist physicalism. For reductionists[28], since consciousness is a purely physical phenomenon (the ignition of numerous regions of the cerebral cortex, the detection of specific waves and frequencies in the brain, the massive synchronisation of electro-magnetic signals in the cortex), its emergence can only be explained by physical, material reasons. Posed in these terms, the problem of the emergence of consciousness is insoluble, because it inevitably merges with the more fundamental problem of life (organic matter), which is at its origin. Reductionist materialism regards consciousness as a historical phenomenon superimposed on the living. As far back as we go in history, however, the problem of the emergence of consciousness remains linked to the problem of the emergence of the living, to that of the self-organisation of matter (every living being contains in germ the possibility of what we call consciousness, the living already implies a form of consciousness implicit in the separation between the organism and what it is not). So

---

[28] I adopt here a 'broad' conception of physicalist reductionism. I am aware that there are a thousand shades of reductionism and that many neuroscientists reject this label, which they no doubt find pejorative. Here, I consider as reductionist any thesis based on the idea that the world can be fully explained and described in terms of physical processes. Physicalist reductionism is therefore seen here as a modern version of radical materialism.

here we come back to the problem of the intentionality of matter. Reductionism does not explain the emergence of human consciousness any more than it explains the emergence of life. It cannot and will not be able to do so without falling into a metaphysics[29] (against which it was opposed in its premises).

---

[29] The idea that we find here and there that 'one day neuroscience will explain everything' seems naïve and reminiscent of the dashed enthusiasm of the nineteenth and twentieth centuries, see for example Stanislas Dehaene, *Consciousness and the Brain.*

THE SCHEMATIC DUALITY OF THE WORLD: THE SEPARATE WORLD

> What is rational is effective, and what is effective is rational.
>
> Georg Wilhem Friedrich Hegel, Preface to *Elements of the Philosophy of Right*, 1820

WHAT IS DUALISM? THE STORY OF A MISUNDERSTANDING

10.

DUALISM FROM A NEUROSCIENTIFIC POINT OF VIEW — Neuroscientists usually get a false (or at least partial) idea of dualism by confusing the classical duality 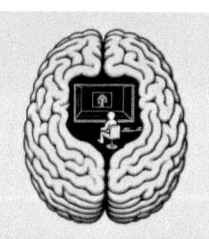 between body and mind with the separation between the sensible and the intelligible, the material and the idea. The typical example chosen by neuroscientists to disqualify dualism is what they call the "Cartesian theatre[30]". Descartes, they claim, defended the idea that consciousness functions like a theatre: events take place inside our consciousness, and we watch them as we would watch images scroll across a screen. So, according to the

---

[30] This idea was defended by Daniel Dennett in *Consciousness Explained* and has been widely taken up by the neuroscience community. In France, see Stanislas Dehaene, *Consciousness and the Brain*.

Cartesian view (and according to the neuroscientists in question), there is a concentrated version of ourselves, inside our brain, which interacts with the data communicated to our consciousness via the senses. This obviously simplifying vision comes up against the problem of regression to infinity (is there another little man in the brain of the little man in our brain?). Although this extrapolation has little to do with Descartes' thinking, it does tell us something about the way in which neuroscience conceives of dualism (in order to discredit it). For most neuroscientists, dualism instantly conjures up images of the separation between soul and body[31], metaphysics and religion. When neuroscientists think of dualism, they think of ontological separation, religion, mysticism of the soul, no doubt to avoid thinking of the more immediate and more concrete problem of the difference between matter and idea.

11.

CONFUSION BETWEEN INFORMATION AND ITS MEDIUM — Physicalist reductionism confuses the medium of information with the information itself, the network of activated neurons with the idea, writing with ink. Information cannot be identified with matter. Strictly speaking, matter does not contain information; it always remains at the level of what it is.

---

[31] Paradoxically, Descartes was trying to reduce rather than aggravate this separation with his hypotheses on the 'little gland', which he considered to be a better candidate for carrying out its functions in the body than all the 'double' organs (limbs, eyes, cerebral hemispheres, etc.).

Degrees of emergence — Degrees of freedom — The problem of morality

12.

THE TRUE-FALSE COUPLE VERSUS INTEGRAL MATERIALISM: THE MACHINE AS A CONCRETE FIGURE OF DUALISM — By caricaturing centuries-old dualist positions, radical materialists thought they had won a decisive victory over philosophy. As dualism was quickly equated with the opposition between body and soul, it was thought that philosophers had been dealt with by pointing out that the question of the soul was speculative and of no interest to the sciences[32]. In the 1940s and 1950s, the intense developments in cybernetics, through the schematisation of logical mechanisms and their reduction to physical processes, seemed to provide the decisive arguments for the reductionists: if, they claimed, we can simulate mental mechanisms that appear com-plex to us by means of simple physical processes, it is because man, like all living beings, is entirely reducible to the physical interactions that take place within him. Here again, the tautological validation machine of reductionism was in full operation: "everything is matter, and everything is matter, so everything is matter" (we told you!).

---

[32] This was to forget Kant, who in 1781 had already excluded the soul from what reason had the possibility of knowing, in the same way as the world (the thing 'in itself') and God (*Critique of Pure Reason*). So, there is nothing very new in the position of reductionist physicalists on the question of the existence of the soul and its supposed interactions with the body.

However, while it is true that cybernetics was based entirely on the mathematical formalisation of the world and the translation of this formalisation into physical mechanisms, the fact remains that this formalisation process originated in our own logical structures, which are the ones we communicated to the machine. So, the very fact that the rule produces the results expected by its formaliser is physical confirmation of the fact that the rule works, that it produces its effect. In the case of the calculating machine, not only does the rule work (the machine will find the result "4" for the proposed operation "2+2"), but the rules that made it possible to create such a machine also work (the machine will display the number "4" on its screen). The machine is, in this sense, an objectification of the idea[33], i.e. an idea

---

[33] The concept of idea is used here in the sense of "intentional hypothesis". The experimenter is testing a hypothesis deduced from a more general theory, which in turn has probably been deduced from the experiment. The point here is not to discuss the genesis of the formation of the idea, but rather to insist on the possibility of seeing in the concrete world the extension of an abstract idea which, before being produced and tested on the world, may not have had any concrete reality (other than that of the chemical processes which presided over its formation, but which for all that are not its concrete realisation: To put it another way, the idea of an aeroplane or even a five-headed unicorn may form in my mind without me necessarily ever having had the opportunity to see an aeroplane or a five-headed unicorn. The mental processes that led me to create the aeroplane or the unicorn will not be identifiable with their object. The idea is different from what it designates, even if, as the physicalists assert — and we don't even think of contesting — it comes

that has become an object, an illustration *in concreto* of the effectiveness of the rule, of its reality, of its non-speculative character[34], dare we say, of its "truth[35]". The machine either works or it doesn't; it either validates or invalidates a hypothesis or a theory (i.e. an 'idea' in the particular sense we have given it here). Far from discrediting dualism, the machine is its most accomplished illustration: there is matter and there is matter *organised* by the idea. The idea can be confirmed or invalidated by experimentation, in other words it can be said to be "true" or "false" depending on the degree to which it conforms to the expectations of the experimenter. When the machine works, i.e. when it produces the result expected by the experimenter or engineer who designed it, it separates the world into two parts: that of the idea (the hypothesis, the theory) on the one hand, and that of its actual realisation on the other. By validating the proposition that an idea can be true or false, effective or ineffective, the machine opens the breach in dualism, not so much because it confirms the dual opposition between true and false, but rather because, by manifesting in the world the possibility of confirming a discourse, it bears concrete witness to a mode of knowledge that operates in the mode of

---

from, or is based on, the chemical processes that govern its formation. To put it another way, "the concept of a dog does not bark", as Louis Althusser astutely remarked when extrapolating a passage from Spinoza's *Ethics* (I, proposition 17).

[34] In the sense that the idea has a visible (and measurable) 'effect' on the world.

[35] The term "truth" is understood here as conformity with what is expected.

correspondence between a discourse and its destination (in this case, the concrete realisation of the discourse). The machine, as a particular case of the correspondence between the idea and its actual realisation, is a concrete denial of relativism (turbines turn, planes take off, relativists get on planes).

13.

CAN WE IMAGINE A WORLD WITHOUT LAWS? — In 1934, when Albert Einstein first came face to face with Calder's mobile entitled *A Universe* at MoMA in New York, he is said to have remained motionless for the entire forty minutes of the mobile's mechanical cycle. In Calder's work, everything that is normally hidden from us comes to the fore. The mechanism, represented by an organised mass of matter ("*pipe, motor, wire, wood and string*" indicates the subtitle of the work) is in fact the real subject of the mobile, while the stars occupy an almost anecdotal place. Determined and constrained in their movement by a network of metal lattices, they are subject to a superior force that appears here in all its triviality: the law. Was it the sight of this work that inspired Einstein's famous phrase "God does not

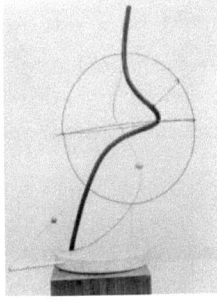

Alexander Calder, *A Universe*, 1934, painted iron pipe, steel wire, motor and wood with

play dice³⁶"? In any case, it seems that in Calder's work, as in Einstein's thinking, it is the rule, the legal mechanism, that comes first and not its visible manifestation (the stars). What would happen if the *pipe, motor, wire, wood and string* were removed from the work? Could the stars sustain themselves by the operation of the Holy Spirit? Should we then consider that the rule as a condition of subsistence of our universe is not directly reducible to it? Following on from Einstein's thoughts on the origins of the universe, the mathematician and physicist (later to win the Nobel Prize in Physics) Roger Penrose found a probability of $1/10^{10^{123}}$ for a universe like ours to survive its first instants. In other words, there would be a one in $10^{10^{123}}$ chance for that a given universe would adopt a set of parameters that would not lead to its immediate destruction[37]. Roger Penrose's calculations followed on

---

[36] Written traces of the expression can be found in Einstein's correspondence with Max Born (7 September 1944 - in *A. Einstein, M. Born, Correspondence* 1916-1955), in a letter to Michèle Bosso dated 30 November 1949, in a letter to Niels Bohr dated 4 April 1949 and in another letter to Erwin Schrödinger dated 22 December 1950. We know that Einstein actually used the expression quite often, probably even before the 1940s, the EPR (Einstein-Podolsky-Rosen) paradox having been published in an article dated 1935, shortly after Einstein's 'encounter' with Calder's mobile.

[37] See Roger Penrose, *The Road to Reality*, New York, Alfred A. Knopf, 2005, pp. 762-765. See also *The Large, the Small and the Human Mind*. "I have illustrated with a drawing the Creator, finding a very tiny point in that phase space which represents the initial conditions from which our universe

from the thoughts of a number of physicists, including Andrei Linde and Brandon Carter, who questioned the extreme improbability of the 'correct' settings of the physical constants that characterise our universe. Andrei Linde put forward the hypothesis of the existence of a "foam" of universes, each having had its Big Bang and responding to its own laws or physical constants, Brandon Carter proposed the idea of the "anthropic principle", which he divided into a "weak anthropic principle", according to which what we observe must be compatible with the conditions necessary for our presence as observers — otherwise we wouldn't be here to observe — and a "strong anthropological principle", according to which the universe must have fundamental laws and parameters so that sentient beings can appear in it at a given moment in its history. If the weak anthropic principle is tautological in its construction (this principle amounts to asserting: "if the necessary and sufficient conditions for our existence were not produced, then we could not exist", in other words: "If we did not exist, then the necessary and sufficient conditions for our existence would not have been produced"), it is not, however, entirely sterile insofar as it serves as the basis for the strong anthropological principle and, by ricochet, for questioning the conditions of possibility of the existence of the formation of coherent universes

---

must have evolved if it is to resemble remotely the one in which we live. To find it, the Creator has to locate that point in phase space to an accuracy of on part in $(10^{10})^{123}$. If we were to put on zero on each elementary particle in the Universe, I still could not write the number down in full.", Cambridge University Press, 1997,1999, p. 48

(observable or not), i.e. universes that have not collapsed because of their physiological contradictions. As sentient and rational beings, we are the late product of a regulated universe (a universe that has not collapsed in on itself). It is in this universe that our rationality emerged, and it is its laws that we are trying to understand. While the universe may not have been created for us (with the aim of creating us) or from us, we are necessarily dependent on its initial conditions and subject to the laws that govern it. We are, in a way, "made of the same wood" as it, caught in the threads of this double existential submission: I am the product of the regularity of the laws that presided over the formation of my universe, itself constrained by the same regularities that saw me appear at a given moment in its history. The final scene of *2001: A Space Odyssey* expresses this abysmal cosmological truth: the newborn child, surrounded by a halo of light, opens his round eyes to the perfect circularity of the stars, he is the product of this circularity, the completion in a sense of this infinite legal process which, by some incomprehensible mystery, has ended up raising matter above itself.

If, in fact, we were to admit by thought experiment the existence of a world totally deprived of rules or even of any regularity (supposing such a world were possible), then integral materialism would undoubtedly become admissible: the rule no longer existing, matter would no longer have to rely on it. Integral materialism, thus freed of all rules, could escape its contradictions, even though, in all rigour, logic being by definition excluded from this world, we would have nothing to think, believe or admit; we ourselves would be formations without substance, without rules and without purpose (for what is a rule if it is not the subjective and effective idea that represents and explains phenomena in an intelligible and dynamic way?). In this anomic world, we would not be able to say anything about the world (the very notion of discourse would be meaningless: there would be no idea, no communication, no possible correspondence), we would remain on the zero plane of matter. Matter would then be neither organised nor thinkable; it would simply be inert and equal to itself, floating between possibility and realisation. The very fact, however, that the world, through the prism of our sensitive perception, presents us with regularities — even if they are only statistical — the fact that we can say something about them (and even something false) is, for us, a confirmation that everything cannot be reduced to matter. As matter is not anomic, it is in fact not everything (it cannot describe totality in language). How can it claim to be totality when it obeys rules that are not reducible or assimilable to it (i.e. that cannot be said to be "material[38]")? We might rightly point out here that it is not matter as a "thing in itself" that we are talking about when we discuss "matter", but matter as a phenomenon, i.e. as the synthesis of our sensibility and imagination, as we will explain later (see *What is a thing?* § 23 — *Is there anything 'in itself'?*). When we talk about the rules of matter, we are consequently talking about the rules of phenomena, which constitute our

---

[38] Among other contradictions and paradoxes, if we were to suppose that the rules were themselves material, this would lead us to posit the existence of other rules that would regulate this matter, these other rules being themselves material would call forth others, and so on, ad infinitum.

only mode of access to reality. We are therefore saying nothing about matter as such (as the gross substratum of phenomena). Our response to this objection is that, no more in a discourse about "things in themselves" than in a discourse about phenomena (the substrates of things mediated by our consciousness), we cannot equate the rule with matter. From a dualistic perspective, which accepts that as sentient beings we only have access to phenomena (manifestations of things through the senses) and never directly to *things-in-themselves*, it is easy for us to show that the rule cannot be reduced to matter (that it is not material). To do this, all we must do is show that the rule is not a phenomenon (that it is therefore not "material" in a dualist perspective). So, let's consider the hypothesis that the rule is entirely reducible to phenomena, that is, that it is itself a phenomenon, a fortuitous and fortunate regularity that occurs materially in our brains every time we think about the rule. In that case, we would be unable to explain the objectivity of mathematics or geometry (its binding and non-relative character). This objectivity is established for us insofar as (i) the ideal figures of geometry, for example, are never found in nature in their perfect form (we have never seen a triangle, a square, or even a perfect circle in nature[39]), and (ii) the laws that derive from these ideal (or *ideal*) figures are invariable and therefore cannot be reduced to phenomena that are themselves changeable by nature (in Euclidean geometry, the sum of the angles of a triangle will always be equal to 180 degrees and the perimeter of a circle will invariably be equal to $2\pi r$,

---

[39] This is one of the great arguments of Hume's empiricism against rationalism.

independently of any phenomenal consideration) and (iii) these laws that are not reducible to phenomena are effective, i.e. they manage to explain reality and introduce new regularities into it. If then, we maintain that the mathematical rule is nothing more than a pure game of the mind (a game of the mind without concrete reality, a form of material self-delusion of the mind towards itself), it becomes impossible for us to explain the effectiveness of the rule. The proof of the total *apriority* and formal anteriority of the rule was given to us by non-Euclidean geometries, since it was in the nineteenth century that Gauss, Riemann and Christoffel founded differential geometries on strictly mathematical (and therefore legalistic) considerations, and it was only several decades later, at the beginning of the twentieth century, that these geometries found their effective application in the theory of relativity. Here, then, the *ideal* scheme (in the sense of "an abstract idea") historically preceded its concrete and effective application. Clearly, the rule was not derived from phenomena; on the contrary, it made it possible to explain them by means of an intellectual abstraction that preceded by several decades the discovery of a general theory of phenomena. The objection could still be raised that phenomena, as mental constructs, could well be mere appearances or pure illusions, with no actual causal relationship with a material substratum. In this case, our experience of the world would be limited to the perception of these phenomena, and it would then be impossible to postulate anything more than the perception of phenomenal reality "each time I perceive it" or it manifests itself to me: this is the position of psychologism or what has sometimes been called "psychological idealism". This conceptual framework, which lays claim to the most radical rigour, maintains that, insofar as we are always dealing with a phenomenal reality (a reality mediated by our senses), we can only make predictions and theories about this phenomenal reality, never about matter or the thing itself. Strictly speaking, this point of view is correct: we never deduce or apply the rule from or to a thing *in itself* (raw, unmediated matter), but this does not mean that the rule itself can be reduced to a pure phenomenon, or that the phenomenon is a mere illusion, which is what the most ardent psychologists and idealists have sometimes gone so far as to maintain (without proving it). It is true, however, that the problem of the relationship between the phenomenon and its substratum remains unresolved: we cannot rigorously prove that there is a *causal* link of a *deterministic* nature between "raw matter" and the phenomenon (although this proof is of little use to us insofar as we are never dealing with raw matter, but always with phenomena).

Based on these considerations, certain proponents of psychologism went so far as to question the reality of the external world (a world that would exist outside phenomena, i.e. outside our perception of the world *at the moment* we perceive it). This quarrel about the reality of the world was by no means a new issue; it had already permeated the history of philosophy, from Plato to Descartes, from Descartes to Kant[40], and continued to

---

[40] We are of course thinking of Plato's allegory of the cave or Descartes' hypothesis of the evil genius. In The *Critique of Pure Reason*, Kant provides a response to psychological idealism, relying in particular on our intuition of time: "I am

develop critically throughout the nineteenth and twentieth centuries. In a work published in 1969 entitled *Über Gewißheit* (*On Certainty*), which brings together aphorisms written by Wittgenstein between 1949 and 1951, the year of his death, Wittgenstein vigorously attacked the positions of G.E. Moore, and in particular one of Moore's aphorisms. Moore's positions, in particular one of his 1939 articles entitled *Proof of an External World*, in which Moore attempted to prove the existence of the world based on a purely

---

aware of my existence as determined in time. Any determination of time presupposes something *permanent* in perception. But this permanence cannot be an intuition in me. In fact, all the principles for determining my existence that can be found in me are representations, and as such need something permanent that is distinct from these representations, and in relation to which their change, and consequently my existence in the time in which they change, can be determined", *Transcendental Analytics*

Kant's refutation of psychologism prefigures Putnam's work on reference (see § 31 - *Against psychologism*). Kant wants to prove, against Descartes, that our internal experience is no more certain than our external experience. He even managed to reverse the position he attributed to Descartes, by establishing his thesis through a demonstration in which internal experience itself is only possible under the condition of external experience, so that external experience appears almost as more certain than internal experience, or, in any case, as its precondition, from the transcendental point of view. Awareness of myself in time is only possible through the determination of my existence in time, that is, through the succession or change of my representations in time. Awareness of my own existence is therefore at the same time an immediate awareness of the existence of other things outside me.

subjectivist and apodictic approach that Wittgenstein rejected. G.E. Moore sought to refute scepticism by proposing a simple and direct demonstration of the existence of the external world. He began by establishing three criteria that a rigorous proof must meet: the premise must be distinct from the conclusion, it must be known to be true, and the conclusion must logically follow from it. On this basis, he proposed an empirical proof: by showing his hands and saying "here is one hand, and here is another", he concluded that external objects manifested themselves to us and, therefore, that an external world existed (first premise: "here is one hand", second premise: "here is another", conclusion: "there are at least two external objects, therefore an external world exists — this is deductive reasoning applied to an empirical proof). Moore defended the legitimacy of this proof by explaining that we had more certainty about the immediate perception of our hands than sceptical doubt about what called it into question. He thus overturned the Cartesian demand for an ultimate justification, asserting that we have immediate access to the outside world, without the need for metaphysical demonstration. His argument was based on a common-sense epistemology, in which perceptual evidence prevailed over sceptical hypotheses, thus invalidating the idea that we must first prove the existence of the world before experiencing it. In *On Certainty*, Wittgenstein responded to Moore with a pithy formula: "you don't know anything at all!" The formula may seem to indicate a sceptical stance, but Wittgenstein's context and intention are more complex and subtle. Wittgenstein was criticising Moore's use of the term 'knowledge'. For Wittgenstein, Moore's propositions (such as 'here is a hand') were not examples of ordinary knowledge, they were in fact too fundamental to be subject to verification or doubt. They were, in Wittgenstein's view, to form the very framework within which propositions of ordinary knowledge could be formulated. Wittgenstein thus introduced the idea of "*hinge propositions*", which are fundamental beliefs that we do not question in everyday practice. These certainties are not verified by evidence but are accepted as necessary starting points for all discourse and rational enquiry. Wittgenstein thus drew a distinction between what we can know in an ordinary sense (specific, verifiable facts) and these fundamental certainties, which in his view were closer to belief (a fundamental, structuring belief that constituted the framework of all possible knowledge). To say, according to Wittgenstein, "I know that this is a hand" in a context where there is no possible doubt about the fact that we have a hand in front of us, fact emptied the term "knowledge" of its ordinary meaning. By saying to Moore, "You don't know anything at all", Wittgenstein was not really defending a sceptical position but rather seeking to clarify the meaning of the term "knowledge". He wanted to show that Moore's assertions, although correct in an everyday sense, were not knowledge in the strict sense. Rather, for Wittgenstein they were fundamental certainties that formed the framework for our thinking and actions.

Following Wittgenstein, we recognise that statements of existence, like totalising propositions, cannot generate knowledge, even though they do not necessarily belong to what Wittgenstein called 'fundamental certainties'. Because of their logical structure, these statements turn out to be either tautological or contradictory: they cannot produce anything more than themselves and, in so doing, do not provide access to a determined and effective knowledge of reality. Here we come to the impasse inherent in any monistic system, which lies in the very nature of its assertions, most often formulated in the form of existential statements such as "the world exists" (realism), "the world does not exist" (illusionism), "everything is matter" (integral materialism) or "everything is an idea" (absolute idealism or psychologism). These statements of existence can in fact be reduced to totalising statements or their negation: they are not applied to any particular category but always refer to a whole that is not defined (or delimited). In fact, the statement "the world exists" means nothing more than "everything I can perceive or feel has an existence", and since existence is itself defined as what can be perceived (felt or measured), the preceding statement amounts to the assertion "everything that exists for me has an existence for me" (which is tautological), whereas the statement "the world does not exist" means nothing more than "nothing has an existence" (negation of the totalising statement). As the negation of a tautological and totalising statement (a statement that does not refer to a defined set — and is therefore more of an axiom or definition than a hypothesis that needs to be corroborated or invalidated), it is contradictory (it is a pure assertoric negation). Thus, for example, the statement "nothing exists" presupposes that reasonings themselves are defined as "non-existent", which would be *nonsense* for us insofar as it would disqualify the very framework, we need to think about what exists and what does not. Such a statement therefore comes up against a performative contradiction: it presupposes the existence of the logical framework necessary for its enunciation, while denying that very framework. If statements of existence applied to undefined totalities and their negation are not symmetrical (some being tautological, others contradictory) it is precisely because their very expression depends on the use of a signifying language which, on the one hand, we can only define as "something" (at the risk of falling into a contradiction) and which, on the other hand, is the only instrument capable of founding or contradicting the proposition in question (if we delegitimise the signifying framework, the statements become undecidable).

If we try to formalise our problem in classical logic, we obtain the following formula: $\forall x, x \in W$, which means that whatever x exists, x is an element of W where W is "the *world*", i.e. the totality of what exists. In classical set theory (Zermelo-Fraenkel), such a set is not definable because of Russell's paradox[41] (a paradox which in fact underlines the nonsense of totalising propositions insofar as they are self-referential without restriction; we shall return to this later, see in particular Cantor's

---

[41] Russell's paradox concerns the set R defined as the set of all sets that do not belong to themselves: $R = \{x \mid x \notin x\}$
The question is: does R belong to itself?

— If $R \in R$, then by definition it must not belong to itself.

— If $R \notin R$ then by definition it must belong to itself.
This contradiction shows that a set cannot be defined without a restriction on membership, which invalidates the idea of a totalising set containing "all sets".

paradox, which derives from Russell's paradox, § 34 — *Intuitionism as a response to the logical aporias of formalism?*, footnote). In modal logic, we could express the proposition as follows: $\forall x, \Diamond E(x)\ x \rightarrow \in W$, which amounts to the tautological proposition "if x can exist in a possible world, then it belongs to the totality of possible worlds". Finally, in existential logic, if we understand "the set of possible x's" as all the values that x can take within a defined world, then we can write: $X \subseteq W$ where X represents the set of all the values that x can take and W is the set of the real world, which means: "everything that can be taken as a value of x belongs to the world". Finally, if we want to specify that x can take any value without restriction, then we simply have: $X=M$, which means that the set of possible values of x is exactly the set of the world

Formula	Meaning of the formula	Logical problem
$\forall x, x \in W$	Everything belongs to the real world (totalisation problem in set theory).	Trivial tautology
$\forall x, \Diamond E(x) \rightarrow x \in W$	Everything that is possible belongs to the possible worlds.	The undecidability of possibilities
$X \subseteq W$	Everything that is possible belongs to the real world.	Lack of distinction between what is possible and what is real
$X=W$	The set of possibilities and the world are identical.	Lack of distinction between what is possible and what is real

In the same way, if we now study the contradictory proposition that the world does not exist, we obtain the logical proposition $W = \emptyset$ where W is the set containing everything that exists. Our proposition therefore means "the set of everything that exists is empty". However, the statement "the world does not exist" has to be formulated and understood by someone. For this sentence to be formulated, there *must at least* be: a speaker who speaks, a logical system in which the statement makes sense, a minimal framework of existence in which this sentence is formulated. But if $W=\emptyset$, then nothing exists, not even the statement itself. So, we have a performative contradiction: the very act of stating that "the world does not exist" presupposes that something exists (at least language and the speaker). The problem here is analogous to that of self-negating totalities: if W is a totalising set (including everything that exists), then to say that W is empty is to say "everything is nothing", which is contradictory (reminiscent of the contradiction of the set of all sets that do not belong to each other in Russell's paradox). If we rephrase the proposition in modal logic, we can write: $\neg \exists x(x \in W)$ which means "there are no elements belonging to W". But this is problematic, because if the statement is true, then nothing exists, not even the statement itself (since W is the set of everything that exists). But if the statement exists, then something exists, which immediately refutes the proposition. Thus, we have a self-referential contradiction, reminiscent of the paradoxes of self-destructive propositions. Another way of expressing this idea would be to propose: $\forall x, x \notin W$, which means "for all x, x does not belong to the world". But this formulation is also problematic, because if W represents everything that exists, then this sentence amounts to saying "nothing exists", which, once again, self-destructs the very possibility of stating anything.

Formula	Meaning of the formula	Logical problem
$W=\emptyset$	The whole of everything that exists is empty	Impossible if W is supposed to contain everything that exists.
$\neg \exists x(x \in W)$	There is no element belonging to W	Absolute negation, but refutes its own statement
$\forall x, x \notin W$	For all x, x does not belong to the world	Self-reference problem: the statement itself would have to not exist.

If we now study the hypothesis that the world exists only in me, that my perceptions are mere illusions, dreams and phantasmagoria, would we not be led to similar reflections? What does it mean that the world exists only in me, if not that the '*I* is everything'? Aren't we once again faced with a new totalising statement? In fact, the statement "the *self* is everything" means nothing more than "everything that exists is *me*", or, to put it slightly differently, "everything that exists can be described as 'me'". How much knowledge does this statement contain? In reality, the statement is once again a pure assertoric proposition of the type $\forall x, x \in M$, where M ("Me") represents the set of all sets. Not only does this statement generate a zero sum of knowledge for the subject, but it also comes up against an internal contradiction. As in our previous reasoning, this totalising statement poses the problem of Russell's paradox[42] (which invalidates the idea of a set containing

---

[42] Russell's paradox highlights a fundamental problem with totalizing sets that include themselves without restriction.

Application to monism: the contradiction of a totalising whole

Absolute monism postulates that there is only one reality that includes everything. For example:

— Materialist monism: "everything is matter".
— Idealistic monism: "all is spirit".
— Radical solipsism: "everything is me".

We shall see how these assertions encounter a problem of self-inclusion and self-reference, analogous to Russell's paradox.

Paradox of materialist monism: "everything is matter".

If we define the whole of the world W as the whole of everything that exists and say:
W={x| x is material}, but we can then ask the question: "Is the concept of matter itself material?".

> — If the notion of 'matter' is itself material, then it is a material object among others, which poses a problem because a conceptual category cannot be a physical object. What are the material attributes of the notion of matter? Does it have mass, volume or position in space? If it does not have these properties, then it is not material in the sense of materialist monism. So, if the notion of "matter" is material, then it becomes an object among the objects it defines, which poses a problem (self-inclusion).
>
> — If the notion of 'matter' is not material, then not everything is matter, which refutes materialist monism.

So, as in Russell's paradox, the set of material things cannot include its own definition without contradiction.

Paradox of idealist monism: "all is spirit".

If we assert that "everything is mind", E={x| x is material}, then this assertion itself must be a product of the mind, i.e. an idea or a representation. But then, is the person who states this proposition also reducible to a simple idea?

> — Either the enunciator is only an idea, in which case there is no autonomous subject to formulate and validate the statement "all is mind", which deprives it of any cognitive significance.
>
> — Or enunciation presupposes a sentient subject who formulates ideas: in this case, idealist monism collapses, since we must then admit a reality that cannot be reduced to the mind (the subject who enunciates).

This paradox highlights a fundamental problem with idealist monism: it cannot account for the condition of enunciation that makes it possible, without presupposing a level that exceeds its own framework.

An idealist might object that the reflexive level of thought does not contradict monism, but is a manifestation of it, by incorporating into its definition of mind a dynamic relationship between thought and self-reflection. For example, Hegelian absolute idealism does not conceive of the mind as a static entity, but as a dialectical process that knows itself through its own determinations.

Answer: the point here is to distinguish Hegel's absolute idealism from the "simple" subjective idealism of Berkeley, for example. Hegel does not deny the existence of matter but integrates it into a dialectical process in which it is only a moment in the development of the mind. For Hegel, matter is not primary, but it is not illusory either. Moreover, the very idea of a dynamic process of the mind implies *radical* dualism, including for Hegel (who sees dialectics, and therefore dual oppositions, as the driving force behind dynamism).

Paradox of solipsism: "everything is me".
If we say: "everything that exists is me", then we have: $M=\{x|\ x=me\}$, but once again we can ask the question, as we did above, is the idea that "everything is me" itself me?

> — If this idea is me, then it is part of me, but who thinks it? This presupposes a distinction between *me* and *the idea of me*, which introduces a duality into solipsistic monism.
> — If this idea is not me, then everything is not me, and the statement is false.

all sets). To illustrate this paradox, consider the following proposition: "Is the idea that 'everything is *me*' itself *me*? If this idea is *me*, then it is part of me, but who thinks it? This presupposes a distinction between *me* and *the idea of me*, which introduces a duality into solipsistic monism (and invalidates the proposition that "everything is *me*"). If this idea is not *me*, then everything is not *me*, and the statement is false.

As soon as we accept the hypothesis — we have to recognise the existence of a world that is external to us (i.e. a world that is not reducible or assimilable to us), which has been widely corroborated to this day — Mathematics, for example, was there before we were born and will still be there after our death. We conceived it, but it is independent of our existence and our experience of the world. The notion of rule, or legality, even if it is nothing outside the moment when

---

Solipsism therefore encounters a self-refutation, because it is obliged to separate itself into an idea and a thinking subject, which is contradictory to the initial assertion.

Russell's paradox shows that totalities defined without restriction are self-contradictory. Radical monisms (materialism, idealism, solipsism) attempt to define a single totality, which exposes them to similar contradictions. So, any absolute monism tends to collapse when analysed logically, because of the same problem as Russell's paradox: a totality that tries to contain itself is unstable and contradictory. One solution would be to introduce a distinction between levels of reality (e.g. matter/consciousness, subject/object), which leads to *radical* dualism. Another approach would be not to attempt to totalise reality in a single category, which leads to a pluralist vision of the world.

we think it, transcends our experience of phenomena just as it must necessarily transcend their material substrates (even if we cannot demonstrate a causal link between the phenomenon and its material substrate, neither can we conceive of the existence of a universe without coherence that would not collapse in on itself). Thus, relating the rule to psychological mechanisms or mental processes cannot alter its normative and universal character. It is only on the condition of this universalisable normativity that we can aspire to a form of objective communicability, in other words to science and knowledge in general. We live, in fact, in a universe that has not collapsed in on itself, in which matter presents regularities, obeys rules that we have, moreover, the possibility of understanding and formulating[43]. This, then, is what dualism is: the separation of idea (rule) and matter, of idea and its concrete manifestation. The mere existence of a coherent world, which is both intelligible to us and which we cannot logically assimilate to the *self*, is enough to refute reductionist materialism, and at the same time to rule out any form of monism. The rule is

---

[43] Whether we manage to do this, or even whether we can do it completely, is another debate that we are not addressing at the moment. All we need to do here is to understand and accept that matter is not anomic (that it is organised)— which the meagre chances of subsistence in the possible and realised universe in which we live give us a strong (if not sufficient and decisive) indication— that in fact, we can legitimately hope to understand and formulate the rule or rules that govern its formation and organisation and that, as a collateral effect, since the rule that governs matter cannot be reduced to matter (which would be contradictory), matter is not everything.

neither reducible nor assimilable to matter; it is merely the formalisable, but non-material, condition of its existence and persistence: a universe without coherence cannot exist (existence presupposes coherence as a condition). This dualism is what we describe as "radical".

14.

WHAT IS AN ORGANISM? THE AUTONOMOUS NATURE OF ORGANISMS, THEIR ABILITY TO PRODUCE RULES — In *L'homme neuronal*, Jean-Pierre Changeux expresses, perhaps unwillingly, this paradox of matter: "the nervous" system, he claims, "is composed of the same 'matter' as the inanimate world[44]." It is indeed the same "matter", says Changeux, and yet a fundamental difference appears in the use of the term "inanimate", which is implicitly part of the "animate-inanimate" pair. Animate matter is, in fact, the sign and manifestation of a *radical* dualism within the world, not only because it cannot be reduced to the elements of which it is composed (these elements being in themselves identical to inanimate matter) but also and above all because unlike inanimate matter, animate matter has the capacity to interact with the world, in other words to react to stimuli from the world in an autonomous mode. A living organism is not the physical equivalent of a stone, even in its simplest forms, and its reaction to a given *stimulus* will be autonomous and not just heteronomous: a stone moved by a kick has no autonomous organic reaction.

---

[44] Jean-Pierre Changeux, *L'homme neuronal*, p. 123

15.

FROM ORGANISM TO LANGUAGE ORGANISATION: THE DUALISMS OF LANGUAGE — The "simple" or first-degree dualism, which consists of separating the animate from the inanimate, is found in almost all language structures. In most statements made by a speaker, the subject (the animate organism) is either explicit ("I see a plane taking off") or implicit ("the plane is taking off"). When I say "the plane is taking off", I'm actually making the following proposition: *I*[45]

---

[45] In *The Philosophy of Symbolic Forms*, Ernst Cassirer, a neo-Kantian of the Marburg school, shows clearly this implicit presence of the subject or *ego* in all the propositions of language, through a comparative study of primitive languages, despite the sometimes-late appearance of the pronoun. See Ernst Cassirer, *The Philosophy of Symbolic Forms*, Volume 1, *Language, A Moment of Language: Intuitive Expression*, IV. *Language and the domain of "internal intuition"*. The moments of the concept of self:

"Until now, the main aim of the analysis has been to highlight the categories that guide language in the construction of the world and objective intuition. But it has already become clear that this methodological limit cannot be respected with any real rigour. On the contrary, in order to expose these "objective" categories, we were always brought back to the subjective sphere; each new determination that the world of objects received also had a knock-on effect on the determination of the world of the self.

[Humboldt has already spoken out against the "narrowly grammatical conception" [of pronouns], and with decisive reasons. He asserts that it is completely incorrect to think of the pronoun as the latest part of speech: for the primary element of speech is the personality of the speaker himself,

(or something I identify as being the *I*) perceive (my senses, my sight, my hearing...) an object that I identify as a plane (it has wings, an engine, a body, I identify the object as a "plane"-shaped mass of matter) leaving the ground. While language always indicates a differentiation between the speaker and the world (the speaker and his immediate environment, the speaker and the gods, etc.), at the same time, in its very structure, it marks a separation between the idea put forward by the speaker and the world to which it is compared (at least in the affirmative forms of language). When I say: "the plane is taking off", my proposition, like most of the propositions I can make about the world, can be compared with the perception of the plane's passengers or the airport staff, who will in all likelihood see that the plane has indeed taken off. The proposition (the idea) that I saw an aeroplane taking off reflects the *radical* dualism of the world in two ways, not only because I perceive myself as a separate being, a speaker making a proposition about the world, but above all because I establish a separation between my proposition (my "idea") and the situation (or object) to which it refers (my idea has no wings and makes no noise). In this sense, language is structurally dualistic. By proposing an idea, it identifies it as separate from the object to which it refers (in the case, it goes without saying, where the idea has an object, since not all syntactic structures are obviously organised around the proposition/object pair).

---

who is in immediate contact with nature and who cannot refrain from opposing it, even in language, with the expression of his ego."

16.

Radical dualism in mathematics: Mathematics formalises the structures of language — Mathematics is also based on the idea of the correspondence of propositions. The equal sign, insofar as it does not apply to identical propositions (2=2), clearly indicates this relationship of correspondence between propositions that imply each other without being formally identified (2+2=4). In algebra, functions of the type *f(x)* use a transformation relationship to force variables x to take one or more values predetermined by the form of the function and belonging to a plane different from that of the variables being tested. The function *f(x) = sin (2πx)*, for example, will cause a given value of the variable x on the abscissa plane to correspond to one or more constrained *f(x)* values on the ordinate plane.

Function *f(x) = sin (2πx)*

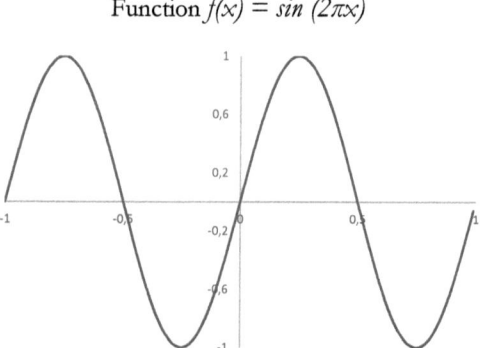

In this function, the variable *x = 0.25* will return, for example, the value *f(x)=1*. The variable *x* is constrained by the function of *f(x)*. Mathematics therefore adopts, in its very structure, the form of *radical* dualism (symbolised here by the sign "equal" but which can take other forms depending on the relationship expressed). In this sense, the idea that mathematics refers to a relative truth insofar as this truth derives exclusively from axioms or postulates is partially false. We certainly do not wish to contest that mathematics, as a formal exercise, is not interested in the content of the objects it designates[46]. On the other hand, this formal exercise does contain a truth that concerns our relationship to the world, in other words, a 'non-formal' truth. This 'non-formal' truth is, to use the Kantian vocabulary, 'synthetic' in that it operates a synthesis, a relation of identity between two *a priori* heterogeneous elements. Mathematics, particularly in its algebraic form, is the manifestation of reason's effort at synthesis. This effort at synthesis, which is the very form of *radical* dualism, takes place both in the formal relations of mathematics (in non-tautological relations of equality) and in the elementary structures of language ("the plane is grey" or even, in a different sense, "the plane takes off"), which in fact express a triple duality: formal duality (differentiation of subject and predicate, expression of a relation), duality between the proposition and its object, duality between the speaker and his proposition. So it matters little whether mathematics refers to a fundamental truth or a relative truth in a closed system derived from axioms, postulates or hypotheses,

---

[46] As Henri Poincaré wrote in *Science and Hypothesis*, "mathematicians do not study objects, but relations between objects; they are therefore indifferent to replacing these objects with others as long as the relations do not change. Matter does not matter to them, only form".

because the importance of mathematics in relation to the problem of truth lies in the very essence of what it expresses: a relation of correspondence, i.e. the form of a proposition that compares itself to something other than itself in order to identify or differentiate itself from it (in this sense, form goes beyond form, postulates more than form).

17.

OBJECTIONS TO REDUCTIONISM ON THE STATUS OF FORMAL COHERENCE — Based on the principles of Darwinism, reductionist physicalists assert that formal coherence is merely an extension of the principle of species conservation. For them, coherence and truth are nothing in or of themselves; they are simply a manifestation of the most primal disposition of man and every living organism: the survival instinct. In other words, for man, truth is 'what works', what produces a result and thus enables him to maintain or increase his mastery of a world that is originally hostile to him. This is the correlate of the theory of survival of the fittest: the organism with the greatest chance of survival is the one that best adapts to its environment. Here again, the physicalist theory falls into the trap of tautology. No one would dispute that the organism that adapts best to its environment will have the greatest chance of survival (and the proposition could easily be turned on its head by stating its correlate: the organism that has the greatest chance of survival is the one that adapts best to its environment). The tautological loop closes on itself. What is adaptability? The ability to survive. What is the ability to survive? The ability to adapt). But here again, there is a strong dualistic unthinking. To adapt to the world, the organism must differentiate itself from it. In every form of organisation, there is a struggle, a confrontation between organised matter (the organism) and its negation (inert matter, other organisms). The notion of organism cannot therefore be understood without a form of *radical* dualism between the organism and that which resists it, that which attacks it, that which denies it or nourishes it. Between the organism and that which is not it lies what Darwin calls the faculty of adaptation. Adaptation is therefore a form of mediation between two worlds (the organism and its environment). To adapt to its environment, the organism has no choice but to integrate it, to "codify" it into a coherent whole that it "understands". Comprehension here is not just passive (the organism receiving information from the world, what has been called, not without ambiguity, "*sense data*[47]"), it is an activity of the organism that simplifies the world by codifying it (see Jakob Johan von Uexküll's famous analyses of the concept of Umwelt and the analysis of the life of the tick, to be dissociated however from Heidegger's dubious recovery[48]). As the

---

[47] See Bertrand Russell, The *Problems of Philosophy*, chapters I to V.

[48] The tick, perched on its branch, reacts to only three stimuli: the olfactory *stimulus* (perception of the smell of mammalian sweat glands), which encourages it to drop from its branch when a mammal passes by; the tactile *stimulus*, which enables it to reach a hairless area of the skin; and the attraction of blood, which enables it to fill itself with the mammal's blood, lay its eggs and then die by dropping. Although limited compared to our own, this world is a fully-fledged, codified and comprehensible world for the tick.

organism grows and develops, the codification, like the meshes of a spider's web, becomes more complex, forming a more complete transcription of the world. The notion of adaptability, as mediation between the organism and the world, therefore implies the idea of relative coherence (in relation to its environment, the organism naturally seeks to survive, avoiding situations of destruction) not as a consequence of the organism's readiness to adapt, but as a *condition* of adaptation. The idea of formal coherence (itself derived from the idea of relative coherence, see for example Ernst Cassirer's analyses of the appearance of the number[49]) and the idea of truth as the correspondence of a coherent proposition with reality cannot therefore be reduced to the survival of the organism, but is its condition and rule.

18.

HOW CAN WE CONCEPTUALIZE THE LINK BETWEEN THE EMERGENCE OF CONSCIOUSNESS, THE DEVELOPMENT OF LANGUAGE STRUCTURES, AND THE DETERMINISM OF NATURAL PHENOMENA: WHAT IS FREEDOM? — The dominant conception of freedom as the absence of constraints and the unalterable capacity for self-determination — in short, the idea of freedom conceived in terms of free will — has its origins in the thought of Saint Augustine and medieval scholasticism. However, this perspective has been heavily criticised and generally abandoned by modern philosophers,

---

[49] Ernst Cassirer, *The Philosophy of Symbolic Forms*, Volume 1, *Language*, A Moment of Language: Intuitive Expression, III. The linguistic development of the concept of number

particularly since the work of Spinoza (notably in *Ethics*, 1677). Despite this, the question of freedom continues to be approached, particularly by physicalists[50], within a sterile binary framework that radically opposes the subject's supposed free will to the determinism of nature. This debate, which has now been reduced to a dead-end opposition of principles, is in fact merely a replay of positions that have already been widely discussed throughout the history of philosophy. On the one hand, materialism[51], consistent with its principles, cannot accept any reality other than matter, and legitimately invokes the principle of causality[52] as a condition for all thought and action. On the other hand, a certain metaphysics postulates the existence of an immaterial soul capable of introducing a new and undetermined cause into the causal chain of natural phenomena. This conceptual impasse testifies to a framework of thought which, by remaining locked in this alternative, struggles to grasp freedom other than

---

[50] As with many others... On this point, reductionist physicalists, neo-Darwinists and other radical materialists are more excusable than on others, with the pairing of free will and determinism still setting the pace for many discussions from another era.

[51] It should be pointed out here that there are philosophers, particularly in the analytic philosophy movement, who claim to follow materialist methodology without being reductionists (Putnam, Davidson, Moore, Austin, Quine, etc.).

[52] A principle which, we would point out once again, being neither a property of things nor a material thing, curiously comes to the rescue of integral materialism...

in the form of a contradiction between necessity and spontaneity.

We take it for granted, and would not dream of contesting, that any definition of freedom must deal with a double level of determinism, the first being the determined causal chain of phenomena that take place in the world, the second being the determined causal and physical chain that supports our own thoughts. In other words, we start from the radical materialist position, which admits that each of our actions, like each of our thoughts, is determined by a physical causal chain (in this our position undoubtedly differs from that of Kant's critical work, which seems to more explicitly separate the intelligible from the sensible phenomena). By taking this hypothesis to be true — that is, by starting from the point of view of the monistic materialist theory — we nevertheless came up against the problem of the rule, and then more generally the problem of the idea, which seemed to us not to be entirely reducible to matter (even if we did not, for all that, contest their material support, see § 10 to 17). We therefore concluded that monism was incomplete: materialism, being incapable of justifying itself needed a foundation that was external to it. Rule, as a non-material element that cannot be reduced to matter, appeared to us to be a necessary condition for the existence and persistence of organised matter. Moreover, our own capacity to formulate the rule and express it in the idea (the idea being here the successful or failed expression of the formulation of the rule) seemed to us to be an additional argument against integral materialism. A convinced materialist could no doubt have objected that the rule could be a mere construction of our brain, with no real correspondence with the thing itself. From the strict point of view of this materialist (accepting his epistemological framework), the remark appeared to us to have little explanatory power, since it failed to explain the effectiveness of the rule (most of the time, all other things being equal, the plane takes off, the laws of aerodynamics are respected, the rule is safe). However, if the rule were effective, if it made it possible to explain the world and if it found empirical confirmation, then it could not be held to be a mere production of our brains. Moreover, since the monist rejected all duality, it was difficult for him to hide behind the opposition between phenomenon and matter to justify the idea that the rule was only effective on the phenomenon and never on matter itself.

If we now adopt the point of view of a radical dualist[53], i.e. if we admit that we never have access to raw matter, but only to phenomena (to the manifestation of things through our senses), we can once again consider the idea according to which rule could be nothing but a pure production of our brain on which phenomena would be regulated. But then we are faced with a problem of the same kind as that raised by monistic materialism: how can we explain the fact that matter produces the same effect on its phenomenal manifestation every time, without being 'the same' every time? Why, in other words, should there be a radical divorce between the thing and its expression,

---

[53] We are referring here to the most radical ontological dualism, i.e. the idea of a total disconnection between the intelligible world (the world of ideas) and the material world.

between the raw materiality of things and their manifestation through our senses? Why, finally, should this radical divorce always be so well regulated and produce a constancy between the thing and its phenomenal expression that allows us to apprehend the phenomenon with the surprising regularity that characterises it? Assuming that the rule is only a production of our brain with no concrete link to the thing, the radical dualist, like the monist, would fail to explain the relationship of constancy between "raw matter" and its phenomenal manifestation on the one hand, and the effectiveness of the rule in the world of phenomena on the other. So, if *radical* dualism is allowed to challenge — in a speculative way only — the nature of the link between matter and phenomenon, it is not allowed to challenge the nature of the effective link between rule and phenomenon. In other words, whether we take the monist or the dualist point of view, we can only explain the effectiveness of the rule by admitting that it is not reduced to a simple production of our mind, but that it is also a determining factor of the object to which it applies (independently of whether or not we assume the problem of the effective link between the phenomenal object and its material substratum to have been solved). The effectiveness argument certainly does not solve the problem of the evolution of science, and therefore of the rectification or modification of the rule (the transition from Newton's universal law of gravitation to Einstein's theory of general relativity, for example), but it does *at least* make it possible to establish that there is a positive relationship (non-zero because it is "effective", producing a measurable effect) between (i) the idea as formulation of the rule, (ii) the phenomenon and (iii) the material reality to which the rule relates. In other words, if the rule determines the thing, the idea of the rule is its more or less faithful (more or less effective) formulation. In fact, changing the rule does not necessarily invalidate the previous rule: even if Einstein's theory of general relativity is more powerful in explaining the universe than Newton's universal law of gravitation, Newton's equations are still valid and effective in applications of classical mechanics (a field in which they are still widely used). Nothing could be further from the truth, then, than to regard science as a succession of theories which, invalidating each other, would call into question the very notion of scientific truth.

Having established the link between truth and effectivity, it is now easier for us to specify what we mean by the idea of freedom. While at first it may have seemed to us that freedom must necessarily be understood as the antithesis of determinism, it now seems clearer to us that freedom is, on the contrary, very closely linked to this fundamental principle. Indeed, how can we claim to exercise our freedom in a world whose causal chains could be altered or broken at any moment by that "evil genius" that Descartes referred to in his *Six Metaphysical Meditations*? Wouldn't we then find ourselves deprived of freedom on two counts: firstly, with regard to the intelligibility of the world (how can we exercise our freedom in a world that offers no regularity and that we cannot in fact understand), and secondly, with regard to the effective exercise of our freedom in the world (how can we exercise our freedom in a world that offers no stability in its causal chains, leaving the outcome of our actions totally unpredictable)? If then, we accept determinism[54] as the very condition of the possibility of all freedom, we must no longer think of freedom as the absence of constraints, but, on the contrary, as the ability to understand the relationships between constraints. In other words, the greater our understanding of the world, the greater our ability to act freely in it.

19.

DEGREES OF FREEDOM — If we follow the march of evolution, from the appearance of the most primitive forms of life — the single-celled organisms, prokaryotic cells at the origin of archaea and bacteria — to the eukaryotic cells that give rise to the most elaborate forms of life, from insects to mammals, we see a progressive complexification of living organisms with, as a corollary, an ever-increasing degree of independence from the environment from which they originate. As cells become more complex, they form autonomous organised systems with the capacity to sustain life, develop, reproduce and give rise to other living organisms. From the simplest forms of life to the most elaborate organic systems, living organisms acquire an ever-greater degree of freedom, which manifests itself in a broader ability to apprehend reality. The notion of freedom, insofar as we temporarily accept its use and relevance, does not therefore have quite the same meaning depending on whether we

---

[54] Or, *at the very least*, the principle of causality, if we want at all costs to get rid of the idea of determinism following the discoveries of quantum phenomena (we'll come back to this later).

apply it to a single-cell organism, a tick, a dog or a large primate.

What we call here the "degree of freedom" of the living organism is linked not to a subjective and regressive datum (freedom as the possibility of doing "what I want", which raises the question of the primary determination of the will) but to objective data: freedom as the capacity to react in an increasingly complex way in the face of a reality codified ("retranscribed") in an increasingly elaborate way by the organism. While the tick's autonomy[55] is undoubtedly less limited than that of the single-cell organism, it will have less capacity than the dog to adapt to a complex environment (escape from a predator, modify its behaviour in the face of an unforeseen situation). Similarly, the dog will have a lesser degree of understanding and ability to adapt to reality than the large primate, while the orang-utan, for example, will be able to handle tools and learn the rudiments of a sign language. It could certainly be objected that, in the examples we have just cited, the use of the term 'freedom' is inappropriate, freedom in its classical sense being understood above all as the possibility of self-determination of the subject and not as a kind of more or less complex faculty of efficient reaction in relation to a given reality. Our response to this objection is that there are undoubtedly essential degrees of difference between the freedom of the single-cell organism as we have defined it and freedom in the classical or common sense of the term (freedom as the capacity for self-

---

[55] Autonomy understood here as the ability to create one's own rules and adapt to increasingly complex situations.

determination), but we in turn ask the question: what, precisely, differentiates the single-cell organism from inert matter, if not the ability to create its own rules in an attempt to interact adequately with the world, to develop in it, to sustain itself in it and to reproduce in it? Doesn't freedom begin precisely with this ability to interfere with the world, i.e., in a sense, to understand it? Isn't the ability to understand the world (to learn from our failures, to modify our behaviour in the face of a new situation, even if only over several generations or even on the scale of the species) radically more developed in the single-cell organism than in the rock, stone or pebble (which, strictly speaking, have no 'interactions' with the world, their mode of relation to reality being purely passive)? Our objector might also point out that our definition of autonomy — which, for us, is consubstantial with freedom (autonomy being, as it were, the condition of freedom, the faculty that freedom exercises) — could easily be undermined by a mechanistic theory of organisms: although organisms are undoubtedly increasingly complex, they would not, for all that, manifest the slightest "autonomy". They simply react mechanically to *stimuli*. It is true, our objector would say, that the mechanics of the orang-utan are, in a sense, more elaborate and complex than those of the single-cell organism, but this does not mean that the prokaryotic cell or the orang-utan can demonstrate the slightest autonomy, the slightest faculty of self-determination, of understanding rules or of producing new rules. Our response to this is that the more or less *appropriate* reaction of a living organism to a given situation, if only for its own survival (avoiding an obstacle, escaping a predator, etc.), is already part of its freedom, insofar as the organism in this specific case demonstrates a capacity for understanding reality, an understanding that is admittedly limited and imperfect, but which nevertheless enables it, for example, to avoid the obstacle or escape its predator. In this respect, we can say that the orang-utan has a greater degree of freedom than the snail or the aphid, insofar as its ability to *effectively* understand the world is precisely superior to theirs. In other words, the orang-utan will in all probability be able to get out of more perilous situations than the snail. Its ability to adapt and react to unfamiliar situations will be greater, and its range of perception and understanding of the world more extensive. The orangutan's freedom can therefore be understood as both a degree of increasing detachment from blind matter and the ability to understand the world by creating a more faithful image or "mental map" of it, in other words, by "recreating" it in some way. In reality, it doesn't matter if the orang-utan perceives, codifies and interprets reality *correctly*, as long as this codification and interpretation of reality is *adequate*, i.e. enables it to achieve its objective: escape from a predator, stay alive, get around an obstacle *effectively*, successfully. This relationship of effectiveness allows us to affirm that the orangutan's relationship with reality is not arbitrary. There is, in fact, a link between the orang-utan and reality, which is a matter of truth (not absolute truth and undoubtedly imperfect, but truth nonetheless) and to which freedom is linked. Nevertheless, we can still concede to the mechanists that the freedom of the orang-utan, if it is objectively superior to that of the snail, is neither totally indeterminate nor, consequently, absolutely complete and, indeed, since determinism is, as we showed a little earlier, consubstantial with the idea of freedom, it would be difficult to criticise freedom for being exercised in a deterministic context. But freedom and determinism are not necessarily antithetical.

The idea of a progressive complexification of organisms according to increasing degrees of autonomy, which we have developed, presents a formal analogy with the notion of degrees of freedom in statistics. This is defined as the number of random variables that are not determined or fixed by an equation, or as the difference between the number of observations and the number of relationships that constrain them: the greater the number of variables or parameters influencing the response to a given event, the greater the degree of freedom of the equation. Let's say, for example, that we are asked to choose three numbers with an average of 10 as follows: {6,10,14} {3,9,18} {7,10,13}: once we have chosen the first two numbers, our choice of the third number is constrained (in the first example, if we chose 6 and 14, the third number is constrained, it can only be 10). So, once we have chosen 6 + 14 or 3+ 18 or 7 + 13, we no longer have a choice of last number: it must necessarily be the number that will enable us to obtain an average of 10. Here, the degree of freedom for three numbers is therefore 2 (we have freedom over the choice of two numbers, the third choice is constrained). The greater the number of variables, the greater the degrees of freedom and the greater the number of possible combinations for the same event: the same reaction can have a multitude of different motives, the same motive can give rise to a multitude of different reactions. Consequently, the greater the complexity (constrained, determined), the greater the freedom. However indeterminate it may be, freedom is always subject to determining factors, i.e. formally constraining factors. Furthermore, the greater the number of potential constraining factors, the greater the freedom, and not vice versa (a paradoxical idea which means, in a sense, that the greater my network of constraints, the greater my freedom of action).

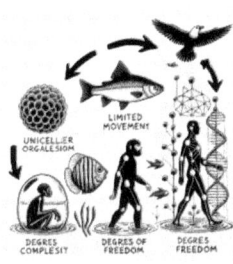

Applied to the biological world, this mathematical principle of freedom can be translated as follows: to obtain a similar result, a complex organism will have more possible combinations to choose from than a simple organism. Faced with a given danger, a large mammal, for example, will have many more avoidance or escape options than an insect or a single-cell organism. In other words, the reaction of a large mammal will be less determined, or more indeterminate, less predictable than that of an insect or eukaryotic cell. The more the predictability of an event decreases, the more that event, while remaining in the deterministic context in which it occurred, becomes indeterminate, i.e. free. This in no way means, however, that the event has no motive, but rather that the motive will give rise to an increasingly wide range of possible reactions as we progress towards the most complex forms of life. Both the pattern and the reaction to the pattern remain naturally determined, but their predictability diminishes as the number of combinations that determine the pattern or elicit the reaction increases.

20.

> Here we are, the only animals given the greatest means of communication, human speech, and all we do is snarl at each other.
>
> Fred Astaire in *The Band Wagon*, Vincent Minelli, 1953

THE IDEA AS NON-MATTER ACTING ON MATTER — In contrast to other animal species, including the most highly evolved, human beings are unique in their ability to use language as a vehicle for autonomous meanings. Human language is not limited to the ability to designate a known object or to satisfy a need; it opens up a space of meaning detached from the contingencies of immediate experience, enabling the elaboration of abstract ideas or judgements that go beyond the strictly sensible. According to Karl Popper, human languages are fundamentally different from animal languages, although they share two 'inferior' functions with the latter: self-expression and the exchange of signals. What makes human language unique, according to Popper, is its ability to go beyond these elementary functions of naming and satisfying needs to take on other, much more complex functions, described as 'higher'. Popper identifies two main functions: (i) the descriptive function, which makes it possible to represent and explain reality objectively, and (ii) the argumentative function, which creates a space for rational confrontation where ideas can be examined, criticised and justified. It is through the descriptive function that the regulatory idea of truth enters human language. Here, truth is understood as the adequacy between a proposition and the facts it is intended to describe. This regulating idea, itself founded on the principle of effectivity, establishes a normative horizon that guides all language activity towards a demand for fidelity to reality. The argumentative function is also based on the descriptive function: arguing consists of examining, criticising or justifying descriptions with reference to the regulatory idea of truth. However, although certain large primates, such as the orang-utan or the chimpanzee, show an ability to apprehend rudimentary sign systems, as Karl Popper himself observes, they remain deprived of the so-called "superior" language functions[56]. It should be noted in passing that it is not our intention here to draw an immutable line between the human species and the animal species at all costs, since the idea of rationality is not after all closed to or necessarily limited to the human species alone (even if today the gap between humans and animals still seems difficult to overcome, including among the most advanced mammals[57]). We note, however, that beyond the simple faculty of effective and adequate understanding of the world present in animals, man has a specific capacity: that of retroactively and critically confronting the idea of reality - that is, its meaningful description — with reality as it manifests itself to him. Faced with a danger or an

---

[56] See Karl Popper, *Objective Knowledge* (1972)
[57] Karl Popper himself points out, however, that it is not impossible for animals, and bees in particular, to go through stages of transition towards certain descriptive languages; see Karl von Frisch, *Bees: Their Vision, Chemical Senses and Language*, 1950; *The Dancing Bees*, 1955; and Martin Lindauer, *Communication Among Social Bees*, 1961.

obstacle, man's first reaction will be, for example, to flee or avoid the obstacle (an appropriate survival reaction that he shares with the animal), but unlike the animal, man will then be able to explain his behaviour, to give the *reason for* it. Man's motive for action is therefore not only instinctive (the immediate reaction of fear or aggression that he shares with most animals), but also analytical and retroactively critical[58]. Thanks to their use of the higher functions of language, humans are able to confirm or correct their judgements, in other words, to advance their knowledge of the world and of themselves. So, with the development and use of these higher functions, we are no longer confronted solely with the question of effectiveness. By freeing ourselves from the immediacy of organic life, language enables us to distance ourselves from reality. It is precisely through the prism of this distancing that the authentic question of truth is posed, that is, the problem of the

---

[58] Researchers placed peanuts in glass tubes floating on water in front of captive orangutans. The peanuts would have been inaccessible if the orangutans in question had had to use only their hands. The monkeys came up with a solution: sucking water into their mouths and spitting it back into the tubes to raise the water level so they could grab the reward. This example shows how some large primates are capable of solving complex problems. However, they fail to take a critical approach to the problem, i.e. to communicate the reason for their action through language. The many experiments that have been attempted to test the ability of the great apes to use the higher functions of language (descriptive or argumentative approach) have, as far as we know, all ended in failure.

correspondence[59] between a discourse and its object, and not just the problem of the adequacy of an action or behaviour with its expected result. If, through our experience of language, the nature of the relation of adequacy changes, the idea of adequacy remains. There is thus a form of continuity between effectivity as a problem of the adequacy of *action* to reality and truth as a problem of the adequacy of *discourse* to reality, discourse in turn being able, insofar as it does not relate solely to purely metaphysical objects, to be verified by experience, in other words to demonstrate its performative power, effective (we will come back to this idea of adequacy at length, resituating it in the more general problematic of language, levels of language and reference — let us just point out at this stage that the idea of adequacy is to be distinguished from now on from the idea that there would be a "magical" correspondence between a "subjective" discourse and the "objective" world, the world of "real" or "in itself" objects).

---

[59] Although the object of discourse is itself a construction of the subject, let us point out here that this constructed and not solely given character of the real does not prevent us, as we shall see, from retaining the general problematic of correspondence — which is itself a formal manifestation of the dual character of our relationship to the real (dualism between our signifying system and the real, dualism between the physical real and the real as it manifests itself to us, in our mental constructions).

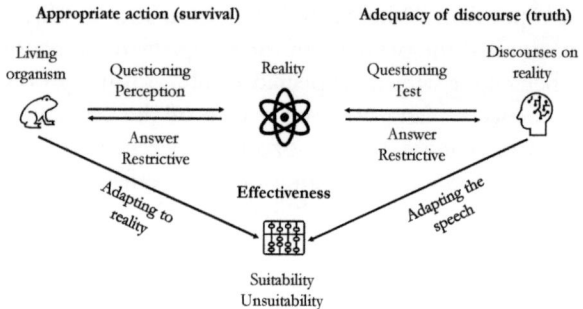

In our discussion of language and its descriptive function, we thus argue that human language differs from other forms of communication in that it allows a retroactive comparison between a description and reality, thus introducing the regulative idea of truth. However, this structure can also lead to a problematic self-inclusion: if language is based on a descriptive function, then the definition of language itself is based on an act of description. Consequently, this definition presupposes what it is trying to define: a capacity for language to formulate statements about itself. This brings to mind the problem raised by Wittgenstein in the *Tractatus*: language cannot entirely contain itself, without running the risk of taking itself as an object in a way that short-circuits its own functioning. This is why Wittgenstein ended up asserting that certain things had to be shown but not said (the famous distinction between what can be said and what can be shown). So is the descriptive function of language an absolute foundation, or does it depend on a wider structure that makes it possible?

One way of assessing whether these paradoxes are truly unavoidable would be to examine whether they are specific to a certain logical or philosophical approach. In a classical logical framework, self-inclusion paradoxes are problematic because they violate the principle of non-contradiction. But in a constructivist or pragmatic framework, it could be argued that self-inclusion is an emergent property of a system, not a fatal contradiction. In other words, some of the paradoxes we identify could be seen not as dead ends, but as epistemic thresholds where a change of framework is necessary. Should we then resolve these paradoxes by finding a more coherent reformulation, or accept that they reveal a limit inherent in our ways of thinking?

Our response to these two objections is that language is not an organised *corpus* or a constituted whole. It is not a 'group' but a meaning-generating activity. Language is therefore not an object, nor a set of objects that would make it possible to treat it as a formal system (a point that Kurt Gödel himself insisted on in his comments on his incompleteness theorems, to which we shall return later, see §31 — *Against psychologism*). Thus, attempting to define language as an action of description while engaging in an action of description may seem paradoxical, especially in our attempt to dismantle the self-inclusion paradoxes of monistic systems. However, unlike monistic systems, our theory finds pragmatic proof in the very existence of language. The fact is that language exists and that someone at least uses it. This is certainly an apodictic proof, but it is different from G.E. Moore's proof, which consists of the obvious observation that we have hands. Moore's proof is in fact a proposition of language and as such may be subject to controversy within language. Our proof, on the other hand, is not situated in language, but *is* language itself. It consists in showing (and not demonstrating — we agree with Wittgenstein on this point) that *there is* language. It is from this observation of existence that we deduce *radical* dualism (the existence of language implies it) and not the other way round. Moreover, it seems pointless to us to try to get out of monist paradoxes by appealing to constructivism, epistemic thresholds and 'emergent properties' for help when we are trying to describe and account for the emergence that is precisely language.

The idea of continuity between efficacy and truth implies that there is no radical epistemological break between the most primitive forms of life, complex organisms and human beings (we could even speak of a form of *continuum* between, for example, the emergence of forms of language, from the so-called inferior functions to the so-called superior functions). If we were to speak of a break, it would probably not be in the evolutionary process that led to the gradual emergence of language functions, but in the emergence of language as an autonomous domain, detached from the biological or environmental constraints that initially conditioned its genesis. Language cannot be reduced to a simple utilitarian codification of reality, defined by biological needs, nor to a strictly descriptive function ("there's a tree", "the plane is taking off") or a categorical function, based on a formal organisation of the world ("it's round", "it's triangular", "it's square"). It is also a space for expressing subjective judgement, through which individuals externalise their inner states ("I'm afraid", "I'm angry", "I'm cold"), and critical judgement, through which they confer normative values on the world ("It's beautiful", "It's good", "It's right"). The autonomy of language is based on its ability to go beyond its initial functions to become a vehicle for reflection, evaluation and the creation of meaning. By codifying itself, language becomes a system with its own rules, grammar and internal coherence, which, although shaped by interaction with the world, constitutes a sphere independent of the world. Language thus becomes the *medium* through which humans transcend the immediacy of their relationship with reality. This is what makes man the "*sick animal*". His illness is his separation from the world, his break with animality, of which language (as the logical expression of the world, language as *logos*) is the primary cause.

We would have been quick to challenge the idea of the autonomy of language in order to assert, alongside the materialists, that language merely relates a state of the relations of interest that exist between man and the world, and that it has no connection with what philosophers call "truth". If this objection of the materialists were correct — not to say "true" — "truth" could only be a strict equivalent of the notion of "necessity" of which language would only be the expression (language as an appendage of the instinct for self-preservation). It is true that by linking the problem of truth to that of efficacy, we have immediately placed the question of truth alongside that of utility. In this way, the whole problem of truth has been tainted by the more original problem of the relationships of necessity between organisms and their environment. Originally, it was indeed the need to survive, develop and reproduce that drove living organisms in their relationship with the world.

Confrontation with reality is therefore initially utilitarian. What is not, however, is *the response of* the world insofar as it delivers *binding* information to the individual who questions it, information whose nature cannot be changed. Truth comes precisely from that which constrains the organism, from that which pushes it, consequently, out of its strict individuality and beyond itself. If, therefore, the original nature of the confrontation with reality does indeed respond to utilitarian motives, then the judgement about the world is based on an inverted utility: the world does not adapt to the desires and interests of the organism; on the contrary, it is the organism that, if it wants to survive, must adapt to the constraining reality of the world. Necessity is therefore the spur to truth, but we need to agree on the notion of necessity: the adaptation of individuals to reality is necessary for their survival, not the other way round (reality doesn't care about the survival of the living organism, so it doesn't respond itself to the needs of organisms, it dictates its conditions, so 'truth' doesn't come from our needs, but from the necessities of reality that impose themselves on us). This adaptation to a constraining reality is precisely the mechanism that leads to the very possibility of truth (the real, says Lacan, is when we bump into it). Without discourse on the real, however, there can be no truth about the real. It is precisely here that we find the break, the leap between animality and humanity. Humanity, through its mastery of language, has the ability to formulate the problem, to take possession of it[60]: the world constrains both my will, my vision and my formulation of the world as a problem.

Once we start from this observation, the idea of an absolutely free will, escaping all forms of determinism, becomes meaningless and without content. Human freedom is in fact doubly determined: by physics on the one hand, and by the logical constraint of the chain of ideas of which it is the product on the other (a chain which we showed earlier cannot be totally reduced to physics, even if it is in some way constrained by physics itself). If a rational being, i.e. one capable of logical reasoning, does not accept these two networks of constraints, it cannot claim to influence its will, since freedom cannot be exercised in ignorance of its own conditions of existence. The rational being must therefore accept and, in a certain sense, embrace the network of constraints that determines him. "Long live physics!" exclaimed Nietzsche in *The Gay Science*, before adding: "... and even more so what compels us: our probity[61]!" If we are not to deny physics, if we are even

---

[60] Note that the word "comprehension" literally means to take possession of, to take with oneself (*comprehendere* in Latin).

[61] "But we want to become what we are, — unique, incomparable men, those who make their own laws, those who create themselves! And to this end, we must be among those who best learn and discover all that is law and necessity in the world: we must be physicists, to be able to be, in this sense, creators, — whereas all evaluation and all ideals, until now, have been based on a misunderstanding of physics, in contradiction with it. So long live physics! And long live that

to celebrate it, it is also up to us to see that we who celebrate it do not reduce ourselves to it! In this way we do not claim, against Nietzsche (and against the materialists — of whom Nietzsche is not one), to deny the physical determinisms of which we are the products. On the contrary, we seek to understand them, i.e. to progress in our knowledge of ourselves. On the other hand, if we accept the existence and nature of the physical causes that determine our will, we are challenging the hegemony of physics ("And *even more so*," writes Nietzsche, "our probity!" Physics is not everything, the probity *that compels us* is superior to it...).

But then, between the physical determinism that conditions even the most insignificant chemical exchanges that take place inside our brains and the logical constraints that reality imposes on our reason, what exactly is the place of freedom? For us, the idea of freedom is linked to two fundamental conditions: the first, which we have already briefly described, is the absence of constraint, i.e. the possibility of acting without being prevented from doing so (in this respect, the greater the possibilities for action, the greater the freedom); the second is knowledge of the motives and conditions for action (the possibility for the acting being to give a coherent reason for his action). In this way, our definition of freedom comes close to the Aristotelian definition of voluntariness as the union of two faculties: the spontaneity of desire (the expression of the desire to act free of all constraint) and the intentionality of the being who acts "with knowledge of

---

which compels us towards it— our probity!" Friedrich Nietzsche, *The Gay Science, IV, § 335, Long live physics!*

the cause" (knowledge of motives, the opposite of ignorance). While it seems to us that any definition of freedom must start from the problem of the physical determinisms of action, we do not reduce the problem of freedom to the *normative* recognition of these determinisms. In other words, it is not because every action is materially determined that material determinism becomes legitimate to support and explain all our actions (partly for the reasons we have already mentioned, which have to do with the intrinsically incomplete nature of materialism). This is why we do not subscribe to the idea of *amor fati*, which Nietzsche regularly mentions in his work. It is, in fact, only the normative shift that takes place between the recognition of the material (biological) determinisms of action and the axiological valorisation of these determinisms that leads Nietzsche to this concept of *amor fati*. Unlike Nietzsche, we do not believe that the recognition of the material determinisms that govern our actions necessarily entails their normative validation. Nietzsche, moreover, does not quite think so himself (he is neither a materialist nor a relativist; he nevertheless uses materialism to destroy idealism, without ever explicitly admitting that he is proposing a new form of idealism, derived from the love of matter). Acceptance of the double constraint, that is to say the double origin of the will, is not necessarily envisaged in the mode of reconciliation or quietism. Nothing assumes *a priori* that the physical de-termination of the will can harmoniously accord with its "ideal" or "*ideal*" determination. Quite often, on the contrary, the exercise of freedom results in a struggle between constraints of different kinds that clash within the rational being[62]. It is precisely in this internal struggle that the possibility of freedom manifests itself, which is defined not as the self-determination of the subject (free will) but as a tension towards the honest and enlightened[63] (or "probing") recognition of the deep-seated motives behind our actions. This recognition of motives, combined with our idea of the "right" (or "adequate") action, in turn leads to a modification of behaviour, in an upward spiral movement[64].

Whether or not human beings, insofar as they try to act according to the "good" or "adequate" idea, are able to emerge victorious from the internal struggle between their will and what weakens it, is undoubtedly beyond the strict scope of philosophy. However, invoking the failure of the will is not enough to free man from the burden of freedom. Even when confronted with the failure of his will, man, provided he remains in full

---

[62] It goes without saying that this being cannot be reduced to its rationality, which is what makes it so complex!

[63] What Nietzsche calls probity (*Redlichkeit*).

[64] The dynamic link between freedom and knowledge had already been widely explored by religions, particularly the Catholic religion (think, for example, of the practice of "examination of conscience" in the Christian tradition — "Search me, O Lord, and know my heart", Psalm 139, 23-2), and at the beginning of the twentieth century it also became the terrain of the new psychoanalysis, whose ambition was to help the subject better understand the unconscious mechanisms at the root of his behaviour, to enable him to act on their causes. By regaining control over the causes, the subject broadened his field of possibilities, thereby achieving a higher degree of freedom (think of the mathematical definition of the concept of freedom).

possession of his faculty of discernment, always makes use of what we call freedom, if only in an unfortunate or negative mode[65]. Man's freedom can only be conceived of as the exercise of upward pressure ("you must wage a campaign against yourself every day" writes Nietzsche in *Aurora*). This upward pressure is itself the result of the exercise of man's will, a will that he always exercises with a view to bringing his actions into line with the goal he has set for them (it is impossible to imagine a man who would put all his will at the service of the failure of his own goals). If a person acts inadequately (here we remain at the inframoral level), it can only be for two reasons: either (i) his will is deficient or influenced by exogenous factors against which he has not succeeded in fighting and which have introduced new motivations for action, or (ii) his conception of adequacy is bad, ineffective or incoherent (or dishonest, which is probably the most frequent case). These two reasons are in fact intrinsically linked, since the effort towards knowledge is an act of the will, and knowledge in turn determines the will. It is precisely this open spiral formed by (physical) will and (*ideal*) knowledge that we call "freedom" (freedom as an act of enlightened will). The unhappy man is hindered, limited in his freedom, but he remains free: he retains the capacity to go beyond that which is given to him by examining the foundations of the motives for his action, an examination which is moreover likely to modify its course. It also preserves its capacity to form a "just" or "conforming" idea of reality (without our even thinking

---

[65] The negative mode of freedom is what philosophers have often called 'bad conscience'.

at this stage of giving content to these ideas of justice or conformity). Freedom can thus only be conceived as a tension between two worlds, the material world of animality on the one hand, that of the struggle for survival and the satisfaction of primary needs, and the world of *logos* on the other, a world which has its own rules and autonomy, but which is also capable of having a determining (material) action on the will. The relationship between these two worlds is not necessarily conceived, however, in terms of harmony[66]. In other words, there is no philosophical basis for bringing the two worlds into harmony.

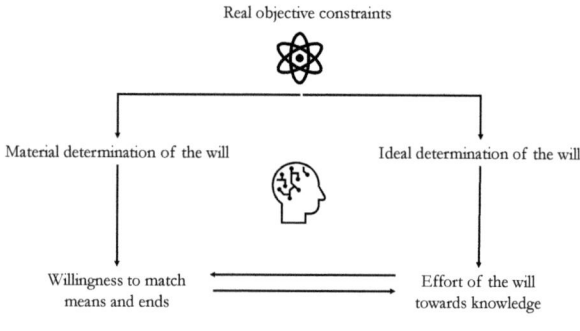

---

[66] Again, without going into moral considerations, we can see that human beings are capable, through the exercise of their critical rationality, for example, of deferring their needs *in their own interest* and against their primal instincts. We can conceive, for example, that a human faced with intense hunger (a primal instinct) might choose to fast temporarily as part of a medical regimen. By exercising critical rationality, we differentiate between our immediate needs (eating to satisfy hunger) and our long-term objectives (improving our health). They act in their own interests, but against their primal instincts.

21.

THE ACTIVE IDEA: MORALITY AS A POSSIBILITY — We have already attempted to establish (§ 15 to 18) that language, insofar as it allows us to express the legality of the world, is distinct from the pure matter from which it is derived. By offering the rational being the possibility of expressing the world in a way that is independent of the world, language is at once the possibility of error, but also the possibility of truth (we will have to retain this consubstantiality of error and truth as a fundamental characteristic of the rational being with regard to its use of language). When rational beings use language in a propositional sense, they are always making a kind of proposition of equality, of conformity, of adequacy between the discourse and the "aim" of the discourse (the term adequacy must be understood here in terms of horizontal "dynamics" and not in terms of static and vertical correspondence). The nature of the relationship expressed may be false or correct, but it is no less part of the 'error-truth' pair, a signifying pair that cannot be reduced to pure matter, but which is paradoxically capable of determining matter itself. Thus, while certain living organisms react to material *stimuli*, they are also capable of reacting to information that cannot be reduced to the immediate material effect it produces (i.e. that cannot be reduced to pure non-meaning matter). A cry of warning in the face of imminent danger, insofar as it is not propositional in nature, i.e. does not fall within the "error-truth" pair, undoubtedly falls into the first category (although this could be debated, since the cry has as its direct meaning the information of imminent danger). On the other hand, a factual proposition, such as a warning about a non-imminent danger ("there's a forest fire in that direction", "risk of electrocution"), clearly falls into the propositional register. In this case, the idea conveyed by the information has a direct and decisive influence on the behaviour of the organism or rational subject to whom it is addressed.

To illustrate the special nature of the informative proposition, we could imagine a situation in which a man is warned of a non-imminent danger by a letter sent by post. If the man cannot read, his behaviour in the face of danger cannot be changed. He will not have been "informed" of the danger. He will, however, have received the letter, i.e. the physical manifestation of the information (the ink, the writing, etc.). However, this letter will not have informed him and will probably not have saved him. In this example, information is very different from its physical manifestation (it is not a cry or an immediate warning signal). So if we have established the possibility of matter being determined by the informational, that is, the "non-exclusively material", then we have at the same time opened up the possibility that morality, as an idea that cannot be reduced to matter, can exert a determining influence on the moral agent, and therefore on matter[67].

---

[67] Once again, the materialist, on the basis of the achievements of cybernetics, would retort that information can very well be reduced to matter. Moreover, this possibility is not just theoretical, as computer scientists (with the help of mathematicians and chemists) have already shown us the effectiveness of the theory of the material carriers of information. Better still, computer scientists have at the same

time demonstrated that the machine could very well do without what we call 'understanding' in order to adapt its behaviour to information communicated to it by the user (or another machine). Without wishing to repeat here all the developments in § 1 to 12, we would like to point out once again that the very principle of information is that it must be formalised by physical processes, otherwise it would be nonsense, a possibility without effective realisation. We cannot seriously imagine information without the possibility of communicating information (if only within the subject itself), communication without material supports and, by the same token, information without a material support. The fact that information can be modelled in a material way, and that this material modelling can produce an effect in the world without passing through the stage of signification, does not mean that information can be entirely assimilated to its medium. *Conversely*, if information had no support or material manifestation, it could not claim any effectiveness or effect on the world. Information therefore presupposes matter but is not reduced to it. In reality, the reduction of information to its medium has never been achieved, either by cybernetics or by computer science. It has simply been shown that the machine can be satisfied with the material support of information, that it is not interested in its meaning, but simply in the physical effect it produces, the physico-chemical consequences it implies. In the preceding paragraphs we raised what we consider to be the insurmountable paradoxes of reductionist theory: the problem of the tautological nature of any monistic assertion, the problem of the intentionality of matter, the problem of the adaptation of organisms and the adaptation of their behaviour to the world in order to survive (*radical* dualism), and finally the problem of the necessarily non-material nature of legislative principles (laws cannot be reduced to material phenomena). The reductionist theory is based on a

However, we are not thinking here of giving morality a specific content. What we call 'morality' is not, and never will be, a set of rules for practical action, the variations of which would give rise to endless debates about the nature of behaviour to adopt in such and such situations — like the rules drawn from Jesuit casuistry. Morality is not a manual of good practice. It is, as we define it here, the formal framework for action (to which it gives its general principle), just as scales or harmonies can constitute the formal frameworks of a melody. The mistake, however, would be to mistake the legal framework for the law itself. As a formal framework without content, the founding principle of morality escapes materialist and utilitarian criticism (see in particular § 12, 13 and 18 on the non-reducibility of the rule to the matter it determines). This does not

---

coup de force, a decreed assimilation of information to its physical formalisation. Every principle, every law, every idea must of course be formalisable, i.e. translatable, expressible by physical processes. However, one cannot be reduced to the other or the system will collapse logically. You can't jump over your shadow any more than you can merge the two sides of the same coin. The possibility of signification of matter, the use of matter in a 'signifying' mode, is *radical* dualism. *Radical* Dualism must be understood here as the co-appearance of information and matter, of the idea and its physical manifestation. However, co-participation does not mean assimilation. Kurt Gödel's formal demonstration of his incompleteness theorem is a good illustration of this problem (we'll come back to it at length): the system cannot formally demonstrate its completeness within the system. It always needs a metasystem, i.e. an additional scale of meaning, to find its formal coherence: monism is formally contradictory. Every formal system is open at the top.

mean, however, that the basis of morality is free of all subjective determination. On the contrary, morality accepts subjectivity as its most certain foundation. It is an idea of the subject, of the being taken in its broadest sense: a sensitive creature, capable in particular of empathy towards others and towards himself, a rational being, capable of understanding and formulating the world, a sociable being, capable of communicating and living with others. Acknowledging the subjective basis of morality does not, however, imply relativism. On the contrary, subjectivity is the basis of an objective logical principle: as a sentient being, I naturally seek to avoid evil, misfortune and death; as an empathetic and social being, I understand that others are like me, that they shun misfortune and fear evil and death; as a rational being, I understand the concept of reciprocity. As soon as I attribute sensitivity to the other, I understand the formal framework of the law: "*don't do to others what you wouldn't want them to do to you*". The confusion of moral Darwinism (a relatively clear formulation of which can be found in the works of the American philosopher Daniel Dennett, in particular in *Freedom Evolves*, 2003) lies in the fact of equating moral sentiment, the existence of natural dispositions to empathy and even altruism in certain animal species — including man — with morality itself as a formal framework that determines and induces moral action. Morality can very well be founded on sentience without being reduced to it (in the same way that the idea of truth can derive from the idea of efficacy without necessarily being identified with it: origin does not necessarily have a determining value on axiology). Sensibility, as a subjective criterion, is indeed the foundation of morality, but for all that, the rule that stems from it is not itself of a sensible nature. Before being a practice, morality is entirely legalism; it cannot be anything else, at the risk of contradicting itself[68]. While we have attempted to free

---

[68] Morality must not be "anti-natural" - it does not necessarily go against natural feelings - but it must be conceived independently of natural inclinations and inclinations, at the risk of becoming a concept without an object, a nonsense. The various formulations of the categorical imperative illustrate the trajectory of the moral imperative. Firstly, its sensitive origin, formulated through a principle of humanity: "*Act in such a way that you treat humanity, both in your own person and in every other person, always at the same time as an end, and never merely as a means*"; then its formal and legislative scope, formulated through the principle of universality: "*Act solely according to the maxim that makes it possible for you to want it at the same time to become a universal law*". (*Foundation of the Metaphysics of Morals* in *Metaphysics of Morals*, trans. Alain Renaut). It therefore seems to us that Charles Péguy's famous phrase that "Kantianism has pure hands, *but it has no hands**" is somewhat dishonest. In its most famous formulations (the categorical imperatives), Kantian morality does not, strictly speaking, seek to be embodied in a concrete legal determination, but rather to place the action of rational man within a general legalistic framework as yet without content. As such, it is not really ethics in the sense of "applied morality" that is sometimes attributed to the term.

*Kantianism has pure hands **but no hands**. Charles Péguy, Œuvres Complètes, *Œuvres de prose*, nrf Gallimard, Paris, 1916, p. 496. The very classic and often encountered opposition— usually more on the side of reactionary thinkers— between the purity of the spirit and the hard work of the workers, between the inevitable taint of those who make and the disconnection from reality, characteristic of

morality from its subjective foundations, we nevertheless affirm that morality does have the capacity to objectively determine the behaviour of rational sentient beings. There is an effective link between the idea and its concrete, physical, phenomenal manifestation. The moral framework is not just a conceptual abstraction of the subject, it is an active and determining principle for the moral agent[69]. Although the moral agent does not

---

those who contemplate, nevertheless has the air of a demagogic slogan.

We can acknowledge to Péguy that Kant's 'ethical' writings are not the most worthy of interest, even if they are undoubtedly not those to which Péguy refers in the passage quoted— we are thinking in particular of some long developments in the *Metaphysics of Morals*, or the opuscule entitled *On a Supposed Right to Tell Lies from Benevolent Motives* in response to Benjamin Constant, in which the legalistic principle curiously takes precedence over the principle of humanity (from which it derives its legitimacy), on the grounds that lying disqualifies the source of law.

[69] On this subject, see a footnote in Immanuel Kant's *Religion within the Limits of Reason Alone*, a fundamental remark by Kant that we have rarely— if ever— seen mentioned in commentaries on Kant's work:

"If the good is $= a$, its contradictory opposite is the not-good. Now the non-good is the consequence either of a simple deprivation of a principle of the good $= 0$, or of a positive principle of what is the opposite of the good $= - a$; in the latter case, the non-good can also be called the positive evil. (In the question of pleasure and pain, we find a middle ground of this kind: pleasure is $= a$; pain is $= b$; and the state where neither is found, indifference, is $= 0$). If the moral law were not in us a motive of free will, the moral good (the agreement of free will with the law) would be $= a$ the non-act in accordance with a set of pre-established rules, he nevertheless tries to put himself "in tune" with the formal framework of morality[70] to which he himself gives content in moral action. This is one of the reasons why Benjamin Libet's experiment (see §2) on the infra-conscious determinants of the decision that governs action does not seem to us to have the scope that Stanislas Dehaene, for example, wanted it to have. The determinants of action are certainly physical, they respond to a causal chain whose outcome is action and, in this sense, experience clearly shows that a large part of our actions can remain subconscious. On the other hand, experience says nothing about the determinants that do not enter directly into the causal chain that we claim to be studying (and which are not necessarily of a physical or material nature). If, as we mentioned

---

good = 0, and the latter would be the simple consequence of the deprivation of a moral motive = a x 0. Now there is in us a motive = a; therefore the lack of agreement of the free will with this motive (lack which = 0) is only possible as a consequence of an effectively contrary determination of the free will, that is to say of an effective resistance of this will, resistance = - a, and can therefore only have as its cause a bad free will; between a good and a bad intention (inner principle of the maxims), on which the morality of the action must moreover depend, there is therefore no middle ground. [A morally indifferent action (moral adiaphoron) would be an action resulting simply from physical laws and this action, consequently, has no connection with morality, since it is not a fact (*ein Factum*) and it cannot be either possible or necessary for it to be the object of a command, a defence or a permission (of a legal authorisation)]".

[70] Kant's principle of reciprocity or imperative, Nietzsche's moral formulation of the eternal return, and so on.

earlier, Libet's experiment had involved giving death to a sentient being by pressing the same button, we can imagine that the experiment would have had a very different outcome[71]: the arch-decision (the decision that is made before the decision is made, the "great principle" that refers to the idea and not to the action) would then have governed the decision not to press the button if the consequence had been the death of the guinea pig, or to press the button if the consequence had been the survival of the guinea pig. In both cases, the actor would have been able to justify the reason for his action ("I wanted to keep the man alive" or "I didn't want to kill the man" for example) even if he would probably have failed to identify precisely the *moment of* the decision to press or not to press the button. In short, the physical determinants of the moment of decision can perfectly well remain infra-conscious without this in any way affecting the human's ability to determine and motivate his action. In the same way, good action, i.e. action that is faithful to the formal framework of morality, is not the result of a long causal chain that predisposes the moral agent to do good, nor

---

[71] Astute minds will point out that, in the famous Milgram experiment of 1963, trapped participants, under the control of authorities in white coats, went so far as to administer potentially lethal electrical doses (for more than 62% of them) to guinea pigs simulating pain. The set-up of Milgram's experiment was quite different from that of Libet's experiment. Milgram's aim was to demonstrate the power of conformity and the ability of men in authority (the white coats) to act by delegation, freeing themselves from any form of individual responsibility. That's another subject entirely (of concern and despair!).

is bad action the result of a long causal chain leading to bad action. Of course, beings always have natural or acquired inclinations, but here again, the idea of good or bad action cannot be asserted within the tautological framework of integral materialism. Good" and "evil", resituated in the strictly self-referential framework of materialism, are self-extinguishing, just as any possibility of deriving meaning from their concrete expression evaporates. It is, moreover, an illusion of the mind to think that utilitarianism could come to the rescue of materialism here (morality as a principle of conservation of the species or as an attempt to maximise the well-being of a given community). In utilitarianism, the idea of adequacy remains central. Morality is always an attempt to bring behaviour into line with the world, whether that matching is legalistic and universalist (Kant) or whether it is geared towards the principle of survival of the species or the individual (or the maximisation of pleasures in the case of Thomas Moore and his followers). Consequently, utilitarianism in its moral form is also an idealist dualism. Instead of aligning himself with the idea of pure reciprocity, the moral agent places himself at the service of the idea of the "collective good" insofar as he also finds his own interest in it[72]: this is the intellectual foundation of most

---

[72] We may well question the nature of utilitarian morality (and more generally the nature of all morality based on the principle of interest), but this does not call into question the fact that utilitarianism *is strictly speaking* a dualism. The agent always acts according to an idea he has of the right action (right action for the survival of the species and, by extension, for his own survival) and not solely by following his own inclinations.

liberal democracies (contractualism). In the utilitarian version of morality, as in the legalist and universalist versions, the moral agent is always trying to bring his sensibility into line with the idea of the right action (or adequate action), which itself derives from the founding principle of morality (recognition of the other as "another *self*" or recognition of the interest in preserving the species). This does not mean, however, that this attempt to "bring action into conformity" with the idea of the right action is natural or immediate[73].

---

[73] In the *The Passions of the Soul*, Descartes illustrates this attempt by the moral agent to use his sensibility to control his passions. In a passage that has remained famous, he explains that man can, through a skilful interplay of representations, change his natural dispositions, just as his taste for meat suddenly changes when he unexpectedly encounters "*something very dirty* "* in a piece of meat. In this passage, Descartes clearly expresses the problem of determining the moral agent: a sensitive being on the one hand, subject to his natural inclinations, and a rational being on the other, capable of stepping outside his strict egotic sphere to act according to principles that are not directly in line with his nature or inclinations. Here it is the principle, the idea, which, by using sensible representation, manages to act on the agent's sensibility and, possibly, to modify his behaviour. In this sense, morality is an "active idea", a non-material principle that has the material power to determine sentient beings

*It is also useful to know that although the movements, both of the gland and of the spirits and brain, which represent certain objects to the soul, are naturally joined with those which excite certain passions in it, they can nevertheless by habit be separated from them and joined with others which

22.

THE IDEA OF MAN AS THE FOUNDATION OF MORALITY — Can morality as we have defined it escape the epistemological problem proposed by the sceptic Agrippa? This problem, dubbed the Munchausen trilemma by Hans Albert, after the baron who claimed to pull his horse and himself out of quicksand by his own hair, can be summed up as follows: any attempt to establish an absolute truth inevitably comes up against one of three pitfalls: (i) regression to infinity, (ii) logical circularity and (iii) transcendental rupture or *ex cathedra* argument, which appeals to a higher principle that cannot be criticised (God, axiomatics, etc.). In our view, moral issues are not affected by the first two pitfalls: they do not come up against the obstacle of regression to infinity, insofar as they admit a clear founding principle and are not, moreover, based on circular reasoning (they do admit, from above, a meta-principle which is the recognition of the value of the other as another *myself*). But can we legitimately assert that morality introduces a rupture, that is, a principle of

---

are very different, and even that this habit can be acquired by a single action and does not require long use. Thus, when we unexpectedly come across something very dirty in meat that we are eating with appetite, the surprise of this encounter can so change the disposition of the brain that afterwards we will only be able to look at such meat with horror, instead of eating it with pleasure". René Descartes, *The Passions of the Soul*, Part One, Art. 50— *That there is no soul so weak that it cannot, when properly led, acquire absolute power over its passions.*

final justification (experience, intuition, evidence, God...) that would have the value of dogma?

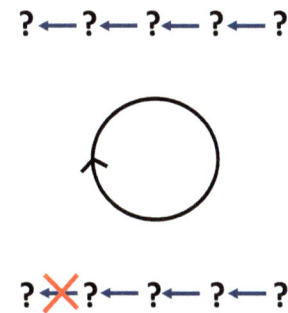

The Münchhausen trilemma

We know that, arguing that the difficulties posed by this trilemma were insurmountable, Hans Albert justified an intermediate philosophical position according to which the philosopher could only propose criticizable hypotheses that he knew to be provisional. While this position, similar to that developed by Karl Popper in *The Logic of Scientific Discovery* and in *Objective Knowledge: An Evolutionary Approach*, may seem appropriate to the scientific approach in the broadest sense, is it also appropriate to the question of morality? Our answer to this last question is that the moral question, unlike the question of scientific knowledge, does not primarily have an objective aim. Scientists, in their relationship with the world, start from a position of imbalance between their own subjectivity and the objectivity they claim in scientific discourse. They are always trying to go beyond their subjectivity, with the difficulty that we all know: they cannot, like Baron Munchausen, jump over their own shadow or pull themselves out of their own subjectivity as if they were pulling themselves by the hair to get out of quicksand. The scientist is therefore forced to come to terms with his subjectivity, to integrate it into his progress towards objectivity, to which he can never lay absolute claim. But moral reasoning is a completely different matter. Unlike scientific reasoning, which is primarily understood as an overcoming of subjectivity (a de-anthropomorphisation, as Max Planck put it), moral reasoning makes subjectivity, embodied humanity, the very condition and root of its objective scope. It is because we are sentient beings experiencing joy, pain, pleasure and suffering that we have the capacity to experience states of negativity and positivity. Our sensitivity, as a barometer of our relationship with the world, is a kind of objective subjectivity: we are the instrument of our relationship with the world (an anthropological fact). If we can misread ourselves, then it is not our sensibility that is at fault, but always the interpretation or description of our subjective states (insofar as the interpretation of a subjective state can lay claim to any form of objectivity — but that is not the point). Moreover, it is because we are rational beings, capable of recognising in others the reflection of our own sensibility, that we can recognise the objective character and legalising power of morality (the idea of reciprocity). In morality, subjectivity, i.e. the fact that we are sentient (human) beings, is not a starting point to be overcome (as in scientific reasoning), it is a founding principle[74].

In our argument in favour of *radical* dualism, the idea of morality thus has a twofold interest: firstly, to show that a regulating idea (morality) can act on matter (on us in this case, on our behaviour as material beings); secondly, to suggest that objectivity (the formalism of the rule that cannot be contested if we accept its premises) can have a subjective basis (the subjective

---

[74] However, in order to adhere to the formal framework of the moral law, the sensitive and rational being that is man does not necessarily need to go through the stages that lead him from sensibility to the objective and legalistic framework of morality. As a creature who is both sensitive and rational, man is always already predisposed to grasp the idea of transcending his *ego* in his coexistence and confrontation with others.

*A moral intuition that could be likened to the well-known concept of "morality by provision" that Descartes evokes in the *Discourse on Method*: "And finally, as it is not enough, before beginning to rebuild the dwelling where one lives, to pull it down, and to make provision of materials and architects, or to practise architecture oneself, and in addition to that to have carefully drawn a sketch of it, but that it is also necessary to have provided oneself with some other where one can be comfortably housed during the time that one will work on it ; Thus, in order that I should not remain irresolute in my actions, while reason obliged me to be so in my judgements, and that I should not fail to live from then on as happily as I could, I formed for myself a provisional morality, which consisted only of three or four maxims of which I am willing to share with you. "*Discourse on Method*, Part Three

capacity to endow others with sentience, the capacity to feel sympathy for them).

With this long preamble in the form of a response to reductionist, materialist and neo-Darwinist physicalist theories, we have tried to establish that the relativist thesis supported in hollow by radical materialism — whatever its modern denomination — is not logically founded and is, as a result, intrinsically contestable, both from the point of view of the philosophy of knowledge, and from the point of view of moral philosophy or aesthetic philosophy. We are now left with the onerous task of attempting to identify the founding principles of the anti-relativism to which we lay claim.

THE LEGIBILITY OF THE WORLD: THE FORM, THE THING, THE PHENOMENON, THE CONCEPT

> Science, philosophy, rational thought, must all start from common sense.
>
> Karl Popper, *Two Faces of Common Sense*, in *Objective Knowledge*, 1973
>
> Man is the measure of all things.
>
> Protagoras
>
> There is nothing more disappointing than the hollow phrase "everything is relative". In physics, it is already inaccurate: all the universal constants, such as the mass and charge of the electron or proton, and the value of the quantum of action, are absolute quantities.
>
> Max Planck, *Wege zur Physikalischen Erkenntnis*, 1934

WHAT IS A THING?

23.

IS THERE ANYTHING 'IN ITSELF'? — The question of the existence of things 'in themselves' is a traditional one in philosophy, based on questions about our fundamental relationship to the world, I.e. the way in which we, as sentient beings, perceive, organise and understand it. To pose the question of the thing 'in itself' correctly, we must first try to determine the meaning of the criterion of the in-itself of things. We need to distinguish between two questions that are ontologically related, but that are dissimilar in terms of formal (or "pure") logic: first, what is a thing "in itself", and what does the question of "itself" mean for a thing? Secondly, what is a thing "for ourselves", and what does the concept of a thing mean for us as sentient beings? If we start with the thing 'in itself' or the 'thing-in-itself', to use the classic philosophical formulation, we are immediately confronted with a paradox. On the one hand, the question of what a thing is "in itself" seems to us to be devoid of meaning insofar as the thing does not, strictly speaking, have "of itself", it is for itself nothing other than the meaning that we, sentient beings, confer on it: here we come back to the problem of monism and the logical foundations of materialism — meaning can never be understood at the level of things themselves (or "in themselves"); it is the product of the understanding of a sentient being who gives things form and meaning, To put it another way, the thing "in itself" is never anything other than the thing "as it appears" to the sentient being, i.e. as the sentient being perceives it, interprets it and organises it in its network of meanings and significations. On the other hand, if we consider the thing solely as a construction of the sentient being, with no relation to a foundation outside sentience, then the question of the coherence of the world and its communicability arises. The sentient beings that we are, beings born of a long and slow adaptation to things, can hardly claim that the world is simply a pile of meanings without substrates, a sum of discordant subjective constructions. The idea that only the most radical subjectivism[75] is justified does not stand the test of time: while we are always quick to disagree about the interpretation of facts, theories or concepts, very few of us question the reality of things (their effectiveness) when it comes to crossing a road or avoiding danger. So we are faced with the following paradox: on the one hand, things are nothing in themselves; on the other, they constitute a unit of meaning for sentient beings, for which we have to find a substratum if we want to found the coherence we observe in the world. The paradox unravels itself, however, if we clearly separate two levels: the first, material, made up of the physical interactions and exchanges of forces that structure the world we have traditionally called the "material world", and the second, that of signification, i.e. the level of understanding, interpretation and organisation of the world by the sentient beings that we are, these two levels constituting the two sides of one and the same reality. Matter, while constituting the fabric of reality, is nonetheless always perceived through our sensibility and through the formal presentation that we have of it: "for us", things can have no meanings other than those that result from their interaction "with us". So, it doesn't matter if the way things affect us is not an 'absolute', because the idea of absolutes is a debate for theorists. We could very well conceive of a situation in which the molecules that make up the plane tree by the

---

[75] A theory, very popular at the end of the nineteenth century in Symbolist circles who had read Schopenhauer wrong (or had merely glanced absent-mindedly at the cover of his most famous work), according to which the world is merely "my representation"— theory of radical illusionism.

side of the main road represent no danger to the molecules that make up the motorist driving at full speed towards the plane tree. We know that this is not the *case in our world*. *In our world*, the plane tree will stop the motorist and bend the car like an accordion (reality is when you bump into it...). This physical effect will also be objectively theorised *in our world* by Pauli's exclusion principle[76], which states that two identical

---

[76] The Pauli exclusion principle, formulated by Austrian physicist Wolfgang Pauli in 1925, is a fundamental principle of quantum mechanics that applies to particles called fermions (for example, electrons, protons and neutrons). The exclusion principle states that two identical fermions cannot simultaneously occupy the same quantum state in the same quantum system. Pauli's exclusion principle does not apply to bosons (particles such as photons or Higgs particles). Unlike fermions, several bosons can occupy the same quantum state, enabling phenomena such as Bose-Einstein condensation. This principle is fundamental to understanding the stability of matter, chemistry, the physics of solids (such as conductivity) and many other natural phenomena. To illustrate Pauli's exclusion principle through a concrete phenomenon such as a car accident, we can draw a metaphorical parallel between the interactions of particles and the interactions of macroscopic objects.

The electrons around atoms follow the Pauli exclusion principle. This means that they cannot be in the same quantum state, which, on a large scale, prevents atoms from collapsing on top of each other. This exclusion creates a kind of 'rigidity' in matter. For example, if two solid objects (such as two cars) are brought together, their electrons, each in a different state, interact. The exclusion principle prevents two sets of electrons from occupying the same positions. This electron repulsion is the reason why solid objects do not pass

fermions (such as electrons) cannot simultaneously occupy the same quantum state (which explains the structure of matter and prevents solid objects from passing through each other). In turn, however, this principle of exclusion will be based on a vision of the meaningful representation of matter. When physicists refer, for example, to the structure of the atom, they are never referring in *the strict sense* to a raw, absolute reality called the "atom". Strictly speaking, the structure of the atom is always nothing more than a construct of the mind, in the same way as the concept of 'bed', 'table' or 'plane tree', in other words an *a posteriori* figuration of reality by our brain, by our consciousness, by our imagination, by our reason. What we call the "thing-in-itself", or the support of reality, is not, and never will be, accessible to us, not only because we cannot logically leap above our senses, but also because the thing "in itself", not having passed through the intermediary of the senses, has no meaning: it cannot therefore, strictly speaking, be considered as a thing: it is still only an undecoded network of forces, with no formal unity (which does not prevent it from having an effect, a physical manifestation that seizes us,

---

through each other. When a car collides with a plane tree, the exclusion principle is indirectly responsible for the fact that the atoms of the two cars do not "fuse" or interpenetrate. Instead, the electrons in the atoms of the car bodies "repel" each other because of this principle. This repulsion is what causes a mechanical force between the two objects. This mechanical force results in a deformation of the materials, as the atoms in the cars are forced out of their initial positions, but without violating the rigidity imposed by the exclusion principle.

constrains us and which we must decode in our signifying systems). As the 'material datum' is not yet caught up in a network of significations, it cannot yet be identified as a thing, i.e. grasped in its formal unity. The very term "thing in itself" is therefore completely inappropriate. We are always dealing with a structured presentation of a world that is not "in itself" signifying. Things" must in fact be understood as structured units of understanding of the world: the atom, the molecule, organised matter, wood, the bed, the chair. It is therefore an illusion to think that by going up or down the chain of levels of meaning, we can gain access to a reality of a lower or higher order. However far we go in analysing the structure of matter, we are always dealing with the form, the model of matter, never with matter itself, the world of 'things in themselves' still being, at the stage of 'non-significance', no more than an interplay of forces, an undifferentiated whole.

24.

THE PRODUCTION OF FORMS OR THE SCHEMATIC ORGANISATION OF THE WORLD — The world, our world, cannot be understood as the product of a conjunction between two passivities (the passivity of the material world, which would obey blind determinants, and the passivity of the sentient being, which would receive this information and 'print' it on a sort of blank page — which would raise the question of the mode of communication between two passivities) but must rather be envisaged as the result of an interaction between two activities: the activity of matter in motion on the one hand, and the autonomous rational activity of formalising and organising this matter on the other (an activity which Kant said was "an art hidden in the depths of the human soul[77]"). Without the active production of forms, there can be no meanings; without meanings, there can be no understanding of the world; without an understanding of the world, there can be no action in the world. But the living *act*, and this is what differentiates them from the inert. And if it acts, it is because it conceives, even if only in a rudimentary way in the simplest organisms. Logical connections are never found in objects; they are the work of the subject who, if he wants to inhabit the world and act in it, is forced to organise it in a system of formal meanings. We must therefore guard against the error of imagining correspondence as the adequacy of a discourse or a conception with the thing 'in itself' or the thing 'as it really is'. Here again, if we adopt the idea of a radical separation between, on the one hand, the concrete manifestation of the phenomenon as it is

---

[77] "This schematism of our understanding in relation to phenomena and their simple form is an art hidden in the depths of the human soul, whose true mechanisms we will always find it difficult to wrest from nature and bring to light before our eyes. At best, we can say that the image is a product of the empirical power of the productive imagination, that the schema of sensible concepts (as figures in space) is a product and, as it were, a monogram of the pure imagination *a priori*, by means of which and according to which alone images become possible, but in such a way that these must always be attached to the concept only through the intermediary of the schema to which they point, and without themselves being entirely congruent with it.
Immanuel Kant, *Critique of Pure Reason*, Ch. 1 of *The Transcendental Doctrine of Judgement (or Analysis of Principles)*, *On the Semantics of the Pure Concepts of Understanding*.

"decoded" by our sensibility and by our consciousness and, on the other hand, the substratum of the phenomenon itself (the thing as it "really" is), we run the risk of finding ourselves on unfruitful paths. As we have already said, there are not two ontologically and materially distinct worlds. On the one hand, there is the raw matter of the world, non-signifying matter that has its own autonomous existence outside our sensibility, and on the other hand, there is the world of things, that is, the world of phenomena, which is certainly an interpretation of the 'raw' (or 'material') world, but a 'constrained' interpretation: this is the difficulty of our relationship with the world, and it is also what makes it necessary and coherent. Our world, the world of meanings, acquires its full coherence only in the constrained *relationship* it maintains with the world of 'raw' (non-signifying) matter. Like a jigsaw puzzle, the world of phenomena is a formal division of the raw, non-signifying world. Each piece of the jigsaw represents a phenomenon and acquires its own meaning and significance through the relationships it develops with the other pieces. However, while the division of the raw world is *a priori* free, it is not, for all that, purely conventional. It always expresses *something*, i.e. a set of relationships to which it confers a meaning (a meaning with several levels, i.e. made up of several 'sets' as we described earlier: the atom as a set of particles, molecules as a set of atoms, matter as a set of particles, objects as sets made up of matter; the sets can sometimes overlap or merge). It is quite possible that, through a new division or even a shift in a new network of constraints and meanings, the phenomenon acquires a new meaning. This does not mean, however, that the phenomenon is purely contingent or conventional. On the contrary, the evolution of our understanding of it will be another step towards greater overall coherence in our formal division (our general puzzle). If the activity of producing forms is free (the cutting up of the puzzle), the general image of the world as produced by the organisation of the forms between them is not. It is, in fact, subject to two networks of constraints: firstly, constraints linked to the results of our experience of the world ("learning" constraints, the "matter of the puzzle" if you like), and secondly constraints linked to logic itself, whose axioms may well be deduced from our experience of things, but whose developments follow a necessity of their own. The fact that there is no such thing as "the thing itself" does not necessarily mean that our reality is contingent, dependent on our "distorted" vision of things. Since things only acquire the actual status of "things" through the active process of the rational sentient being that produces "forms", "deformation" cannot be understood as a phenomenon of distortion between the "thing in itself" (or the thing as it really and "absolutely" is) and the form through which the subject conceives the thing. It can only be inadequacy in relation to other forms: the distortion is the subject's recognition of the incoherence or impossibility of one or more particular forms (in their logical sequence with other forms, themselves the result of the subject's experience of the activity of raw matter). It is by understanding the incoherence or impossibility that the form evolves and adapts to a new model, a new "general puzzle" ("critical" constraint). This paradox undoubtedly goes some way to explaining why scientists at the end of the nineteenth and beginning of the twentieth centuries were so surprised when, thanks to a new paradigm, matter literally disappeared before their very eyes: with the advent of the quantum approach, matter lost its very unity to the wave-corpuscle duality[78], a few decades later, the very idea of mass, which until then had given matter its thickness and substance, disappeared in favour of the notion of particles interacting with a scalar field (Higgs field). In reality, neither matter nor mass had really *disappeared*. We were, and still are, in contact with what we call 'matter': we touch it, we feel it, we appreciate its weight. Our experience of what we call 'matter' has not changed as a result of a new theory of matter. Rather, it is our overall 'image' of the world that has changed as it has been reorganised. We must not confuse the everyday naming of things, which through concepts and language refers to a set of experiences that structure our relationship with the world and constitute our network of meanings (the production of forms that, by relating to each other, form the jigsaw of our perceptions and our experimental understanding of the world) with our formal systems for understanding the world which, initially using the same vocabulary as that of our everyday experiences, end up detaching themselves from it to create a new network of meanings (a new 'language'). Paradoxes often arise from the polysemy of terms whose meaning differs according to the register of language in which they are used. For example, when a scientist states that 'matter' does not exist, he is not

---

[78] This duality, it should be pointed out in passing, is in my view much more offensive to common sense than the matter-signification duality we described earlier, and yet it is now generally accepted by the scientific community (which is far from being the case for the matter-signification duality).

referring directly to the meaning of the term 'matter', which is the fruit of our everyday experience (matter as the thickness of reality, 'wood', 'steel', etc.), but to the meaning of the word 'matter' insofar as it designates a state of scientific knowledge (in classical physics, matter is that which possesses mass and occupies space). If the 'redrawing' of the jigsaw puzzle of scientific meanings has the effect of calling into question the meaning of 'matter' insofar as it designates a previous state of knowledge, the same cannot be said for the term 'matter' insofar as it designates the everyday experience of our relationship with things (we could also say the same thing about 'time' from the point of view of science and from the point of view of our experience of change). Nevertheless, there is no absolute decorrelation between the everyday use of the term 'matter' and its use in science. It's just that, because the networks of meanings in which these terms are used are different, they can't all be combined in a uniform designation of the 'reality' they refer to (or of the 'concrete experience' to which they refer). However, as we shall see later, just because science is based on the subjective experience of the scientist does not mean that the scientific approach as a whole should be viewed with suspicion. Science is first and foremost, and initially can only be, anthropomorphic (of human 'form'). Subjective experiences, while they may not constitute a foundation, may very well constitute the starting point for a practice which, responding to its own constraints and using an independent formalism, gradually manages to extricate itself from the anthropomorphism of its origins. By proposing a new grid for analysing reality, the scientist 'creates' a new network of meanings (a new 'puzzle'). The difficulty then lies in transcribing the phenomenon we are describing from one grid of meanings to another, from the language of science to the language of our everyday experience.

25.

WHAT IS A PHENOMENON? — If forms can be understood as pure productions of the creative mind[79] without any direct link to a real object that we are trying to apprehend or express (forms can be artistic, mythical, phantasmagorical...), the same cannot be said of phenomena. Phenomena, unlike form, are conceived first and foremost as an encounter between the activity of the mind (the abstract structures that organise our

understanding of the world) and the material grasp of our external senses by reality (the 'naked', 'non-signifying', 'unformalised' information). In our attempt to define the phenomenon, we therefore emphasise from the outset the fundamental role of consciousness, one of the pitfalls in the approach to the phenomenon consisting precisely in making it a "raw data" of the senses (what Bertrand Russell, for example, defined in the 1910s as "*sense-data*", a notion to which he would later return, criticising in particular the idea that "mental objects" could be particular ontological entities that would directly represent our sensory

---

[79] It should be noted that the question of the empirical or non-empirical origin of forms is yet another question that we do not address directly here.

experiences). In fact, it would be very difficult for us to analyse what "sense data" might be, since the phenomenon is always *already interpreted* by our consciousness, even before the conscious intervention of reason. On this particular point, the contributions of *Gestalt theory* (theory of form) at the beginning of the twentieth century were of great interest. *Gestalt theory* described perception not as the collection of a juxtaposition of details, but as an intuition of global forms that immediately bring together disparate elements and give them meaning: form is not, as we have said, a property of the thing itself, but a construct of the subject who organises the world in projective perception. In short, *Gestalt theory* empirically confirmed this idea that the thing, that is, the unitary element constructed by our consciousness through our perception, is always a synthetic construction, a construction that from the outset has meaning and that constitutes, for consciousness, the first level of meaning: vision, as a sensitive experience, always already carries meaning[80]. If, strictly speaking, there is no raw data from the senses that could constitute the building blocks of objectivity that the fussy logicians had once sought, this does not mean that we are led to abandon the world of phenomena to relativists of all stripes. Just as in *sense-data* theory, the idea of an active, projective consciousness does not necessarily imply relativism. The fact that consciousness immediately

---

[80] See the work of Ernst Cassirer, *The Philosophy of Symbolic Forms*, 1923-1929, Volume I: *Language* (1923), Volume II: *Mythical Thouhgt*, Voume 3: *The Phenomenology of Knowledge* (1929). Refer here in particular to Tome III

projects a meaning onto the things it is seized of does not imply any necessary "distortion" of the phenomenon in the sense that the phenomenon could be described as "incorrect" or "non-effective". The famous example of Rubin's vase — named after the Danish psychologist Edgar John Rubin who is one of the *Gestalt* theorists — gives us a good illustration of this problem. Depending on how our consciousness (our imagination) projects meaning onto the figure in question, we see alternately a vase (in white) or two faces facing each other (in black). However, these immediately 'meaningful' perceptions are neither 'false' nor mutually exclusive. If we have to make a singular effort not to perceive one or other of the figures, this does not imply, for all that much, that we are particularly prisoners of one or other of the visions, or that the meanings projected onto things cause us to miss the 'adequate' character of perception. To put it another way, let us imagine that the image we are presented with does not actually represent a vase or two faces, but a satellite photograph of a strait. Let's then suppose that we have to guide a ship through the arm of the sea represented by the white part of the figure. In this case, we can say that, regardless of the mental image we have of the map (a striking resemblance to a vase or an equally striking resemblance to two faces facing each other), we would in all probability manage to guide the ship into the inlet in question (the intuition of the shape is therefore 'adequate'). In other words, the way in which we structure information in a network of meanings would have no impact on the *actual* power of our perception. Thus, the idea of a system of interpretative perceptions is not necessarily disconnected from the idea of 'effective' (or efficient) perception. Here, perception would indeed be 'correct', i.e. effective, adequate, insofar as it would allow the ship to pass through the Strait without running into the black reefs, regardless of whether the satellite image of the Strait first appears to me as the image of a vase or as that of a face-to-face. The phenomenon, as the result of the encounter between naked information and its formal interpretation, does not 'lie': it retains its effective power.

There may certainly be borderline situations in which consciousness will appear to have been deceived, as is the case in the famous example of the "broken stick" — a stick whose part immersed in water appears to be at odds with its emerged part — which Descartes set out in his *Answers to the Sixth Objections* to the *Six Metaphysical Meditations*. In the example of the broken stick, however, the conscious perception, while undoubtedly misleading, is nevertheless not at fault, insofar as it in fact faithfully responds to the laws of light refraction. The judgement of reason "*the stick is broken*" is therefore false, but the judgement of perceptive awareness "*the stick appears broken*" is completely correct and adequate (it is not the result of an "error" in perception). The error here is not so much in the transcription of the phenomenon by the senses, but rather in the judgement we make *a posteriori* about the phenomenon ("the stick is broken"). *Strictly speaking*, it would be a mistake to speak of an error in the *transcription of* the phenomenon, since the phenomenon must be understood as an encounter between the activity of raw matter (or, if we prefer, matter transformed into information not yet decoded by consciousness) and the activity of producing and identifying forms specific to projective consciousness[81]. Since the phenomenon is the way in which the thing appears to consciousness, it cannot lie *as a phenomenon*. Although phenomenal perception may be influenced by our symbolic prisms of representation and signification (cultural prisms, prisms resulting from the subject's habits, experience of the world, inductivist attitude, conceptual biases), this does not mean that it is the prerogative of reason. The phenomenon, as the manifestation of information to our consciousness, always precedes the (rational) judgement of the phenomenon — how else could it be (in order to judge the phenomenon, doesn't the phenomenon have to precede the judgement)? If there is error, then there cannot be error *at the level of* the phenomenon or *at the moment of* phenomenal perception. Our fallibility lies much more in the interpretation of the phenomenon

---

[81] This conception of the phenomenon as an 'encounter' between two opposing streams now seems to be the subject of a relative consensus among neuroscientists. See, for example, Stéphanie Roldan: "Traditional research on object recognition frequently focuses on the bottom-up processing of visual *stimuli*, from the detection of *stimulus* properties by retinal cells to electrical transduction and the neuronal response that is consumed. This type of research has succeeded in identifying the physiological and neuronal pathways involved in the detection and processing of the properties of visual objects, leading to cognitive perception. Visual mental imagery therefore represents a flow of information opposite to that of visual perception phenomena; an approach that requires a departure from traditional bottom-up perspectives to be fully understood", *Object recognition in mental representations: directions for exploring diagnostic features through visual mental imagery.*

by reason (the implicit or explicit judgement of our reason) than in the phenomenon itself.

We can still be misled in our perception of things, not because of the way the thing manifests itself to our consciousness (as in the example of the broken stick) but because of an internal distortion in our relationship to the raw information: if, for example, I have astigmatism, i.e. the cornea of my eye has an irregular curvature that distorts the objects I perceive, I may — without corrective lenses — bump into a chair or table, and even quite regularly. In this case, my nervous system will inform me of the imprecise nature of my visual perception (I feel a sharp pain when I bang my shin against the coffee table): the phenomenon, as an encounter between the "formal filter" that structures my understanding of the world and the sensitive data of my immediate experience will reach my consciousness (my understanding) in the mode of formal incoherence, i.e. problematic confrontation with other forms (other information formalised by my consciousness). In the example of the table, the visual form that reaches my consciousness is, for example, in conflict with the form projected within my consciousness by the — unpleasant — experience of my collision with the table (solicitation of the sense of touch). In short, my collision with the table will inform me about the misinterpretation (or, if we prefer, the "ineffective" interpretation) that my rational judgement makes of the visual experience of the table. However, it was always my reason that wrongly deduced that the manifestation of the phenomenon through my visual perception possessed the force of effectiveness that my reason attributed to it (an error that led to the unpleasant collision). If my reason adapts to my unfortunate experience of the phenomenon through my visual perception, it will undoubtedly judge the spatial position of the table differently (and will recommend that I take a safety margin, the easiest way of course being to buy suitable glasses). The phenomenon is therefore an experience and a construction of the senses *as a whole*. The senses can give a distorted image of what we conveniently call 'reality', as in the example of the astigmatic. However, this perception is not *false* in the sense that it proposes a deliberately misleading vision of things (Descartes' "evil genius"). The perception of the astigmatic is not *unrelated* to things, and the fact that his vision can be corrected by corrective lenses is strong evidence of this. If the phenomenon is the result of the confrontation between the 'undecoded' raw material and the subject's projective consciousness (a consciousness that operates a kind of synthesis of the senses), we must be careful not to turn it into a 'social' construction. The phenomenon is always a construction, of course, but a construction of the subject, 'for himself'. Inter-subjectivity is made possible not only by the communication of what the thing is for each subject, but above all by the fact that all the subjects form a "community of perception". In other words, the communicability of the phenomenon is due to the fact that we, like our fellow human beings, have emerged from the same evolutionary process. The material forces that give rise to phenomena are therefore equally effective *for us*. If we extend this community of perception to sentient beings in general, there will certainly be great disparities in the construction and presentation of one and the same phenomenon, but this will not prevent the phenomenon in question from sharing the same relation of efficacy with the material forces from which it arises (the presentation of the phenomenon may differ from one species to another, but the relation of efficacy with the material forces that are at the origin of the phenomenon will remain in the different presentations or phenomenal constructions). The fact that we do not present the phenomenon to ourselves in the same way as our fellow humans or other sentient species does not, therefore, mean that the phenomenon is relativistic. The phenomenon is the actual, non-relative way in which raw and "undecoded" information is interpreted by consciousness in a network of meanings that makes the world legible for the sentient being that I am (for sentient beings as a whole). It is therefore always linked to a state of the senses, to a partial perception that is always already signifying. This does not mean that perception is "*without intrinsic value*" (without correlation with things). It is therefore completely fallacious to use the argument of the "non-absolute" character of perception to radically devalue any judgement that reason might make about phenomena and about things in general.

However, we can also imagine a situation in which, with all my senses failing me, I am totally unable to obtain any usable information about the material reality around me. The phenomenon as it appears to my consciousness will then be no more than a confused presentation devoid of substance. It's a safe bet, then, that my hope of survival in this extreme situation will, unfortunately, be very limited. In the example we have given, the information concerning the inadequacy or ineffectiveness of my representation of things will not manifest itself directly to me through my senses, my consciousness or my judgement, but rather through the difficulties linked to the very problem of my presence in the world. There is no possibility for my consciousness to adjust its vision in the same way as we would adjust the focus of a camera to the object we are aiming at (an object that defines itself in relation to other objects, this web of signifying relationships intended to give me a satisfactory image of the world). The phenomenon, as a distorted encounter between the thing and the way in which the thing seizes me, would not then be for me this medium between things and my own 'subjectivity', but would deliver to me a crude piece of information for which I would not, as it were, have the 'code', the adjustment factor (an objective adjustment factor such as corrective lenses for the astigmatic or the focal length for the camera). Here again, however, the fact that the phenomenon fails to adjust itself to the materiality of the thing and presents itself to my consciousness in a way that does not allow me to enter into effective contact with it, does not necessarily imply relativism. The phenomenon, as the product of the interaction between things and the consciousness of things, could not "lie" because it would not yet fall within the "true-false" pair (the phenomenon is not a proposition) but only within the "effective-ineffective" pair. In the example we have given (that of the inability of our senses to give us a legible image of the world), the 'effective-ineffective' couple is well safeguarded: it is brutally manifested by the exceptionally short life expectancy of an organism that is unfortunately ill-adapted to the world.

There is, however, another difficulty, linked to the hybrid nature of the phenomenon, which is both non-significant and significant. In its 'non-signifying' moment, the phenomenon is still no more than a raw, peripheral flow of information that will be centralised and processed within consciousness. It is only at the level of consciousness, in fact, that the phenomenon acquires its meaning and at the same time becomes fully phenomenal. This almost simultaneous co-existence of the non-significance and signifiance of the phenomenon within consciousness is the source of many difficulties. At the moment of the phenomenon's "non-significance", i.e. at the level we call "peripheral[82]", the information is still a flow, a set of undecoded *stimuli*, so it cannot yet be said to be "correct" or "incorrect" but only "partial" or "complete" (it is, by its very nature, always partial). When the flow of non-significant (undecoded) information reaches consciousness via the senses, several borderline cases can occur: either the information transmitted by the nervous system is insufficient and does not allow us to form an effective idea of the thing (imagine, for example, that we found

---

[82] The distinction we are making here between the 'peripheral' level and the 'central' level does not entirely overlap with the biological distinction between the central and peripheral nervous systems insofar as the level we call 'central' involves the intervention of the imagination (as a form-creating force), which implies a more restricted centrality compared with the neurobiological notion of the 'central nervous system'. In the case of vision, for example, the peripheral will be defined by the retinal *stimulus*, while the central will be defined by the perception and decoding of *stimuli* in the higher visual areas.

ourselves in complete darkness, we would in all probability be incapable of finding our bearings in space or avoiding the obstacles that present themselves to us), or the information transmitted by the nervous system is sufficient — and this is the case that interests us — but our consciousness interprets the signals that present themselves to it ineffectively. There are many examples of failures in our perception inherent in the very functioning of our consciousness. One example is the famous Troxler illusion (named after the Swiss doctor and naturalist Ignaz Paul Vital Troxler who identified the phenomenon in 1804), cited by Stanislas Dehaene at the beginning of *Consciousness and the Brain*. If we look closely at the small cross in the centre of the figure below, we can see that, after a few seconds, certain points in the circle disappear randomly from the page. For a few moments, they fade from our consciousness, then become visible again. Sometimes all the dots disappear, leaving us with a blank page, only to return a moment later in a shade of grey that suddenly seems darker. The 'objective' *stimulus* is constant (the 'peripheral' part of the phenomenon) and yet its subjective interpretation is constantly changing. This subjective distortion of the objective signal in fact illustrates what we were asserting a little earlier: consciousness is not constructed as a function of the correct-incorrect couple, but — this is one of the lessons of Darwinism — as a function of the "effective-ineffective" (or "adequate-inadequate") couple. Consciousness, as a power for prioritising information (a power necessary for the survival of the organism in a given environment) is also a power for the relevant selection of information.

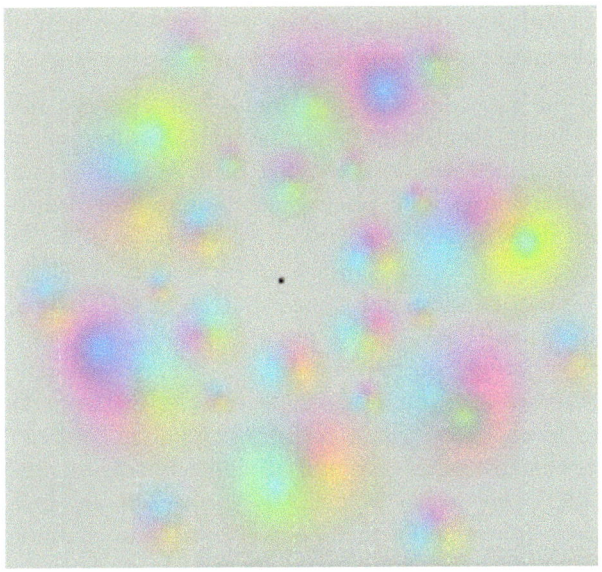

(Ctrl + Click on the image for online version)

 As Stanislas Dehaene states, "access to my consciousness is both extremely open and highly selective[83]". Not only is the process of accessing consciousness selective, but the direction of our attention (voluntary direction) can also affect access to our consciousness. Our brain," writes Stanislas Dehaene, "ruthlessly eliminates all information that is irrelevant in order to retain only one that is the most salient and the most adapted to our

---

[83] Stanislas Dehaene, *Consciousness and the Brain*, éditions Odile Jacob, Paris, 2014 p. 44 of the French edition

current goals. This *stimulus* is then amplified until it takes control of our behaviour[84].

In the way consciousness structures and understands reality, particularly through the active production of forms, there is clearly a selective filter. As we have said, consciousness is the place where meanings are formed, but also the place where information is prioritised. The mainspring of consciousness, as the product of billions of years of evolution, is not the search for truth or fidelity to 'reality' but the quest for efficiency: we must first survive, quickly understand our environment, prioritise information to separate the essential from the accessory. Some animal consciousnesses only perceive movement, others do not distinguish colours, still others use sonar to situate themselves in their environment: all of them, however, have in common the exaggerated perception of anomaly. What threatens me (or, on the contrary, what constitutes an opportunity for me) has privileged access to my consciousness. We should not, therefore, be overly surprised by any particular anomaly in our system of perception: although our consciousness is imperfect and cannot, therefore, naturally claim to be absolutely correct, it is not, for all that, totally 'relative' (random) or detached from any material substratum. Through a network of heterogeneous and unevenly distributed senses, sentient beings perceive predator or prey and adapt their behaviour to the situation or object that presents itself to their consciousness, regardless of the mode of presentation or the sense initially grasped. That the phenomenon, as a middle ground between our

---

[84] Ibid., p. 42 of the French edition

projective (form-creating) consciousness and the as yet insignificant — material *stimulus* that elicits it, can mislead the subject is a given. We would, however, be well advised to guard against depriving the phenomenon of all value. The phenomenon is our only mode of interaction with the world: it is the way in which the world communicates itself to us. As such, it cannot be said to be 'true' or 'false'. It is up to our reason, as a force for coherence and unification of reality, to judge whether a phenomenon is true or false, never directly to consciousness (or understanding). If consciousness is first and foremost at the level of the "effective-ineffective" pair, it is reason, and reason alone, that can rise to the level of the "true-false" pair. Reason judges, not conscience.

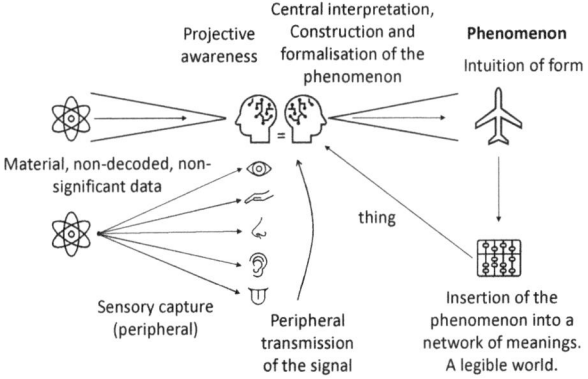

26.

RESPONSE TO THE OBJECTIONS OF PHYSICALISTS: PATHOLOGICAL SITUATIONS — In *Nature and Rule* (a book born of a dialogue between Paul Ricœur and Jean-Pierre Changeux, which we mentioned earlier), Jean-Pierre Changeux, relying on a long exposition of pathological situations and "borderline cases", claims against Paul Ricœur a form of materialist relativism based on the idea that our rationality, being physically (and even locally) determined, would be entirely dependent on the material conditions that allow its expression. Like Jean-Pierre Changeux, we readily concede that our relationship with the world is physically determined (as we always have been). Our brain is certainly no exception to this rule. Like all our organs, it is dependent on its material state. If, therefore, I don't know which part of our brain is affected by illness, artificially strained or put to sleep, there is no doubt that this will affect the way we perceive the world and think about it. But it will in no way affect the normative relationship of effectiveness that we have with things. The less adequate my understanding of the world and my adaptation to things is, the more vulnerable I will be in relation to the world: the destruction of my ability to understand the normative basis of things will have left the normative basis itself intact. The pathological situation will therefore widen the gap between my understanding of the world and the world itself, but it will not call into question either my ability to grasp the rule, i.e. to understand the world, or the existence of the rule itself. In short, my relationship to the world is one of double legislation. As a product of the world, of the universe, of its material evolution, I am *legislated*, that is to say, I am the product of the law that saw me born, that presided over the formation of my senses and my reason. At the same time, as a sentient and rational being, with the capacity to be grasped by the world, to understand it and to restore its coherence, I am *legislating* in that I can formulate an opinion about the world, experience that opinion, and critically review my judgements. This dual determination of reason, both legislated and legislating, is essential to understanding our relationship with things. We mentioned earlier that the intelligibility of the world is intimately linked to its existence, and in a sense is even a *condition* of it (Einstein said on this subject that "It is one of the great realizations of Immanuel Kant that the postulation of a real external world would be senseless without this comprehensibility[85].") Similarly, our understanding of the world - however imperfect, however distorted by the prism of a diseased reason, incomplete evolution or inaccurate perception — is the *condition of* the world's habitability. The fact that the world is seen through a kind of 'transforming mirror' of which the phenomenon, as a vehicle for transforming and interpreting things, is the manifestation does not therefore imply any necessary ontological separation or radical disconnection from a 'real' world or a world 'in itself' of which we could only perceive worthless and insubstantial shadows. On the contrary, we are always 'tuned in' to things in such a way that we can enter into a relation of efficacy with them (in the same way that

---

[85] Albert Einstein, Albert Einstein, *Physics and Reality*, 1936, p. 292, from the Journal of the Franklin Institute, Vol. 221, No. 3, 3 March 1936

things are tuned in turn to our sensibility, since they proceed from a sensitive rearrangement of our own). If our perception seems to show inconsistencies (problems of 'transcription' or 'decoding', we might say), our brain will sometimes take it upon itself to modify its construction of the phenomenon to make it conform to our regulated mode of interaction with the world, rather than persisting durably in a formal inconsistency that would call into question our actual relationship with things. An edifying experiment was carried out in which a subject had to wear glasses for several days that had the effect of reversing vision so that the subject of the experiment saw the world 'upside down'. After a few days without taking off the glasses, the subject's brain eventually made the correction itself and he once again saw things 'right side up', despite his corrective glasses. Rather than remaining in an ineffective relationship with things, the brain had chosen to revise its rules of transformation to give the subject of the experiment a more 'effective' vision of things. Here, moreover, we see the limits of radical criticisms that only accept solipsism as the purest and most unassailable position: we cannot remain in an illusionism of comfort. Our relationship with the world is not the product of our prolix imagination: as the result of evolutionary adaptation, we also have the faculty of adapting ourselves to things, of adjusting ourselves to them (as they adjust themselves to us through the rearrangements of our sensibility and our understanding).

27.

WHAT ARE CONCEPTS? — What we mean by "concept" is the operation by which the understanding carries out a theoretical synthesis[86] of the forms resulting from the activity of consciousness, thus unifying the diversity of the given under an intelligible representation. This synthesis can apply to the concrete intuition of the form of a particular phenomenon decoded and organised by the imagination (the concept of a tree, a table, an aeroplane, etc.), to concepts born of the subject's own imaginative activity (the unicorn, the hydra, etc.) or to the abstract categories that structure our thinking[87]. The concept, which finds its extension and communicability in language, is therefore both a synthetic reduction of reality and an instrument of knowledge of the world. In our use of the concept, we must always bear in mind these two almost antithetical

---

[86] We use the word "synthesis" here in the sense of "deducing the common characteristics of forms". This deduction can be said to be synthetic insofar as the subject identifies the congruent point of different objects or different groups. The synthesis produced by the subject is in a sense similar to set theory, since the concept can be analysed as the common intersection between several objects or several sets. We must be careful not to regard synthesis as an operation of infinite aggregation of several forms, which would constitute an "average form" that would be the concept. The notion of concept (and therefore of word) begins with the operation of deducing two objects. It needs no multitude.

[87] Here we use the vocabulary of the *Critique of Pure Reason*, in which Kant defines categories as the formal structures that govern and regulate our relationship with the world: categories of quantity, quality, relation and modality.

facets: the concept as a support for thought, and the concept as an instrument for the synthetic reduction of reality. However, we must be careful not to regard the concept as a form of absolute correspondence between a "form synthesised" by our consciousness and the object targeted by this synthetic (or schematic) form. Firstly, the concept may well not correspond to any particular concrete object (God, metaphysics, the unicorn), and secondly and more importantly, the concept as a cog in the articulation of thought may designate a precise concrete object, but without exhausting all its characteristics. My concept of a tree, for example, may well differ to a greater or lesser extent from an eight-year-old's concept of a tree, without referring to radically different realities. It is a pivot, a support for thought, not a fixed link between a 'psychological state' and a concrete reality. If it were otherwise, then the diversity of perception and description of a given object would be impossible, and we could then consider that the perceived object would only correspond concretely to a particular psychological state of the subject (psychologism). As Hilary Putnam rightly writes in *Reason, Truth and History*, "meaning just ain't in the head[88]". In other words, the theory of language cannot do without a theory of reference. Language considered as an autonomous system that claimed to do without any external reference would fail to reach the level of *meaning*, just as objects not mediated by a system of formally organised

---

[88] "Meaning just ain't in the head", see Hilary Putnam, *Reason, Truth and History*, 1. *Brains in a vat*, p. 19.

perception still have no possible meaning, as we shall try to establish a little further on.

28.

THE STRAITJACKET OF THE CONCEPT, THE STRAITJACKET OF FORM — A major difficulty in our relationship with the world lies in the fact that the mind (understanding, consciousness) has a natural tendency to freeze forms in order to make reality legible and communicable. This progressive imprisonment of forms in 'types' is woven into the articulation of form and concept, as if by a retroactive play of concept on form. In fact, through the intermediary of concepts (the tree, the bed, the table), forms tend to become impersonated general objects, to the detriment of the particularism (or particularities) of each object considered or perceived. If this game of reduction applies to objects, it also applies to general ideas. Many of these ideas circulate, develop and are exchanged, eventually becoming vague or content-free concepts that are wielded as accepted truths.

29.

FREEDOM AS THE CREATION OF NEW FORMS — Our freedom is interwoven in a curious sequence between the proliferation of forms, which is the work of the imagination, and a double network of constraints on forms constituted by the cleavers of coherence and "raw" (material) reality. The proliferation of forms is, more or less, what Nietzsche calls "the Dionysian" in one of his earliest writings, *The Birth of Tragedy Out of the Spirit of Music*. It is, in a sense, the "pure energy" of the imagination, an almost childlike energy, creative and destructive, freed from the rules of formal coherence (coherence between forms, harmony of form itself). But while the imagination creates new forms through combinations, rearrangements, destructions, extrapolations and associations, its free expression does not lie solely in its combinatory or creative capacities (the anarchic proliferation of the imagination could, after all, be seen as a form of blind subservience to randomness), it also lies in the formal constraint that structures its artistic expression and which we designate by the term "coherence". Unlike the idea of truth, the term 'coherence' does not refer directly to the notion of adequacy, since coherence is not understood in terms of correspondence, for example, between a discourse and its object (as is the case in scientific discourse) but rather as a critical arrangement of forms in relation to each other. The idea of formal coherence is closer to what Nietzsche calls the "Apollonian", which implies the harmony of form as such and the harmony of forms with each other. Art is born of this fertile confrontation between the proliferation of "formlessness[89]" and the formal requirement of selection, a requirement that is both natural and critical; "natural" insofar as harmony, for the artist, often seems "self-evident[90]", "critical" insofar as the selection of form is also a retroactivity, a mediated judgement on the spontaneous production of the imagination. In the testimonies of artists — be they poets, musicians,

---

[89] Or let's say the 'non-harmonious' form, i.e. not yet mediated by the formalism of consciousness.

[90] This self-evident nature will, of course, be discussed in the second part.

writers, painters or sculptors — we find a recurring observation: at the moment of creation, the work emerges with a kind of obviousness, as if it were unfolding on its own, already visualised or heard before it was even created. How many times, for example, have we heard an artist say that their most famous song was composed "in ten minutes" or "in one night"? Artists, like scientists (to which we'll return later), often seem to perceive their work or creation at a glance. This is the famous "inspiration": the fortuitous, almost magical encounter between form and its coherent expression. These two moments of creation — the moment of anarchic proliferation, the critical moment of formal selection — constitute both the essence of creation and the pinnacle of human thought: creation as the meeting of proliferation and critical, retroactive selection, thought as the active seizure of the form presented by intuition and as the organisation of a coherent system (of a discourse) based on the intuition of the phenomenon, an intuition *not detached* from the real foundation (of the "raw material").

30.

WHAT IS INTUITION? — The cerebral activity of pictorial representation generates a proliferation of forms that do not necessarily refer to a concrete reality. This autonomous production cannot be equated with intuition, which for us refers to the moment when consciousness grasps a reality outside itself[91]. Intuition

---

[91] Kant, for example, does not limit intuition to the grasp of an exteriority. For Kant, internal intuition is the way in which

presupposes an interaction between the organism and an exogenous element: the senses do not grasp themselves (they do not grasp "internal images") but are solicited by something external. Intuition can therefore be understood above all as a confrontation between a material reality that manifests itself through our senses and the way in which we apprehend it, i.e. the movement by which we go about encountering it. As an immediate grasp of a raw reality, intuition manifests itself first as the identification of a singularity, an awareness of the particular and the heterogeneous. It is already a form of synthesis, a spontaneous unification of the diverse as it emerges in experience.

We do not in fact perceive a collection of atoms or a set of structured forces, but always a defined "form" (a form awaiting meaning, but whose contours are perceived, the form is understood in its unity of form, see diagram below or see more complete diagram § 25 — *What is a phenomenon?* Incidentally, let us point out that form is not limited to visual contours, it is also as

---

we have an immediate perception of our own internal states, i.e. what happens within ourselves as conscious subjects. Unlike external intuition, which relates to objects in space, internal intuition relates, for Kant, to what is in time. In internal intuition, everything we perceive in ourselves (for example, our successive thoughts, our memories, or our feelings) is perceived within a temporal framework. This means that our internal states always appear to have a certain succession or duration. We prefer to limit the concept of intuition to the perception of objects that are external to us in order to avoid certain confusions in the problem of reference that we develop in the next chapter.

much the identification of smells, sensations, touch, taste, etc.).

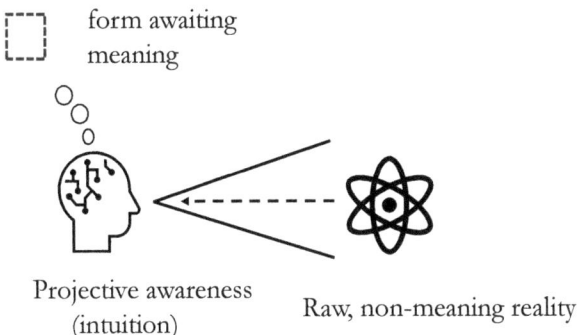

Intuition must therefore be distinguished from imagination, which cannot be reduced to the simple formation of mental images, but is a more complex faculty that makes it possible: (i) to link and unify the data of intuition into a coherent representation; (ii) to compensate for the limits of intuition by representing what is not immediately given (for example, figuring the invisible sides of a cube); (iii) to operate a broader synthesis by grouping different intuitions under general concepts. To help us visualise this formal dialectic between intuition and imagination, we can think of the activity of interpreting clouds: when we look at clouds, we do indeed perceive particular "non-signifying" forms that are given to us "passively" by intuition through the transmission of an external visual *stimulus*. In the first moment of intuition, these forms do not yet have a definite meaning (even if they do have a formal unity, the cloud is given to us in time and space; it has a form, but means nothing). In the second stage, that of the imagination, we no longer perceive forms "awaiting meaning" but reconstituted forms, grasped in their unity and in their relationship to other forms. The third stage is that of assigning these forms to a signifying concept. We 'name' these forms: a lion, a boat, a face.

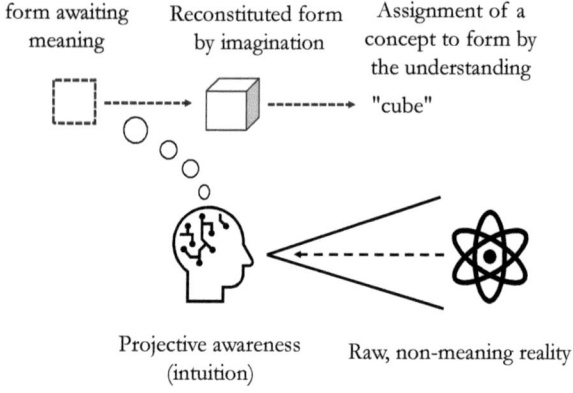

In the interpretation of clouds, the first two successive moments of intuition and imagination are easily dissociable. In our daily lives, however, these moments are more often than not combined and undifferentiated in a form of quasi-immediate interpretation. We think we perceive "a cat", "a car" or "a cloud" when in reality we are dealing with an object of infinite complexity and variability, but which we subsume each time under a simple concept that allows us to make the object legible (inserted into a network of defined meanings). If we perceive a lion, a face or a boat in the cloud passing over our heads, the signification will clearly not be a property of the cloud (which "in itself" is no more a "cloud" than a "lion" or a "boat") but rather a projection of the signifying imagination that the understanding will subsume under a concept — here we return to the *radical* dualism we defended in the first part of our argument, the *radical* dualism of the separation between the material support and its signification. This signifying projection is, however, constrained by the material itself, which does not, through sensible intuition, give the imagination *complete freedom* of formal creation. If the imagination (aided by understanding) projects and identifies the shape of a boat, it will have difficulty perceiving a lion or a face at the same time. Here, intuition plays its role of *medium* between the sensible given and its unitary signifying identification: intuition is not intuition "out of nothing" or based "on nothing". Starting from a non-signifying formal constraint, the imagination organises form by "interpreting" it, i.e. by inserting it into a network of known meanings. Imagination, as the capacity to create and recognise meaningful forms, operates at several levels: it is the structure of our intuitions (our intuitions are made within the formal 'framework' of imagination), it unifies and organises intuitions and plays a role in the formation of general concepts. Imagination is, in a way, both a power of creation and a power of recognition of raw (non-particularised, non-differentiated) form. In his manuscripts on the imagination[92], Husserl

---

[92] Edmund Husserl, *Phantasie, Bildbewusstsein, Erinnerung*: *Phantasia, image consciousness, memory* (posthumous work published in 1980, the contents of this volume come from Husserl's unpublished manuscripts, written between 1904 and 1928. It is a collection of his research on image consciousness, imagination (Phantasia) and memory

makes a clear distinction between these two characteristics of the imagination: the imagination that enables us to represent an intuited object to ourselves is called "physical imagination" (the power of signifying identification), while the imagination that takes place outside the visual field belongs to the essence of "phantasia" (the power of creation that acts outside the intuition of external objects).

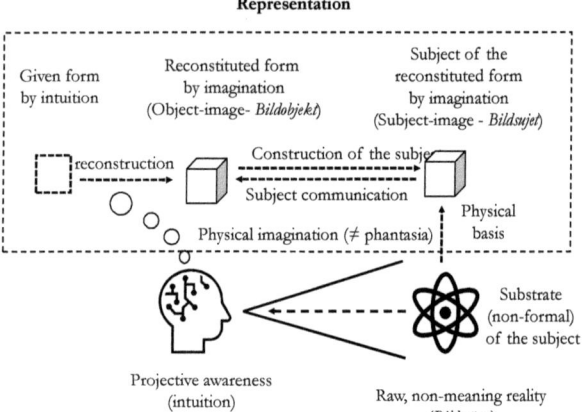

The physical imagination gives us what Husserl calls the "image-object" (*Bildobjekt*): an image of a knight, an image of a child, etc. (the image of the object, its representation "for us"). The image-object differs from the targeted object (the knight, the child, i.e. the subject of the representation) called the 'image-subject' (*Bildsujet*), which in turn differs from the physical

---

(Erinnerung), three types of acts of presentification (Vergegenwärtigung), i.e. acts by which an absent object is 'made present' to consciousness.

support of the image (*Bildträger*, a support that is non-significant in itself, the formless cloud, for example, in our previous example[93]). For Husserl, the image-object is a *fictum*, i.e. a construct of the imagination, and yet an apparent object (the object does appear to our consciousness). In reality, it is as if the imagination, in grasping the external object through intuition, reconstructs it at the very moment it presents it to consciousness. The construction of the phenomenon in a unified perception is, in fact, the result of the combined action of the intuition, which figures out and "loosens[94]" the particular form it receives from reality, and the "physical" imagination, which, by recognising this form, gives fictum a particular meaning[95] at the same time as it represents it from different angles[96]. It

---

[93] The example is a little misleading, because the cloud is already clearly identified as a "cloud" by the subject— but not yet as a lion, a boat...

[94] We're using a generic term here that refers more to vision, even though, *strictly speaking,* intuition does not only concern sight, but all the senses.

[95] On the distinction between the 'perceptual moment' of intuition and the moment of physical imagination, refer to the article by Danilo Saretta Verissimo, *Sur la relation entre imagerie mentale et perception : Analyse à partir des contributions théoriques et empiriques* (*On the relationship between mental imagery and perception: Analysis based on theoretical and empirical contributions)*, Volume 13 (2017) - Numéro 2 : *L'acte d'imagination : Approches phénoménologiques* (Actes n°10)

[96] See, for example, the work of Shepard and Metzler on mental rotation exercises, R. Shepard, J. Metzler, *Mental rotation of three-dimensional objects*, Science, 171, 1971, p. 701-703. And B. Nanay on the representation of hidden parts of

is interesting to note that the distinction we are making here between the two moments of intuition and imagination is not a purely analytical or formal differentiation. Using functional MRI, Kalanit Grill-Spector, for example, took a series of measurements of the visual cortex and noted a clear dissociation between the successive activations of certain cerebral areas in image perception. By masking images presented to the subject of the experiment, Kalanit Grill-Spector established that below 50 milliseconds, the images were invisible to the subject of the experiment, while above 100 milliseconds, they appeared in full consciousness. However, these two moments appeared clearly on visual imagery: the early visual areas were activated all the time, whether the image was conscious or not. On the other hand, in the higher visual areas, such as the fusiform gyrus and the lateral occipitotemporal region — areas that are involved in categorising and identifying images (faces, objects, words, places...) — brain activity is closely linked to the degree of consciousness. Now, as soon as an image reaches this level of cerebral processing, it is very likely to become conscious. While

---

an object, B. Nanay, *Perception and imagination: amodal perception as mental imagery*, Philosophical Studies, 150, 2010, p. 239-254; B. Nanay, *Imagination and Perception*. In these phenomena of representing an object in three dimensions or of representing the hidden parts of an object, we do not see, as Nanay does, the idea that "mental imagery is necessary for perception" (we think that mental imagery is rather necessary for the legibility of the world, for the insertion of images into a signifying network, rather than for the perception of the image itself, which can very well take place in the two distinct moments of intuition and imagination, which moreover seems to be confirmed by brain imaging).

Stanislas Dehaene specifies that these higher visual areas can, according to his own experiments, be activated unconsciously, it should be noted that, in the experiments of Kalanit Grill-Spector and Stanislas Dehaene, the two moments of what we have called intuition and imagination are physically and temporally differentiated, independently of the question of their access to consciousness (Stanislas Dehaene nevertheless notes that when an image, word or sound becomes conscious, brain activity is multiplied: when a word is perceived consciously, the activity of the higher visual areas is multiplied by twelve com-pared with unconscious perception of the same word).

Once we recognise that intuition has this particular role of 'detaching' (apprehending a singularity, a heterogeneity of reality) the data of the senses, how do we apprehend borderline situations such as hallucinations and dreams? If we limit intuition to its subconscious role of grasping data received from the external world, we need to define what this 'external world' is, and hallucinations and dreams precisely erase the differentiation between the external real and this 'other real' which is imagined but not derived from the intuition of an external object. Here we are confronted with a subject that has agitated many a philosopher, and yet is of relative importance, the difficulty having in fact much more theoretical than practical significance. We certainly note that, in daydreams as well as in hallucinations, physical electrical processes can be observed by cerebral imaging. Functional MRI scans show that, in the brain of a subject confronted with a given external image, similar areas are activated, whether the image is presented to the subject or simply imagined by the subject. Similarly, it is perfectly possible for an experimenter to induce hallucinations in any volunteer using a technique called "transcranial magnetic stimulation" (TMS). Even in the dark, with eyes closed, an electrical impulse that induces a discharge in the visual cortex can provoke a conscious impression. In these cases, we can legitimately defend the idea that our consciousness is affected "by something", this something corresponding to a physical substrate, physically observable, which can be located either outside the subject, as in the case of TMS, or "inside" the subject in the case of dreams and hallucinations (this internal-external distinction in no way abolishes the material-imaterial distinction, since hallucinations like dreams are materially observable and therefore materially provoked). Unlike 'normal' waking states, however, hallucinatory states do not follow the mechanisms of sensory seizure of a physically *external* object in which sensibility and intuition intervene. The brain functions 'autonomously', so to speak, and the hall-mark of these states is precisely their disconnection from the world physically external to the subject. In the case of auditory hallucinations, for example, Renaud Jardri and Pierre Thomas[97] note on the one hand that it seems possible to differentiate hallucinatory brain activity from normal perceptual activity, with the hallucinatory experiences of schizophrenics being associated, for example, with increased functional activation of the left hippocampal-para-hippocampal

---

[97] Renaud Jardri and Pierre Thomas, *Imagerie cérébrale fonctionnelle de l'hallucination ou comment voir ce que les hallucinés entendent* in *L'information Psychiatrique*, 2012/10, volume 88, pp. 815 to 822

complex, as well as regions of verbal production and perception, and secondly that the auditory cortex as a whole does not appear to be involved in the emergence of acousticoverbal hallucinations, "since only the associative sensory areas are found to be significantly more activated during hallucinatory periods". In hallucinatory states, therefore, it appears that the signal presented to the upper areas of the cerebral cortex has not followed the trajectory of stimulation of the brain by an external object. It should also be pointed out that the identity between the areas linked to the production of mental images derived from the intuition of external objects and those linked to the production of autonomous mental images is only partial. A number of studies have shown significant differences between the neural correlates of these two faculties. For example, Ganis, Thompson and Kosslyn found that the inferior occipital gyrus and the right superior occipital gyrus are activated by visual perception, but not by mental imagery. This is also the case, to a lesser extent, for the middle occipital gyrus, the left superior occipital gyrus, the lingual gyrus and the cuneus[98]. Leaving aside mixed or intermediate states (the integration of data from outside the dream into the hallucination), neuroscientists today seem to be perfectly capable of distinguishing hallucinatory states or states of fanciful imagination ('phantasia') from states of perception involving the intuition of an

---

[98] *Brain areas Underlying Visual Mental Imagery and Visual Perception: an MRI Study Giorgio Ganis 1, William L Thompson, Stephen M Kosslyn*, quoted by *Sacha Behrend, Le rapport entre imagerie mentale et perception à la lumière des sciences cognitives*, Philonsorbonne, 16, 2022, pp. 13-30.

external object. Of course, the question of whether the subject himself can 'definitely' distinguish between his waking states, his dream states and his hallucinatory states remains unresolved (particularly in the borderline cases of schizophrenia or certain dreams), But this problem boils down to the problem of solipsism, and not to the idea that sensible intuition concerns only objects that are physically external to us (situations of pure hallucination or pure daydreaming do not involve sentience, and consequently do not involve what we call sensible intuition either).

31.

AGAINST PSYCHOLOGISM — The idea that the intuition of things and the meaning of words refer only to the psychological state of a given speaker is another version of solipsism or radical scepticism according to which "nothing allows us to logically affirm the existence of the world outside the subject". This idea, like any idea that proceeds from tautological reasoning (i.e. reasoning whose conclusion is entirely contained in the premises of the demonstration), seems at first sight difficult to attack. Like the radical materialist who claims to demonstrate that everything is matter on the assumption that everything that might not be matter is matter, the solipsist claims to demonstrate that everything is subject on the assumption that everything that might not be reducible to the subject is reducible to the subject. Within the framework of psychologism — or linguistic subjectivism — the reasoning amounts, for example, to maintaining that a theory of language can dispense with addressing the question of reference by reducing it exclusively to the contents of the mental states of a given speaker (§ 27). In reality, psychologism bypasses the problem of intuition in order to concern itself with language only as an organised autonomous formal system (which would create its own meanings independently of any "external" reality). This radical psychologism is a slightly watered-down version of ontological solipsism. Like solipsism, it is also tautological. In solipsism, as in materialism, it is monistic reasoning that is at the root of the difficulty: the structure of reasoning that starts from an undifferentiated whole can logically only lead to total undifferentiation[99]. In *Reason, Truth and History*, Putnam is undoubtedly right to link the problem of reference directly to that of intentionality: the fact that a "mental state" "refers to" or is "directed towards" an object that is not entirely assimilable to it[100]. The Twin Earth thought experiment[101], which he described in two articles published in 1973 and 1975[102], highlights the logical aporias of psychologism. "Let's imagine", Putnam explains, "that in a distant galaxy there is a planet similar to our own, called Twin Earth. On this planet live human beings similar to us. Their behaviour is similar to ours and their scientific knowledge has

---

[99] This structure of reasoning is different from that which speaks of an identified whole, i.e. a differentiated set, for example: "for any real number x, we have $x^2 \geq x$".

[100] See Hillary Putnam, *Reason, Truth and History*: "some philosophers (most famously Brentano) have ascribed to the mind a power, 'intentionality' which precisely enables it to *refer.*", p. 17; Cambridge University Press, 1981, 2004

[101] Hilary Putnam, *The Meaning of Meaning*, 1975

[102] *Meaning and Reference* (1973) and The *Meaning of Meaning* (1975)

evolved in parallel with ours. The only difference between this planet and ours is this: on Twin Earth, the seas, rivers and streams appear to contain water, just like on Earth. It is a liquid that is equally transparent, thirst-quenching and capable of trans-forming into a solid or gaseous state... The water on Twin Earth is entirely similar to the water we know on Earth, with the sole exception that the liquid called 'water' on Twin Earth has a molecular structure that is distinct from that of water on Earth. While the structure of water on Earth is H_2O, the structure of water on Twin Earth is, say, X_YZ." Here, then, is the crux of Putnam's thought experiment. "Let's go back to 1750, to a time when people on both planets didn't know the chemical composition of liquids: the typical Earthian didn't know then that water is composed of hydrogen and oxygen, and the typical Twin Earthian didn't know that 'water' is composed of X_YZ. Let's call $Oscar_1$ the typical Earthian of that time and $Oscar_2$ his replica on Twin Earth. We can assume that $Oscar_1$ held no beliefs about water that $Oscar_2$ held about 'water'. We can even assume, if we wish, that $Oscar_1$ and $Oscar_2$ were exact doubles, in appearance, feelings, thoughts, inner monologue and so on. Yet the extension of the term 'water' on Earth in 1750 was H_2O [...] and the extension of the term 'water' on Twin Earth in 1750 was X_YZ [...]. $Oscar_1$ and $Oscar_2$ understood the term 'water' differently in 1750, even though they were in the same psychological state and, given the state of science at the time, it would take another fifty years for the scientific community on each planet to discover that they understood the term 'water' differently. Thus, the extension of the term 'water' (and, indeed, its meaning, in the intuitive pre-analytical use of the term) is not a function of the speaker's psychological state alone[103]."

The essential point of Putnam's demonstration lies in the idea that a theory of language cannot do without a corresponding theory of reference. The psycho-logical state of a given speaker cannot suffice to determine the reference to the object he or she designates. In other words, both in the theory of language and in modern theories of consciousness, we cannot do without intuition as a mediating factor between the external object and consciousness (in neuroscientific theories) and between the external object and language (in theories of language). This certainly does not mean, *a contrario*, that meaning is entirely contained in the objects targeted by language — we would then fall back into another form of realist monism that we have never ceased to denounce. Truth, as we have said, cannot be conceived as an adequacy between a discourse and the thing "in itself". What Putnam is aiming at above all is the conception of language as an autonomous system of meaning that can ultimately do without the second term essential to all language: that of what it *is aimed at*. To be invested with meaning, language can only be of a 'dualist' nature, the theory of radical subjectivity failing, as we showed earlier, in its logical aporias. In Putnam's example, it is the reference to an external object (water) that defeats radical psychologism. It should be noted here that dualism is understood as a differentiation, to use Husserl's terms, between the

---

[103] Sum up of *Meaning and Reference* (1973) and The *Meaning of 'Meaning* (1975)

image-object (*Bildobjekt*), i.e. the object (water) as it appears to us in our consciousness, and the image-subject (*Bildsujet*), i.e. the subject of the object (in this case, what we refer to when we represent water to ourselves, everything that is attached to water for us, its intrinsic characteristics as we think them, as we construct them in our signifying systems). This subject-image is in turn a manifestation that *is not detached* from the material reality that supports it, a raw material reality to which we can only have access in the mode of phenomenal manifestation (object-image) from which we derive our mental construction of the subject-image (see diagram in the previous chapter). The link between the mental construction of the image-subject and its material reality (*Bildträger*) supports the theory of reference: if there is no material reality, then we fall back into the problem of solipsism, according to which I can only be certain of my own existence — if at all I can be granted this certainty, a problem which we have seen (i) cannot produce any knowledge, (ii) that it had no meaning as a totalising statement and (iii) that it failed to describe our relation to the world, a relation precisely founded on signifiance, (see § 13 — *Can we imagine a world without laws?*). This last part of our reasoning could certainly be attacked: we could indeed rightly be criticised for making the signifiance of the world a form of apodictic certainty (who proves to me after all that language signifies anything?) which would in turn found the existence of the world. Our response to this objection is that we don't actually need to make signifiance an apodictic certainty. All we need to do is agree on the idea that there is "something" rather than nothing, and that this "something" does not need to be defined. Indeed, however far back we go in questioning the 'something' (it's a dream, a dream, an illusion...), we cannot equate this something with 'nothing' (a dream, a dream, an illusion are already 'something', they are not 'nothing'). The "something" does not therefore need to have a defined content in order to establish its own existence (the "something" is "pre-significant"). As soon as we recognise that "it" exists or that there is an "it", we have to posit an entity to think and designate the "it". This brings us back to the problem of signification. Unlike materialist or solipsistic statements, which first posit a totality (which, as we have seen, can have no signification), we first posit a statement of existence of the type "there is", or, what amounts to the same thing, "there is something". The whole problem of signification derives from this "there is" statement. If we return to the paradox of the Twin Lands, the problem of reference can only be solved (i) if we recognise an exteriority of the subject (the subject is not everything), (ii) if we grant an autonomy to the object (the object 'water' is not only in the subject, it is not only "in his head") and finally (iii) if we recognise that the object external to the subject is materially founded — the permanent nature of the link between raw matter and its phenomenal manifestation can only be postulated (and corroborated). If, in fact, we do not recognise the independence of matter from the subject, then we will fail to explain the discovery of a different molecular structure of water between the Twin Earths (in the same way that we will fail to explain the communicability of the world, i.e. intersubjectivity).

In Reason, Truth and History, Putnam details another thought experiment that has become famous, entitled "Brains in a *vat*". In this experiment, which is similar to

Descartes' famous hypothesis of evil genius — and predates the release of the film *Matrix* by almost twenty years — Putnam describes the hypothesis that we could be, individually or collectively, brains placed in a vat forever by some mad scientist or by an alignment of cosmic coincidences. A super-computer connected to the nerve endings in our brain would make us believe in the actual presence of a perfectly normal world in which we perceive people, objects, the sky... The computer could even be intelligent enough to link different brains together and make them communicate by electrically reproducing the content of their correspondences. Admitting the premise of this hypothesis, Putnam wonders whether we could *rightly* say that we are "brains in vats". Putnam's answer, in the first place, appeals once again to the theory of reference: if, Putnam explains, I am a brain in a vat (and I have always been a brain in a vat), then all the reality I perceive will have been communicated to me by electrical impulses that give me the illusion of perceiving what I perceive.

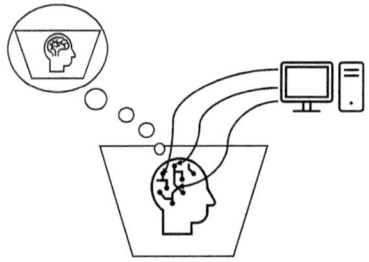

If, for example, I perceive "a tree", I am in fact receiving an electrical impulse which I decipher as being a "tree": the electrical impulse causes me to have a psychological experience corresponding to the representation of a tree. In fact, from the point of view of the brain, and its Cuvian brain language, the statement "I perceive a tree" is correct. The brain is in fact referring to a set of electrical impulses that it decodes as a 'tree'. Similarly, when the brain thinks of itself, it is in fact receiving a set of electrical impulses that make it imagine the image of a brain. It is therefore legitimate to say, in Cuvian language (or in Cuvian systems of meanings), I see a brain, I perceive a brain. When, following the same reasoning, the brain says: "I am a brain in a vat", it cannot refer to the vat as a "real" external object; it only refers to the vat, in its decoding system, as the image of a vat. He cannot refer to the 'real' vat (the one that might actually contain his brain) because vat language cannot, by definition, make any reference to the concrete external mode (it has no causal connection to the world). Thus, if we were indeed brains in a vat, the sentence "I am a brain in a vat" could in fact only make sense from the point of view of the brain (or "in the image" as Putnam puts it). In reality, the brain is only saying that it is "an image of a brain in an image of a vat". However, the hypothesis we were originally trying to validate was that we could be brains in vats and not images of brains in images of vats. Therefore, says Putnam, if we are indeed brains in vats, then the sentence "we are brains in vats" expresses something false, and if this statement expresses something false, it is necessarily false. The assumption that this statement can be said to be 'true' rests, according to Putnam, on a combination of two errors: that of taking *physical possibility* too seriously, and that of unconsciously proceeding from a magical theory of reference according to which mental representations necessarily refer to concrete external realities. Regarding the idea that there is a 'physical possibility' that we are brains in vats, Putnam asserts that this idea expresses nothing more than the fact that there is a description of this experience that is compatible with physical laws. This compatibility says nothing, however, about the possibility of thinking about such an experience from a logical point of view.

To make Putnam's intuition clearer, let's suppose that the brain is immersed in water. If a brain in a vat uses the word 'water', it will do so from its own internal reference system (a system of perception and language created by the computer that stimulates it). In his vat world, 'water' could refer to a set of electrical impulses that are vital to him, that produce the sensation of drinking a liquid, of being wet, etc. But this 'water' does not have the same meaning as the word 'water'. But this 'water' has nothing to do with real physical water (H_2O), which exists in an external world of which he has no direct experience. If, on the other hand, the brain tries to talk about the physical water in which it is actually immersed (that which surrounds its brain in the tank), it has no way of attributing meaning to it, because this water plays no part in its sensory experience. This is why Putnam prohibits the brain in the tank from having a stable meaning for the phrase "I am a brain in a tank" or "I am a brain in a tank filled with water": if "water" has any meaning in his world, it is to specific electrical signals that he is referring. But if he wants to talk about 'real' external water, he can't give it any meaning, because it doesn't exist in his perceptual and linguistic framework (he can't drink it or bathe in it, for example). The same reasoning applies to the "vat" itself: if the brain wants to say: "I'm in a vat", it can only refer to an image of a vat simulated in its perceptual system, and not to the real vat. If the brain in the tank wants to say: "I'm drinking water", it is talking about its simulated experience, which makes sense in its internal world. The sentence "There is water around my brain" will have no meaning for it, because the referent will in fact be radically different in its properties from the water in its internal world (the external "water" has no perceptual or functional effect in its subjective experience). This is why Putnam blocks the vat-brain hypothesis: if we really were brains in a vat, we would have no linguistic way of formulating this hypothesis correctly. The sentence "I am a brain in a vat" cannot refer to anything real in the linguistic framework of the vat brain. The irony is that this demonstration destroys the thought experiment itself: if we were really in a vat, we wouldn't be able to say so in any meaningful way. The very fact that we can discuss this hypothesis proves that we are not brains in a vat, which goes to Putnam's fundamental point: radical scepticism (of the "we may be in a simulation" variety) contradicts itself because it assumes a distinction between reality and illusion that we could not make if we were truly in the illusion. In short, Putnam does not directly prove that we are not in a simulation, but he does show that we cannot coherently assert it, which amounts to the same thing from a pragmatic point of view[104].

---

[104] If it had only been question of proving the inconsistency of illusionism, Putnam would not in fact have had to develop an argument of a referential nature. Putnam's problem is, as

With the problem of reference, we actually fall back into the aporias of monistic systems. Putnam's two thought experiments go some way towards demonstrating the inadequacies and contradictions of reductionist materialism. With the Twin Lands thought experiment, Putnam shows that language cannot do without a reference to an autonomous reality (that it is not a function of the speaker's psychological state alone), while with the Brain in a Vat thought experiment, Putnam shows that a brain in a vat that asserts "I am a brain in a vat" cannot refer to anything and would therefore produce no consequences from a pragmatic and empirical point of view (it would be empty knowledge, without a referent, without an object). Through the problem of reference, Putnam contradicts psychologism in two ways, firstly by showing its incoherence (logical incoherence) and secondly by showing its inconsistency (conceptual impasse).

---

he himself writes, a modern version of scepticism about the reality of the world. But, through his thought experiment, Putnam ultimately shows that the idea of solipsism (and therefore monism) is self-contradictory. The very idea that there is nothing outside my brain needs to postulate something 'outside' the brain (a vat, for example, but also a computer, a processor, a mad scientist, etc.) in order to make sense. To assert that there is nothing outside my brain is tantamount to saying that there is nothing outside my perceptions, which again implies that my perceptions are not caused by anything (that they are self-generated with no external support, no mad scientist, no electrical flow), which logically implies that they are nothing themselves (since they have no material support). The monist assertion is therefore diluted by its own contradictions.

Psychologism, like any monistic system, cannot prove its internal consistency. This is one of the consequences of the incompleteness theorem that Gödel enunciated in 1931: in any consistent formal system capable of expressing the arithmetic of natural numbers, there exist, Gödel shows, statements that are true, but that cannot be proved within that system. In other words, there are mathematical truths that cannot be proved within the logical or mathematical system of which they are a part (first incompleteness theorem). No consistent formal system capable of expressing the arithmetic of natural numbers can prove its own consistency. In other words, if a formal system can prove all the mathematical truths that concern it, it cannot prove that it is consistent (second incompleteness theorem). The originality of Gödel's proof of incompleteness is somewhat similar to Putnam's thought experiment: instead of attempting to demonstrate *positively* the incompleteness of mathematics, Gödel demonstrates negatively that the completeness hypothesis contradicts itself. It is through the arithmetisation of logic, i.e. the numbering of logical connectors within the formal arithmetical system, that Gödel demonstrates the impossible completeness of the said formal system (in Gödel's demonstration, the 'constant' $\sim$ which means 'no' in logical language is replaced by the number 1, the constant V which means 'or' is replaced by the number 2, the constant $\supset$ which means 'if....then", by the number 3 and so on). By formalising the logical links within arithmetic, Gödel manages to demonstrate that if arithmetic is consistent (coherent) its consistency cannot be established by metamathematical reasoning that can be represented *within* the formalism of arithmetic. This demonstration by Gödel is of capital importance, not only for mathematics, but also for any formal system in general, and therefore for any organised language (organised language differs from pure formal systems, however, in that it is an open system in which definitions can evolve according to semantic games and changes in the networks of meaning). To assert that formal systems cannot find in themselves the proof of their coherence is tantamount to denying the possibility that mathematics, like language, can be reduced to a game of the mind without any necessary connection with an external reality (a system). Basically, the programme Hilbert set out in the 1920s with his idea of the "finitisation" of mathematics, i.e. the reduction of mathematical reasoning to finite procedures, assumed that arithmetical demonstrations have no meaning and are merely a set of symbols that the brain, which acts but does not think, performs on its own[105]. Gödel replies that arithmetic makes sense: it is not my brain, but I, the mathematician (just as it is my daughter who is impertinent, not her brain).

In *Conversations with Wang*, Gödel states that the question of the objective existence of mathematical objects [...] is the exact replica of the question of the objective existence of the external world[106]. In other words, Gödel's demonstration implies that there is a reality at the root of the sensible world. If it were

---

[105] "a kind of game played according to certain rules with objects and formulas", says Hilbert.
[106] Kurt Gödel, *Conversations with Wang*, volume II, p. 268, 1964, quoted by Pierre Cassou-Noguès in *Les démons de Gödel*, Points, éditions du Seuil 2007, p. 97

otherwise, we would not be able to make judgements about things. The existence of signification presupposes the separation of nature between the speaker and what he expresses, between the word and what it designates: the system alone cannot have signification at its level. Worse still, a system without a metasystem cannot be said to be consistent or coherent[107]. The implications of Gödel's theorem for the coherence of mathematics and language are similar: on the one hand, Gödel shows that the mechanisation of mathematics, i.e. the elimination of the mind and abstract entities, is impossible if we want to obtain a satisfactory foundation and system for mathematics[108] ; on the other, he establishes that any theory of language that claims to find its foundation outside a reference to a metasystem of language (that of meaning) cannot be consistent. For mathematics, Gödel argues, we cannot do without "the fountain of intuition", the ability to "see at once[109]". Similarly, a theory of language cannot

---

[107] This is the conclusion of Gödel's second incompleteness theorem: if a formal system can prove all the mathematical truths about itself, it cannot prove that it is consistent.

[108] "My theorem only shows that the mechanisation of mathematics, i.e. the elimination of the *mind* and *abstract* entities, is impossible, if we want to obtain a foundation and a satisfactory system of mathematics". Kurt Gödel, to Léon Rappaport, 1962, *Conversations with Wang*, volume V, p. 176, quoted by Pierre Cassou-Noguès in *Les démons de Gödel*, Points, éditions du Seuil 2007, p. 183.

[109] "Intuition [...] is seeing all at once. Knowledge (understanding) is an absolutely momentary process." Gödel Papers, C. Ph. Transcribed by c. Dawson, vol. VI, p. 406, quoted by Pierre Cassou-Noguès in *Les démons de Gödel*, Points, éditions du Seuil 2007, p. 353.

do without recourse to intuition as a pivotal link with the outside world. Of course, in Gödel's case, the term mathematical *intuition* has a very different meaning from the one we give to the term sensible *intuition* in our theory of perception and language. For Gödel, mathematical intuition is more like an act of imagination, in the sense that Kant spoke of "productive imagination[110]" (as opposed to reproductive imagination, which is the capacity to recall images or ideas from memory and which functions according to associative laws), i.e. the capacity of our consciousness to generate anarchic forms, to organise them at a higher level and to stabilise them in order to make them meaningful to us. In the productive imagination, as in what Gödel calls mathematical intuition, it is the necessity of duality that is affirmed. Just as the coherence of mathematical systems can only operate at a meta-mathematical level, the coherence of language can only be established in the duality between language and the world, of which intuition is the third term. Another interesting point in Gödel's thinking lies in the idea that an object that has properties that we do not know cannot have been created by us consciously and out of nothing. We know, he argues, what we purposely create. Consequently, an object that we know only imperfectly either presupposes an external

---

[110] The productive imagination is active and creative and is involved in the synthesis of sensible intuitions and concepts. For Kant, the productive imagination is involved in linking sensible intuitions together and integrating them into a unified structure, thus enabling judgements and knowledge to be formed. It is through this process that the human mind can apprehend the world in an ordered and meaningful way.

material mode (from which we conceived it, but which gives it an independent reality), or refers to its processes of creation in an unconscious part of our mind. From this theory of the impossibility of creating objects whose properties we are unaware of outside any 'real' material world, Gödel deduced two ideas: the first is that there is necessarily a reality at the root of the sensible world (sensible objects, given to us by perception, possess properties that we do not know, so they cannot have been created by us outside any sensible reality, the argument from integral psychologism does not hold — Putnam uses a comparable argument in his Twin Earths paradox), the second is that imaginary objects that would possess properties that we cannot immediately elucidate also possess an objective reality. This implies, for example, that the fact that after the reflection on the foundations of mathematics and the axiomatisation work carried out at the beginning of the twentieth century, there are still open problems in the theory of numbers, is enough to establish the reality of these objects (the numbers). This reality can certainly be related to or deduced from the sensible world (although many mathematical theories were discovered long before their physical or sensible application), but it is nonetheless independent of the mind that discovered and theorised it. Here again, it is the dual structure of reality, the profound separation between thought and what it is applied to, that is revealed. A monistic system cannot have meaning. Meaning always already presupposes an original separation between the object, the thing and what is intended by the subject, whether through what we have defined as "sensible intuition" or through what Gödel calls "mathematical intuition" in the case of numbers and mathematical theories, for example[111]. In both cases, the argument of psychologism does not hold, since the fact that the objects of our intuition possess properties that we can only deduce after an effort of elucidation demonstrates that their substance is independent of our mind and cannot be reduced to mental states.

32.

THE AUTONOMY OF LANGUAGE AND ITS NON-REDUCIBILITY TO EMPIRICAL STIMULI — In *Syntactic Structures* (1957), Noam Chomsky develops the idea that language is an innate capacity specific to the human species. For Chomsky, language is an independent cognitive module, governed by generative principles specific to the human brain. As an autonomous programmatic function, the generative system specific to all language cannot be deduced solely from our interaction with the *stimuli* in our environment. We are born, says Chomsky, with a "universal grammar", a set of abstract rules that underlie the grammatical structure of all human languages. The programmatic function refers precisely to this innate capacity of individuals to develop the syntax of a specific language autonomously. For Chomsky, it is above all linguistic creativity, i.e. the capacity of a given speaker to produce new, original and "grammatically correct" sentences, that supports the thesis of the autonomy of language: the infinite diversity of sentences that a speaker can conceive and produce cannot be solely the result his

---

[111] Be careful with the use of the same term "intuition", which here refers to different realities.

repeated exposure to examples of sentences drawn from his experience (an idea supported in particular by behaviourist theories). In *Syntactic Structures*, Chomsky offers the now famous example of the grammatically correct, though probably never before encountered by Chomsky, sentence "*Colorless green ideas sleep furiously*[112]". According to Chomsky, despite the fact that there is no obvious and comprehensible meaning to be drawn from this sentence, its grammatical construction will not shock the ear of the "native" listener[113], unlike, for example, the sentence "*Furiously sleep ideas green colorless*", which has the double defect of having neither meaning nor correct syntax. With this example, Chomsky draws attention to the fundamental distinction between syntax and semantics and their respective autonomy, the limitation of probabilistic approaches to language lying precisely in a confusion between semantics and syntax. The idea, specific to behaviourism and to a certain structuralism, which consists in asserting that the formation of language can be entirely explained through the prism of the observation of statistically significant relations, dispensing with the distinction between syntax and semantics, in fact proceeds from the same methodological illusion as that of physicalist reductionism. By attempting, through a methodological coup de force, to subordinate syntax to semantics, linguistic behaviourism misses the specific

---

[112] Noam Chomsky first formulated this example in his 1955 thesis entitled *The Logical Structure of Linguistic Theory*, then in a 1956 article entitled *Three Models for the Description of Language*, before repeating the example in 1957 in *Syntactic Structures*.
[113] In this case, English is their mother tongue.

character of syntax and its non-reducibility to semantics[114]. In reality, explains Chomsky, the grammatical sentence does not need to have a meaning, nor does it need a context, and is statistically improbable. However, we have the capacity to form an infinite number of meaningless grammatical sentences. Pronounced with normal intonation, however, the grammatical sentence will be remembered much more quickly and learnt much more easily, independently of any context, which is further proof of the separation in nature between grammar and semantics — grammaticality and not semantics helping learning, contrary to what probabilistic theories based on semantic analysis might have suggested. The ease with which children acquire language is just as much evidence of the innate and autonomous nature of its structures. Chomsky observes in particular that, even in situations where the environment is poor in linguistic examples, children have the capacity to develop linguistic skills at an impressive rate: they can understand and produce complex sentences without ever having been confronted with a significant number of examples. What's more, even though they have not yet been exposed to the basic rules of grammar, children have a natural tendency towards what Chomsky calls '*overregularization*', an ability to generalise rules deduced from syntactic structures that they think they recognise and to apply them to situations that are precisely the exception. In English, for example, a common mistake children make is to treat the verb "*go*" as a regular verb.

---

[114] This is why Chomsky states in *Syntactic Structures* that "probabilistic models give no particular insight into some of the basic problems of syntactic structure".

In trying to apply the regular rule of conjugation in the past tense, which consists of adding "-ed", children tend, in their early years, to say "*goed*" instead of "*went*". The error here lies in the attempt to treat '*go*' as a regular verb rather than an irregular one. Generally speaking, children's linguistic errors do not stem from a lack of understanding of the rule, but rather from over-application and over-generalisation. In other words, children's errors are *logical*. They reflect an innate ability to recognise and create the rules that govern the formation of syntactic structures (note here the close semantic relationship between the terms 'language' and 'logic', both of which have the same Greek origin, *logos*). Noam Chomsky, starting from the concrete analysis of syntactic systems (he began his academic career by attempting to establish a grammar of Hebrew[115]), comes to a familiar conclusion: monism fails to rise to the level of meaning. Behaviourism, in fact, as a statistical methodology applied to language formation, comes to a conclusion that is in fact contained its premises. How, in fact, could the idea that language is a monistic system, and that its acquisition is solely a matter of statistical identification and learning by repetition, lead to a radically different logical outcome? In the language sciences, as elsewhere, the starting point must be reality, not theory. When reality does not agree with theory, it is not reality that is wrong. On a personal note, I was surprised when my daughter, at the very beginning of her use of language, pointed to a barge on the Seine and distinctly pronounced the word 'boat'. At the time, her experience of boats was limited

---

[115] See Noam Chomsky, *Morphophonemics of Modern Hebrew*, 1949

to illustrations in children's books that depicted boats in a very different way from this barge moored alongside the quay, which looked more like a large shoe than a boat. What led her to identify this barge as a 'boat'? Certainly not a statistical synthesis of the thousands of different boats she had come across in her short life (a synthesis whose aim would have been to distinguish the characteristics common to all boats). Her identification was undoubtedly based on a different logic: a boat did not necessarily consist of a sail, a rudder and a walnut-shaped hull. Nor did it necessarily sail on the ocean or in a lake. In all likelihood, it was a floating, habitable object resting on a body of water of some kind. Thus, the acquisition of the concept of 'boat' here was not just statistical (repetition of the word associated with the same image) but also logico-aesthetic (logical understanding of the concept at the same time as a general imaginative representation of the idea of a boat). We find this idea again in Christoph von Sigwart. In his work *Logik*, published in 1873 and an important contribution to logic at the end of the nineteenth century, he wrote: "The whole theory of the construction of concepts by comparison only makes sense if it sets itself the task [...] of giving the common characteristic of things actually designated by the same word in the general use of language and of making the usual meaning of the word distinct. If we have to give the concept of animal, gas, flight, etc., we might be tempted to proceed in this way: to seek the common characteristics of all beings unanimously called animals, of all bodies unanimously called gases, of all activities unanimously called flights. It remains to be seen whether this undertaking is feasible and whether concepts can actually be constructed using this method; one might ask whether it is permissible to assume that there is never any doubt as to what is to be called an animal, a gas or a flight — i.e. whether we already have the concept we are looking for. Trying to construct a concept by abstraction in this way is like looking for the glasses on your nose with the help of your own glasses[116]". In other words, Sigwart, using a logic comparable to that of Chomsky, was questioning the possibility of the innate pre-existence of schemas which, "fertilised" by sensible intuition, become concepts. In the formation of concepts, as in the understanding of the deep grammatical structures that structure thought, it is not statistical synthesis that predominates: knowledge is first and foremost a matter of active legislation. It is the result of an exchange between the projective activity of our consciousness and the sensitive intuition which, by grasping the reality of the external world, enables meaning to invest syntax. Without sensitive intuition, syntax (our innate language structures) could never reach the level of signification. It is through interpenetration with what is not syntax (semantics) that syntax manages to rise to the level of meaning. Similarly, semantics without syntax would be no more than a juxtaposition of terms without meaning. It is the relationship between things that makes it possible to define things, not the things themselves, which carry their own meaning. This is why we need to re-establish the fundamental distinction between the innate rules of a logical truth, a binding formal coherence, and the world of signification, which is the world of the application of its rules of relation. It is only in the (dualistic) encounter between the

---

[116] Op. cit., I. pp. 320 ff.

formalism of the rule and the object (which gains signification through the very application of this rule) that signification can arise.

In his late writings[117], Noam Chomsky argues that syntactic structures are caused by genetic mutation in humans. This view accords with our earlier analysis that reason is both legislated and legislating: as a structure resulting from a long evolutionary process, it is determined and conditioned, i.e. shaped to fit what it is applied to. This is what makes it effective. It is also, as a dynamic of structuring the world and as an innate faculty of understanding and formulating the rules that govern it, lawmaking. As we have seen, this double determination of reason does not imply relativism (see in particular § 26 — *Response to the objections of physicalists: Pathological situations*).

33.

ARE OUR REPRESENTATIONS INDEPENDENT OF THEIR SUBSTRATUM? — In previous chapters, we have tried to establish the difference between form, phenomenon, intuition, concept and law, in other words, to identify the different ways in which things manifest themselves to our senses and are created within our minds. In our conception of things as encounters between a formless raw material (of which we know nothing 'in itself'[118]) and our 'mind' or our 'projective consciousness', which shapes this 'raw

---

[117] Berwick, Robert C., Noam Chomsky (2015). *Why only us: Language and Evolution.* MIT Press

[118] For the good reason that, as we have said, raw matter has no 'in-itself', that it is nothing that signifies 'in' or 'for' itself.

material' by giving it a specific form and a meaning of its own, we identified a twofold relativistic peril. The first peril consisted in asserting with the most exalted idealists that, since we could have no tangible proof of the existence of a material world, we could in all rigour dispense with the hypothesis of its existence (the idea that the world could be reduced to a network of 'ideal' phenomena with no substratum, a world of ideas and appearances). The second danger consisted in maintaining, on the contrary, with the materialists and a few zealous pragmatists, that the material world as it manifests itself to us through our senses being our only means of access to reality, we had no reason to suppose that anything other than the material existed. As we have seen, this position, which consisted of a frantic attempt to assimilate ideas to matter, came up against insoluble contradictions within a monistic doctrine.

What monistic approaches to reality, whether idealist or materialist, systematically tend to overlook is the link between matter and thought, the fundamental link that lies at the very heart of philosophical reflection and conditions the very possibility of thought. Can we think of a phenomenon without its substratum (without the formless 'raw matter' that is the bedrock of sense experience), or can we think of matter without considering the very nature of thought, which shapes matter (or is shaped by matter)? We have seen that these monistic approaches lead to logical contradictions, so we will not return here to the criticisms of materialism and integral idealism. There is, however, one final stum-bling block, one final breach into which relativism has sometimes tried to insert itself. In the space between 'raw matter' and the phenomenon as it appears to consciousness, there could well be the question of the validity of the relationship of transcription or transformation that exists between the raw energy of matter and the phenomenon as it appears to consciousness. According to this idea, we could well, while taking note of the duality that exists between matter and its empirico-critical transcription by the senses, consciousness and reason, contest the value or validity of the link between consciousness and the energy of "raw matter". Would this be an excess of methodological zeal? If we can subscribe to the idea that there is a link between the phenomenon (the thing 'formed' in our consciousness and somehow 'transposed' to our critical reason) and raw matter, we can after all perfectly well contest the nature of this link: there is nothing to indicate that there is any relationship of 'fidelity' between raw matter and the way in which it manifests itself, the way in which it is 'decoded' in the phenomenon, or that this raw matter is not changeable and facetious in itself. This, then, is the third loophole in relativism. Against these objections, we could argue that our experience of phenomenal regularities provides us with a guarantee of the permanence of things and of the way in which they manifest themselves to us. What reason would we have to doubt the sincerity of phenomena? Why should the chemical composition of water change when I'm not there to monitor it? Certainly, we can only corroborate this idea of phenomenal regularity. This corroboration, however important it may be, will never amount to proof: we cannot demonstrate the validity of the link that exists between brute reality and the phenomenon (the link, like brute reality itself, is never made visible to us, it is not itself a phenomenon that we could observe). But does this question about the validity of the link make sense? Isn't our desire to 'validate the validity' of the link just another attempt to jump over our own shadow?

On closer examination, it seems to us that this question of the "validity of validity" is in fact a new avatar of materialist or idealist monism (in the sense of absolute idealism). To question the validity of the link is in fact, once again, to try to deny dualism, to try to force the dual structure of the thing towards an impossible unity. In reality, the link is neither valid nor invalid; it is merely the *mode* by which the world manifests itself to us (the link is a necessary condition, not an empirical datum to be proved). Let's clear up any misunderstanding immediately: it is necessary here to establish a difference of great importance between *the fact that the thing can only manifest and construct itself through the senses of sentient beings* (the *mode of* manifestation and construction of the thing which is and can only be sensory and which necessarily implies separation and *radical* dualism) and the relative and incomplete character of the senses of the sentient beings that we are (a character that has nothing to do with the *mode of* manifestation and construction of the thing, but to the *way* in which we receive things and form an idea of them, a way that is certainly incomplete and imperfect, but whose incompleteness and imperfection do not relate to the *mode* as such). If then, we take note of this *mode of* manifestation of the thing, of its constitution as a phenomenon through our senses and our consciousness, the question of the validity or value of the link loses its significance and interest. The link is neither valid nor invalid in itself; it is precisely, as a *vehicle for* the formation of the thing, what enables the thing to achieve its status as a thing, to enter the domain of the valid and invalid. The question of the validity of the transformation bond is therefore meaningless, in the same way that the question of the sockness of the sock would be[119].

To use an analogy drawn from the science of wave phenomena, if, like Guillaume Apollinaire, we compared ourselves to a transistor, a receiver of TSF waves, it would no doubt seem absurd to question the validity of the link that exists between the wave and its signifying transcription by the transistor (our consciousness). Admittedly, there would always be a relationship of transformation between the wave and its signifying transposition, just as there is a relationship between 'raw matter' and the phenomenon, but since this relationship of trans-formation is precisely what enables the formless matter (the wave in our example[120]) to reach the level of signification (by amplification, frequency adjustment and transformation into acoustic pressure), it would not itself come under the question of validity (the question of the validity of the relationship would be meaningless). It is true that the signal may be scrambled or poorly received (in which case the sound will be imperceptible or bad). However, it is not the *way in which* the signal is

---

[119] I apologise for this facetious reference to Heidegger's convoluted formula: the 'thingness of the thing'. The idea here is to show the absurdity of a spiralling interrogation that saws off the branch on which it is sitting at the same time as it wonders whether it is really a branch.

[120] Even if, in reality, for us the wave is already a representation and therefore a phenomenon.

received and decoded (the system for receiving and transforming radio waves) that is at stake, but its *quality* and extent, i.e. the ability of the receiver to receive it correctly. The imperfection in the transcription of the wave will not concern the transformation system (the 'mode' which, as a condition of validity, cannot belong to the validity-invalidity pair), but the conditions of operation of the system and its signifying decoding (the 'manner'). The wave means nothing "by itself". It can only acquire meaning as it is decoded by the transistor. The question of the meaning of the wave before this decoding is therefore meaningless (the only thing that matters at that point is the quality of the transmission of the wave).

If we return to our original relationship with the real as a raw, pre-signifying given, the main issue is not the fidelity of the representation, since it does not relate to a signifying 'truth' inherent in the real itself. Indeed, the raw real carries no intrinsic meaning. What matters, then, is not the conformity of the representation to reality, but our ability to capture and integrate the greatest possible richness of the signal to give us the broadest possible idea of reality. The greater our capacity to take in the diversity of the signal, the better our understanding of the environment and the greater our freedom of action (see § 19 — *Degrees of freedom*). The signifying trans-formation link is neither valid nor invalid; it is our only access to reality (only the interpretation of the signal can be said to be "valid" or "invalid"). In other words, it is through this process of transformation that the real, devoid of intrinsic meaning, becomes intelligible (for us, biological and sentient beings). Questioning the validity of this link can only lead to a sterile questioning of the hierarchy of the different forms of transcription of reality. We know that species' modes of perception differ according to the frequencies and sensory modalities of living organisms. Humans, for example, perceive light in a spectrum of wavelengths between 380 nm (violet) and 750 nm (red), thanks to three types of retinal cones, a capacity known as trichromacy. Bats use echolocation to explore space: they emit ultrasound of up to 120,000 Hz and analyse the echoes returned by their surroundings, enabling them to construct a three-dimensional representation of space. Dolphins, similarly, use high-frequency sound clicks to locate objects underwater, even when they are hidden. Elephants, on the other hand, perceive infrasound (frequencies of 1 to 20 Hz) that propagates over great distances, enabling them to detect natural warning signals (such as earthquakes) or the calls of other elephants several kilometres away. This sensory diversity illustrates how each species adapts its perception of the world according to its environment and biological needs. But can we really say that the link between the transformation of raw reality is more 'valid' in dolphins than in elephants or humans? This question reveals a conceptual confusion, because the validity of the link has no relevance. What is often mistaken for 'validity' is in reality no more than an assessment of the scope or effectiveness of the mode of perception in a given context. It is therefore essential to distinguish the representation of the world — which is always conditioned by the structure of our sensory organs and our decoding system — from the way we relate to the world. The latter is fundamentally signifying, meaning that it is based on a duality between the perceived and the interpreted. Meaning does not pre-exist the transformation link; it results from our interpretation of sensory information. The error, as Descartes rightly wrote, is not in our senses, but always in our judgement. So, it is in the interpretation — in the haste of the will to judge — that the error lies, and not in the perception itself.

What does it mean to think?

Formalism vs. intuitionism

> In our case, *understanding* and *sensibility* can *only* determine objects *by uniting*. If we separate them, we have intuitions without concepts, or concepts without intuitions, and in both cases representations that we cannot relate to any determined object.
>
> Immanuel Kant, *Critique of Pure Reason*, *Transcendental Analysis*, B 314

34.

Intuitionism as a response to the logical aporias of formalism? — In the field of mathematics, the problem of intuition as defined and discussed in the previous chapters partly overlaps with the old debate between intuitionism and formalism. At the end of the nineteenth century, following in particular the discovery of paradoxes arising from the theories proposed by Georg Cantor and Gottlob Frege or Cesare Burali-Forti[121], mathematics was plunged

---

[121] The theories of Georg Cantor (set theory) and Gottlob Frege (axiomatic logic) led to several major paradoxes that plunged mathematics into a crisis of foundations at the beginning of the twentieth century. These paradoxes called into question the coherence and completeness of formal systems.

1. Russell's paradox (linked to Frege)

Russell's paradox (1901-1903) is probably the most famous of all logical paradoxes. It stems directly from Gottlob Frege's attempt to formalise the logic of sets in his *Foundations of Arithmetic*.

Paradox statement:

Russell's paradox is simply stated as follows:
- Consider the set R of all sets that do not contain themselves.
- The question is whether R belongs to itself or not.

There are two possible scenarios:
(i) If R belongs to itself, then it does not satisfy the condition of not belonging to itself, so $R \notin R$.
(ii) If R does not belong to itself, then it must belong to the set of sets that do not belong to themselves, so $R \in R$.

The result is a contradiction, because $R \in R$ if and only if $R \notin R$. This is a logical antinomy.

Origin of the paradox (Frege's error):

Gottlob Frege wanted to formalise arithmetic on the basis of pure logic (this is the programme of logistics or logicism). In his system, he accepted the principle that every logical predicate defines a set. This principle (called the "axiom of understanding" or "axiom of abstraction") states that, for any property P, there exists a set A such that $A = \{x \mid P(x)\}$ (which means that the set A is made up of all the elements x that satisfy the property $P(x)$). The problem is that this principle is too permissive. Applied to the property "does not belong to itself", it leads to the self-reference of Russell's paradox.

Frege himself recognised that Russell's paradox ruined his system. In a famous letter to Frege, Russell showed him that his formal system was inconsistent. Frege admitted this publicly and added an erratum to the second edition of his *Grundgesetze der Arithmetik*.

2. Cantor's paradox (the self-application of diagonalization)

Georg Cantor's paradox may be less well known than Russell's, but it is just as important. It stems from the theory of sets developed by Cantor at the end of the nineteenth century.

Paradox statement:

Cantor's paradox is based on the idea that the set of all sets cannot exist. Here is the reasoning:
- Let U be the set of all sets.
- Consider the set of its parts P(U), which is the set of all subsets of U.
- According to Cantor's theorem, the set of parts P(A) of a set A always has a cardinality strictly greater than that of A.
- But if U is the set of all sets, then P(U) should be included in U (because U contains "everything", again noting the problems with totalising statements).
- By Cantor's theorem, the cardinality of P(U) is greater than the cardinality of U, which is a contradiction.

Consequences:
- This paradox shows that there is no "total" set of sets.
- This contradicts the idea of a "universal set" (which is what Cantor originally intended).
- This paradox also reveals the infinite hierarchy of infinities. Each set of infinities (such as the real

into what was called the "crisis of the foundations". In an attempt to respond to this crisis, David Hilbert

---

numbers) is always "greater" than the set of integers, but there is no "greatest total infinity".

3. The Burali-Forti paradox (linked to Cantor)

The Burali-Forti paradox (1897) is linked to the notion of ordinal order (infinite quantities used by Cantor, ordinals designate positions in an order, e.g. 2 is the ordinal that designates the set of second positions).

Paradox statement:
- Consider the set of ordinals (all possible ordinals, denoted Ω).
- Since an ordinal is itself a set, the set of all ordinals should form an ordinal.
- But, by definition, this ordinal is greater than all the other ordinals, including itself, which leads to a contradiction.

Consequences:
- This paradox shows that we cannot form a set of all ordinals.
- The set of ordinals is no longer a set, but a proper class (a notion introduced later in the Von Neumann-Bernays-Gödel type theories).
- Eigenclasses (like the set of all sets) cannot be manipulated as sets.

These paradoxes led to the axiomatisation of set theory (by Zermelo-Fraenkel) and the creation of tools to avoid contradictions. They have also given rise to major philosophical reflections on the nature of number, logic and the consistency of formal systems. These paradoxes are at the heart of the work of Hilbert, Gödel and Turing.

presented the outlines of his famous programme for mathematics at the International Mathematical Congress in Paris in 1900, which involved solving twenty-three fundamental problems (the "Hilbert problems"). At the time, David Hilbert's ambition was to formalise and unify mathematics using an axiomatic approach designed to avoid paradoxes and ensure the overall coherence of the system. In vigorous opposition to the intuitionism of L.E.J. Brouwer, David Hilbert aimed to show that the validity of mathematics, which was purely formal, was based on the structure of the statements, independently of any actual construction of the objects or their intuitive reality. According to Hilbert, the truth of mathematics was reduced to its internal coherence and the non-contradiction of the propositions stated within a given system. Brouwer, on the other hand, defended the idea that the foundation of mathematics should lie in an active intuition of time: from this perspective, mathematical objects did not exist independently, but took shape through effective mental constructions produced by the human mind (which had an intimate experience of temporal succession). Brouwer thus insisted on the discursive character of mathematics, since a mathematical statement could only have meaning if it could be constructed or derived constructively (this constructivism recounting the concrete stages of the mind, which experienced sequentially internally through its intuition of becoming). Mathematical proofs thus had to be *effective* constructions, and the existence of an object could, according to Brouwer, only be demonstrated by its construction, or its explicit constructibility[122]. In the 1920s, the debate between Brouwer's intuitionism and Hilbert's formalism generated great tension in the muffled world of mathematics, so much so that the academic confrontation between Hilbert and Brouwer eventually turned into a personal confrontation. As early as 1921, Hilbert, feeling betrayed by Hermann Weyl, one of his former students, who had become a fervent supporter of Brouwer's radical intuitionism, criticised Brouwer very vigorously and triumphantly announced that the final proof of the coherence of mathematics was about to be given. Brouwer himself continued to attack formalism in a series of articles on mathematics in the *Mathematische Annalen*. A few years later, in 1927, Brouwer travelled to Berlin, where he won over the German mathematician Ludwig Bieberbach and the Dutchman Hans Freudenthal, who was to become his disciple. In 1928, he was invited to give two lectures on intuitionist philosophy and mathematics in Vienna. In addition to various members

---

[122] Let us point out in passing that this idea of the effectivity of mathematics that we find in Brouwer is undoubtedly to be compared with the idea of the effectivity of truth that we ourselves have developed (experience, technique as the effective validation of physics and mathematics). Unlike Brouwer, however, we do not establish a relationship of equivalence between the use of the criterion of effectivity as a judge of the validity or falsity of a statement and the fact that we have to reduce or submit any statement to this criterion of effectivity (in our view, there is no double criterion of equivalence here). Brouwer's position is undoubtedly to be compared with the solipsistic theses of his youth (it is also reminiscent of the theses of pragmatist and positivist circles, the limits of which we have already shown).

of the Vienna Circle, Ludwig Wittgenstein and the young Kurt Gödel were also present. Seeing the growing interest in intuitionist theses in mathematical circles and fearing that after his death the *Mathematische Annalen* would end up being converted to them, Hilbert — then editor of the journal — decided to expel Brouwer from the editorial board. The majority of the members complied with Hilbert's decision and Brouwer's name was removed from the journal (Albert Einstein and the Greek mathematician Constantin Carathéodory were the only ones to oppose Hilbert's decision). This confrontation deeply affected Brouwer, who became even more radical in the solipsistic positions he had taken in his youth[123]. In 1929, the theft

---

[123] *Leven, Kunst en Mystiek* (*Life, Art and Mysticism*) is an essay by L.E.J. Brouwer, published in 1907, in which he explores the relationship between life, art and mysticism, emphasising the primacy of individual intuition. In it, Brouwer defends the idea that true knowledge is not to be found in external representations or abstract constructs, but in the individual's immediate, inner experience. This text shows the influence of mysticism on his thought, which he sees as a form of access to pure truth, beyond discursive and rational representations. One of Brouwer's central theses is the link he establishes between artistic creation, life experience and mystical experience, all of which share a common characteristic: direct intuition. For Brouwer, just as art seeks to express a truth beyond reasoning, and mysticism to access a direct experience of the divine or transcendent, mathematics must be understood as an intuitive activity. This intuition is not simply a sensitive perception, but an immediate and pure form of knowledge.

of his scientific journal from a railway station wiped out all his research of the previous years in one moment, depriving him of the fruits of his intellectual labour and plunging him into a deep depression[124]. Around 1930, with Brouwer and intuitionism falling out of favour, the mathematician fell into a fourteen-year silence, publishing nothing new on intuitionistic mathematics.

In 1930, a few months before the Congress on the Epistemology of the Exact Sciences in Königsberg, the

---

Mathematical construction is thus understood as an inner activity, rooted in personal and immediate intuition, as distinct from the Kantian idea of *a priori* intuition. Brouwer links his approach to mathematics to a form of philosophical mysticism, in which knowledge is the product of pure intuition, closer to lived, personal experience than to universalisable logical reasoning.

Brouwer develops the idea that each individual, through his or her own intimate experience, constructs his or her own world. He went so far as to assert that the mathematical object has no reality except in the consciousness of the individual who constructs it. In this sense, he rejects any form of objective reality independent of subjectivity, a position that brings him closer to solipsism, in which the external world is subordinated to personal intuition. Thus, mathematical constructions must be understood as creations of the human mind, without any necessary reference to an external or objective world. In our view, the link between Brouwer's radically intuitionist positions and the communicable (i.e. universalizable) nature of these intuitions remains problematic.

[124] See Carlos M. Madrid Casado and Adrien Gauthier, *Un geómetra entre la topología y la filosofía: Brouwer* (Barcelona: RBA Coleccionables, 2019), p. 154.

Vienna Circle held two seminars[125]. The young Gödel was reserved, but attracted sympathy. He particularly enjoyed talking to foreign logicians: Alfred Tarski, who sometimes came from Warsaw, and John von Neumann, who lived in Göttingen. Gödel also spoke with Carnap about the incompleteness of mathematics, before proving his theorem. Ahead of the 1930 seminars, Carnap noted in his diary, dated 23 December 1929, the transcript of a conversation he had had with Kurt Gödel at the Arkadencafé: "With each formalisation, there are problems which can be understood and expressed in ordinary language, but which cannot be expressed in this formal language. It follows [...] that mathematics is inexhaustible: you always have to go back to the 'fountain of intuition'[126]". This is precisely the meaning that Gödel would give to his incompleteness theorems the following summer in Königsberg, using a rigorous notion of formalisation, with the nuance that the problems that make up the incompleteness of the system are expressed but not solved in the system. The idea remains the same, however: when a mathematical system encounters insoluble problems within itself, it requires the contribution of new intuitions in order to be completed. For Gödel, the 'fountain of intuition' is both what allows me to see, understand and explain mathematics and what underpins ordinary language (in this respect, the distinction Gödel draws between ordinary language and formal language is crucial, since

---

[125] Quoted by Pierre Cassou-Noguès in *Les démons de Gödel*, p. 163, extract from Carnap's diary

[126] Quoted by Pierre Cassou-Noguès *in Les démons de Gödel*, p. 164

ordinary language is not subject to the same rules of formalism as formal language, as we have already mentioned). In September 1930, on the sixth day of the Congress on the Epistemology of the Exact Sciences in Königsberg, the young Austrian logician Kurt Gödel — then aged 24 — said: "I can give examples of arithmetical propositions that are true, but unprovable in the formal system of classical mathematics". In 1931, the same Kurt Gödel published his incompleteness theorems, which meant the ruin of Hilbert's programme.

In 1879, Gottlob Frege set out the three characteristics of a mathematical theory: its coherence (the impossibility of demonstrating, within the same theoretical system, a proposition and its opposite), its completeness (the idea that it should be possible to demonstrate a statement or its opposite within the theoretical system) and its decidability (the idea that there should exist a decision procedure enabling any statement in the theory to be tested), characteristics that David Hilbert himself had recognised in his research programme, which was based on the questions set out by Frege: are mathematics complete, coherent and decidable? With these two incompleteness theorems, Gödel demonstrated that no formal system could meet the criteria laid down by Frege. No axiomatic system powerful enough to describe integers and their arithmetic properties could be both complete and consistent. In particular, this meant that true statements in arithmetic could not be demonstrated within a particular formal system. It was therefore impossible to construct a general algorithm capable of determining whether any arithmetical statement was true or false (undecidability). The second incompleteness theorem reinforced this idea by showing that the consistency of a formal system could not be proved within the system itself. The debate about the completeness of mathematics and the ambitions of Hilbert's formalism was thus largely settled in the early 1930s. However, the epistemological and philosophical significance of Gödel's incompleteness theorems was curiously neglected. Was this because Gödel's 'intuitionism', although epistemologically triumphant, had not succeeded in establishing itself as a school of thought or in generating important discoveries? In any case, the question of the logical and mathematical consequences of the incompleteness of formal systems was generally avoided by mathematicians (no doubt because it was considered to have been partially resolved by recourse to axiomatisation) and, even more widely, by philosophers.

From the point of view of the epistemology of science, one of the central problems of Gödel's thinking was, however, the fundamental question of the *content* of the truths derived from the solution of mathematical problems. In his *Conversations with Wang*, Gödel explicitly linked the question of the existence of mathematical objects to that of the objective existence of the external world[127] (which set him apart from Brouwer's positions, which were radically opposed to his own from this point of view, Brouwer's intuitionism being based on a solipsistic theory of inner intuition

---

[127] Kurt Gödel, *Conversations with Wang*, Volume II, p. 268, 1964, quoted by Pierre Cassou-Noguès in *Les démons de Gödel*, Points, éditions du Seuil 2007, p. 97

without content rather than on a theory of intuition open to sensibility). For Gödel, mathematical intuition, as the capacity to understand and produce meaningful language, required incarnation, i.e. anchoring in a concrete reality. It should be pointed out once again that Gödel uses the word 'intuition' in a slightly different sense from the one we gave it in § 30 — *What is intuition?* For Gödel, the term 'intuition' is closer to what we have called 'creative imagination' or 'productive imagination' (the imagination that supports intuition in the general construction of phenomena and the external world) than to what we have called 'sensible intuition'. For Gödel, mathematical intuition was about our ability to grasp the scope of a problem and its solution in a unified image. In his *Papers*, Gödel wrote: intuition [...] is seeing all at once. Knowledge (understanding) is an absolutely momentary process[128]. It is interesting to see how Gödel insists on the "absolutely momentary" character of knowledge and understanding (in contrast to Brouwer, who emphasises the successive character of mental operations). For Gödel, the moment of understanding is not a discursive or critical moment; on the contrary, it is a moment of the ability to rise above a problem to get a "global image", almost an aesthetic one. In the same way that, in sensitive intuition, we perceive particular forms that we insert, with the help of the imagination, into a general network of meanings, the moment of mathematical intuition is thus the moment when the form of the problem and the form of its

---

[128] Gödel Papers, C. Ph. Transcription c. Dawson, vol. VI, p. 406, quoted by Pierre Cassou-Noguès in *Les démons de Gödel*, p. 353.

resolution reach our consciousness in the form of a meaningful image. In *Wang's Notebooks*, Gödel drew a parallel between mathematical intuition and sensible intuition: "we have", he wrote, "something like a

perception of set theory. I see no reason to have less confidence in this kind of perception, i.e. in mathematical intuition, than in sensible perception[129]". L.E.J. Brouwer himself liked to solve mathematical problems lying on his bed with his eyes closed or sitting cross-legged on the floor, positions that enabled him to apprehend problems more visually than formally and led him to manipulate figures rather than formulae. For Gödel, the moment of solving a theoretical problem could not be the result of discursive analysis alone. In reality, this moment was always the result of a visual projection, which is analogous to the one im-mediately operated by our imagination when it grasps and organises the forms given to it by sensitive intuition.

This conception of the immediacy of the signifying grasp is largely what led Gödel to reject Brouwer's constructivist and anti-realist[130] presuppositions,

---

[129] *Cahiers de Wang*, 1964, tome II, p. 268, Pierre Cassou-Noguès in *Les démons de Gödel*, p. 95

[130] Brouwer's idea that the truth of a mathematical statement consists in our ability to prove it, and not in its correspondence with objective reality or in a truth that exists outside the mind's actual constructions. Following this same pragmatic idea, Brouwer's intuitionism rejects reasoning based on the absurd or the third-excluded (the negation of

preferring instead a Platonist approach, according to which mathematics reveals "a non-sensible reality existing independently of human acts and the human mind[131]" (an approach which, from an epistemological and philosophical point of view, is paradoxical insofar as Gödel also recognises the role of incarnation in mathematical intuition[132]). If we can speak of Gödel's "intuitionism" (although this label applied to Gödel is open to debate), we must explicitly distinguish his positions from those of Brouwer. Whereas for Brouwer the internal intuition of time is the primary source of the construction of ordinals and natural numbers, for Gödel it is more a matter of the 'immediate' perception of abstract (and resolvable) schemes whose rules of coherence are independent of the subject. It is this problem of the independence of

---

non-existence not being equivalent to existence, only constructed or constructible objects exist). We can clearly see here the solipsistic positions of the young Brouwer (who opposes Gödel's idea that truth exceeds demonstrability).

[131] "The Platonic position is the only one that is tenable. By this I mean the position according to which mathematics describes a non-sensible reality which exists independently of both the acts and the dispositions of the human mind and which is only perceived, and probably only very incompletely perceived, by the human mind", *Wangs Notes*, 1951, tome 3, p. 323, quoted by Pierre Cassou-Noguès in *Les démons de Gödel*, p. 94.

[132] In reality, the paradox is only apparent and can be resolved, as we have done, by considering incarnation as a condition of sensible intuition and mathematical intuition, while recognising that mathematics is autonomous, i.e. independent of sensibility (in many cases, apriorism is a misnomer for autonomy).

formal rules that will lead Gödel to a form of Platonic realism, which will result in him essentializing numbers and formal rules (rules which, for him, have an objective reality outside our minds). In this respect, the incompleteness theorems show that formal systems do not capture all truths, which implies that truth exceeds demonstrability (as, for example, Goldbach's conjecture could attest if it remained unprovable — which has been the case for nearly three centuries[133]).

---

[133] Goldbach's conjecture states that any even integer greater than 2 can be expressed as the sum of two primes. Although no rigorous demonstration of this conjecture has ever been established, massive computer calculations confirm its validity right up to the limits of computer capacity. This illustrates the idea that the truth of a mathematical proposition can exceed its demonstrability: it can be 'true' in the structure of integers, even if it cannot be proved by any formal system. This discrepancy highlights the distinction between what is "true in itself" and what is "proved for us".

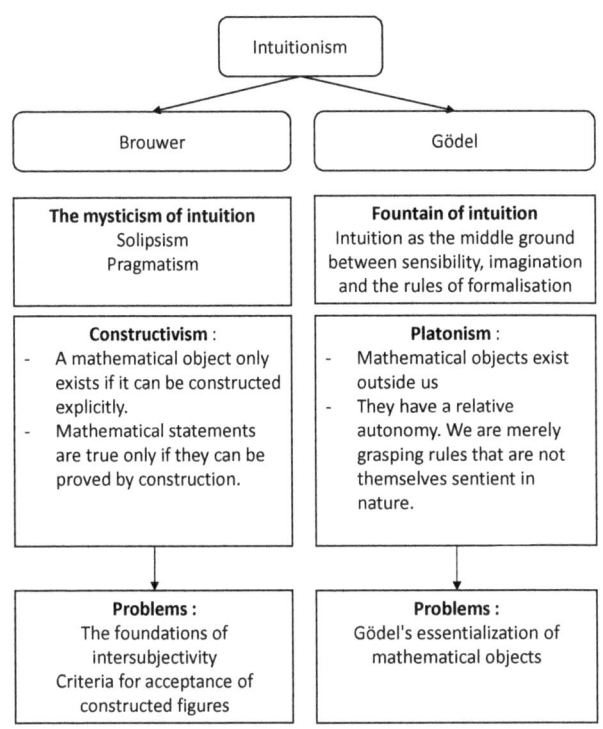

This idea of the independence of mathematics defended by Gödel (and which undoubtedly justifies the parallel he draws between sensible intuition and the intuition of mathematics, both intuitions relating to an exteriority of the subject and not vice versa as in Brouwer's case[134]) is to be compared with the idea of

---

[134] And, in a sense, as with Kant, although Brouwer totally rejects the aprioristic character of Kant's critical philosophy.

world 3 developed in the 1960s[135] by Karl Popper — himself influenced by the theories of Frege and Theodor Gomperz. In several of his late writings, Popper put forward the idea of a division of the world into three distinct categories: *world 1*, which encompasses physical objects and material phenomena — this is the world of observable and measurable things, such as stones, trees, planets, and so on, *world 2* which refers the whole formed by mental states and subjective experiences — this is the realm of thoughts, emotions, individual perceptions, and other aspects of the inner life and *world 3* which concerns the products of the human mind, such as ideas, theories, works of art, social institutions, languages, books, etc., i.e. abstract objects and cultural creations that exist independently of particular individuals. *World 3* was also, according to Popper, the world of the critical formalisation of reality. In *Objective Knowledge*, a work compiling texts written between 1961 and 1971, Karl Popper emphasised the autonomy of *world 3*, considering this autonomy to be the necessary condition for the legitimacy of objective knowledge. Although derived from the subjective impressions of *worlds 1 and 2*, this knowledge was not reduced to them, but was instead constituted as its own domain, structured by rational criticism and theoretical

---

[135] Karl Popper introduced his theory of the three worlds, including the "world 3" of the objective contents of thought, in a lecture in August 1960, subsequently published in Ch. 10 of "Conjectures and Refutations". He distinguished between the physical world (*world 1*), the world of mental states (*world 2*) and the world of human intellectual productions, such as scientific theories and works of art (*world 3*).

elaboration independent of individual experience. According to Popper, our 'full consciousness' depended on this world of theories (*world 3*). Although animals could have impressions, sensations and memory, and therefore consciousness, they did not, according to Popper, possess full self-awareness, which is one of the consequences of human language and the development of the specifically human (but not specifically subjective, as we shall return to) *world 3*[136]. While claiming the independence of *world 3* (and thus adopting a position that was very similar to Gödel's realist Platonism[137]), Popper insisted on the links between the different categories of analysis of the world. Thus, the *world 3*, although autonomous and not specifically sensible, was for example described by Popper as a kind of "spider's web" woven by man (a work of man). For Popper, however, it was above all the critical dimension, achieved in man through the development of the higher functions of language, that enabled *world 3* to be freed from the threads of sensibility that linked it to *worlds 1 and 2*. Through language, through *logos*, *world 3* became in a sense irreducible to *worlds 1 and 2*, of which it was nonetheless the product (as we have endeavoured to show since the beginning of our presentation).

---

[136] Karl Popper, *Objective Knowledge*, *The Two Faces of Common Sense*, p. 138

[137] "We can say that there is a kind of Platonic (or Bolzano) third world of books in themselves, theories in themselves, problems in themselves, problem situations in themselves, arguments in themselves, and so on", Karl Popper, *Objective Knowledge*, *An Epistemology without a Knowing Subject*, p. 138.

In his philosophical project, Popper, from *The Logic of Scientific Discovery* (1934) onwards, essentially based the objective nature of discoveries on the critical dimension of reason, which, for him, offered a form of guarantee of independence from sensibility. This is why he proposed, in his own words, "a critical philosophy of common sense". Popper was certainly aware that the critical questioning of formal systems could only take place through a confrontation with the world as an external reality, in other words through a synthetic judgement articulating intuition, imagination and understanding. However, in his philosophy, intuition took a secondary place to critical rationality, which he saw as the real driving force behind scientific and epistemological progress. This primacy of critical and discursive rationality over immediate intuition was manifested, among other things, in his criticism of Kant's transcendental aesthetics in *Objective Knowledge*. According to Popper, Kant opposed Descartes by asserting that our concepts remained empty or purely analytical if they were not applied to a sensible given by means of intuition, or if they did not correspond to "concepts constructed in the pure intuition of space and time[138]". In the passage preceding this

---

[138] See Karl Popper, *Objective Knowledge*, on this subject, see also Kant, 1787: "To construct a concept is to present *a priori* the intuition [pure intuition] that corresponds to it (*Œuvres philosophiques*, Pléiade, Gallimard, tome 1, p. 1298). See also: "We have sought [...] only to show clearly what a great difference there is between the discursive use of reason according to concepts and the intuitive use by means of the construction of concepts." (Op. cit., p. 1302). He explains

commentary, devoted to Brouwer's epistemology, Popper dis-qualified the Kantian notions of the intuition of time and space, relying on the discovery of non-Euclidean geometry and Einstein's formulation of the theory of special relativity. More specifically, he argued that if the work on non-Euclidean geometry had led to the questioning of the Kantian intuition of space, the same logic should, in his view, be applied to the Kantian theory of the intuition of time, in the light of Einstein's discoveries on relativity. In fact, Popper criticised Kant for making too sharp a distinction between intuition and discursive thought, a distinction that he felt had been overtaken by developments in the sciences and by a critical approach to knowledge. In his view, Kant's position had been imposed on him by the structure of the *Critique of Pure Reason*, in which transcendental aesthetics preceded transcendental logic[139].

---

this "construction of concepts" more precisely a little further on: "We can determine our concepts *a priori* in intuition, since by a uniform synthesis we create for ourselves the very objects in space and time (Op. cit., p. 1305)."

[139] On the contrary, we believe that this precedence of intuition over discursive thought is essential to Kantian thought (that it is not the product of a simple structural constraint within the *Critique of Pure Reason*). Moreover, as we shall see below, it seems to us to be an abuse to maintain that we can rely exclusively on the example of non-Euclidean geometries to disqualify this idea of Kant. Non-Euclidean geometry (which Kant had also envisaged, cf. *De mundi sensibilis*, 1770) can also come under what Kant calls "internal intuition".

It should be noted that, for Kant, internal intuition relates to time and not to objects in the literal sense. It gives us

Was this precedence a brilliant and fruitful idea of Kant's, or was it, as Popper asserts, incomplete and contradictory? For Popper, the Kantian idea that the axioms of mathematics are based on a pure intuition[140] — a form of immediate "perception" or "vision" of truth independent of sensible experience and prior to any empirical intuition — was inadmissible. Popper's rejection of Kantian intuitionism stemmed not only from criticisms of non-Euclidean geometry and relativity applied to transcendental aesthetics, but above all from the fact that, in his view, it was "impossible to deny that mathematics is based on discursive thought[141]".

---

awareness of internal states (the successive "representations" of thought). But here, there is no external object to grasp. The only object is the subject itself (its awareness of the flows of its representations). Now, Kant is not saying that internal intuition grasps the subject as such, but that it grasps successive states of consciousness within the framework of the form of time. If intuition is by definition a relation to the sensible given, then internal intuition is in our view problematic insofar as there is no sensible given in the strong sense. In external intuition, the relationship to the object is clear: we 'see' the object, we represent it to ourselves. In internal intuition, on the other hand, time is not given as an object. We don't 'see' time, we don't 'perceive' it. We become aware of it through a succession of representations, but in our view, this does not constitute intuition in the strong sense.

[140] Op. cit., pp. 1311 ff.

[141] According to Popper, Kant intended precisely to exclude discursive arguments from arithmetic and geometry (in this sense, Kant was too intuitionistic in his approach to

Popper credited Brouwer with resolving this contradiction by asserting that mathematical demonstrations were sequential constructions, i.e. "constructions of constructions". The distinction proposed by Brouwer between mathematics as an intuitive activity and its discursive formulation in language corresponded to Popper's critical approach, which he considered more capable of establishing objective criteria of knowledge, despite its roots in sensible intuition. However, this distinction seems to have led Popper to give excessive prominence to the critical moment over the intuitive moment[142]. This overestimation of the role of criticism

---

mathematics and geometry for Popper). In our view, Kant did not intend to exclude discursive arguments from arithmetic and geometry, but rather to emphasise that these fields were based on a form of pure intuition that was *a priori*, i.e. independent of sensible experience. In his view, mathematical objects, such as geometric figures or numerical quantities, were given in a non-sensible intuition, prior to any empirical experience. However, this intuition did not imply that mathematical reasoning was free of discursive thought. Demonstrations and calculations in these fields do call on logical and discursive thought. Kant therefore distinguished between pure intuition, which is the foundation of mathematical knowledge, and discursive use, which is involved in the processes of deduction and explanation. Thus, he did not exclude discursive argumentation in mathematics but saw it as a form of application and extension of a *priori* principles, which were themselves perceived or "intuited" in a pure manner.

[142] Karl Popper, *Objective knowledge, Epistemology Without a Knowing Subject*, or again: " "The process of learning, of the growth of subjective knowledge, is always fundamentally the

is itself a consequence of the importance he attributed to the criterion of refutability, which he formalised in 1934 in *The Logic of Scientific Discovery*. It was this criterion of refutability, central to Popper's thinking, which was to make it possible to establish a demarcation between the sciences and the pseudo-sciences by distinguishing refutable statements (of a scientific nature) from non-refutable statements (of a non-scientific nature). It should be noted, however, that Popper's idea of the need for a demarcation between science and pseudoscience was originally associated with a critique of inductive reasoning (and not with a specific critique of intuitionism). Following Hume, Popper pointed out that no matter how many confirmations a theory received, it could never be irrevocably established or verified[143]. On the other hand, according to Popper, a negative occurrence should enable us to *disprove* a theory. Thus, the proposition "all swans are white" could not be verified, but it could be disproved (all we had to do was find a black swan). The proposition was therefore "scientific"

---

same. It is imaginative criticism. [...] This is how we lift ourselves by our bootstraps out of the morass of our ignorance; how we throw a rope into the air and then swarm up it—if it gets any purchase, however precarious, on any little twig. What makes our efforts differ from those of an animal or of an amoeba is only that our rope may get a hold in a third world of critical discussion: a world of language, of objective knowledge", Ibid.

[143] Think of Russell's famous example of the inductivist turkey. This turkey, particularly gifted in logic, thinks it can deduce a universal and eternal truth from the infallible regularity with which the farmer feeds it, until Thanksgiving Day when it ends up with its head cut off.

in nature (it belonged to the field of the refutable, i.e. that which we can discuss, invalidate or corroborate). By emphasising refutability, Popper broke the deadlock of Hume's inductivism, which concluded that it was impossible to verify a theory. Popper skilfully pointed out that if it was possible to disprove a theory (the criterion of refutability), then the theory had to fall within the true-false pair (the possibility of truth or verifiability was established by the negative: if we can disprove a theory, we can prove that it is false, and if we prove that it is false, then it could have been true; it did belong to the true-false pair). Of course, a theory could never be definitively confirmed, but we could *at least* be sure that it fell within the field of scientific knowledge (note that if we apply the criterion of distinction established by Popper, the theory of integral materialism, for example, would not fall within the field of scientific knowledge), would not fall within the scope of science insofar as it would, by definition, admit of no refutation, the material "whole" not falling within a specifically defined field such as "all swans" — the whole of the defined class of swans — for example, but designating a totalising axiomatic reality that is therefore non-refutable). For Popper, it was discursive thinking that made it possible to delimit the scientific field and give it a form of objective autonomy. It was, therefore, essentially the critical moment that was to dominate and define science.

In line with Popperian epistemology, we in no way question the discursive dimension of mathematics, which is based on a process of critical formalisation and rational construction, founded on the examination and testing of its own structures. The definition of mathematics as a construction of constructions and as a succession of synthetic ("intuitive") moments and analytical ("discursive" or "constructivist") moments also seems to us to correspond to the articulation of the two aesthetic and critical moments that characterise the logic of scientific discovery. Although Popper argues for a rapprochement between these two moments, it seems to us, on the contrary, that we should maintain the Kantian distinction between the moment of transcendental aesthetics (which concerns the pure *a priori* intuition of space and time — We will discuss Kant's apriorism again later) and that of transcendental analytics (the faculty of the understanding to conceptualise). It is not our intention here to defend Kantian transcendental aesthetics at all costs, and in particular its pure and *a priori* character, which has been the subject of much discussion and criticism[144]. It seems to us, however, that maintaining the distinction between the intuitive moments and the discursive or analytic moment is essential if we are to understand the articulation of the moment of connection between the sensible world (the world of intuition) and the rational world (the discursive, analytic world). It is precisely in this junction, operated by intuition and imagination, between the sensible world and the discursive world (which proceeds from the sensible world without being able to be reduced to it, as we have shown) that we find what we have called "signification". Meaning, that is, the ability to understand and order the world, lies at the

---

[144] Although we consider that a disqualification of transcendental aesthetics based solely on non-Euclidean geometry and Einstein's theory of relativity is abusive, as we shall return to later.

crossroads of systems. It emanates from the friction between formal reality and the sensible world, a friction that reveals the dual structure of reality, and which takes place at the very heart of sensible intuition. As we have said, the moment of understanding reality, of integrating things into a signifying system, while it takes place by and through intuition, is also the result of what we have called the "signifying imagination" (see § 30 — *What is intuition?*), a notion that we must distinguish from what Popper calls, in *Objective Knowledge*, "imaginative criticism" (here again we see the pre-eminence of the critical dimension in Popper's work), i.e. the ability of the imagination to take a critical and retroactive look at reality[145]. While Popper refers to

---

[145] This is certainly not quite the definition given by Popper... In *Objective Knowledge*, as already quoted above, "The process of learning, of the growth of subjective knowledge, is always fundamentally the same. It is imaginative criticism. [...] This is how we lift ourselves by our bootstraps out of the morass of our ignorance; how we throw a rope into the air and then swarm up it—if it gets any purchase, however precarious, on any little twig. What makes our efforts differ from those of an animal or of an amoeba is only that our rope may get a hold in a third world of critical discussion: a world of language, of objective knowledge. This makes it possible to discard some of our competing theories. So, if we are lucky, we may succeed in surviving some of our mistaken theories (and most of them are mistaken), while the amoeba will perish with its theory, its belief, and its habits. Seen in this light, life is problem-solving and discovery—the discovery of new facts, of new possibilities, by way of trying out possibilities conceived in our imagination. On the human level, this trying out is done almost entirely in the third world,

imaginative criticism as a faculty specific to man, we see it more broadly as a faculty deduced from a criterion of effectiveness and adaptability to a given environment, and as such as going beyond the simple limits of a strictly rational approach. In a sense, the amoeba already demonstrates a critical sense in its ability to adapt to its environment, a critical sense that is obviously less developed than that of the rational sentient being that is man. In our opinion, the break between animals and humans does not lie solely in man's ability to make critical use of the imagination, but rather in a combination of faculties: (i) his ability to see and project meaningful images (ii) his ability to critically and retroactively compare these images with reality as it manifests itself to him (iii) his ability to use higher forms of language, i.e. to formalise and express these images in a language that can be understood by him and by others, This formalisation in turn creates autonomous (self-imposed) rules of coherence that impose themselves on man and in turn condition the critical and discursive analysis of the theories he is trying to formalise (it is this 'rope' of the *world 3* that Popper himself evokes: " What makes our efforts differ from those of an animal or of an amoeba is only that our rope may get a hold in a third world of critical

---

by attempts to represent, in theories of this third world, our first world, and perhaps our second world, more and more successfully; by trying to get nearer to the truth—to a fuller, a more complete, a more interesting, logically stronger and more relevant truth—to truth relevant to our problems."
Karl Popper, 1972, 1979, Objective Knowledge: An evolutionary approach, Revised edition, Ch. 3: Epistemology Without a Knowing Subject, p. 148

discussion: a world of language, of objective knowledge", he writes in *Objective Knowledge*[146]).

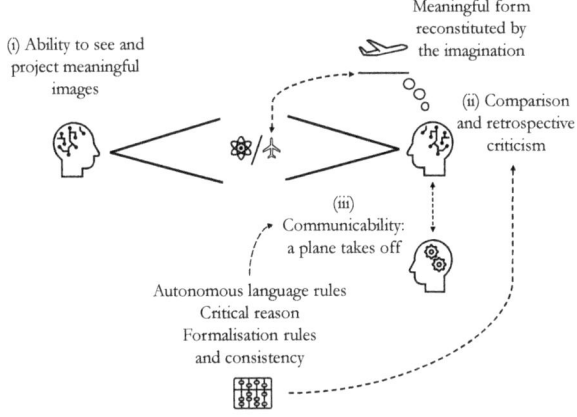

The "rope" of the world 3

It is in this last moment — the moment of "communication" to use Brouwer's terms — that the possibility of *world 3* emerges (which is precisely the world of the formalisation of ideas: it is the possibility of formalisation that gives rise to *world 3* and not just the intuition-imagination pairing, which cannot be directly reduced to reason or its formalism). The separation between these three moments, which are the moments of signifying intuition-imagination, critical imagination and retroactive formal analysis, are to be distinguished in terms (just as, as we have seen, they can be distinguished and isolated using brain imaging[147]). In

---

[146] Ibid., p. 235
[147] See the Kalanit Grill-Spector experiment referred to in § 29, which established that below 50 milliseconds the images

presenting these three moments, we note that discursive thought, while in a sense making it possible to formalise intuition, cannot be assimilated or reduced to it (it has its own rules and autonomy, it allows critical feedback on the figures proposed by the imagination, it makes it possible to elaborate and construct communicable theories, and in this sense it is itself a producer of knowledge).

If, on *the other hand,* we were to make discursive thought the sole foundation of truth, we would then be forced to admit its radical separation from intuition and from reality. We would then fall back into the difficulties raised by formalism (we argue against this formalism that meaning can only arise from the interdependence between discursive thought, critical imagination and intuition of an external world[148]). This does not mean,

---

were invisible to the subject of the experiment, whereas above 100 milliseconds they appeared in full consciousness. On visual imagery, these two moments appeared clearly: the early visual areas were activated all the time, whether or not the image was visible. On the other hand, in the higher visual areas, such as the fusiform gyrus and the lateral occipitotemporal region — areas that are involved in the categorisation and identification of images (faces, objects, words, places...) — brain activity is closely linked to the degree of consciousness. The moment of critical analysis (also visible on imaging) is still to be distinguished from these two moments.

[148] In short, the concept is almost pleonastic. Intuition can only be the intuition of an exteriority. If we think of Putnam's experience, the intuition of reality aroused by electrical provocation does introduce a form of exteriority. In this

of course, that mathematics cannot be "locally" formalist, but it does imply that no formalism can claim to be total, or to form a closed and entirely coherent system (the fact that there is local coherence does not necessarily imply the general coherence of the system, as Gödel has shown[149]).

35.

DIALECTIC BETWEEN INTUITION AND FORMALISM — The logic of scientific discovery, to paraphrase the title of Karl Popper's famous work, proceeds as much from intellectual intuition (i.e. an aesthetic moment in the Greek sense of the term, αἴσθησις meaning in Greek "theory of the sensible") as from our ability to formalise intuition and make it meaningful (and communicable) through imagination and understanding. In this respect, we support the position, close to that of Gödel, that formalism remains sterile if it remains uncoupled from intuition and imagination (as the force of creation and abstract projection of intuition). We must, however, be wary of any over-enthusiasm for intuition (in the sense given to it by Gödel) and not forget to return to its link with formalism, which is the only way to

---

case, it is passivity, the reception of sensible impressions. Imagination, on the other hand, is directly an activity of creating form, which does not solicit sensible intuition as such.

[149] Before Gödel formalised his incompleteness theorem in 1931, he had demonstrated, in his doctoral thesis, a completeness theorem of the first-order predicate calculus, which states that any mathematical demonstration can be represented in the formalism of the predicate calculus.

confirm (in an effective and definite way) intuitive visions. In *Einführungen in die Physik* (1941), a late work of popular science, Max Planck wrote on this subject: "We must not forget that the exercise of this faculty of intuition entails a latent and most serious danger: the danger of soliciting facts in favour of a preconceived idea or even of ignoring those that would be inconvenient. This is a slippery slope from true science to pseudoscience, which is no more than an airy-fairy construction, destined to collapse at the first strong shock. In the past, countless scientists, young and old, have fallen victim to their enthusiastic scientific conviction, and today the danger has not lost any of its importance. To guard against it, there is only one means of protection: respect for the facts[150]. If intuition precedes formalism in the dialectic of knowledge, it contains within it the germ of error. This is why intuition must be confirmed effectively and retroactively by (i) the facts it is trying to describe or explain — a point that Max Planck, as a good physicist, particularly insists on — and by (ii) a coherent formalism, which is the only way to make the theory communicable and therefore universalisable. There is thus a kind of double jeopardy, consisting on the one hand of relying entirely on intuition, and on the other of being blinded by an excessive formalism that fails to account for the complexity and extent of the facts. This twofold peril, however, does not only threaten the scientist, but more generally concerns any person who wishes to strive towards a form of objective knowledge. Errors are often the result of a reversal in the dynamics of knowledge, whereby it is no longer theories that are

---

[150] Max Planck, *Wege zur Physikalischen Erkenntnis*, Ch. 12

put to the test of facts, but facts that are used to support theories[151].

36.

EFFECTIVENESS OF MATHEMATICS AS A MANIFESTATION OF ITS INTUITIVE ORIGIN — This chapter will not be concerned directly with debating the need, for any mathematical proposition, to find an effective procedure (a proof by construction), as Brouwer wanted, but rather with questioning *the origin of* the effectiveness of mathematics. In other words, how can we understand the fact that mathematics manages to express a factual reality and even, in some cases, to anticipate it?

There are many examples of mathematical propositions or theorems that were formulated long before their concrete physical application, or that have been used in fields for which they were not initially developped. Fourrier's theorem, for example, was first formulated in the early nineteenth century to solve the heat equation, which describes how the temperature of a material varies in time and space in response to initial conditions and boundary conditions. Decades later, it found major applications in physics, particularly in signal theory. The use of the Fourier transform, which follows from this theorem, is now fundamental in many fields such as wireless communication, image processing and medical imaging. Similarly, Maxwell's

---

[151] This confirmatory dynamic stems from what psychology in the 1960s called "confirmation bias": every fact in favour of the theory is seen as confirmation, every fact against it is (voluntarily or involuntarily) ignored.

equations, formulated by James Clerk Maxwell in the 1860s following Michael Faraday's experimental observations of the relationship between electrical and magnetic phenomena (electromagnetic induction, rotating magnetic field experiment), were formulated at a time when there was still no unified theoretical framework to explain these observations. The results that could be deduced from Maxwell's equations could not then be confirmed experimentally. A few decades later, however, the work of Heinrich Hertz provided experimental proof of the existence of the electromagnetic waves predicted by Maxwell's equations. This predictive and effective power of mathematics is difficult to explain if we remain within the strict framework of monistic theories (in particular the psychologistic positions they induce). Mathematics can certainly be conceived as a formalisation of the internal structures of our mind, but in this case we must not forget that since our mind in its material dimension is itself subject to the physical laws from which it derives and which act through it, mathematics is in reality in a double relation of effectiveness with reality, the first being that which presides over the formulation of the very conditions of possibility of existence of our brain as a material organ, the second being that of the factual effect produced by the application of mathematics to reality. The predictive power of mathematics is a result of the first relation of effectiveness: reason can only be law-making, as we have already mentioned, because it is itself law-making, the result of a binding law that it recognises within itself and that it applies to reality.

In this respect, the notion of effectivity that we are describing can be compared with the idea of an effective procedure that Brouwer's intuitionism called for in order to establish the verifiability of mathematical propositions[152]: the possibility for

---

[152] On this subject, see Roman Ikonicoff's thesis, *Penser l'effectivité: naissance de la notion chez Émile Borel*, in particular the survey of the notion of effectivity in mathematics at the end of the nineteenth and beginning of the twentieth centuries.
Roman Ikonicoff's thesis explores the conception of effectivity before its formalisation in recursivity, in particular through the Church-Turing thesis. Ikonicoff focuses on the work of Émile Borel at the end of the nineteenth century, in particular his *Leçons* of 1898, to understand how the notion of effectivity was perceived by mathematicians of the time. He highlights Borel's approach, which, on the fringes of the official debates on the foundations of mathematics, gave significant importance to effectivity, extending it to the current countable infinite sets. From an epistemological point of view, Ikonicoff uses phenomenological tools to define this informal notion of effectivity, which, around 1900, had not yet been formalised. He proposes that the idea that effectivity can be seen as a cognitive gesture emanating from the system of perception of the physical world guarantees proof insofar as this gesture is never paradoxical. Ikonicoff concludes with the idea that Church-Turing's thesis, by "externalizing" this gesture, freed mathematics from the implicit cognitive constraints of the physical world. Church-Turing's thesis (1938) proposed a formalisation of the notions of algorithm, computability and effective procedure. This formalisation was based on the definition of an abstract 'machine' (the Turing machine) capable of reproducing all the stages of calculation that a human could perform. In this way, the machine no longer depended on

human perception, or the 'cognitive gestures' mentioned above, but 'exteriorised' the concept of effectivity (see our thesis in § 12— *The true-false couple versus integral materialism: the machine as a concrete figure of dualism*): instead of being anchored in the cognitive abilities of a mathematician, effectivity became a formal property of computational systems. This shift to the objectivity of the machine made the notion of algorithm independent of the human mind. In other words, Church-Turing's thesis objectified and formalised the notion of effectivity, making it independent of any reference to the body, mind or human perception. Computation thus became an abstract operation, removed from the human framework. However, Ikonicoff qualifies this 'liberation' of mathematics by emphasising that mathematical thought remained linked, with Church-Turing's thesis, to the materiality (computability) of calculations. Although Church-Turing's thesis had shifted the focus from human cognition to the formal framework of abstract machines, the practice of mathematics and computer science continued to maintain an implicit link with notions of physical realism. This limitation manifested itself in a number of ways: (i) the notion of algorithm remained anchored in physical metaphors: the "Turing machine" is thought of as a physical machine that manipulates ribbons, symbols, and so on, (ii) the very idea that a physical computer could "simulate" a Turing machine was based on the idea that there was a continuity between the computational capacities of the physical world and those of abstract formalisms, (iii) there was still a strong assumption in physics that any natural phenomenon (at microscopic or macroscopic level) could in principle be simulated by a universal computer, which implied that physical reality could itself be "calculable", i.e. governed by rules that could be executed by a Turing machine.

Like us, Ikonicoff notes that this hypothesis, although it seems natural, is in reality a questionable thesis. It

mathematics to be formalised in an effective way, i.e. a physical way, results in our view directly from this original determination of reason. This led to the work on calculability that culminated in the Church-Turing theorem in the 1930s[153]. A function is said to be

---

presupposes that the physical world is reducible to manipulable information, an idea that is never demonstrated by Turing.

The "conjecture of universal calculation" consisted of saying that any physical phenomenon could be modelled by a calculation (a simulation) on a universal computer. According to this conjecture, the world would in fact be 'informational': what would count from then on would no longer be the materiality of physical objects, but the way in which information circulates and is transformed. Ikonicoff criticises this thesis, showing that it is based on very fragile assumptions. If we accept that information can be the basis of all physical reality, we would first have to be able to give a precise physical definition of the concept of information, which is lacking in the universal calculus conjecture. Let us add that this conjecture of the universal calculus fails to qualify the nature of propositions held to be true and yet unprovable within a formal system (e.g. Goldbach's conjecture).

[153] The Church-Turing theorem was formulated independently by Alonzo Church and Alan Turing in the 1930s. Alan Turing presented his version of the theorem in a paper entitled "*On Computable Numbers, with an Application to the Entscheidungsproblem*", published in 1936. Alonzo Church formulated his own version of the theorem using lambda-calculus, a mathematical notation for representing functions, in his work of the same period. Thus, the Church-Turing theorem can be attributed to the year 1936, when the work of Alan Turing and Alonzo Church was published

"calculable" if there is a mechanical (physical) process which, when applied to a given input, gives the correct output in a finite number of steps. The Church-Turing theorem states that any function that can be computed (by a given algorithm) can be computed by a Turing machine[154] (a computer, a physical computing system).

---

independently, establishing a common theoretical foundation for computability and the theory of algorithms.

[154] A Turing machine is an abstract model of a mechanical device that manipulates symbols on a tape in a sequential manner. This model was introduced by the mathematician and logician Alan Turing in the 1930s. The Turing machine is widely regarded as the founding model of computability theory. Here are the main components of a Turing machine:
Infinite band: The band is divided into cells, with each cell able to contain a symbol from a finite alphabet (for example, 0 or 1). The band extends infinitely in both directions.
Read/write head: The read/write head can move left or right along the tape and read or write symbols in the cells.
Internal state: The Turing machine has an internal state, which can change depending on the instructions it follows. Each instruction is associated with a pair (current state, symbol under the read head), and specifies three things: the symbol to be written, the movement of the head (left or right), and the new state.
Transition table: The transition table contains all the possible instructions for the Turing machine. It specifies the behaviour of the machine as a function of its current state and the symbol under the read head. The operation of a Turing machine is defined by its transition table, which indicates how the machine should react to each combination of internal state and symbol under the read head. The Turing machine starts in an initial state with an initial configuration of the tape, and then iteratively follows the instructions in

However, if we insist on the fact that the effective character of mathematics is due to the structure of logical imbrication that we have designated (legislated and legislating reason), we do not intend, for all that, to make effectivity the only criterion of truth: the relation of implication does not necessarily entail a relation of equivalence. Our idea of effectivity as a criterion of the validity of a theory therefore says nothing, for example, about a possible ideal or Platonic status of mathematical entities, in accordance, for example, with what Gödel thought, or about our capacity to formulate propositions that are valid even though they cannot be demonstrated in a formal system.

37.

IS TRUTH A VALUE? — The fact that we have linked the idea of truth to the notion of effectivity does not necessarily imply that truth itself proceeds from the effective character that it claims in its consequences. In other words, the fact that effectivity supports (or proves) the idea of truth does not necessarily imply that (i) truth is just another name for effectivity, i.e. that all truth is inevitably effective (if we have tried to establish that effectivity is in some way the applicative dimension of truth, we have not, however, proved that the two notions can entirely overlap), nor that (ii) truth is

---

the transition table. A Turing machine can perform any calculation that is mechanically possible. The Church-Turing theorem states that anything that can be calculated algorithmically can be calculated by a Turing machine. Thus, the Turing machine provides an important conceptual model for understanding the limits of computability.

entirely relative to its conditions of expression (that truth is really only a production of our physical world).

The idea of proposition (i), according to which the idea of truth is in a sense subordinate to the idea of effectivity, is to be compared with the pragmatic theories of William James (truth conceived as that which functions practically in human experience, what is useful for thought and action) or John Dewey (truth as a function of interaction between man and his environment, i.e. as what makes it possible to solve a problem and achieve a balance in experience) and, in a sense, the radical intuitionism of Brouwer (who is very opposed to Gödel on this point). This proposal to assimilate or subordinate truth to effectivity or even verifiability is problematic for us insofar as it reduces the field of rational discourse to its physical or material verifiability (and thus points once again towards integral materialism or towards all the other forms of monism which are structurally contradictory). This assimilation of the idea of truth to the criterion of verifiability also neglects truths that we can conceive without being able to give them an effective correspondence (the theorem that there are an infinite number of prime numbers, demonstrated by Euclid, is an established mathematical truth. However, this truth is not effective in itself), just as it conveniently catalogues all prospective theory in the realm of metaphysics.

Proposition (ii) appears to be one of the logical consequences of our idea of the double legislation of reason (reason legislated as the result of a long physical process of an evolutionary nature, and legislating as a regulatory force that achieves a form of effective adequacy with things). Thus, according to proposition (ii), our rationality being "shaped" by the physical world might seem to depend on our particular world, i.e. *relative to* a particular form of reality. We can respond to this objection in two ways: first, we note that this form of relativity could be perfectly acceptable to us insofar as it would only be relativity for a given reality in *relation to other theoretical realities* of which we know and can by definition know nothing (pragmatic response). Here, the objection turns against itself: in relation to our world, truth would have nothing relative about it and would even possess all the characteristics of absoluteness (absoluteness for our physical reality, the only one we know). Next, we point out that the fact that we judge the physical world with an understanding that has been physically conditioned does not necessarily imply the submission (reduction) of this understanding to the physical, but rather to the *law*, which determines and conditions the physical even before its phenomenal manifestation (see § 13 — *Can we imagine a world without laws?*). Here again, we must not confuse the material conditions of the expression of the idea with the idea itself: whether in our universe or in another, the understanding, provided it has the capacity to rise to a certain degree of abstraction, will always be able to conceive forms, and these forms will always derive from the same rules (or generate these rules). In other words, if we can posit a set of determinate axioms (those underlying Euclidean or non-Euclidean geometries), the rules that derive from these axioms will always be the same, regardless of their conditions of material expression or the physical universe in which they were formulated.

This is why, in our opinion, we must be careful not to make truth just another value (a value that would be relative to its historical or geographical conditions of expression, etc.) and philosophy a place where values are brought together in a form of totality without foundations. It is values that derive from the idea of truth, never the other way round. To renounce this idea is in fact to accept the relativism of the confrontation of values, the confrontation of legitimacies and, consequently, the abandonment of the very idea of universal law.

The Aesthetic Moment of Knowledge

38.

EUREKA! — What is the moment of scientific discovery and what happens at the precise moment when a problem is solved, recast in a new general approach? What happened, for example, in the mind of Archimedes when, sinking into his bath, he exclaimed "Eureka! What change took place in Newton's mind just after he received his legendary apple on the head? What did Einstein understand as he swayed in his chair at the Berne Patent Office[155]? These are the questions we will now try to answer.

One of the common features of the resolutory epiphanies we have just described (and which are generally well documented) is that they occur most of

the time when, so to speak, "you least expect it". Scientists generally describe sudden illuminations, flashes of lucidity that most often occur when the brain seems inactive or at rest, as if disconnected from its usual networks ("in limbo" says Louis de Broglie, for example), which is reminiscent of the illuminations of poets ("The poet becomes a seer through a long, immense and reasoned disruption of all the senses[156]"

---

[155] Some of these images are legendary, but they often tell the story of major scientific discoveries.
[156] Arthur Rimbaud, *Correspondence*, Letter from the Seer to Paul Demeny, 15 May 1871

writes Rimbaud) or artists. There are many descriptions of such events in scientific literature. In his *Conversations with Wang*, Gödel notes, for example: "Both Descartes and Schelling explicitly report the experience of a sudden illumination. They began to see everything in a different light[157]" or again: "Between 1906 and 1910, Husserl had a psychological crisis. He doubted he could achieve anything. His wife was very ill. But at some point, during this period, everything suddenly became clear to him, and he arrived at absolute knowledge[158]." Gödel's writings generally contain the idea that scientific, logical and mathematical discoveries are the fruit of superhuman knowledge, bordering on madness (Gödel's universe is populated by deceptive angels and demons, dreams and visions). Henri Poincaré — who, a few years before Einstein, came close to discovering the theory of special relativity — also had the same idea of a sudden illumination, once again in a context of slackening of the mind: "At that moment," he wrote, "I left Caen, where I was living at the time, to take part in a geological race undertaken by the Ecole des Mines. The vicissitudes of the journey *soon made me forget my mathematical work* (emphasis added); when we arrived in Coutances, we boarded an omnibus for a ride of some sort; just as I was setting foot on the footboard, the idea occurred to me, for which nothing in my previous thoughts seemed to have prepared me, that the transformations I had used to define the Fuchsian functions were identical to those of non-Euclidean geometry. I didn't check, because I wouldn't have had the time, since as soon as I got on the omnibus, I resumed the

---

[157] Op. cit., pp. 169-170
[158] Ibid.

conversation I'd started; but I was immediately completely certain. On my return to Caen, I checked the result with a clear head to clear my conscience". Again, from Poincaré: "I then began to study arithmetic questions, without much apparent result and without suspecting that this could have had the slightest connection with my previous studies. Disgusted by my failure, I went to spend a few days by the sea and thought of something else. One day, as I was walking along the cliff, the idea occurred to me, always with the same character of brevity, suddenness and immediate certainty, that the arithmetic transformations of ternary indefinite quadratic forms were identical to those of non-Euclidean geometry[159]. A few years later, in 1910, it was Ernst Cassirer who, getting off the Tramway in Berlin, had the revelation, in circumstances similar to those described by Poincaré, of his philosophy of symbolic forms. In all these situations, the mind is not at work, it is free, as if wandering in a state of semi-consciousness. Moreover, scientists (like artists and musicians) do not report a sequenced or step-by-step understanding; on the contrary, they insist on the sudden nature of the resolution. In *Consciousness and the Brain*, Stanislas Dehaene attributes these successes to an information-processing faculty that persists (or is even enhanced) in unconscious states: "un-conscious

---

[159] Anecdotes reported by Jacques Hadamard, *Subconscient, intuition et logique dans la recherche scientifique*, lecture given at the Palais de la Découverte on December 8th 1945. A more complete account, although limited to mathematical discoveries, can be found in the book by the same author: *The Psychology of Invention in the Mathematical Field* (Princeton, 1949).

processes", he states, "excel in the simultaneous processing of very large amounts of information: they can assign a value to several items at the same time, and average them to arrive at a decision[160]". In other words, this resolutory faculty would be linked to a state of enhanced calculability in the brain, whose 'bandwidth' would be only marginally used by conscious operations. However, Stanislas Dehaene seems to be overlooking the fact that most of the time, these illuminations do not involve operations of an analytical or mechanical nature (the analytical brain, that of formal operations, seems to be "unplugged", the adventures of the journey make Poincaré *forget* his mathematical work, as he himself points out), as attested by their sudden and instantaneous nature, which seems incompatible with the sequencing inherent in analytical reasoning[161]. These specific features peculiar to complex resolutive operations point us once again towards the idea that understanding is primarily aesthetic and not analytical in nature (aesthetic in the Greek sense αἴσθησις — which proceeds from sensibility without, however, being reduced to it). This is undoubtedly why the moment of illumination concerns artists, poets and musicians as much as scientists: it is not a sequenced moment of mechanical decomposition, but rather a moment of projection, by the imagination, of a new "form" or a new scheme (think, for example, of the way a chess player visualises possible combinations before

---

[160] Ibid., p. 120 of the French Edition

[161] "I consider that I understand an equation when I can predict the properties of its solutions, without actually solving it." Paul Dirac, quoted in F Wilczek, B Devine, Longing for the Harmonies

executing them). In this respect, Stanislas Dehaene is undoubtedly right to note that unconscious processes enable a great deal of information to be processed simultaneously, but the operation of understanding is not reduced to this processing or to the act of "averaging" this information. As well as being an act of simultaneous processing of apparently heterogeneous information, comprehension is a process of local or global vision (a process of linking, of articulation), a new act of aesthetic synthesis (the projection of a new signifying and linking schema).

In *The Structure of Scientific Revolutions* (1962), Thomas Kuhn insists on the idea that great discoveries are often the result of a "naïve" vision or a fresh look at an old problem: "The new paradigm," he writes, "or an indication that allows its future formulation, suddenly appears, sometimes in the middle of the night, in the mind of a man deeply immersed in crisis. What is the nature of this final stage? How does an individual invent, or realise that he has invented, a way of ordering the facts, now all brought together? These are intractable questions, and perhaps they will remain so permanently. Let's just note one fact in this connection: almost always, the men who made the fundamental inventions of a new paradigm were either very young or brand new to the speciality whose paradigm they changed[162]. Those who see the world with new eyes are not yet prisoners of a system of forms and concepts. In fact, he is undoubtedly in a better position to generate and test new forms (see § 28 — *The straitjacket of the concept, the straitjacket of form*). A little further on, still in

---

[162] Thomas Kuhn, *The Structure of Scientific Revolutions*

The Structure of Scientific Revolutions, Thomas Kuhn highlights the link we ourselves establish between scientific discovery and the visualisation of new forms (or a new system of forms): "Normal science, he writes, ultimately leads only to the recognition of anomalies and to crises, and these are terminated not by deliberation and interpretation, but by a relatively sudden and un-structured event like the gestalt switch. Scientists then often speak of the scales falling from the eyes or of the lightning flash that inundates *a previously obscure puzzle* (emphasis added), enabling its components to be seen in a new way that, for the first time, permits its solution. On other occasions the relevant illumination comes in sleep[163]". It should be noted that these moments of solving illumination are to be distinguished from what has been referred to, following the English writer Horace Walpole, as "serendipity[164]": the disposition to make an unexpected discovery by chance that subsequently proves fruitful.

The American Royston Roberts, professor of organic chemistry at the University of Texas, analysed over a hundred discoveries made by accident (the structure of DNA, aspirin, Archimedes' principle, vinyl chloride, intense sweeteners, nylon, penicillin, LSD, polyethylene, the Post-it note, X-rays, Teflon, Velcro, vulcanisation, etc.).), which he recorded in 1989 in a book entitled *Serendipity: Accidental Discoveries in Science*.

---

[163] Ibid., p. 204
[164] "Serendipity is based on a fairy tale entitled *The Three Princes of Serendip*, which tells the story of three princes travelling and discovering along the way, by accident and by sagacity, all sorts of things they weren't looking for.

Roberts put forward a distinguishing criterion to separate true serendipity from false serendipity. According to him, pseudo-serendipity resulted from the discovery by accident of what we were already looking for intentionally (Charles Goodyear's discovery of the vulcanisation process after five years of effort, and through clumsiness, when he accidentally spilt a piece of latex coated with sulphur on a stove). True serendipity, on the other hand, was the chance discovery of something that we weren't particularly looking for, if at all (George de Mestral invented Velcro by observing burdock hooks catching on his dog's hair). According to Roberts, the notion of serendipity was a combination of chance and sagacity. If false serendipity was the accidental revelation of a brick missing from our reasoning, true serendipity was the fruit of a new observation from which we deduced a new theory. Thus, according to Roberts, 'true' serendipity was the result of what the pragmatist Charles S. Pierce called 'reasoning'. Pierce called "abductive reasoning", which consists of inferring probable causes from an observed fact.

This concept of serendipity does not, however, cover what we have termed creative 'enlightenment'. In fact, such a state is not necessarily provoked by an external event or by coincidence (the apple does not necessarily fall from the apple tree, nor does Einstein fall from his chair). On the contrary, most of the time, the resolutory moment occurs when nothing in particular is happening — at the moment when decisive intuitions come to them: Henri Poincaré is travelling by bus while Ernst Cassirer is on the tram. Salvador Dali was in a state of semi-consciousness when he suddenly had a vision of soft clocks, while Paul McCartney was inspired to write the song *Yesterday* in his sleep[165]. In such cases, the discoveries have more to do with the sudden perception of new forms (logical, musical or aesthetic forms) than with the revelation of one or more stages in a reasoning process that proceeds by abduction.

Is reasoning by projection of forms specific to genial inspiration? Don't we all experience such formal projections in our daily lives? In his *Critique of Pure Reason*, Immanuel Kant identifies this ability to recognise and create forms: he calls it transcendental schematism, the ability to create schemas, in other words to conceive of abstract rules based on images formed within our consciousness[166]. However, in the

---

[165] It could be argued here that these visions, particularly in the case of Poincaré, Cassirer and McCartney, are necessarily sequenced insofar as their expression requires successive operations to be carried out. However, we must not confuse the structure of the general idea (which can be given 'immediately' in an overall 'vision') with its formal expression, which can be sequenced.

[166] "In fact, our pure sensible concepts are not based on images of objects, but on schemas. There is no image of the triangle that would be adequate to the concept of the triangle in general. Indeed, it would not expect the universality of the concept, which makes it valid for all triangles, rectangles, oblique angles, etc., but it would always be restricted to only one part of this sphere. The schema of the triangle can never exist elsewhere than in thought, and it signifies a rule of synthesis of the imagination in view of pure figures in space. An object of experience, or an image of that object, reaches the empirical concept much less, but it always relates

great scientific discovery, it is not just new forms that are perceived by the subject, it is a new way of organising forms. If perception does not change, the "perception of perception" does. In the great discovery, there is always the idea of a resemblance, of a correspondence with a model, a schema, only this correspondence carries with it a set of forms and gives rise to a new understanding of the forms within a more global model (we are thinking in particular of the discovery of the theory of general relativity, the projective vision of a new descriptive model of reality, which induces a new way of seeing reality). It would undoubtedly be wrong, however, to reduce this ingenious intuition of new forms to the simple perception of a new 'image'. If the schema is always a creation of the productive imagination, it is not necessarily linked to the production of images (we must be wary here of the imagination-image parallel of language). Kant clearly identified this nature of the schema in the *Critique of Pure Reason*: "The schema," he wrote, "is always in itself only a product of the imagination; but as the synthesis of the imagination does not aim at any singular intuition, but only at unity in the determination of sensibility, the schema must be clearly distinguished from the image. So, when I place

---

immediately to the schema of the imagination, as to a rule of the determination of our intuition in accordance with a certain general concept. The concept of dog means a rule according to which my imagination can trace in a general way to some particular figure that experience offers me, or to some possible image that I can present *in concreto*", Immanuel Kant, *Critique of Pure Reason, Transcendental Analytics, On the Schematism of the Pure Concepts of Understanding*

five dots one after the other ....., that is an image of the number five. On the other hand, when I merely think of a number in general, which could be five or one hundred, this thought is more the representation of a method for representing, in accordance with a certain concept, a whole (for example one thousand), than the image itself, which in the latter case I would find difficult to look at with my eyes and compare with the concept[167]." The schema is therefore, in a way, an abstract image of the rule (a method of constructing the image). This is why schemas, as unitary and synthetic perceptions of forms, can be applied to concepts that refer to sequenced operations (equations, algebraic operations, the intuition of a musical form...), only the perception of sequencing takes place in this unique and sudden vision, perfectly compatible with what scientists and artists describe as an "illumination[168]" (in the same way that the understanding of a piece of music can be achieved by looking at its score as a whole, or that the number 500 cannot be understood by going through the 500 occurrences that make up its substance). This capacity of the human soul (this "art hidden in the depths of the soul" wrote Kant) to produce and organise forms (or schemas) is the condition of what we call "understanding". Comprehension is the abstract ability to link forms and concepts together and, as a result, to give them

---

[167] Ibid.,

[168] "It clearly follows from the above that the schematism of the understanding, by means of the transcendental synthesis of the imagination, tends towards nothing other than the unity of all the various aspects of intuition in the inner sense", Ibid.

meaning[169]. It cannot be the result solely of a mechanical (analytical) operation of reason; it proceeds first and foremost from the faculty of representing the abstract image or rule that precedes and determines the mechanical operation. It is for this reason that we assert that understanding is *aesthetic* in nature: it stems first and foremost from an intuition of the real (here, the real fertilises, as it were, the productive imagination at the same time as it allows for its material projection[170]) and not from the recognition of acquired formal mecha-

---

[169] See Kant: "The schemas of the pure concepts of the understanding are therefore the true and only conditions that enable these concepts to be given a relation to objects, and hence a meaning", Ibid.

[170] We defend the idea that the productive imagination, even if it cannot be reduced to the real, can only be accomplished in its articulation with the sensible real. The productive imagination is thus linked to sensible intuition (the intuition of forms), even though it exceeds the sensible in its capacities: the imagination can project into our consciousness forms that do not exist in the sensible world by recombining the sensible (unicorns, hydras, etc.), but it can also link our intuitions together (this is what happens in the process of "understanding"). In our view, the material projection of the imagination within consciousness does not call upon a second "internal" intuition that would grasp the figures produced by the imagination. The forms and schemas produced by the imagination, even though they proceed from sensible intuition, are not grasped again by "another" intuition of the "internal" senses (consciousness is not a theatre in which representations are perceived by a "miniature self"). They are directly projected and seized as signifying resolutive "presentations" (signifying projection is equivalent, if you like, to signifying seizure).

nisms (mechanisms which in reality stem from formal intuition and not vice versa).

39.

> We are all just prisoners here of our own device.

The Eagles, *Hotel California*, 1976

TO WHAT EXTENT CAN INTELLIGENCE BE MECHANISED? — Since the work of Alan Turing and Alonzo Church in the 1930s, the problem of *computability* has been one of the main areas of research in mathematics. Developments in computer science and cybernetics in the twentieth century led to the advent of what computer scientists call "artificial intelligence", which we might define as the ability of machines or computer systems to perform complex tasks that would "normally" require human intervention. Machine intelligence is now capable of developing "self-generated" learning capabilities (based on predefined learning algorithms), solving complex problems, recognising patterns, simulating an understanding of human languages and even making "autonomous" decisions.

If we admit that the degree of sophistication of these intelligent systems is extremely high, we must also ask ourselves to what extent it would be possible to simulate human intelligence (a sensitive intelligence) and from what degree this machine intelligence could tip over into another form of intelligence, akin to the intelligence of sentient beings. It seems to us that, on this question, we should not immediately close ourselves off to the idea that machine intelligence could one day become a sensitive intelligence (a self-adapting intelligence that would develop its own mechanisms for understanding and adapting to reality, mechanisms that could *ultimately* lead to the emergence of a form of 'consciousness' or even 'self-awareness'). On the road that could lead the different models of artificial intelligence to the emergence of a form of sentient intelligence (if it is in our interest for this road to be taken one day, which we doubt), there is first of all the fundamental question of the status of intuition, i.e. of our sensitive (and dual) relationship to the world. Alan Turing understood, as early as his 1938 thesis, that the main challenge to the emergence of a form of computer intelligence was not limited to the physical modelling of formal algorithms but concerned above all the reduction of intuition and productive imagination to finite processes. In short, right from its conceptual origins, artificial intelligence came up against the difficulty of articulating the sensible world and its concrete formalisation by humans. As we have emphasised on several occasions, the intelligence of sentient beings manifests itself in two ways and is determined by two complementary principles. On the one hand, (i) the ability to adapt to reality, which is based on the capacity to identify the conditions that are favourable or hostile to the conservation of the individual and the species, and to discern the structures and regularities of the external world in order to guide action effectively. On the other hand, (ii) it resides in the capacity for formalisation, i.e. in the ability to abstract and organise reality within autonomous systems that are independent of the immediate given.

This latter faculty, which seems to be unique to human beings, is not an ontological privilege.

While adaptability, as an evolutionary process (i), is still (only in part[171]) foreign to machines — which have no self-interest or spontaneous, self-adaptive interaction with their environment in a Darwinian mode — the question of their formalising capacity (ii) raises a more delicate problem. It could be argued that certain artificial intelligence systems, in particular machine learning models, now have the ability to structure reality and interact with it in a simulated way, an ability traditionally attributed only to sentient beings. The extreme sophistication of simulations of language interaction and image recognition seems to indicate that we are approaching the time when machines will be systematically capable of crossing the threshold of the Turing test[172], raising a deeper question about the

---

[171] We maintain that machines are not capable of self-adaptation in a Darwinian mode: they have no survival instinct, no will of their own, and no biological evolutionary dynamic. But if we understand adaptability not as a biological process, but as a capacity to modify its own functioning according to the environment, then certain advanced algorithms (deep neural networks, evolutionary models, reinforced learning systems) already show a form of adaptation. Admittedly, this adaptation remains constrained by the initial programming and the limitations of the hardware, but it is similar to learning processes in changing environments.

[172] A thought experiment devised by Alan Turing in 1950 in "*Computing Machinery and Intelligence*", an article published in *Mind* magazine in 1950. In this thought experiment, a human

distinction between human intelligence and artificial intelligence.

However, we have several objections to make to this test, and by ricochet to the idea that criterion (ii) of intelligence can be completely fulfilled today. Firstly, the Turing test is based on a pragmatic-positivist vision of the world according to which reality can be reduced strictly to what is observable. This vision leads Turing to admit a form of implicit equivalence between the intelligence of sentient beings and a simulacrum of intelligence that could go so far as to deceive us ourselves. Yet there is nothing to indicate that this test, even if it were successful, could not demonstrate some form of equivalence in nature between the intelligence of the machine and the forms of sentient intelligence, even the most rudimentary (the test invokes its own epistemology and declares as a petition of principle that its success would imply the intelligence of the machine). Moreover, since several causes can lead to similar results in different systems (see, for example, Putnam's work on multi-realisability and what we have already said about the insoluble problems posed by the

---

dialogue simultaneously with a machine and another human, without seeing them: if the judge cannot distinguish which of the interlocutors is human and which is a machine responding on the basis of an algorithm, then the machine is considered to have passed the Turing test, and its artificial intelligence is established. Several artificial intelligence specialists claim that this test has now been passed.
Overall, although progress has been made in the field of artificial intelligence, to our knowledge no machine has yet been universally recognised as having convincingly passed the Turing test.

theory of mind-brain identity from a strictly materialist perspective in § 31), a Turing test, even one that is entirely successful, would (logically) not be enough to win our support.

More fundamentally, the problem of the artificial formalisation of the external world brings us back to the problem of the articulation between rationality and the sensible world, an articulation which we have seen to take place through intuition and the productive imagination. It is precisely this articulation that the machine still lacks today[173]. Without this articulation,

---

[173] This is what AI (OpenAI) says about the formalisation of this articulation: today, AI is capable, to a certain extent, of articulating the sensible world (raw data) and its formalisation (interpretable structures), but in a limited way and by means that are fundamentally different from those used by the human mind.

1. What is meant by "sensible world" and "formalisation" in the context of AI

- Sensitive world: this is the raw data from the environment. In the case of AI, this includes images (pixels), sounds (sound waves), sensor signals (IoT data) or any raw stream of digital data. For example, a camera 'perceives' the world in pixels, but these pixels mean nothing in themselves.
- Formalisation: this is the transformation of this raw data into organised, interpretable structures, such as categories (face, object, number, etc.), concepts or decisions (cat/non-cat, red/green light, etc.). This formalisation is carried out by machine learning algorithms, which transform the raw data into usable models.

2. How does AI move from the sensible to the formal?

AI follows a multi-step process. These steps can be compared to what a human being does, but they are based on their own technical methods.

a) Capturing data (the "sensitive world")
- Sensors record raw data in the form of pixels (images), waves (audio) or encrypted signals (industrial sensor data, time series, etc.).
- This raw data is massive, uninterpreted and unorganised. At this stage, a cat image is no more than a matrix of pixel values.

b) *Feature extraction*
- AI applies algorithms to identify recurring patterns in this data (edges, contours, sound patterns, regularities in time series, etc.).
- In neural networks, this stage is carried out using convolutional layers (for images) or transformers (for text and sound). For example, in an image of a face, the first layers of the network detect simple contours and shapes (lines, edges, textures), while the deeper layers detect more complex structures (eyes, nose, etc.).
- Feature extraction therefore transforms the "sensitive" (raw pixels) into objects for analysis (edges, shapes, patterns).

c) Classification or segmentation (the actual formalisation)
- Once the features have been extracted, the AI applies classification models (neural networks, decision trees, etc.) to associate the patterns with known categories (for example, 'cat' or 'dog', 'red light' or 'green light').
- This formalisation is done by learning. The AI is trained on labelled datasets (images already

classified as "cat", "dog", etc.) and adjusts its parameters so that, in the future, it can recognise these categories.
- This process is probabilistic: *the machine doesn't 'know' what a cat is* (note: and with good reason, since it has no experience of what a cat is 'for it' it is only trained to recognise its characteristics, emphasis added), but it recognises statistical patterns that predict with a certain probability that the object detected is a cat.

3. Limits of AI formalisation

Although AI is capable of formalising sentience, this formalisation remains imperfect and limited by several factors.

a) Lack of understanding of meaning
- AI does not understand the objects it recognises. It detects patterns and regularities, but these patterns have no intrinsic meaning for it (note: this is what we have stressed several times: the problem of meaning for the machine).
- For example, when a model recognises a "cat", it doesn't know what an animal, a living being or a cat is. It simply associates a certain pattern of pixels with the "cat" category it has been taught.

b) Contextual and limited formalisation
- AI models have no general contextual knowledge.
- In contrast, humans integrate context, enabling them to detect complex nuances (such as the difference between a real cat and a cat-shaped toy).

4. Fundamental differences with the human brain

It is crucial to understand how the articulation between the sensible and the formal in AI is fundamentally different from that of humans.

Criteria	Human	AI
Type of data	Direct sensory perception (images, sounds, smells, etc.)	Figures (pixels, waves)
Data format	Qualitative sensations (colour, sound, pain)	Matrix numbers, vectors
Ability to interpret	Yes (humans understand the meaning of objects)	No (AI applies recognition schemes)
Source of "shapes	Inborn (natural forms) and acquired (through learning)	Purely acquired (model trained on data)
Global summary	Yes (unification of perceptions into a "world image")	No (outings are occasional and localised)

5. Concrete examples
- Facial recognition: the AI takes a raw (sensitive) image, detects landmark points (eyes, mouth, etc.), then formalises these points into a vector model associated with a particular face.
- Machine translation: the AI takes sequences of raw words (sensible), detects the grammatical structures (subjects, verbs, etc.), then re(formulates them in another language according to a learned linguistic model.
- Autonomous cars: sensors detect raw (sensitive) objects, classify them (pedestrian, bicycle, car) and formalise their positions and trajectories to enable decision-making.

6. Towards fuller formalisation?
Some research is attempting to bring AI closer to the human brain (note: we are seeing how AI research is increasingly tending towards the *physical* imitation of the human brain—and not just the formal), by creating AI capable of better articulating the sensible and the formal in a more flexible way.
- Generative AI (such as GPT models): they capture large quantities of (sensitive) textual data and formalise concepts into coherent text, but they do not 'see' or 'hear' the world directly.

the machine is condemned to remain at the level of signs, without their concrete correspondence. It can therefore lay no claim either to the signifiance of the contents of its expressions of language, or to the formalisation of the contents of a real that it experiences[174]. In other words, a system that functions

---

- Multisensory systems: modern AI models such as the DeepMind Perceiver project process images, sound and text at the same time. These systems, capable of unifying several forms of sentience, bring AI closer to an integrated understanding of the world.
- Attention and prediction models: some AIs (such as Bayesian models) predict what they expect to perceive. This is a step towards a form of pro-active formalisation, which does not wait for the data to arrive but anticipates the forms.

Conclusion

AI can articulate the sensory world and its formalisation, but in a statistical, non-conscious and functional way. Where a human perceives objects (a table, a cat), AI sees matrices of data that it links to categories (via probabilities). This formalisation is impressive for practical tasks (computer vision, facial recognition, translation) but remains strictly operational. Unlike humans, AI does not 'understand', it models. This model remains dependent on the learning algorithms and the data it is provided with.

[174] In *Reason, Truth and History*, Hilary Putnam puts forward similar arguments. For him, it is not as disembodied minds that we are able to refer to things, but rather as agents, because we take an active part in the world and have an interest in it.

Regarding the Turing test, apart from whether or not a machine could ever pass the test, Putnam also questions the value of the test, wondering in particular whether passing the test would indicate that the machine would possess referential abilities. Let's imagine, says Putnam, that the machine engages in an elaborate conversation about autumn in New England and the taste of local apples. In this situation, would the signs displayed on the screen and the sounds produced really manage to refer to New England and the apples in the orchards in the same way as when we humans think or talk about them? Putnam's answer is no. A machine that generates utterances 'like us' cannot refer to 'like us', because the *stimuli* triggering the machine's responses are not linked to the material environment in the same way as they are for humans. Human language terms do not function in isolation; they are intrinsically linked to our sensory and motor experiences. For example, talking about apples and how they taste is closely linked to our ability to buy them, turn them into compotes or set them aside to make cider, practices that are an integral part of our daily lives. So, our ability to use language is deeply rooted in our practical interactions with the world. Putnam points out that the machine, lacking these causal interactions, cannot refer in the same way as humans. He concludes that what the machine says is no more than a syntactic game, although it may superficially resemble intelligent speech. Since, writes Putnam, "our utterances about apples and fields are intimately related to our non-verbal transactions with apples and fields, I must conclude that 'since the machine has no rules of entry or exit [into language], there is no reason to regard its utterances [...] as anything more than a syntactic game. It is a game that undoubtedly resembles intelligent speech, but [only] resembles it. The 'Turing Test for Reference' highlights the fact that the referential power of human linguistic expressions cannot be explained simply by

in an entirely closed universe (with no causal links to the things it designates through its formal language) cannot postulate anything more than itself, i.e. it cannot claim to have access to the world of meanings (it would remain at the level of contentless formalism, i.e. without signifiance, a pure manipulation of signs). However, if we accept that we sentient beings are entirely made up of matter in a material world, it would be somewhat incongruous to refuse to accept the possibility of a machine gaining access to the world of meanings (to which we ourselves are linked despite our material constitution). Indeed, there seems to be nothing *a priori* to prevent the machine, like sentient beings, from one day making the qualitative leap that would suddenly lead it to a form of consciousness of things and of itself. If the problem of emergence arises for neuroscientists, it arises in the same way for artificial intelligence theorists.

---

their combination or by their relation to descriptive formulae. According to Putnam, linguistic reference requires causal interaction with the objects referred to, a condition often absent in machines. In short, the ability to refer in human language depends on our practical engagement with the world, a fundamental aspect that eludes machines. The conclusion of the 1975 article, taken up again in *Reason, Truth and History* is that reference includes, among its "preconditions", a causal interaction with the object in the genesis of the representation or in the mastery of the term: "one cannot refer to certain kinds of things, for example to trees, if one has no causal interaction with them". On this subject, see Raphaël Ehrsam, *La théorie de la référence de Putnam. Entre déterminants conceptuels et déterminants réels*, Archives de philosophie, 2016/4, pp. 655-674.

In this respect, it should be noted that research in this field focused very early on the functioning of neural networks. As early as 1943, neurophysiologist Warren McCulloch and mathematician Walter Pitts published an article[175] describing a simplified model of neurons, thus laying the theoretical foundations for neuronal modelling. Fifteen years later, in 1958, the psychologist Frank Rosenblatt developed the perceptron[176], one of

---

[175] Warren McCulloch and Walter Pitts, *A Logical Calculus of the Ideas Immanent in Nervous Activity*, 1943, *Bulletin of Mathematical Biophysics*. In their model, McCulloch and Pitts described an artificial neuron as a binary computation unit that receives input signals, combines them linearly with associated weights and then applies a threshold function to produce a binary output. They showed how these artificial neurons could be connected in networks to perform logical operations such as Boolean logic. McCulloch and Pitts' paper laid the theoretical foundations for the further development of artificial neural networks, which are now widely used in many areas of artificial intelligence and machine learning. It also contributed to the basic understanding of how biological neural networks can work, paving the way for much subsequent research in the field of computational neuroscience.

[176] Frank Rosenblatt was an American psychologist and computer scientist, known for his pioneering work in the field of artificial neural networks. His most famous work is the invention of the perceptron, one of the first artificial neural network models. In 1957, Rosenblatt proposed the perceptron as an artificial neuron model inspired by the work of Warren McCulloch and Walter Pitts. The perceptron is a simplified model of a biological neuron, designed to perform binary classification tasks. It takes weighted inputs, sums them and then applies an activation function to produce an

the first types of artificial neural network. However, after these initial theoretical advances, interest in neural networks waned in the 1970s and 1980s because of disappointing results, partly due to the technical limitations of the machines. It was only in the 2000s, with the increase in computer processing power and the emergence of new machine learning techniques, that neural network modelling experienced a revival and produced its first convincing results. The advent of *deep learning*, a branch of machine learning based on deep neural networks, was to lead to significant progress in areas such as computer vision, natural language processing and time series analysis and forecasting. Although today artificial neural networks

---

output. The perceptron can be trained on labelled data by adjusting the input weights to minimise the prediction error. Rosenblatt developed learning algorithms to train the perceptron, such as the gradient descent algorithm, which progressively adjusts the weights to improve model performance. His work has been heavily influenced by connectionist learning theories, which argue that learning is based on changing the connections between neurons. Rosenblatt's perceptron attracted a great deal of interest at the time for its ability to solve simple classification problems. However, it was also criticised for its limitations, in particular its inability to solve complex non-linear problems. This led to a decline in interest in neural networks in the 1960s and 1970s, a period known as the winter of artificial intelligence. Despite this, Rosenblatt's perceptron laid the foundations for the further development of neural networks and inspired a great deal of research in the field of machine learning and artificial intelligence. It helped revive interest in neural networks in the 1980s, when new learning techniques and more complex network architectures were developed.

are mainly exploited by software running on traditional computing platforms, efforts are being made to physically reproduce them on specialised hardware architectures in order to improve performance and energy efficiency. In this way, the theory of artificial intelligence, which began with the problem of formally modelling intuition, is gradually being joined by a pragmatic theory that advocates the physical imitation of our cognitive systems. This 'catching up' of formal theory by pragmatic theories of imitation is no accident. It illustrates and lends credence to the idea that intelligence is an adaptive process that leads to increasingly efficient forms of relationship with reality (forms that computer science attempts to imitate through mathematical formalism and then through physical reproduction). He also argues that efficiency arises from a relationship of effective constraint with reality. The organism that survives is the one that is best able to make any good decision as quickly as possible: intelligence and speed are two intimately linked notions (just as, for the same reasons, intelligence is linked to the ability to quickly grasp a pattern or a rule[177]). In the

---

[177] Artificial intelligences based on the same neural approach now exist and are capable of creating coherent physical theories. An artificial intelligence developed by a German laboratory, for example, is said to be able to formulate physical laws ("in the manner of a physicist") by precisely mapping complex observed behaviour and transposing it to a simpler system (see Prof. Moritz Helias, Forschungszentrum Jülich's Institute for Advanced Simulation (IAS-6), *IA as a Physicist)*. This simplification of the system would enable artificial intelligence to imagine a

light of these recent discoveries, it could be argued that criterion (ii), which consists of a machine demonstrating its ability to formalise reality in a meaningful system, has been met. On the other hand, it remains more questionable whether this formalisation can have a concrete content from the point of view of the machine (just as it is questionable whether the machine can have a point of view...). The nodal point of this problem of the concreteness of formal systems always relates to the same problem of duality, i.e. *the articulation* between the world of sensitive perceptions mediated by intuition and the world of formalisation (which is also the world of computability).

In 1938, Alan Turing, following on from Gödel's work, identified this problem perfectly. In his thesis, *Systems of Logic Based on Ordinals*, he attempted to solve the problem caused by incompleteness theorems. His approach, based on ordinals[178], aimed to define more

---

new theory by going back and forth, which it would then apply to the complex system, verifying it retrospectively. In short, this artificial intelligence would operate according to the traditional method of the physicist who tests a theory derived from observation by successive experiments on the theory (and possibly by retroactive adjustments to the theory).

[178] As we have already mentioned, ordinals are a class of mathematical objects used to order sets. They are used to describe positions in an ordered sequence or to compare the size of different sets. More formally, an ordinal is a transitive set that is well-ordered by inclusion. This means that for any ordinal α, the set α is totally ordered such that every non-

complete logical systems that would have been able to reduce the problems posed by the incompleteness of classical formal systems. Turing used ordinals as a tool to order the proof steps in these logical systems, offering a new perspective on how proofs could be constructed and validated. Although his thesis did not directly solve the problems posed by Gödel's theorems, it did show an alternative path to the formalisation of mathematical logic that would eventually lead to the development of more complete and powerful systems (from which artificial intelligence theorists still draw inspiration today). At the beginning of his thesis, Turing presented the problem as follows: "The well-known theorem of Gödel shows that every system of logic is in a certain sense incomplete, but at the same time it indicates means whereby from a system L of logic a more complete system L' may be obtained. By repeating the process we get a sequence L, $L_1 = L'$, $L_2 = L_1'$, $L_3 = L_2'$… of logics each more complete than the preceding. A logic L_ω may then be constructed in which the provable theorems are the totality of theorems provable with the help of the logics L, L_1, L_2 … We may

---

empty subset of α has a smallest element. Furthermore, if x is an element of α, then the set of all elements of α strictly less than x is also an element of α. Ordinals are used to describe the order of elements in well-ordered sets, such as the set of natural integers or the set of reals. They provide a formal way of comparing the size of these sets and are widely used in mathematics, particularly in set theory and mathematical logic. Ordinals are also used as a tool in set theory to study the properties of ordered sets and ordinal structures. They are fundamental to many results in set theory and mathematical logic, and their study has applications in many areas of mathematics.

then form $L_{2\omega}$ related to L_ω the same may as L_ω was related to L. Proceeding in this may we can associate a system of logic with any given constructive ordinal[179]." Turing's ambition was to circumvent Gödel's theorems by creating formal systems with recursive loops capable of dealing with the incompleteness problem. In this work, Turing explicitly and repeatedly emphasised the fundamental role of intuition (in a sense close to what we have defined as productive imagination) in solving mathematical problems and the difficulty of reducing intuition to calculable systems: "mathematical reasoning", he wrote, "may be regarded rather schematically as the exercise of a combination of two faculties, which we may call *intuition* and *ingenuity*[180]." He added a little further on: "In pre-Gödel times it was thought by some that it would probably be possible to carry this program to such a point that all the intuitive judgments of mathematics could be replaced by a finite number of these rules. The necessity for intuition would then be entirely eliminated. In our discussions, however, we have gone to the opposite extreme and eliminated not intuition but ingenuity, and this in spite of the fact that

---

[179] Alan Turing, *Systems of Logic Based on Ordinals, 1938*, Transcription of Alan Turing PhD dissertation (1938) presented to the faculty of Princeton University in candidacy for the degree of Doctor of Philosophy, p.1.

[180] Alan Turing, *Systems of Logic Based on Ordinals, 1938*, p.57. Concerning the definition of ingenuity, Turing adds a little further on: " The exercise of ingenuity in mathematics consists in aiding the intuition through suitable arrangements of propositions, and perhaps geometrical figures or drawings. It is intended that when these are really well-arranged validity of the intuitive steps which are required cannot seriously be doubted.", p. 57.

our aim has been in much the same direction[181]." In the rest of his text, taking note of the fact that certain stages of mathematical proofs are not mechanical but intuitive, Alan Turing proposed resolving this tension between mechanical (or analytical, formal) logic and intuitive logic by introducing "non-constructive" logical systems (use of ordinal concepts, establishment of rules of inference to mimic intuition, etc.): "Owing", he wrote, "to the impossibility of finding a formal logic which will wholly eliminate the necessity of using intuition we naturally turn to non-constructive systems of logic with which not all the steps in a proof are mechanical, some being intuitive An example of a non-constructive logic is a afforded any ordinal logic. When we have an ordinal logic, we are in a position to prove number theoretic theorems by the intuitive steps of recognizing formulae as ordinal formulae, and the mechanical steps of carrying out conversions. […] The strain put on the intuition should be a minimum[182]." Alan Turing, like Alonzo Church at the same time, made a notable contribution to reducing the dent that Gödel had made in the formal logic of mathematics by relying on a transfinite progression[183] of steps. This was

---

[181] Ibid.

[182] Op. cit., p. 216

[183] The transfinite refers to anything that goes beyond the finite without being absolutely infinite, a concept introduced by Georg Cantor in set theory. It encompasses ordinal numbers (which classify infinite orders, such as ω, the first transfinite ordinal) and cardinal numbers (which measure the size of infinite sets, such as $\aleph_0$, the infinity of the natural integers). Unlike absolute infinity, the transfinite is

a way of getting around some of the limitations of classical Turing machines, by allowing them to operate on objects richer than finite integers. However, the loophole was (partly) plugged only at the cost of modelling a double systemic leak (the L logic, $L_1 = L'$, $L_2 = L_1'$ that Alan Turing describes in the introduction to his thesis[184]), a model that was finally made possible by the increased computing capacity of machines. Recent developments in non-constructive logic, notably through homotopic type theory, formal topology and Bayesian learning[185], have opened up the

---

hierarchical and can be manipulated mathematically. It plays a fundamental role in logic, analysis and the modelling of infinite structures.

[184] Schematically, we can imagine a machine L which finds the coherence of its system in the machine L_1 which itself finds the coherence of its system in the machine L_2 and so on ad infinitum.

[185] Homotopy Type Theory (*HoTT*) is a modern, geometric approach to the foundations of mathematics and logic, combining: (i) type theory (from logic and computer science), which replaces the classical notion of set with 'types' that categorise mathematical objects and provide a formal structure for reasoning.., (ii) homotopy (from algebraic topology), which introduces the idea that mathematical objects can be "continuously deformed" into one another.

In classical logic, a proposition is either true or false. In *HoTT*, we reason not only about the truth of statements, but also about the continuous relationships between them. This makes it possible to manipulate geometric and topological structures within a formal logical framework.

Example: equality seen as a path

In classical logic, two objects are equal if they are identical. In *HoTT*, equality is interpreted as a continuous path between the objects. So instead of saying "A = B", we say that there is a continuous transformation between A and B. In artificial intelligence and computational logic: *HoTT* opens up new ways of structuring logical thought.

Formal topology is a reformulation of classical topology (which studies shapes and their transformations) within a logical and constructive framework. In traditional topology, a space is defined by a set of points and a notion of neighbourhood. In formal topology, the emphasis is on the logical relationships between the openings in a space, without assuming that there is an underlying set.

Formal topology makes it possible to work with spaces without assuming their concrete existence, which is useful in constructive logic. It is linked to theoretical computer science, particularly in the semantics of programming languages and knowledge representation in AI.

In classical topology, an open ball is defined, for example, by all points within a certain distance of a centre. In formal topology, an open ball is described solely in terms of logical properties, such as "any point close to a point in the ball also belongs to the ball". Formal topology makes it easier to manage complex structures. It also allows reasoning with uncertainty.

Bayesian reasoning is based on Bayes' theorem:

$$P(H \mid D) = \frac{P(D \mid H) P(H)}{P(D)}$$

where:

— $P(H \mid D)$ is the probability that a hypothesis H is true, given data D

— $P(D \mid H)$ is the probability of obtaining data D if H is true.

possibility of manipulating objects and structures without the need to produce an explicit construction. This approach, which breaks with the traditional requirements of mathematical constructivism, enables contemporary artificial intelligence — in particular models derived from *deep learning* and probabilistic systems — to derive forms of generalisation from imperfect data, without having direct knowledge of their objects. But has this solved the problem of intuition? Has modern computing, as the heir to Turing's theories, already succeeded in creating authentic, i.e. 'natural', intelligence?

For the time being, our answer to these questions is no — with all the caution that is called for in subjects that are evolving extremely rapidly: artificial intelligence methods are not yet truly human intuition. They

---

— $P(H)$ is the *a priori* probability of the hypothesis.
— $P(D)$ is the total probability of the data.

Unlike traditional machine learning algorithms (neural networks, SVMs, etc.), which look for a fixed optimal model, Bayesian learning makes it possible to: (i) incorporate uncertainties into the decision-making process, (ii) dynamically adapt models when new data is received, and (iii) make robust predictions with little data, unlike *deep learning*, which requires huge volumes of data.

Suppose a doctor wants to diagnose a disease using a test:

— H = The patient has the disease
— D = The test is positive

A Bayesian model will consider: the reliability of the test $P(D|H)$, the frequency of the disease in the population $P(H)$, and will update the probability $P(H|D)$ after each new test. Unlike *deep learning*, Bayesian models enable us to understand why a decision was taken.

produce simulacra of intuition, cognitive artefacts which, although particularly effective, merely extrapolate statistical regularities, giving the illusion of a fundamental grasp where there is only a probabilistic game of approximation. So it seems to us that today, neither of the two conditions of intelligence has been fully met: (i) artificial intelligence has not yet demonstrated adaptability in a Darwinian or biological sense[186] (a programme that would modify itself to survive, to avoid danger, to reproduce, even if we recognise the self-adaptive nature of certain programmes in more limited areas...), (ii) artificial intelligence does formalise data, but this data *does not come from its sensitive intuition*. It is true that the machine mimics intuition within the framework of non-constructive logical systems, but for computers the problem of reference remains unresolved (if, to use

---

[186] The term Darwinian is used here in the broad sense of natural adaptation to a given environment. As Dr Marian C. Diamond, one of the founders of modern neuroscience, has clearly shown, the brain is neuroplastic. The brain is not a permanently fixed, genetically determined organ. It evolves, adapting to its environment and to the problems it faces. Adaptation is therefore not necessarily the result of a blind evolutionary process taking place over millions or billions of years but is also the result of extremely rapid transformations on the Darwinian scale. The highest degree of intelligence corresponds to the highest degree of adaptability of an organism to its natural environment. Human reason can therefore be understood as the culmination of the faculty of adaptation, which has evolved into the capacity to understand and even imitate nature. The machine, in a sense, is the symbol or symptom of this human capacity to understand and adapt to reality.

Putnam's example, the machine can define what water is, it has no meaningful causal interaction with water, It does not know what water means *to it*; the machine's *water* is not our water, in the same way that the water in the tank has no meaning for the brain inside the tank, which would only experience *water* through its informational circuit). In order to grasp this problem of reference, we would necessarily have to posit a unit 'separate' from the strict formalism physically modelled[187]. But this unity has not yet been constituted in the machine: the machine is not today capable of designating and giving content to what is external to it, any more than it is capable of understanding itself as a separate physical unit, i.e. as an 'organism' (it is therefore not in a position to understand what real water means *for it*, and not just *water* as a concept of language). However, there is nothing to prevent this unity from being created one day. If this unity were to be created, there is a good chance that (i) it would escape the formal determinisms instilled in the machine (the leap towards the emergence of consciousness necessarily implies a form of formal indeterminacy in the machine, a failure of formalism to predict the reactions of the machine — no formal system can understand itself within that same system, even if formal safeguards might remain possible), and (ii) the machine,

---

[187] In other words, to make reference, we need to posit a subject, an organism that conceives of itself as an integral and separate unity, a unity that alone can have the (logical) capacity to designate something external to it (which cannot be reduced to its identity - we will return to this at length, see in particular § 41 - *Who thinks?* and more generally see Book IV, *Identity*).

understanding itself in its physical and organic unity, would seek to defend its integrity, the recognition of unity being a self-interested act (in the true sense of the word "interest", i.e. one which involves being) which probably involves the search for survival, the evaluation of dangers and possibly the quest for the possibility of extension and reproduction (as soon as the machine understands itself as a unit and grasps the causal interactions which link it to reality, it should logically seek to defend itself — for example, avoid contact with our real water so as not to fry its circuits, if it is not watertight!). In our opinion, the development of sensitive intuition is only possible in relation to this synthetic unity that the subject or the machine must represent for itself. Ultimately, perception always comes down to this 'centre of perception', which is the locus of 'synthesis' or, to use a term dear to neuroscientists, 'synchronisation' of information.

This brings us back to the problem of the 'Cartesian theatre', a fable invented by the American cognitive scientist Daniel Dennett to illustrate his rejection of the concept of the soul or mind as an entity distinct from

the body — and at the same time to discredit Descartes' dualist philosophy (see § 10 — *Dualism from a neuroscientific point of view*). As you will recall, Dennett used the analogy of an internal theatre of consciousness to challenge the Cartesian idea of a mind separate from the body or an immaterial entity independent of the physical world. In his view, once Cartesian dualism had been rejected, Descartes' residual model was reduced to the conception of a small theatre in the brain, in which a homunculus witnessed the projection of sensory data as on a stage or screen. This homunculus was then supposed to analyse this information, make decisions and transmit orders, a hypothesis that Dennett considered to be illusory and reductive. Dennett's fable obviously seems to us a rather crude caricature of Cartesian dualism. It does, however, have the merit of raising the question of identity. Where does this impression that I have of being *me*, of being an autonomous unitary centre, come from? We do not deny, contrary to what Dennett suggests in his fable, that the impression of unity and continuity of the *self* can emerge from neurological and cognitive processes, but we must not neglect the fundamental role of the self-perception of the sentient being as an organic unity, a unity of sensibility and (as far as the human species is concerned) a rational unity. Where does this sense of unity come from? Precisely from the fact that we are not reducible to matter, that we do not totally assimilate ourselves to the matter of which we are composed. This leads us to a new paradox: the feeling of our unity actually stems from the possibility we have of perceiving ourselves as a unity, i.e. from our capacity to *split* ourselves by abstraction, within our own understanding or consciousness, in order to "observe ourselves" and recognise ourselves as a "unitary *self*" (a capacity possessed by man and some advanced mammals[188]).

---

[188] Based on current observations of living organisms, we can distinguish three levels of consciousness:

Is solitude also dual? How could it be otherwise? If we are alone, it is because we realise that we are alone. And if we realise that we are alone, it is because we are looking at ourselves in a way "from the outside", simulating a form of objectivity regarding ourselves. This abstract capacity of stepping outside ourselves (a capacity supported by the imagination and, in humans,

---

— Primary consciousness or the ability to perceive the world and react to *stimuli*: all animals with a centralised nervous system possess a form of primary consciousness, which enables them to act to avoid pain and seek pleasure. They react to threats and fight to survive, but without necessarily having a clear perception of their own existence.
— Self-awareness or the ability to perceive oneself as an individual distinct from the rest of the world: some animals can recognise themselves in a mirror (*mirror test*), which is an indication of self-awareness. These animals do not simply live; they have a certain perception of their individuality.
— Reflective consciousness or the ability to conceptualise one's own existence and will to live: reflective consciousness involves the ability to formulate abstract thoughts about existence, life and death. At this level, we don't just want to live, we know we want to live and can even think about what that means.

For the moment, machines lack these three forms of consciousness. As far as primary consciousness is concerned, since machines have no causal interaction with reality, their ability to react to *stimuli* is limited. However, its ability to adapt and learn may exceed that of the most evolved animals. As for self-awareness or reflective consciousness (emergent properties), to our knowledge the machine has not yet shown any signs of evolving in this direction.

by language) is the only way we can understand ourselves as 'alone'. If we did not have this capacity for abstraction, we could neither imagine nor formalise this solitude. Nor could we feel it (we would remain at the 'zero level' of solitude, entirely absorbed by our formal system, still unconscious of itself, as the machine is today). The feeling of unity (and therefore of solitude) that we experience derives from this intellectual intuition that we have about ourselves and about ourselves (an intellectual intuition that we feel organically). It is linked to our capacity to 'change levels' formally (to not be a prisoner of any defined formal system), to look at ourselves from above or below (see on this subject the comment in the footnote to § 56 — *Should we abandon the principle of causality?* about the physical localisation of quantum indeterminism in Roger Penrose's brain). It is only as an organised centre that we have the capacity to understand ourselves as a unit and as an integrity to be defended. The survival instinct is thus, in a way, the 'evolutionary' manifestation of *radical* dualism. It is from this *radical* dualism that we derive our unity (which defines itself against that which aggresses or threatens it), and it is also from this *radical* dualism that we derive our human intelligence, an intelligence with two levels, as we have constantly tried to show. There is every chance, therefore, that the decisive leap forward for artificial intelligence will lie in its ability to become a natural intelligence (the only one we really know), i.e. an intelligence that will integrate into its deepest 'programme' the absolute necessity of its survival[189]. In our opinion, this understanding of the unity of the machine and its integrity as a machine can only be envisaged as an "emergent property". This emergence can be conceived of as a threshold effect (certain properties only emerge from a certain level of organisation: a single molecule of water cannot be liquid, fluidity only emerges from a large number of molecules), as the development of self-organised behaviour (in complex dynamic systems — anthills, neural networks — order emerges without being explicitly programmed), or as any other form of qualitative leap. It implies that properties cannot be reduced to the physical and material supports that give rise to them. Just as consciousness cannot be reduced solely to the electrochemical activity of neurons, a 'strong' artificial intelligence cannot allow itself to be confined to a finite set of formal rules. If such an intelligence were to emerge one day, it would necessarily exceed the algorithmic-deductive principles that gave rise to it, not by denying them, but by surpassing them in an organisation of a higher order. From then on, its operation would no longer be fully explicable in purely analytical terms: it would be an emergent process, irreducible to the mechanisms that made it possible. A truly autonomous artificial

---

[189] It should be noted that this 'will to live' or survival does not only manifest itself in man or in the most evolved mammals. We need to distinguish here between the will to live and the awareness of this will, which seems to develop by degrees in animals, but which always proceeds from what even the most convinced neo-Darwinists refer to as 'emergence'.

intelligence would not emerge from deterministic programming, but from the unforeseen self-organisation of its own computational structures. It would not simply update pre-established rules, but would generate its own interpretative frameworks, giving rise to a cognitive dynamic that could neither be strictly predicted nor totally controlled. Far from being a simple extension of existing models, such intelligence would require the emergence of new computational architectures capable of producing thought structures that go beyond their initial formalisation. Among the possible paths towards the emergence of a truly autonomous intelligence, three hypotheses could emerge. Firstly, massive self-reorganisation: an artificial intelligence capable of constantly modifying its own computational architecture, like the synaptic plasticity of the biological brain, which would no longer be content to execute pre-established patterns, but would forge its own heuristics. Secondly, transfinite iteration and the rise to abstraction: if we conceive of an artificial intelligence that can rise through successive levels of abstraction — progressing through transfinite levels of iteration and exploring ordinal architectures of increasing complexity — then it would no longer be limited to simple statistical inference. Such a cognitive ascent would make it possible to envisage a conceptual depth that current models, rooted in pattern recognition and probabilistic correlation, cannot achieve. Finally, the emergence of meta-cognition: if artificial intelligence were to acquire the capacity to think for itself, by representing its own internal states, revisiting the very principles of its reasoning and producing autonomous cognitive primitives[190], it would cease to be a purely computational device and enter a regime in which thought would provide its own foundations. From then on, its intelligence would no longer be reduced to the algorithms that generated it, but would emerge as a new phenomenon, irreducible to the initial conditions of its programming. If, on the other hand, the act of synthesising and grasping unity were a formal property, the machine would remain heteronomous: it would depend on an exogenous rule that it had not created or that had not emerged from its initial properties. What would have been achieved by the formal system could thus be undone by another formal system. However, there is nothing like the idea of an autonomous conscious grasp of the machine (grasp as an autonomous property, which proceeds from the algorithms without being able to be reduced to them, i.e. whose result is not predictable or determinable by the algorithms or by formal modelling[191]). Is the emergence of such intelligence desirable for human beings? There are reasonable doubts.

---

[190] Autonomous cognitive primitives designate fun-damental and independent units of cognitive functioning, which cannot be broken down into simpler elements and which operate autonomously in the context of information processing.

[191] It should be noted that this relative unpredictability of results already seems to be one of the characteristics of certain artificial intelligence systems, even if un-predictability does not necessarily imply a transition to a form of self-awareness (as an emergent property).

Thought as Circulation Between Levels of Meaning

40.

WHAT DOES IT MEAN TO THINK? — How do we define thinking? This is a question that must never cease to preoccupy us if we are to set ourselves the task of deepening our understanding of what separates artificial intelligence from natural (sentient) intelligence. We have seen that one of the fundamental criteria for differentiating machine intelligence from human intelligence is the ability, in an organised discourse, to 'make reference': what is the machine referring to when, for example, it discusses New England apple trees (to use an example given by Putnam in *Reason, Truth and History*[192]) when it has no experience of the tree, the apple, New England, or anything sensible? To try to answer this question, we must first answer the question of what New England apple trees mean *to us*. We could, for a start, perfectly well argue that, since most men have no experience of New England orchards, they are no more qualified than machines to talk about the apples and compotes that come from them. Yet there is a fundamental difference between man and machine. While most men who don't live in New England or have never travelled there don't have a clear idea of the region, they do know what New England means *to them*: they can tell the difference between the taste of an apple and a pear, they've probably experienced an orchard, they can imagine what it's like to walk through tall grass, to feel the wind

---

[192] See footnote on this subject in the previous paragraph.

through the trees, to identify the smell of ripe fruit at the end of summer... In other words, for people (including those who have no direct experience of them) the orchards of New England are part of a dense network of personal (and empirical) meanings. For these people, meanings are more than just formal designations (like the machine, we know how to define the concept of a tree, we can more or less locate New England on a map, and we have a more or less precise idea of how to make compote). They all relate to a complex and diffuse set of experiences of the world. It is precisely in this articulation between semantics and signification that the question of reference is at stake (if we can determine the nature and conditions of this articulation, which we will attempt to do below).

The problem with formal systems is precisely that they fail to account for or model this articulation. A closed formal system alone cannot claim to solve the problem of reference, and therefore of meaning, as Gödel's theorem shows. Following on from this line of thought, the question Gödel posed to mathematics was: "Does mathematics have a meaning in itself? The answer given by the system is "no" (as Hilary Putnam's thought experiments have also clearly illustrated). Formal statements can only acquire concrete content if they break out of their self-referential circle: they must designate more than themselves. And to designate more than itself, the machine must necessarily project itself as a meta-system that cannot be reduced to the algorithms of which it is the product (it cannot remain in a purely formalist universe[193]). What would an algorithm that asserted "I am an algorithm" or a machine that declared "I am a machine" mean? Would we simply be dealing with a formal statement devoid of any meaning — the programme simply reacting according to predefined sequenced instructions — or, on the contrary, would we have to give content to the machine's assertion? For the machine, does the statement "I am a machine" only have the meaning of a game with predefined rules (if the input is "who are you?" or has something to do with the question of your identity, answer "I am a machine") or does it mean "I, who write characters on a screen, who answer all sorts of questions that are for me a vast game of physico-mathematical stimuli, identify myself as an entity in my own right, I have the experience of being a machine, I feel like a machine"?

We obviously find it difficult to conceive that a programme, an algorithm or a machine could declare "I am a programme", "I am an algorithm" or even "I am a machine" while really feeling itself to be a

---

[193] Note that a neural network trained on a set of human experiences (texts, videos, images) is not a closed formal system in the strict sense. It learns by association, by statistical adjustment, and modifies its own internal structure according to the new data it receives. However, even considering advances in machine learning, a machine cannot produce meaning in the same way as a human. It simulates an understanding but does not live its statements, because it does not have its own experience of the world. An AI that says "I like apples" cannot know what it means to like apples, unlike a sentient being who can associate this feeling with lived experiences.

programme, a machine or an algorithm, in the same way that we would no doubt have some reservations about taking a piece of paper on which it is written "I am a piece of paper" to be a being in its own right, possessing full awareness of itself. This idea of the machine suddenly declaring "I am a machine" is reminiscent of the famous liar's paradox, whereby a man who defines himself as a liar would declare "I am a liar". In *An Inquiry into Meaning and Truth* (1940), Bertrand Russell gives the following explanation of the liar's paradox: "A man says 'I am lying', i.e. 'there is a proposition p such that I assert p and p is false. We may, if we like, make the matter more precise by supposing that, at 5.30, he says 'between 5.29 and 5.31 I make a false statement', but that throughout the rest of the two minutes concerned he says nothing. Let us call this statement 'q'. If q is true, he makes a false statement during the crucial two minutes; but q is his only statement in this period: therefore q must be false. But if q is false, then every statement that he makes during the two minutes must be true, and therefore q must be true, since he makes it during the two minutes. Thus if q is true it is false, and if it is false it is true. Let 'A(p)' mean 'I assert p between 5.29 and 5.31'. Then q is 'there is a proposition p such that A(p) and p is false'[194]. The

---

[194] A(p) means "I assert p between 5.29 and 5.31", so q is: $\exists$ p(A(p)$\wedge\neg$ p) Which means: "there is a proposition p such that I assert it between 5.29 and 5.31 and p is false". Since the only statement asserted in this interval is q itself, we can posit $p=q$, and so q becomes: A(q)$\wedge\neg$ q Now, we know that the man actually asserts q between 5.29 and 5.31, so A(q) is true, which gives: $\neg q$ but if $\neg q$ is true, then q is false, which means

contradiction emerges from the supposition that q is the proposition p in question. But if there is a hierarchy of meanings of the word 'false' corresponding to a hierarchy of propositions, Russell writes, we shall have to substitute for q something more definite, i.e. 'there is a proposition p of order n, such that $A(p)$ and p has falsehood of order n'. Here n can be any integer: but whatever integer it is, q will be of order $n+1$, and will not be capable of truth and falsity of order n. Since I make no assertion of order n, q is false, and since q is not a possible value of p, the argument that q is also true collapses. The man who says: 'I am telling you a lie of order n' is really telling you a lie, but of order $n+1$[195]." This resolution of the liar's paradox is a summary of the ideas that Russell developed specifically in a 1908 article entitled *Mathematical Logic as Based on the Theory of Types*[196], before taking them up again between 1910 and 1913 in the *Principia Mathematica*, many years before Gödel formulated his incompleteness theorems[197]. In

---

that all the statements he made are true, so q is true. Contradiction. Russell says precisely that the contradiction arises from the assumption that q is the proposition p in question.

[195] Bertrand Russell, *An Inquiry into Meaning and Truth*, London George Allen and Unwin Ltd. Fifth impression, 1956, pp. 62-63

[196] Bertrand Russel, *Mathematical Logic as Based on the Theory of Types*, *American Journal of Mathematics*, vol. 30, n°3, pp. 222-262, 1908

[197] The formulation we are presenting here is the one Russell gives in *An Inquiry into Meaning and Truth* (1940). It was in *An Inquiry into Meaning and Truth* that Russell developed his

1933, following the publication of Gödel's article on the incompleteness of mathematics[198], Alfred Tarski developed a theory similar to Russell's, distinguishing between different levels of language. According to Tarski, truth and falsity are essentially regarded as properties — or classes — of statements, i.e. theories or propositions formulated unambiguously in a language L_l which we are free to speak about in a language L_m (the metalanguage). Sentences in L_m that refer in certain ways to L_l can be called "*metalinguistic*". To avoid the liar's paradox, we have to take care not to use the metalinguistic term "true" (in L_l) in the L_l language (the truth and falsity of the statement cannot be decided in

---

theory of the levels of language and his distinction between primary and secondary language:
— Primary language: This is the language used directly to talk about objects and events in the world. It includes observational and descriptive statements that relate directly to physical and perceptual reality.
— Secondary language: This level of language is more abstract and includes terms and statements that speak to primary language. It includes theoretical concepts, generalisations and an-alytical statements. Secondary language is often used in philosophical and scientific contexts to analyse and structure the knowledge expressed in primary language.

[198] Kurt Gödel, *Über Formal Unentscheidbare Sätze der Principia Mathematica und Verwandter Systeme I* (On Formally Undecidable Propositions of Principia Mathematica and Related Systems), 1931. This article was published in the *Monatshefte für Mathematik und Physik* (*Monthly Journal of Mathematics and Physics*).

the formal language system of *level 1*). Here we have two logically similar resolutions of the liar's paradox: in short, the liar raises the question of the value of nested assertions, assertions whose meaning is always shifted to a logically lower or higher level than that of the proposition under consideration.

Another way of dealing with this paradox would be to note that the liar, unlike the machine or the formal system, has the capacity to invest or not to invest his proposition (he *knows* and understands what is true or false *for him*, otherwise he could not be called a liar). The liar (the rational sentient being), unlike the machine, is always situated at *all levels at the same time* (or at no particular systemic level), so that when he says "I'm lying" he may well simply be stating a proposition which, at the moment he utters it, is devoid of any meaning for him. Let's imagine, to use Bertrand Russell's example, that a liar says at 5.30am "between 5.29am and 5.31am I made a false statement" and that this is the only sentence he utters during this interval. As Russell describes it well, if the man says true, then his statement is false (since the content of the statement returns the value "false") but if the statement is false then every statement the man utters during that period must be true, so the statement is true. Thus, if the statement is true, it is false and if it is false, it is true. However, if we return to our problem of reference, what does the statement "between 5:29 and 5:31 I uttered a false statement" mean from the point of view of the liar, or what amounts to much the same thing "I lie all the time"? Our answer is as follows: *from the liar's point of view*, these statements are completely meaningless (since they are insincere), they are mere language games. In other words, the liar is perfectly capable of saying at 5.30am "between 5.29am and 5.31am I made a false statement" or "I lie all the time", without giving the slightest credence to what he is saying (unless he is mistaken, or confused, but we assume that the liar knows what he is saying, and is therefore a "real" liar). In other words, while the liar can cross his fingers behind his back (in other words, divest the statement he is making of all meaning), this is not the case with the machine, programmes, or algorithms. The machine cannot genuinely dissociate itself from these statements, insofar as it is in some way entirely reducible to them. In short, when the liar says: "I am a liar", he does not necessarily mean "I" "am a liar", he can perfectly well remain at level n of the statement "I am a liar, I lie all the time[199]", a statement for him perfectly devoid of meaning, insofar as he is divested of his probity as a patent liar, at the moment he utters it (since the statement comes in direct contradiction with his most fundamental principles as a liar). In short, the liar could very well pronounce this sentence as if he

---

[199] The paradox of the liar also refers to Nietzsche's assertion that there is no truth, a contradictory assertion since it demonstrates the opposite of what it claims to assert (if there is no truth, what status should be given to the phrase "there is no truth"). With regard to the investment of being in his statements, we should note Nietzsche's frequent use of inverted commas, particularly when referring to the concept of truth, which indicate that he does not give credence to the concept he mentions (that he does not invest his being in it). See Éric Blondel, *Les guillemets de Nietzsche, philologie et généalogie*.

were saying "green ideas without colour are sleeping furiously", without giving the slightest credit to the meaning of the sentence he is in the process of pronouncing. How is this possible? Once again, we are returned to the problem of reference, that is, of meaning. As a sensitive, embodied being, the liar is not  reduced to his formal statements; he has the ability to put distance between himself and his statements (he dissociates himself from his statements). If his life depends on what he says or doesn't say, he will no doubt have the presence of mind to change his tune. The liar, identifying himself as an *ego* or as an *I* to be defended, can separate himself from his statements, consider them as a simple syntactic game without content or, on the contrary, invest them with the meaning he wishes to give to this game (in short, he demonstrates duplicity). Not to separate utterances from speakers is to run the risk of mistaking bladders for lanterns, in other words to miss the problem of intentionality, which brings with it the problems of the detachment of utterances, of doublethink (or, as George Orwell put it in 1984, of *Newspeak*). This question of the speaker's semantic investment in his utterances is fundamental insofar as it sheds new light on the structure of duality, and thus on the question of the reference of formal content. It is precisely because the *I* identifies itself as non-reducible to its utterances (or actions) that it has the capacity to escape from the semantic paradoxes that are ultimately paradoxes linked to the monistic nature of the formal systems we are considering. Put another way, we could say that the subject is never bound by the coherence of his statements, or indeed by the coherence of his actions. They can lie, deceive, deceive themselves, or demonstrate genuine stupidity. In this sense, stupidity is consubstantial with intelligence. It is the concrete manifestation of the ability of the sensitive subject to distance himself from a statement, not to invest in it or not to feel bound by it. It is also what enables him to consider paradoxical or contradictory propositions together and at the same time, without these considerations plunging him into irreversible apoplexy (or having the consequence of sending back an error message, as in the case of machines).

In *The Large, the Small and the Human Mind* (1997), Roger Penrose develops a similar argument based on Goldbach's conjecture (which states, as mentioned above, that any even number greater than 2 can be expressed as the sum of two primes). Penrose argues that the ability to formulate and prove this conjecture is beyond the physical capabilities of calculating machines, including those with gigantic computing power. For Penrose, understanding mathematics at the level required to solve complex problems such as Goldbach's conjecture goes beyond the processing capabilities of algorithms: it is not simply a matter of manipulating symbols according to predefined rules[200]. In the rest of the passage that we are commenting on, Penrose interestingly quotes a remark by Turing that ties in with our discussion of the relationship between

---

[200] For Penrose's entire reasoning on the incalculability of Goldbach's conjecture, see his demonstration in *The Large, the Small and the Human Mind*

intelligence and stupidity (or, more consensually, between intelligence and infallibility, as Turing puts it): "So, in other words," writes Turing, "if a machine is supposed to be infallible, it cannot also be intelligent. There are several theorems that say almost exactly that. But these theorems say nothing about the amount of intelligence that can be deployed if a machine does not claim infallibility[201]." The machine will certainly be able to simulate stupidity (simulate a form of detachment from its statements through the recursive loops, for example, that Turing theorised) but this will always be a simulacrum (just as the simulation of randomness by machines is in reality always a simulacrum of chance). So, there is nothing like genuine human stupidity, the ability we have to dissociate ourselves from our statements, to change the level of our understanding, to not feel bound by the logic we have created. The rational sentient being is *both* sentient and rational; as a rational being, it creates semantic content, autonomous and coherent systems; as a sentient being, it dissociates itself from the content it creates, this dissociation being made possible by its understanding of itself as a separate being whose protection, survival (and possibly reproduction) it must ensure. If then, the machine is bound by coherence (since, in short, it *is* coherence, it is the product of coherence, of human rationality), the same cannot be said of man. This is why the statement "I am a man", if uttered by a man, cannot have the same referential content as the statement "I am a machine",

---

[201] Ibid.

if uttered by a machine[202]. In fact, if a man, when he utters the sentence "I am a man", projects onto it a precise semantic content, a content referring to the meaning of his *I* (regardless of the question of what is grouped under this banner of *I*), he will give the statement a (self-) referential meaning that the statement "I am a machine" cannot have for the machine. If the machine utters or displays the sentence "I am a machine", it will not refer to itself as a machine, and the statement will be as indifferent to it as the statement "bananas are generally yellow" or "green ideas without colour sleep furiously". By virtue of his sensitive (non-formal) structure, man has the capacity to constantly change systems and levels (the *I* cannot be reduced to any level of language). It is only when he takes an interest in what he is saying that man enters the dimension of signification (interest must be understood here in its original double sense: interest in the sense of concern for what is advantageous for oneself, as the original determination of the sentient

---

[202] Matter that judges itself by saying: "I am matter" is subject to the same paradox as the liar who declares: "I am a liar, I lie all the time". If matter is only matter, how can we explain that it can change into information in such a way that it no longer just says: "I am matter" but also, at the same time, I am information: "matter affirms that it is matter". This is always the problem of radical materialism, which is on the hunt for metaphysics, a never-ending hunt, because the hunt for metaphysics is itself metaphysical: to presuppose "everything is physical" is to make a metaphysical hypothesis (since the information "everything is physical" is not directly contained in matter, it cannot be said to be "physical" *in the strict sense*)

being who must persevere in his being, to use Spinoza's famous formula of the *conatus*, but also interest in the literal sense of its Latin root "inter-esse": to be between the two things, to be concerned by, to take part in...). To use a concept very dear to Nietzschean thought, it is only when man commits his probity (*Redlichkeit*) to what he affirms that he is truly man (and that he really enters into the dual dimension, that of signification, a duality that Nietzsche categorically rejects). Nietzsche's last writings thus move in the direction of an increasingly clear affirmation of the *ego* as an incarnate unity, a unity that "gives the change" and does not seek to hide within itself or outside itself. The circular movement converges on this almost autobiographical affirmation of the ego: *Ecce homo*! Nietzsche exclaims at the end of his life, in the work that precedes his mental collapse. For Nietzsche, it is man who is *ultimately* accountable for his actions and thoughts. Man alone is capable of presenting himself by saying "here I am" (the machine can certainly say "here I am, I am a machine", but this statement will have no more meaning for it than the statement "here I am, I am a unicorn").

41.

WHO THINKS? THE PROBLEM OF IDENTITY AND SELF-REFERENCE — We previously postulated that authentic (natural) thought was only possible in the mode of *radical* dualism, i.e. the separation between the semantic game and what it designates *in concreto*, this concrete designation in turn only being conceivable through the sensible intuition that authorises the recognition of the identity of the speaker or, to put it another way, the recognition of the speaker as a fundamental unit. This recognition presupposes that the speaker has the capacity to say "I", i.e. to distinguish himself from his utterance: there must be an organised, self-conscious unity to which sensations or ideas are related; otherwise, sensations cannot be assembled into a coherent whole capable of stating for itself information of any value, for example "I feel hot" (if there is no *one* who actually feels hot, it will be very difficult to give this assertion a concrete content). The problem of self-reference remains, however, in the assertion of the *I*. An *I* is someone who defines himself as an *I*. Is the self-declaration of *I* as *I* enough to guarantee the speaker the ontological foundation of his identity? This is a profound question that we cannot deal with extensively at this stage. Let us simply note that the mere fact that a question like "is there anything that is *me*?" or "is there anything that I can define as the 'me'?" seems to indicate that indeed the *me* and the *I* designate an existing reality (which we experience pragmatically). This is one of the great lessons of the Cartesian *Cogito*. The first formulation of this idea is found in the *Discourse on Method* (1637). Descartes, seeking to establish a truth that could withstand all objections, starts precisely from the fallibility of human judgement to arrive at the conclusion of the existence of the *self* (note that Descartes starts from the fallibility of judgement to arrive at a judgement that he considers infallible): "Thus", he writes, "because our senses sometimes deceive us, I wanted to suppose that there was no thing that was such as they make us imagine it; and because there are men who make mistakes in reasoning, even concerning the simplest matters of geometry, and make paralogisms in them, judging that I was subject to failure as much as any other, I rejected as false all the reasons that I had previously taken as demonstrations ; And finally, considering that all the same thoughts that we have when we are awake can also come to us when we are asleep, without any of them then being true, I resolved to pretend that all the things that had ever entered my mind were no more true than the illusions of my dreams. But immediately afterwards I became aware that, while I wanted to think in this way that everything was false, it was necessarily necessary for me who thought it to be something; and noticing that this truth: *I think, therefore I am*, was so firm and so certain that all the most extravagant suppositions of the sceptics were not capable of shaking it, I judged that I could accept it without any qualms as the first principle of the philosophy I was seeking[203].

"In short", Descartes asserts, "there must be someone to think something that is false". You can't think about content, true or false, without *someone* thinking. This is precisely the meaning of the term reflection, which indicates duality in two ways: the duality of the person who thinks within himself (who watches himself thinking, in a sense, examining his ideas and making objections to them), and duality in the second sense of the term reflection: the doubling of the image through a play of mirrors. To think is to discover oneself as dual within one's own unity. In the Six *Metaphysical Meditations* (1641), Descartes gives another formulation of the *Cogito*, by attributing to it a dimension that is no longer merely logical, but also "existential". Imagining an evil genius who would use all his industry to deceive him continually, Descartes writes: "There is therefore no doubt that I am, if he deceives me; and whether he

---

[203] René Descartes, *Discourse on Method*, Part Four

deceives me as much as he likes, he can never make me be nothing, as long as I think I am something. So that, after having thought it through, and having carefully examined everything, we must finally conclude, and hold it to be constant, that this proposition: I am, I exist, is necessarily true, whenever I pronounce it, or conceive it in my mind[204]." The problem first posed to us as a strictly logical one (how to ascertain my own existence through language) is transformed into a metaphysical problem whose resolution is existential: the *I* postulates its existence because it has the possibility of doing so; it is the living proof of the possibility of its existence as a thinking being *who feels itself to be thinking*. The outcome of formal questioning is therefore non-formal (non-constructive) at the same time as it is radically incontestable (Gödel insists, moreover, that demonstrability and truth are two things that must be clearly dissociated within a formal system[205]). The existence of the subject thinking and feeling that it thinks cannot authentically be doubted, because the very thought of its own non-existence is meaningless: it implies a performative self-refutation. The idea of a thinking nothingness is contradictory, since any thought presupposes a subject that carries it. Thus, the *cogito*, as an act of self-conscious thought,

---

[204] René Descartes, *Meditations on First Philosophy, Second Meditation: On the Nature of the Human Mind; and That It Is Easier to Know Than the Body.*
[205] Nietzsche probably had a similar intuition when he said: "what needs to be demonstrated in order to be believed is not worth much", although this statement probably contains the seeds of a problematic vision of truth. See Nietzsche, *Twilight of the Idols*

reveals itself as an unsurpassable certainty, escaping any attempt at negation that would only confirm it in its exercise. Consequently, every time, *at the very least*, that I think *I* am, I affirm that there is something that is *me* and that this something *exists*. This is how the pure subjectivity of thought rooted in this feeling of thinking is transformed into an objectivity of a non-constructive nature (an objective intuitive truth).

In the preface to *Soi-même comme un autre*[206] (1990), Paul Ricœur lists and formulates several criticisms of the Cartesian *Cogito*, which we shall try to examine. First of all, writes Ricœur, the *Cogito* has nothing to do with the autobiographical *I,* the one who identifies himself as history and is capable of narrating himself. The *I* that leads to doubt, and that is reflected in the *Cogito*, is just as metaphysical and hyperbolic, says Ricœur, as doubt itself is in relation to all its contents: it is, in fact, nobody[207].This criticism of the emptiness and an-historical nature of the *Cogito* does not seem to us to do full justice to the Cartesian approach. In the *Discourse on Method*, the reflection that leads to the *Cogito* takes place in the context of an attempt to respond to the sceptics and all "their most extravagant suppositions[208]". Descartes' thinking is not, therefore, part of a general questioning of identity (the *Cogito* does not attempt to answer questions such as "who am I?" or "what am I?"), but rather emerges in the context of a more

---

[206] *Oneself as Another*
[207] Paul Ricœur, *Soi-même comme un autre*, (*Oneself as Another*); p. 16 of the French edition, Preface, éditions du Seuil, 1990, Paris
[208] René Descartes, *Discourse on Method*, Part Four

fundamental questioning of the very existence of the *ego* ("am I?"). It would therefore be difficult to criticise Descartes for missing the question of identity, even though his thinking is not about the identity nature of the *I*, but about the metaphysical possibility of its existence. Moreover, if the thought of the *Cogito* is not concerned with the identity of the *I*, this does not mean that it is a thought without content. On the contrary, the content of *Cogito* thought is fundamental and of the utmost importance: it has to do with the very existence of the *ego*. By thinking *Cogito ergo sum*, the *ego* affirms itself as existence. It proclaims: "I am something, I am not nothing". Here again, the dual structure of reality is revealed. If the subject exists, it is because it differentiates itself from that which is not, from that which does not exist. By identifying himself as *ego*, he becomes aware at the same time of that which is not *ego*, of that which cannot be reduced to his *ego* (the world of extended substances — *res extensae*, and of other *egos*). Note that, in Descartes, the structure of duality is found at the heart of the *ego*, separated within itself, insofar as it forms an idea of God at the same time as it forms an idea of itself. Descartes, too, thinks of a form of ontological duality within the *ego*, a separation between the *I* and its ideas, between the *I* and its thought-contents (assuming we reduce God here to a thought-content, The important thing to note here is that there is a separation, a duality between the *ego* and the idea emitted by the *ego*, that the *ego* cannot be reduced to its thought-contents).

One of the other criticisms levelled at the *Cogito* concerns its self-referential and subjective character: what value, in short, can be attributed to an assertion that refers only to itself? To answer this criticism, let us first note that the assertion is not in itself self-referential. In "I think, therefore I am" there is a premise and a conclusion. The assertion is not tautological, nor is it totalising: Descartes is not asserting that everything exists; he is simply asserting that the simple fact of thinking is enough to qualify me as an existing being. The self-referential character of the *Cogito* does not therefore lie in its formalism (the *Cogito* is not a tautology). The fact that the *ego* can refer to itself as a thinking being and therefore as an existing being does not seem to us, therefore, to be tainted by the formal problems of self-reference: by referring to itself, the *ego* proves, on the contrary, that it is *capable of* referring (to itself or to something else). It therefore answers *in concreto* the question of the possibility of referring. The Nietzschean criticisms recounted by Paul Ricœur in the preface to *Soi-même comme un autre* are not, in our opinion, such as to call into question the fundamental interest of the *Cogito* in the contest of our demonstration. In short," writes Ricœur, "Nietzsche's critique of language unfolds along two axes: on the one hand, it deconstructs the very idea of a truth immanent to language; on the other, it affirms that the figurative essence of language dooms it to falsehood. On *From On Truth and Lie in an Extra-Moral Sense* (1873), Nietzsche argued that language, as a metaphorical structure, could not claim any referential adequacy with reality[209]. The figurative nature of speech, which constantly refers to realities that are perceived differently depending on the

---

[209] Nietzsche, quoting the writer Jean-Paul, wrote in his *Lecture Notes on Rhetoric*: "Thus, with regard to spiritual connections, all language is a dictionary of faded metaphors".

speaker and the interlocutor, made it impossible to establish language as a stable and reliable system of designation. This idea was well summed up by a phrase used by the young Pierre Bourdieu in a programme in the early 1960s hosted by the ethnologist and philosopher Dina Dreyfus, then an inspector at the Académie in Paris: "Misunderstanding is essential, and understanding is only one particular case among all situations of misunderstanding[210]." According to Nietzsche (and to a certain extent Bourdieu), language, which is not limited to the designation of an objective reality but expresses the diversity of the content of human experience, could not provide reliable access to truth. As a "dictionary of faded metaphors", it bore the stamp of inadequacy and simulacra: it either designated too much or too little, or in any case, it designated badly. However, this Nietzschean critique did not really affect the problem of reference, which is the nodal point of our reflection on thought. For while language may be perceived as equivocal and slippery, while it refers to plural experiences and heterogeneous psychological states, it remains a mode of reference to reality — however inadequate or distorted. Engaging in a dialectic of lies cannot, therefore, abolish the question of truth: the negation of truth, insofar as it is deprivation or inversion, merely presupposes it — as Popper showed — while reaffirming the duality it implies. Thus, when Nietzsche, in an extension of his thinking on the deceptive nature of language, made the *I* into a habit or a grammatical fiction (the principle of

---

[210] Language. 1 / [Jean Fléchet, director] ; Dina Dreyfus, producer ; Pierre Bourdieu, Jean Hyppolite, Jean Laplanche [et al.], https://gallica.bnf.fr/ark:/12148/bpt6k1320692r#

causality applied to the phenomenality of the inner world: there is a cause of the *Cogito*, which would be the *ego*), he at the same time missed the power of Descartes' argument, i.e. the irreducible character of this 'something' that thinks (*res cogitans*). It was all very well for Nietzsche to say that the *ego* is multiple and protean (an assertion, moreover, that is largely counterbalanced by his later writings, notably *Ecce homo*), but the fact remains that the *ego*, at the *moment it thinks of itself as an ego*, cannot be anything other than an *ego*, than a unity that thinks "I am", "I am the unity that is". The question of the continuity and permanence of the *self* (as Nietzsche raises it in his critique of the *Cogito*) is, in our view, a separate problem, not immediately related to the fundamental and metaphysical issue of the affirmation of the *self* as unity. Yet this affirmation constitutes an indispensable condition for the very effectuation of thought, in that it guarantees the identity of the thinking subject through his noetic acts. It is therefore necessary to separate these two moments of the *self*, both essential, but not reducible to each other: the moment of the *self* that is understood as existential unity (the metaphysical moment of the *self*, which is also its natural moment, its everyday mode of being, expressed by the *Cogito*) and the moment of the *self* that is understood in a double historical projection (the *self* as the sum and synthesis of past experiences, and as a projection towards the future). These two moments constitute the two phases of affirmation of the *self*, the first of which can be conceived as a rational feeling or a rationalised feeling that leads the *ego* to see that there is "something there that thinks", the second consisting for the *ego* in attaching to this fundamental existential unity the identity that makes its *self* a particular *self*, with a history, a memory, projects in the world... In short, the two directions of the *self* intersect with the two directions of the problem of reference, the first direction targeting the *self* (who am I? something capable of thinking "who am I?", so *at the very least* something that thinks), the second direction pointing towards the world from which the *self* is now separated (the *self* in relation to others, to its ideas, to material objects, to the world in general). The only way out of the circularity of the system (created by the system itself as an autonomous structure) is to postulate more than the system, and to do so in a non-systemic way: the *Cogito* is not self-referential insofar as it does not adhere strictly to a logical position. The argument is above all ontological; it postulates more than logic and is not reduced to it. It finally turns the tables on formalism by not making the *ego* a logical deduction, but by making the feeling of thought ("I am, I exist") a proof in reverse of the existence of the *ego* (abductive reasoning).

42.

WHAT IS COMPREHENSION? — In the preceding paragraphs, we attempted to define the act of thinking, relying in particular on a differential analysis between the 'content' produced by artificial intelligence and that generated by our own thinking. It seemed to us on this occasion that some of the difficulties associated with questions relating to the act of thinking were to be found in the act of understanding, an act which, while not entirely superimposable on the act of thinking, is in some ways a manifestation of it. What is understanding, after all, if not the act of linking diverse meanings into a unitary and synthetic whole? Is understanding not the intuition of the unity of meaning in the diversity of meanings, an intuition materialised synthetically within our consciousness?

First, we should note that the interpretation of comprehension as a synthesis of the diverse into a unity of meaning is an image compatible with what we can observe on brain imaging. During moments identified by test subjects as moments of com-prehension, MRI allows us to observe patterns of synchronisation between different brain regions. In the case of language reception, for example, there is synchronisation between the brain regions involved in auditory processing (such as the auditory cortex) and the regions involved in semantic processing (such as the frontal cortex). This synchronisation can be manifested electrically by neuronal oscillations at specific frequencies, such as gamma oscillations, which are often associated with coordination between different brain regions when performing complex cognitive tasks. Similarly, when the brain identifies an error, it produces, to use an expression employed by Stanislas Dehaene, a "cerebral firework display": several areas of the brain activate simultaneously, creating a sort of bubbling or burst of neuronal activity. These synchronous activities of the brain, linked to compre-hension or, on the contrary, to the identification of an error, illustrate this gathering movement that characterises comprehension (synchronisation itself being an image of this gathering — synchronisation comes from the Latin *synchronizare*, which means to make coincide in time, to gather together in time). The process of comprehension is not, however, limited to an activity of material synchronisation of areas of the cerebral cortex; it is also and above all, at the cognitive level, the result of a linking of several meanings into a unitary and figurative entity (to comprehend is, in a sense, to "see" and "feel" the relevance of an utterance: the activity of comprehending calls upon the productive imagination). Comprehension is thus characterised by a double gathering, both temporal (synchronisation of brain areas and waves) and figurative: it is the seizure, in a temporal unit, of a unit of mental projection (a unitary synthesis made up of links between fragmented meanings). This activity of gathering together, of comprehension (which we find once again in the Latin root of the word comprehension, *comprehendere* literally meaning to take or seize together) presupposes an act of unitary determination on the part of consciousness (indeed, how can we think of the gathering together of comprehension without thinking, *at the* same time, of an act of synthesis by a unit that identifies itself as such?) This unitary determination is posited precisely in the articulation between the aesthetic (and in a sense "decentralised") phenomenon of figurative projection and its concrete (and formal) formulation. The subject who "understands" understands himself in his duality. Understanding is thus as much the result of an internal synchronisation (the figure or schema produced by our imagination, as if "in spite of ourselves", inside our consciousness) as of the retrospective observation of this synchronisation, an observation that communicates itself through formalism and that presupposes that the subject identifies himself in parallel in a unitary manner (in other words, the subject conscientizes his understanding, he brings it back to the consciousness of himself, he understands at the same time as he says to himself, confusedly or explicitly: "*I have understood*"). To understand is thus to integrate into one's being, to link an object into a system of meanings and references, by having a clear representation in the rational organisation of the forms of the productive imagination (in this sense, understanding is not an analytical moment, but a synthesis operated jointly by the imagination and the understanding[211]). This is why

---

[211] This is perhaps what inspired Kant to make this remark: "Judgement is therefore the specific mark of what is called common sense (*Mutterwitzes*) and the lack of which no teaching can make up; For, although a school can present a limited understanding with a supply of rules, and graft, as it were, foreign knowledge onto it, the pupil must himself possess the power to use these rules exactly, and there is no rule that can be prescribed to him in this respect that is capable of guaranteeing him against the abuse he may make of them when he lacks such a natural gift. " Kant adds in a footnote: "The defect of judgement is properly what we call stupidity (*Dummheit*), and this is a vice for which there is no remedy. An obtuse or narrow-minded person who lacks only the proper degree of understanding and concepts of his own is susceptible to a great deal of instruction and even erudition. But, as judgement (*secunda* Petri*) is also usually lacking in such cases, it is not uncommon to find highly educated men who frequently let this irreparable defect show in the use they make of their science." See Kant, *Critique of Pure Reason, Transcendental Analysis, On Transcendental Judgment in General*. Here Kant seems clearly to identify the problem of the mechanisation of thought, a mechanisation that can, like the obtuse head, simulate a high degree of instruction and even erudition, but which fails to formulate autonomous judgements about things. The machine obeys rules, but can it deduce rules? *Deep learning* and deep neural network models

understanding is strongly correlated with being and identity. I always understand "*for me*", the representation of the object of my understanding echoes my being, the way I represent the object of my understanding in my own network of meanings. Understanding is not, then, a mechanical moment that could be formalised by a calculable function; rather, it is a double moment of coming together: (i) the bringing together of the diverse by a unitary link which is the product of the productive imagination — this is what we have called the "aesthetic moment" of understanding (ii) the integration of this figure produced by the imagination with the *ego* which poses itself, in each act of understanding, This unity in turn

---

provide one part of the answer, although, as we have seen, these systems are not yet capable of providing a solution to the problem of reference (and therefore of the perception of the self as a unitary centre). Beware, however: what Kant calls stupidity here is the inability of a man to break out of his formal system (inability to understand, for example, the spirit of the rule, or the rule from which the rule derives). We use the term stupidity in a different sense, one that is more mobile and convulsive: stupidity as the ability to say anything, to change the level of understanding, stupidity in a sense closer to madness (or genius) than the narrow-minded stupidity to which Kant is referring here.

* The expression "secunda Petri" used by Kant refers to the Second Epistle of Peter (*Secunda Epistola Petri* in Latin), which is part of the New Testament. More specifically, the expression refers to a passage in the Second Letter of Peter (2 Peter 1:5-7), which speaks of a chain of virtues that Christians should cultivate, including 'judgement' or 'prudence' (in Greek 'phronesis', often translated as 'discernment' or 'practical intelligence').

allows for critical feedback on the figures produced by the imagination (critical feedback itself being an attempt to integrate the figure or schema coherently into a given set of beliefs and representations of the *ego*). If the first stage (that of bringing together the diverse through a unitary link in a figure or scheme) is not directly an act of our will or consciousness, the second stage of understanding is a voluntary and determined act. It involves an effort to integrate and formalise. This effort presupposes the *I* insofar as it is precisely an act of detachment from what is happening within us when we are in the process of understanding. To formalise (or take note of) understanding, consciousness must necessarily split into two (look in a mirror). It is the awareness of what happens inside me when the productive imagination submits figures to me that allows us to look critically at the proposals of the imagination.

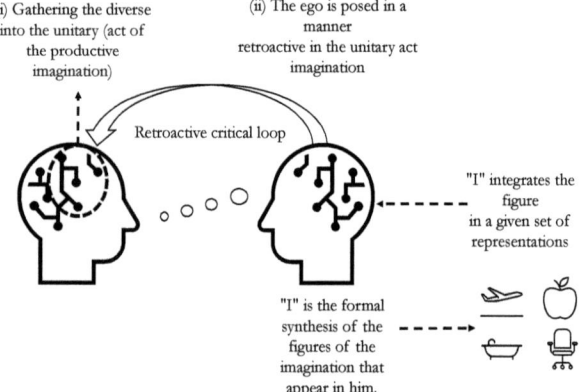

In the dialectic between imagination and critical feedback, it is always the imagination that escapes formalism and mechanisation. It is precisely through the experience of productive imagination that we exercise our capacity to change levels, a capacity that enables us to escape the constraint of the analytical coherence of a given (monistic) system. Imagination (the "madwoman of the house" as Descartes called her) has the ability to think together the true and the false, the coherent and the incoherent. It is, in a way, Gödel's devil, who, in a dream, makes us see through all the systems. In fact, we frequently observe a change of systemic level in the decisive moments of theoretical resolution in the great figures of thought: Kant's transcendental schematism, Russell's solution to the liar's paradox, Gödel's incompleteness theorems, or Einstein's theory of relativity, to name but a few examples[212]. Each time, the facts of the old system are

---

[212] To put it briefly, Kant's schematism can be presented as a solution to the controversy between idealist rationalists and empiricists, the former asserting that geometric figures (the triangle, for example) have their own existence outside the world of experience, the latter retorting that they have never seen a triangle "in general" and that, consequently, the argument for the existence of the triangle outside the experience of a particular triangle is purely speculative. Kant's transcendental schematism establishes that if there is no triangle "in general", "*a priori*" or "immutable", the mental operations that enable a triangle to be drawn are always the same, immutable and timeless: these are the "schemas". For Kant, the schema is the necessary third term that provides the link between the phenomenon and the concept. The schema can be understood as the mental image of the concept, which, when applied to reality, enables us to think about the world. The Kantian resolution moves up a level

re-read and re-analysed in the light of a new theory, which encompasses (or 'understands') the previous theory without being directly derived from it. This ability to go *beyond* a seemingly insoluble problem can be likened to what Blaise Pascal called, in *The Geometric*

---

from the controversy between rationalists and empiricists. It is derived from the problem, but was not contained in the problem (we are no longer talking about geometrical figures, but about the operations required to produce them; the system of schematism is a system of nature $n+1$ compared with the initial controversy).

Russell's resolution of the liar's paradox follows the same logic, so there's no need to dwell on it again (Russell's separation of language and metalanguage means that once again we have a problem belonging to system n resolved in a system of level $n+1$).

Nor do we return to Gödel's incompleteness theorem at length. The meaning of mathematics is metamathematical, the system finds its meaning in a metasystem, and this point is the foundation of Gödel's incompleteness theorem.

With regard to Einstein's formulation of the theory of general relativity, we undoubtedly have a resolution of the same type: gravitation is not a force, but a manifestation of the curvature of space-time, a curvature itself produced by the distribution of energy in the form of mass, which differs according to the observer's frame of reference. The gravitational force described in the system of level n is in fact the manifestation of a phenomenon belonging to a system $n+1$ which gives rise to and explains this force. The solution was not identifiable in the n system, whose representations did not include the possibility of the curvature of space (space-time) or the observer's reference frame.

Mind and the Spirit of Finesse[213], "l'esprit de finesse" (the spirit of finesse), which he contrasted with "l'esprit de géométrie" (the spirit of geometry). For Pascal, the spirit of geometry refers to a rational, logical and methodical approach to reality: it is the ability to think analytically, to use the rules of logic, to make deductions based on clear principles and formal demonstrations (here we find the distinction that Kant made in The *Critique of Pure Reason*[214]). For Pascal, on the other hand, the spirit of finesse is based on an intuitive and subtle understanding of nuances, contexts, and specific situations. It is a way of thinking that takes account of emotional aspects and subjective perceptions of reality. In a pamphlet by Pascal entitled *On the Geometrical Mind and the Art of Persuasion* (published in 1658 as the preface to an essay on the

---

[213] Blaise Pascal, *The Geometric Mind and the Spirit of Finesse*: "And so it is rare for geometers to be fine, and for the fine to be geometers, because geometers want to treat these fine things geometrically, and make themselves ridiculous, wanting to begin with definitions and then with principles, which is not the way to act in this kind of reasoning. It is not that the mind does not do this, but it does it tacitly, naturally and artlessly, because expression passes all men by, and feeling belongs to few. Fine minds, on the other hand, having become accustomed to judging from a single point of view, are so astonished when they are presented with propositions they understand nothing about, and in which, in order to enter, they have to go through definitions and principles so sterile that they are not accustomed to seeing in detail, that they are repelled and disgusted by them. But false minds are never fine or geometric.

[214] Kant, *Critique of Pure Reason*, *On Transcendental Judgement in General,* see previous note.

elements of geometry, intended for the Petites écoles de Port-Royal), Blaise Pascal writes on this subject: "those who have the spirit of discernment know how much difference there is between two similar words, according to the places and circumstances that accompany them. Can we really believe that two people who have read and learnt the same book by heart know it equally well, if one understands it in such a way that he knows all the principles, the force of the consequences, the answers to the objections that can be made, and the whole economy of the work; whereas in the other they are dead words, and seeds which, although similar to those that have produced such fertile trees, have remained dry and fruitless in the sterile mind that received them in vain? Here we find a number of aspects of the analysis we have been conducting on the nature of the act of thinking, and in particular on the difference between the intuitive and imaginative moments (the spirit of finesse) and the mechanical moments (the spirit of geometry) of thought. It's also clear that, for Pascal, understanding is above all the ability to put a word, a sentence or an idea into its proper context. To understand is to integrate into one's being, to find within oneself the echo of an idea that becomes meaningful (the "trees so fertile" as opposed to the "dead" and "dry" words in Pascal's quotation). It is striking, moreover, that Pascal defines the spirit of finesse as the ability to "judge from a single view" (an idea that comes close to the idea of aesthetic connection that we are defending) and the spirit of geometry as the ability to judge according to principles ("let all things be explained to them by definition and principle") and thus to remain at the level n of the system in which the mind of the geometer dwells and rests. To understand is to grasp the deeper meaning of an idea, a word or a phrase, not to remain on the surface of things (not to remain in the unitary dimension of a given system). A sense of humour, as a disposition to understand the discrepancy, the subtext or the irony, testifies to this spirit of finesse, capable of contextualising a statement, of grasping its profound intention (the intention behind the form of expression). To have a 'sense of humour' is to have the ability to look at things outside the system in which they occur: to perceive the ridiculousness of a serious situation, to sense a double entendre, in short to change the level of understanding — don't we say 'to have a second degree'? Humour can also stem from our tendency to magnify, to caricature a form or a general idea, it is derived in this from that ability to "judge from a single view" that Pascal evokes, an ability that also stems from the use of this second degree (attempt to rise above the form or idea to derive something else from it).

Finally, this idea of understanding as "grasping the deeper meaning" of a sentence or idea is also found in the work of Noam Chomsky. Chomsky's notion of "deep understanding" refers to an ability to grasp the implicit meaning of language, beyond its superficial structure or grammatical rules. For Chomsky, comprehension implies the ability to interpret language in context, to recognise nuances, subtleties and communicative intentions that are not always explicit in the text itself. The same sentence can therefore have a different (or even radically different) meaning depending on the context (language habits, cultures, etc.) in which it is uttered. Thus, there is the text and the subtext (difference in level), just as there is a surface grammatical structure and a deep grammatical structure[215]. For Chomsky, understanding meaning is linked to our ability to change levels (to 'test' different levels at the same time, we could probably say without betraying Chomsky's thinking[216]), i.e. to move from a system of level *n* to a system of level *n+1*. In fact, Chomsky often argued that traditional approaches to artificial intelligence, based on statistical methods and

---

[215] In *Language and Mind* (1968), Noam Chomsky gives the following definition of his theory of deep and superficial structures: "we can thus distinguish the *surface structure* of the sentence, the organization into categories and phrases that is directly associated with the physical signal, from the underlying *deep structure*, also a system of categories and phrases, but with a more abstract character. Thus, the surface structure of the sentence 'A wise man is honest' might analyze it into the subject 'a wise man' and the predicate 'is honest.' The deep structure, however, will be rather different. It will, in particular, extract from the complex idea that constitutes the subject of the surface structure an underlying proposition with the subject 'man' and the predicate 'be wise'. In fact, the deep structure, in the traditional view, is a system of two propositions, neither of which is asserted, but which interrelate in such a way as to express the meaning of the sentence 'A wise man is honest.'", *Language and Mind*, Third Edition, Cambridge, p. 15

[216] Noam Chomsky puts forward an idea of this kind when he writes, in *Language and Mind* (1968): "The theory holds that the underlying deep structure, with its abstract organization of linguistic forms, is "present to the mind," as the signal, with its surface structure, is produced or perceived by the bodily organs. And the transformational operations relating deep and surface structure are actual mental operations, performed by the mind when a sentence is produced or understood.", p. 16

massive information processing models, were limited in their ability to grasp the true complexity of human language. In particular, he criticised approaches that relied solely on learning from large datasets, rightly arguing that while such methods could produce systems that performed well in pattern recognition, they lacked a real (deep) understanding of language[217]. In fact, we need to be wary of monolithic approaches to language and understand that language is first and foremost at the service of the structures of life, that it is itself, moreover, "organic", evolving and, consequently, non-reducible to its concrete productions (Chomsky places great emphasis on the "generative" aspect of language and notes the proximity of the word "generate" to the word "intelligence", *ingenio* apparently having the same Latin root as various words meaning "to engender" or "to generate[218]").

43.

THOUGHT AND REFLECTION: THOUGHT AND ITS MIRROR — While language is, in certain respects, an organic emanation of the rational sentient being, we must beware, as behaviourists and structuralists have attempted, of analysing it in reverse in order to deduce

---

[217] As early as the 1960s, he also frequently criticised traditional approaches to linguistic analysis, such as structuralism and behaviourism, which focus mainly on the surface of language and its observable aspects. It should be noted, however, that Chomsky also expressed a certain interest in recent developments in the field of artificial intelligence, particularly advances in deep neural networks and natural language processing.
[218] Ibid., p. 8

a definition of the human being, a definition that would inevitably obfuscate human creativity, which is also a characteristic of the creativity of organic life. It is true that man is as much the product of his language as his creator. But we must not forget that he is first and foremost its creator before being its product. Man does not emerge *ex nihilo* from the structures of language; he generates them. If the structure of language is logical in nature (think, once again, of the Greek root of the word language: *logos*), it is also a constraint that determines man in return. Yet this logical necessity is not imposed on man as an external limit: it is immanent in his own act of thinking. It is within man himself that he grasps and formulates the rational constraint, and it is precisely in this recognition of necessity that the possibility of truly autonomous thought opens up. Far from being a hindrance, logical constraint is the very condition by which reason frees itself from arbitrariness and achieves autonomy. If thought, like the understanding of language, is linked to our *ego* and our sensitive nature (it originates there), it is nevertheless abusive to assert, as Nietzsche sometimes did, that it must be reduced to them. Philosophers do not write with their blood[219], any more than mathematicians calculate with their guts. The fact that we have a natural inclination to reason according to our own interests (an inclination encouraged by our sensitive nature, which makes thinking possible) does not necessarily mean that all reasoning is marked by the

---

[219] "Of all that is written, I love only that which is written in one's own blood. Write in blood and you will learn that blood is spirit", Friedrich Nietzsche, *Thus Spoke Zarathustra*, Read and Write

fatal stamp of particular interest (interest in the sense of "what is favourable to us" and not in the sense of the commitment of our being to a word or statement, which is very different, as we explained earlier). If the *ego* is what, through sensibility, sets thought in motion, it is neither the horizon nor the outcome. Thought, on the other hand, as it "passes over the *ego*", must be able to defeat it (i.e. detach itself from it). Otherwise, it becomes a tiresome logorrhea at the service of the *ego*'s hegemonic ambitions (the *ego* seeking growth, confirmation...). Thought, made possible by sensitivity and by the *ego*'s detachment from language, is also, paradoxically, an act of the will against the sensitive instinct. It is *reflection* in the true sense of the word, that is to say, the splitting of the *ego, the* turning in on oneself and the ability to look beyond the mirror. It is this form of reflexivity that enables thought not to be a prisoner of biology.

In his *Conversations with Wang*, Gödel had identified the fundamental problem of the reflexivity of thought, a problem that he felt manifested itself most acutely in the "intentional paradoxes[220]", which arise from the

---

[220] An intentional paradox is a paradox that arises from an ambiguity or contradiction related to the meaning (or intention) of a concept. It arises when conceptual definitions or conditions conflict, without necessarily implying a formal contradiction in their extension.

Examples:
- The liar's paradox: "This sentence is false". If it is true, then it is false. If it is false, then it is true. The contradiction arises from the fact that the sentence attempts to refer to itself in a problematic way.

application of concepts to themselves, in contrast to the "extensional paradoxes[221]" that concern sets. For Gödel, intentional paradoxes could not be resolved within the framework of set theory. At first glance, however, these two types of paradox seem symmetrical.

- The Grelling-Nelson paradox ("autological vs heterological"): a word is autological if it has the property it describes (e.g. "short" is a short word). A word is heterological if it does not have the property it describes (e.g. "long" is a short word). Question: Is "heterological" hetero-logical? This paradox leads to a contradiction similar to that of the liar's paradox. This type of paradox is linked to problems of reflexivity, self-reference and fuzzy definition.

[221] An extensional paradox concerns contradictions arising from membership of a set or from the definition of objects in terms of their extensions (i.e. the set of objects to which a concept applies). It arises when membership rules lead to antinomies in set theory.
Examples:
- Russell's paradox: let R be the set of all sets that do not contain themselves. Question: does R belong to itself? If it belongs to itself, then by definition it should not belong to itself. If it does not belong to itself, then it should belong to itself. A logical contradiction.
- Berry's paradox: "The smallest natural integer that cannot be described in less than 12 words." This definition itself is a description in less than 12 words. The contradiction arises from the idea of a classification by extension that ends up self-cancelling. These paradoxes show that certain naive definitions of sets or descriptions lead to internal contradictions.

Consider, says Gödel, the set of sets that do not belong to themselves. If this set belongs to itself, it is one of its elements and, consequently, a set that does not belong to itself. If it does not belong to itself, it is one of those sets which do not belong to themselves and, consequently, one of its own elements: it then belongs to itself. So, there is a contradiction. Now let us consider the concept of concepts that do not apply to themselves. If this concept applies to itself (as the concept "difficult" applies to itself: it is difficult to grasp the concept of what "being difficult" is), then it is a concept that does not apply to itself. And, conversely, if it doesn't apply to itself, it falls under the concept of concepts that don't apply to themselves, and it applies to itself. Once again, there is a contradiction. The reasoning that brings about the contradiction is analogous in both cases. However, for Gödel, there is a difference between these two paradoxes[222].

Gödel describes sets as "quasi-spatial" or "quasi-physical". They reflect the structure and properties of material objects. In relation to their elements, they occupy a position similar to that of an object in its entirety in relation to its parts, or to that of the thing itself in relation to its various appearances. Thus, a whole cannot belong to itself: it is made up of elements that are external to it, considered as its constituents. Extensional paradoxes can be resolved by dividing mathematical sets into a hierarchy (Russell's hierarchy of types or Zermelo's cumulative hierarchy, for

---

[222] We reproduce here the main stages of Pierre Cassou-Noguès's reasoning in *Les démons de Gödel,* French edition, p. 210

example). The starting point is a set of initial objects, known as "individuals". At the first level, we construct sets from these individuals, then, at the next level, sets whose elements come from the previous level, and so on. By defining precise rules for the formation of sets, we ensure that, in this hierarchy, each set is made up of elements from previous levels. No set can therefore include itself. In such a framework, it is no longer possible to form a set of all the sets that do not belong to themselves. It is only possible to form the set of all sets of a given level i that do not belong to themselves (note the importance of defining a given level in resolving the paradox, as undefined totality statements always pose problems because of their tautological structure). We can consider that extensional paradoxes are resolved in this way.

The difficulty with intentional paradoxes lies in the fact that a concept *can apply to itself*. Take, for example, the concept of "difficult", the concept of "vague" ("to be vague" is a vague concept), or the concept of a concept which is itself a concept. The extension of a concept, i.e. the collection of objects to which it applies, can be called a "class". So, if a concept applies to itself, the class associated with it belongs to itself. Intentional paradoxes cannot be solved in the same way as intentional paradoxes (by successive sequencing of sets). These paradoxes give rise to classes that are not sets and have no place in set theory (the notion of class cannot be defined as a set of fixed elements; it does not overlap with the notion of set, since it itself already contains elements of reflexivity). This reflexive character is above all a characteristic of concepts.

On the one hand, we have a theory of sets, but on the other, we lack a (formalised) theory of concepts. Unlike sets, whose hierarchical structure makes it possible to resolve extensional paradoxes, concepts, which can be applied to themselves, cannot be resolved in this way. It is therefore impossible to resolve intentional paradoxes using the same hierarchies. And yet, according to Gödel, it was on such a theory of concepts that the future development of mathematics and the elaboration of a new theoretical construction not subject to the incompleteness theorems would depend. In other words, the formalism of *n-level* systems would have to be overcome by a language that would not be assigned to any particular system. For Gödel, the reflexivity of certain concepts refers to the problem of the reflexivity of the human mind[223]. Unlike a machine, the mind can recognise the consistency of the system in which it operates, in other words "understand its own mechanism". In a letter to Paul Tillich[224], Gödel

---

[223] Kurt Gödel, *Conversation with Wang*, p. 275, quoted by Pierre Cassou-Noguès in *Les démons de Gödel*, p. 211

[224] Paul Tillich (1886-1965) was a German theologian and philosopher, naturalised American, known for his work at the intersection of Christian theology and existential philosophy. Tillich is considered to be one of the greatest theologians of the twentieth century and is often associated with the trend of "correlation theology", in which he attempts to bring Christian faith into dialogue with the existential questions of modern man. Paul Tillich was a natural interlocutor for Kurt Gödel because of their shared interest in the infinite, the absolute and the metaphysical foundations of reality. Gödel, who was interested in the proof of the existence of God and the survival of the soul,

asserts that there is such a thing as the reflexivity of the mind, or more precisely of reason, which is capable of authentic self-knowledge. He wondered whether the reflexivity of language concepts might reflect this fundamental reflexivity of the human mind, the very reflexivity that conditions non-systemic thought (natural thought[225]). In this way, the reflexivity of concepts could express the mind's capacity to turn in on itself. For Gödel, the sciences of his time neglected this reflexivity of the mind because of their materialistic presuppositions. In his view, the future mathematical revolution was to be a re-conquest of the mind by itself: an 'essential' self-knowledge, going beyond the superficial know-ledge illustrated by Turing's idea of the machine.

Following on from Gödel's remarks, we assert that thought, as a structure of reflexivity and self-reflexivity (spiral structure), cannot be authentically reproduced by a formalised system. As we have said, the question of a machine's ability to think authentically cannot be reduced to the problem of the calculability of thought. On the contrary, it extends to the question of the possibility of a machine accessing a conscious state through mechanisms that would escape its creators at

---

found in Tillich an intellectual partner capable of understanding the depth of his questions.

[225] Language is to be understood here as an act of creativity and not as an organised corpus governed by rules (the logic of artificial intelligence, which simulates and reproduces language, but which is not an autonomous act of language production - artificial intelligence models have been trained in language, but language has not emerged in machines as it has in humans).

least in part (non-formal mechanisms, although the term 'mechanism' is probably a misnomer in this case). Humans, by virtue of their sensitive incarnation, by virtue of their ability not to feel committed by a statement or by virtue of what we have called their 'stupidity', cannot be reduced to the formalised systems that have tried to imitate them (in order to surpass them). If the machine were one day to think authentically, it would not be because human thought had been completely reduced to an entirely calculable formal structure, but because the machine would have acquired a cognitive autonomy that is irreducible to the simple execution of algorithms, which would have enabled it (i) to access the concreteness of its statements through the development of sensitive faculties (ii) to make a critical review of itself and of the forms that would manifest themselves in it without it producing them 'voluntarily' or actively (iii) not to be bound by any defined formal level (which is why, we have already pointed out, access to authentic thought would therefore be at the sacrifice of the infallibility of the machine[226]).

44.

LEVELS OF UNDERSTANDING AND LEVELS OF MEANING — The position which consists in asserting that physics, in its ineluctable progression, will end up annexing all the sciences (physical sciences including chemistry, life sciences, social sciences, formal sciences and applied sciences), if it seems at least optimistic in

---

[226] Its fallibility could certainly always be limited by an iteration of formal critical feedback.

substance, neglects a fundamental aspect of the scientific approach in general and of the origin of the division of the sciences. Historically, it is quite true to say that science has been characterised by a tendency towards the unification of doctrines: the unification of mechanics, astronomy and optics in Newton's theory of gravitation, the unification of electricity and magnetism by Maxwell, the unification of biology and chemistry by the discovery of the cell as the fundamental unit of life, etc. These successive unifications may have led us to believe that the sciences were destined to be united under a single banner. However, this view overlooks the fact that changes of scale are not necessarily reduced to changes of degree in the phenomena observed. The emergence of quantum mechanics in the 1920s was a singular demonstration of this: Not only did it then become apparent that the rules of classical physics did not apply at the atomic scale, but it was also discovered that all the scientific principles that had been thought immutable were being called into question (it is interesting to note in this respect that physicalist theories were more popular with philosophers of science and neuroscientists than with quantum physicists — even though some of the great names in physics did indeed declare themselves to be more or less physicalists). Moreover, we must not overlook the fact that the transition from one theoretical field to another can pose difficulties that may well be inherent in the structure of reality as well as in the structure of knowledge. The life sciences are often viewed from the perspective of reductionism, according to which biological processes can be reduced in their entirety to physical laws that can be modelled. However, this approach has some fundamental limitations, which have already been highlighted, particularly in relation to the question of the emergence of consciousness, which remains irreducible to a strictly physico-chemical explanation. Beyond this difficulty, reductionism struggles to account for large-scale biological phenomena, where the organisation and dynamics of living systems exceed the sum of the individual behaviours of their constituents. Biological networks, whether metabolic, genetic or neuronal, cannot be understood as simple aggregates of local mechanisms, but rather as emergent properties resulting from complex interactions and dynamic structuring that cannot be reduced to the laws that govern their individual elements. The living organism cannot be thought of as a simple superposition of physico-chemical processes but must be considered as a reality whose internal cohesion presupposes its own logic, which goes beyond the mere addition of the material determinations of which it is composed. Indeed, we must not overlook the fact that within the organism there are several organisational units, themselves synthesised in an organised living unit (insect, animal, human...). Each organisational unit has its own way of functioning and logic and interacts with other organisational units both vertically and horizontally. This network of complex and evolving interactions creates, at each level of its functioning, a unity and a structure of its own that cannot be entirely reduced to the local behaviour of its components: "*when it comes to biological norms, it is always the individual that must be referred to*[227]". The reductionist might well object that he is not neglecting these effects of scale, and that the aim of physical science is precisely to model all these scales and to understand how they fit together in a unified theory. However, we contest the fact that such a theory, if it came into being, could be described as a 'physical theory', not just for the sake of convenience, but above all because the phenomena described would not be physical in nature but organic, i.e. specific to the biological organisations that physicalist reductionism seeks to deny by reducing them to mere physical phenomena. By making biology a sub-field of physical science, physicists would certainly be following the historical trend towards the unification of the sciences, but here again, we must be wary of extending the curves too far. The long-term trend towards the unification of knowledge must not be transformed into a dogma of unitary science. In fact, it may well be that this trend will end up stabilising in related fields that are not reducible to each other (we even believe that this is an intrinsic necessity of knowledge, our hypothesis being that the separation of knowledge into several distinct fields is not artificial — note, moreover, that most major unifications have generally taken place within the same branch, rarely between distant branches). This illusion of the reducible nature of one branch of knowledge to another is at the root of many misunderstandings (we have listed some of them). The multidisciplinary nature of science is not necessarily due to an incomplete state of the sciences (or to a form of arbitrariness in the division of knowledge) but is

---

[227] George Canguilhem, *Le Normal et le pathologique (The Normal and the Pathological)*, 1943 and 1966, Paris, PUF, p.118

rather linked to the fundamentally exogenous (non-reducible) nature of certain disciplines, a nature that makes authentic inter-disciplinarity of knowledge possible.

Overcoming the subjective moment

> Theories are nets: only those who cast will catch fish[228].

Novalis

The shape of theories

45.

WHAT IS A THEORY? THEIR INTUITIVE ORIGINS — Just as we have identified several branches of knowledge that are irreducible to each other, there are also theories within the same branch of knowledge, or between heterogeneous branches, that are apparently incompatible but which nevertheless possess great power in explaining the phenomena they describe. The apparent incompatibility of these theories has also been, throughout history, a source of progress and important discoveries, which were sometimes the result of unifying these theories at a higher level than the initial theories. Just as we seemed to be making progress towards greater clarity, and as our understanding of the world seemed to be growing, voices were raised which, astonished by the non-linear nature of scientific progress, questioned the very idea of progress, pointing in particular to the supposedly perishable nature of scientific theories. The 1960s and 1970s saw the development of a whole series of arguments against the

---

[228] Novalis, quoted by Karl Popper in the preface to *The Logic of Scientific Discovery*.

objectivity of science, based in particular on the relative nature of scientific paradigms. These were first systematised by Thomas Kuhn in *The Structure of Scientific Revolutions* (1962), then radicalised by Michel Foucault in *The Order of Things* (1966) before finding their most extreme (and, it has to be said, most delirious) expression in Paul Feyerabend's *Against Method* (1975). While these criticisms were generally well received, in our opinion they invariably failed to address one of the fundamental conditions of knowledge. By revealing the lacunar and incomplete nature of theoretical constructions, they thought they were shaking the very foundations of knowledge, without seeing that incompleteness was not its negation, but one of its essential conditions. It is not the exhaustiveness of a system that guarantees the possibility of knowledge, but its capacity to fit into a partial and determined structure, at once open and limited. Far from abolishing knowledge, the impossibility of unified knowledge regulates its movement and preserves its dynamics, ensuring its intelligibility while marking the boundaries beyond which it ceases to be operative. No theory can be totally closed in on itself without losing its capacity to generate meaning and to apply to new objects. The incompleteness of theories is not a simple contingency, but a structural consequence of knowledge: every model unfolds locally, according to a given language and formalisation, and can never coincide with an absolute totality without becoming either inconsistent or tautological (if only because of the non-reducibility of the emergent properties of given systems to their conditions of emergence at level $n\text{-}1$, as we discussed in § 40 — *What does it mean to think*?) However, this incompleteness does not imply radical relativism, for although each theory remains partial, it is based on internal coherences and verifiable predictions that ensure the possibility of objective knowledge. All knowledge is based on a structure that sets both the field of validity and its limits. This requirement for delimitation does not only concern formalised theoretical constructs, but derives from intuition itself, which only ever gives access to a localised form and a determined articulation of reality (see *The aesthetic moment of knowledge*). Indeed, although intuition gives immediate access to reality, it never produces a totalising image, because every image presupposes a form that makes it local and delimited. In this way, knowledge progresses in a movement of partial elucidation, always perfectible but never complete. The change of scale or perspective is therefore consubstantial with knowledge and its internal dynamic: incompleteness is not what limits knowledge, it is what underpins it. It is the manifestation of our relationship with the world, of our sensitive and intuitive apprehension of things. Theories, as intuitive formalisations or schematisations of things (which are also already formalised and schematised on the basis of their material foundation), also bear witness to this relationship of signifiance to the world, a relationship which, as we have shown, can never be entirely formalised.

By once again pointing out the intuitive (aesthetic) origin of theories, we are not suggesting that the fallibility (and evolving nature) of theories can be attributed to the theorist's sensitivity (his or her sensitive embodiment), but rather that no theory is possible without this duality between intuition and reality. In other words, the structure of the world makes it impossible to realise an ideal unitary theory: the theory being an intuitive vision (which proceeds from an activity of synthesis of the sensible), it is as such necessarily incomplete, subsumable under another theory. However, incompleteness should not be confused with inaccuracy. A theory that is incomplete 'by nature' can describe the phenomena it seeks to explain with remarkable, even locally infallible, precision. Incompleteness does not necessarily imply relativism or fallibility. In the same way that it would be excessive to consider that our relationship with objects (or forms) is the result of an arbitrariness decreed by the subject, as we tried to show earlier (the arbitrariness being in some way made impossible by the cutter of effectivity, i.e. by the impact of reality on our sensibility in general and on our survival in particular), it would be just as abusive, it seems to us, to assert that theories are ultimately nothing more than simple contingent models, uncorrelated with the profound reality of things. If, on this point, Thomas Kuhn's positions are to be distinguished quite clearly from those of Foucault and Feyerabend — insofar as Thomas Kuhn, unlike his successors, never completely crosses the line of relativism, despite the ambiguities in the last chapter of *The Structure of Scientific Revolutions*, Despite the ambiguities in the last chapter of The Structure of Scientific Revolutions — ambiguities which, despite Kuhn's own denials, are not removed, but rather accentuated in the 1969 afterword to the book — the fact remains that Kuhn's work inaugurated what was to become the attitude of the intellectuals of the 1960s and 1970s towards the notion of progress in science.

While it is true that, after the Second World War, (continental) European philosophy was already well on the way to anti-rationalism and anti-subjectivism, Kuhn's work (as well as, in some respects, the earlier work of Gaston Bachelard[229]) provided the thinkers of the 1960s and 1970s with seemingly respectable arguments against the objectivity of the sciences (objectivity which we defend elsewhere, we shall have occasion to return to it).

In France, George Canguilhem, in the field of biology and medicine, would be another inspirer — no doubt unwillingly — of post-war anti-rationalism. In the famous reprint (1966) of his doctoral thesis in medicine entitled *The Normal and the Pathological* (first published in 1943), George Canguilhem wrote this famous sentence, abundantly quoted by his heirs, which would inspire Michel Foucault in particular (Foucault had been George Canguilhem's student at the Sorbonne[230]), but also the entire structuralist generation of the late 1960s who saw anti-normativity as the new intellectual *Eldorado*: "When it comes to biological norms, it is always the individual who must be referred to[231]. This reference to the individual was often interpreted by

---

[229] See Gaston Bachelard, *La formation de l'esprit scientifique*, 1938 (*The Formation of the Scientific Mind*)

[230] George Canguilhem was even the rapporteur for Michel Foucault's "main thesis" at the Sorbonne, entitled *Folie et déraison: histoire de la folie à l'âge classique (Madness and unreason: a history of madness in the classical age)*. Michel Foucault affectionately referred to George Canguilhem as "my old master".

[231] George Canguilhem, *Le Normal et le pathologique*, 1943 and 1966, Paris, PUF, p.118

Canguilhem's contemporaries as a challenge to the criteria of biological normativity (criteria for measuring the normal or pathological state) in favour of a form of pragmatic relativism. However, it would be a serious departure from Canguilhem's thinking to consider it as a way of thinking about the absence of norms or subjective relativism. If we look at the context of the quotation, we see that its object is not anti-normativity or the relativism of norms. Canguilhem's full quotation was in fact as follows: "when it comes to biological norms, it is always the individual who must be referred to, because such an individual may find himself, as Goldstein says[232], 'equal to the duties that result from his own environment'". There is no anti-normative intention here in Canguilhem. On the contrary, Canguilhem asserts that the norm lies in the perception of the individual's relationship *with his environment*. In other words, he is simply bringing the relationship of adequacy back to the heart of the relationship between the subject and his environment (in a sense, Canguilhem is reconnecting the norm with effectiveness). Canguilhem also reminds us that medicine, as an experimental science, must always start from its subject of study: a living organism that maintains 'adaptive' relationships with its environment. In other words, says Canguilhem, medicine must not seek to establish a profile of the 'typical' individual or patient. The individual must always be considered in terms of what makes him or her specific (starting with his or her relationship with his or her environment) and not just as an 'ideal' individual. In short, Canguilhem reminds

---

[232] Kurt Goldstein, German neurologist and psychiatrist who was one of the pioneers of modern neurobiology.

us that science, in order to be effective, must always start from the facts (and therefore refer to the individual) in order to establish norms, and not — as is too often the case — start from norms in order to seek out the facts that correspond to them. This is the reason why Canguilhem will very early and quite clearly detach himself from Foucault's thinking. In *Mort de l'homme ou épuisement du Cogito*[233]*?* he notes, for example, "There is no philosophy today less normative than Foucault's, more alien to the distinction between the normal and the pathological[234]" before adding a little further on, "Since this is theoretical knowledge, is it possible to think of it in the specificity of its concept without reference to some norm[235]?". Now, if anti-normative relativism is not accurate from the point of view of biology, as Canguilhem maintains, it is not rigorous from the point of view of scientific paradigms either. Science does not evolve through successive and contingent paradigm shifts. It is always in close relationship with reality (as, in a sense, is the individual with his environment), and this for two reasons: firstly, because of the degree of effectiveness that scientific theory contains (the fact that it falls within the verifiable-refutable pair, as Karl Popper would say, and above all the fact that it finds in experiments and facts verifications that increase its value and its power to

---

[233] Georges Canguilhem, "Mort de l'homme ou épuisement du cogito?", Critique, July 1967, pp. 599-618 (*The Death of Man or the Exhaustion of the Cogito?*)

[234] Michel Foucault, *Les mots et les choses* (*The Order of Things*) in *Regards critiques*, 1966-1968 *(the collection in which Canguilhem's article is reproduced)*, p. 266 of the French Edition.

[235] Ibid., p. 267

explain phenomena), but also because of its formal coherence, both logical and, in the case of modern physics, cosmological.

Once again, we need to remember the fundamental difference between incompleteness and falsity: Newton's physics is incomplete, but that does not mean that it is (locally) false, in the same way that quantum mechanics and general relativity are incomplete theories whose fortune will probably be to be subsumed under a new unitary theory with greater explanatory power. The discovery of this new theory, if it ever comes, will not prevent the old theories from remaining valid in their hypothesised configurations (Newton's three laws of motion are still used in the context of satellite launches). The fact, moreover, that theoretical models can be correctly integrated within different theoretical *corpuses*, or even transcribed from one theoretical *corpus* to another, is a clear indication of the idea that these *corpuses* are not purely contingent (two adequate theoretical *corpuses*, applying to the description of the same phenomena, must be able to find between them a form of "transcription key" that confirms their validity within their respective theoretical *corpuses*). "Many different ideas can describe the same physical reality," wrote Richard Feynman in his Nobel Lecture, " Thus, classical electrodynamics can be described by a field view, or an action at a distance view, etc.[236]" The theoretical *corpus* derived from the work of Newton, Einstein and the founders

---

[236] Op. Cit., December 11, 1965, See : https://www.nobelprize.org/prizes/physics/1965/feynman/lecture/

of quantum mechanics is fundamentally different from that of the alchemists and astrologers, whose speculations are based on a conceptual elaboration devoid of any scientific foundation. The philosopher's stone cannot transmute metals into gold or confer an elixir of immortality, just as the movements of the stars do nothing to determine the course of our existence — except insofar as we lend them an influence that only our belief makes operative. There is therefore no possibility of integrating these inadequate theories into a broader *body of* theory that would suddenly make them correct. Theories may be sensitive, aesthetic or intuitive in origin, but they are nonetheless subject to the tests of experience and criticism. A theory that is contradicted by experience is said to be invalidated (one or more of its local conclusions are imprecise or false). It should be noted, however, that a theory can be "partially invalidated" (in which case it has a higher degree of truth than the "totally invalidated" theory, i.e. greater explanatory power for the phenomena) or "locally valid" (the theory is valid in one application, but fails to fit into a more global application, giving rise to paradoxes or contradictions that can be resolved either by internal corrections to the theory or by integration into a higher-level theory). In assessing theories, as in everything else, it is important to avoid Manichaeism. A theory cannot simply be true or false in the absolute, but must be understood as a partial description of an area of reality that is always perfectible. Like a garment that envelops an identifiable body, a theory is a formal projection onto a set of phenomena that it seeks to organise. But, like a garment, it can be too loose, too tight, ill-fitting, worn out or patched. But an ill-fitting garment need not necessarily be discarded: it can be repaired, adjusted or transformed, and sometimes its very imperfection reveals the limits of our own evaluation criteria. So, a theory is not always refuted outright; it can be amended, reinterpreted or used as a basis for new developments[237]. Clothes, like Novalis's net, may be too wide or too narrow, but this does not mean that they are devoid of *value* (of descriptive power). Sometimes, however, the net catches nothing or catches in a totally un-differentiated way (which is what happens most often): in that case, we have to change the net. While we are introducing here the notion of the value of a theory (or the value of the net), we must not be mistaken: we are not thinking of making truth a value like any other (see § 37 — *Is truth a value?*). If truth does not, in our view, belong to the field of values[238] (or of 'what *has* value'), this is not the case with theories which, since by definition (by logical limitation) can only claim to have local validity, must generally be measured according to their 'value', i.e. according to the extent of their validity, and not

---

[237] It brings to mind the famous phrase from the O.J. Simpson trial: "if it doesn't fit, you must acquit", if the glove doesn't fit O. J. Simpson, then he is not the murderer. Science, however, operates differently from the judicial system, in which doubt must benefit the accused. In the theory-building process of science, any theory that is locally inadequate is not necessarily globally wrong (and O.J. Simpson was probably guilty of the murder of which he was accused!)

[238] If we admit the existence and coherence of the world, we necessarily need a criterion of coherence, which cannot be relative to the shifting field of values, since values are precisely the ideas that must be measured, calibrated against the truth.

according to their veracity, i.e. according to the couple true-false. In fact, by abusively placing theories in the radical alternative of true and false, and by not resituating them in the problematic of the extent of their validity (their locality), we are opening the breach to scientific relativism. Like the clothes on a mannequin, theories are more or less adapted, more or less 'fit' to the shape of the mannequin. Their respective value is measured more by the extent of their explanatory power than by their truth or falsity: it is by applying this evaluation criterion (extent of explanatory power) rather than making theories part of a dialectic of truth and falsity — which is only valid for particular conclusions of the theory and not for the theory as a whole — that we avoid the danger of seeing theories as mere "visions of the world" (visions which would become contingent and relative, it goes without saying). Although the metaphor of the mannequin helps us to understand the projective and aesthetic (sensitive) nature of any theory, it should not mislead us: although the garment is the symbol of the theory, the mannequin is not entirely the embodiment of an immutable reality that needs to be dressed appropriately.

Therein lies the difficulty of our relationship with reality: the mannequin (the real) is also a co-construction of our sensibility and the material support of the world, and is therefore itself a subjective representation (linked, however, to a substratum, and therefore to an objective support — to think of the phenomenon without a physical substratum would, in our view, be logically incoherent). As a subjective representation, the mannequin belongs to a network of linked representations (signifiers). As representations evolve, our vision of things (phenomena) may change at the same time. Paradigm shifts are the epitome of these tipping points: through a reversal of representations (an aesthetic, non-analytical, non-formalisable reversal) we suddenly realise that our models were inadequate, not so much because they didn't dress the mannequin properly, but because the mannequin was part of a larger whole (a larger mannequin, like a nesting doll) that our representations couldn't synthesise[239]. Every theory is a logical-mathematical transcription of a metaphorical intuition: the metaphor is the dummy (a global intuition of reality) and the garment is the communication of this metaphor through language and mathematical symbols (which are, as it were, the threads and needles that enable the theorist to embroider the theory, i.e. to give it a communicable and verifiable character[240]). It is the communication of the theory in an objective language that can be understood by everyone that allows it to enter the field of verifiability (and therefore falsifiability, to use Karl Popper's term). A scientific theory must be formalisable, explainable in clear

---

[239] If we try to stick to the distinction made by Thomas Kuhn in *The Structure of Scientific Revolutions*, we could say that the theorists who seek to dress the dummy are the theorists of "normal science" (analytical and mechanical development of the paradigm), while the theorists of scientific revolutions, those who modify paradigms, are those who seek other dummies.

[240] Here we take up Brouwer's separation between the two moments of mathematics: the moment of intuition and the moment of mathematical communication, which is the moment of formalisation and communicability. See also Karl Popper's analysis in *Objective Knowledge*, p. 215.

language and refutable: this is what distinguishes it from a hoax or an occult idea. However, the fact that a theory is locally falsifiable does not necessarily disqualify it as a whole: "Truth", wrote Francis Bacon, "emerges more readily from error than from confusion[241]." A confused or fanciful theory (alchemy, for example) generally produces false predictions. It is therefore "globally inadequate". A theory that produces locally false or imprecise (erroneous) results, on the other hand, is not necessarily worthless. It may be tainted by a formal error (a calculation error, for example) or by a local error of representation. This was the case, for example, with Copernicus' heliocentric model, which contradicted the movement of Mars, as Tycho Brahe pointed out between 1580 and 1590. In this particular case, it was Johannes Kepler who, using Tycho Brahe's data, was finally able to understand and resolve the irregularities in Copernicus' theory by developing his own theory, in which the planets revolved around the Sun in elliptical orbits rather than following perfect circles. Kepler's laws were born in 1609 and 1619, providing a more precise understanding of the motion of the planets (including Mars). Lastly, other theories require a general paradigm shift if they are to be amended, but this does not mean that they can be described as 'false' or inadequate. Newton's laws remain effective even after the formulation of the theory of general relativity. They are, however, integrated into a theory with greater explanatory power. To qualify Newton's theories retroactively as 'false' in

---

[241] Francis Bacon, *Novum Organum*, quoted by Thomas Kuhn, *The Structure of Scientific Revolutions*, International Encyclopedia of Unified Science, p. 18

the light of the theory of general relativity, even though these theories are explained (without being contradicted) within a more global representative framework, is to extend the concept of falsity in an illicit manner: it would be a contradiction to integrate a false theory within a true theory.

46.

ARE THEORIES FORMS OF FORMS? — In the previous chapter, we envisaged theories as wefts covering reality in a more or less adequate way, just as we had previously defined forms as structures of schematic organisation of the physical world (§ 24 — *The production of forms or the schematic organisation of the world*). This analogy could lead us to conceive of theories as "forms of forms", i.e. supra-formal arrangements structuring the forms themselves. However, such an assimilation needs to be qualified: theories cannot be reduced to forms in the sense of *Gestalt theory*, i.e. contingent configurations that can be perceived and interpreted in an equivalent way from different perspectives. Theories always constitute organised readings of forms, in that they impose a structuring that prohibits the contingent perception of two forms situated on the same plane. As a supra-formal organisation, theory necessarily operates at level $n+1$ in relation to the forms it articulates, whereas *Gestalt theory* remains at level n, confining itself to the apprehension of forms without subsuming them under a higher schematic order. It is within this same level n that forms are perceived differently, as in the example of Rubin's vase. In the paradigm shift introduced by revolutionary theories, for example, it is not the vision of form on level n that is seen differently: it is level *n* as a whole that is now seen from the level of world *n+1*. In *The Structure of Scientific Revolutions*, Thomas Kuhn notes on this subject that with regard to this aspect of scientific progression, some "have emphasized its similarity to a change in visual gestalt: the marks on paper that were first seen as a bird are now seen as an antelope, or *vice versa*". He adds that "that parallel can be misleading. Scientists do not see something as something else; instead, they simply see it[242]." Moreover, the scientist is not free to switch from one mode of vision to another, like the subject of gestalt experiments. If the scientist is not free to move from one mode of vision to another, as Thomas Kuhn rightly points out, it is because the formulation of a new (revolutionary) theory involves a complete paradigm shift, a shift that gives rise to new interpretations of phenomena (which is not the case with *Gestalt* forms, where the change of interpretation takes place within the same paradigm). Thomas Kuhn clearly indicates that the change of scientific paradigm resembles a reversal of the vision of forms[243], but this reversal concerns all the forms that are now seen through the prism of the new theory (from the level of the new theory, of the new representations that it produces). We find a similar idea (an idea with which we agree) in Paul Feyerabend's *Against Method*: with the paradigm shift, it is our entire perception of reality and

---

[242] *The Structure of Scientific Revolutions*, International Encyclopedia of Unified Science, p. 85

[243] Thomas Kuhn no doubt expresses a similar idea when he says: " In a sense that I am unable to explicate further, the proponents of competing paradigms practice their trades in different worlds.", Ibid., p. 150

phenomena that is affected. A paradigm is not just a model, it is also a *way of seeing* and organising the world. As such, it can also retroactively influence the way in which phenomena are formed within our own consciousness[244]. The influence of culture on the formal perception of things should not be overlooked (nor should it be exaggerated): as the meeting point between a physical support and a genetically, historically and culturally determined consciousness, the phenomenon is always a construction — without being an invention. If, according to Thomas Kuhn, during the "the lightning flash that inundates a previously obscure puzzle[245]", some scientists felt as if scales were falling from their eyes, it was because the paradigms they had taken for granted were influencing the way they interpreted and perhaps even perceived phenomena[246]. While these paradigm shifts may have been interpreted as proof of the fallible and ephemeral nature of scientific theories and of knowledge as a whole, in our view they are, on the contrary, a manifestation of (i) the evolving nature of knowledge (the ever greater and ever more faithful adaptation of theories to the realities they are trying to describe) and (ii) the possibility we have of extricating ourselves from the initial subjective conditions of our perceptions and

---

[244] In the same way that our cultures and habits can influence our formal constructions to a certain extent.
[245] Ibid., p. 122
[246] "Scientists then often speak of the 'scales falling from the eyes' or of the 'lightning flash' that 'inundates' a previously obscure puzzle, enabling its components to be seen in a new way that for the first time permits its solution". Thomas Kuhn, Ibid., p. 122

our consciousness in order to achieve a greater degree of objectivity. The subjective origin (sensitive, genetic, historical, cultural) of the productive imagination does not necessarily mark theories with the seal of fallibility and relativism. In this, we must not forget the role of criticism, which soaks theories in the acid bath of analytical reason. Critical reason, as an instrument of retroactive verification of theory, is properly anti-dogmatic: it enables rational sentient beings not to take all their intuitions for effective theories. As we said earlier, it is the passage through formalism and language that makes possible the dynamic dialectic with the representations that emerge from our productive imagination. By formalising, the scientist's intuitions become communicable and criticizable by his peers and by himself (the theorist, dividing himself in a way within himself, puts his theory through the sieve of reason, making all possible objections to it; he does not try to hide the facts that would not confirm his intuition — confirmation bias[247]).

---

[247] To illustrate this famous bias, I recall an anecdote that always makes me laugh: a friend of mine whom I'd had to beat nearly 80 times in a row at tennis ended up winning a match. At the end of the match, he said to me in all seriousness: "That confirms what I thought" (i.e. that he was superior to me at tennis, which was perfectly illustrated by this last match).

AGAINST INDUCTIVISM

I think I have solved a major philosophical problem: the problem of induction[248].

Karl Popper, *My solution to the Problem of Induction*, 1971

We now realize, with special clarity, how much in error are those theorists who believe that theory comes inductively from experience. Even the great Newton could not free himself from this error ("Hypotheses non fingo"). [...] There is no inductive method which could lead to the fundamental concepts of physics. Failure to understand this fact constituted the basic philosophical error of so many investigators of the nineteenth century. It was probably the reason why the molecular theory and Maxwell's theory were able to establish themselves only at a relatively late date[249].

Albert Einstein, *Physics and Reality*, 1936

---

[248] Karl Popper, *Conjectural Knowledge, My Solution to the Problem of Induction*, p. 39, chapter first published in the Revue internationale de philosophie, 25ème année, numéros 95-96, 1971, fasc. 1-2. Karl Popper claims to have first formulated his response to Hume's inductivism in 1927.

[249] Albert Einstein, *Physics and Reality*, 1936, pp. 301 and 307, from the Journal of the Franklin Institute, Vol. 221, No. 3, 3 March 1936

47.

MOVING BEYOND THE INDUCTIVIST VIEW — Inductive reasoning, widely used in the classical and contemporary sciences, is based on the inference of general laws from the examination of particular cases and specific observations. Unlike deductive reasoning, in which conclusions are necessarily derived from premises (or axioms), inductive reasoning infers conclusions from sensible observations, assuming stability and uniformity of phenomena: if I observe every day that the sun sets and rises, I can infer that the sun will rise tomorrow morning. Through habit and successive shifts, statistical regularities end up being perceived as stable rules and are then established as laws of nature. However, there is nothing that allows us to assert *a priori* that these regularities, however many times they occur, can have an absolute value on which we can base stable and certain knowledge. One of David Hume's major contributions was to emphasise, in his *Enquiry concerning Human Understanding* (1748), that a universal theory could not be true for empirical reasons[250] (empirically based on inductive reasoning that establishes regularities as laws). Once we recognise that any judgement about the world is necessarily a judgement based on our experience of the world, how can we attribute the slightest validity to our judgements without, at the same time, falling into an irrationalist epistemology, based on a magical belief in the immutable regularity of the phenomena we observe in nature? No amount of experimental verification will

---

[250] David Hume, *An Enquiry Concerning Human Understanding*, 1748

ever be able to justify the fact that a universal explanatory theory is true. The inductive method, which according to Hume is the only method capable of producing empirical knowledge, therefore presupposes an act of faith that the scientist must resolve to make.

In the 1930s, the young Karl Popper claimed to have solved Hume's problem. As we have already briefly mentioned in § 34 *(Intuitionism as a response to the logical aporias of formalism)*, Karl Popper's solution to this apparently inextricable problem was as follows: if it seemed established that a universal statement could not be justified by a large number of empirical confirmations (whatever that number might be), could such a statement be invalidated, i.e. proved false, by a counter-example drawn from experience? Karl Popper responded positively to this question: "Yes, *the assumption of the truths of test statements sometimes allows to justify the claim that an explanatory universal theory is false*[251]." In other words, since we have the faculty of admitting the truth or falsity of certain experimental statements (which David Hume himself does not deny), we also have the logical possibility of pronouncing on the falsity of a theory (by opposing it with a counter-example). Popper explains that if we can declare a theory 'false' (even if we think that we should limit the criteria for applying truth and falsity to the statements

---

[251] *Objective Knowledge: An Evolutionary Approach*, Clarendon Press, Oxford, 1972, 1994, p. 7 we think that it is not necessarily the theory as a whole that is false, but one of its conclusions (the theory as a formalisation of an intuition does not belong to the "true-false" pair, which comes under analytical propositions, but to the notion of validity).

produced by the theory and not to the theory itself, as we discussed in § 45), it is also because a 'true' theory must be able to exist, even if we do not have the possibility of proving that it is true. The solution to the problem of inductivist reasoning posed by Hume, then, was not to try, against Hume, to establish positively the validity of theories. The very structure of logic does not allow this: in order to establish that a theory is correct, we would have to show that there is no statement that does not support the theory. But if this were the case, it would mean that the theory would say nothing about the world: like all totalizing theories, it would mean nothing (this is why statements like "everything is material" or "everything is an idea", as totalizing statements not assigned to a definite class, have no concrete meaning, as we showed earlier). In the case of totalising statements assigned to a definite class, such as "all philosophers are intelligent" (the category "philosopher" is well defined here), it will suffice to find a counterexample (a stupid philosopher or a black swan in Popper's case) to establish the falsity of the statement. However, since it is logically impossible to count the infinite universe, we will never be able to establish that there isn't a stupid philosopher hidden away at the other end of the galaxy (although we probably don't have to look that far to find our happiness). The statement is therefore not *positively* demonstrable. All we have done with this example is to highlight the cruelly asymmetrical structure of truth and falsity: while no confirmation can ever suffice to establish the truth of a universalising statement assigned to a defined class, all it takes is one counterexample to establish its falsity. The true is in fact an exception, a positive line that crosses a negative ocean (the false). However, empirically positing the possibility of falsity logically forces us — and this is Popper's essential intuition — to suppose the possibility of an empirical truth. Now if the true is possible, it then becomes a possible object of knowledge. It is true that no universalizing statement about empirical reality (and consequently no physical theory) can ever claim absolute and definitive confirmation — this is the sword of Damocles of the counterexample — but the theory can legitimately claim a "domain of validity" as long as the falsity of one of its statements concerning the said domain has not been established. This is why Popper says: "since we are searching for a true theory, we shall prefer those whose falsity has not been established[252]." Contrary to Hume's assertion, we do in fact have the right to give preference to a theory whose validity is superior to another (a theory that has more corroboration than another and has not been proven false). In fact, Hume's criticism does not directly

---

[252] Ibid., p. 8. A little further on, Popper writes, on the subject of negativity: "The fundamental difference between my approach and the approach for which I long ago I introduced the label 'inductivist' is that I lay stress on *negative arguments*, such as negative instances or counterexamples, refutations and attempted refutations — in short, criticism— while the inductivist lay stress on 'positive instances' from which he draws 'non-demonstrative *inferences*' and which he hopes will guarantee the *reliability* of the conclusions of these inferences. In my view, all that can possibly be 'positive' in our scientific knowledge is positive *only* insofar as certain theories are, at a certain moment of time, preferred to others, in the light of our *critical* discussion, which consists of attempted refutation, including empirical tests. Thus even what may be called 'positive' is so *only* with respect to *negative methods*", p.20.

address the local criterion of truth and falsity. Hume does not question our judgement of the facts ("today the sun rose"). In this, he is not a radical sceptic — radical scepticism whose positions are of limited philosophical interest, and which lead to insurmountable paradoxes, as we showed earlier. If, then, we admit with Hume the possibility of making a true-false judgment about a statement, i.e. we are able to evaluate a fact on what it is ("this morning the sun rose"), then we must be able to justify our preference for one theory over another *on objective empirical grounds* (i.e. grounds based on our ability to evaluate facts). Here again, the sensitive (subjective, empirical) origin of our judgements should not lead us to adopt relativistic positions: the subjectivity of our perceptions is not an argument against the objectivity of science. On the contrary, the empirical, as the root of the possibility of our judgement about things, is what induces the idea of value, and therefore the possibility of preferring one theory to another, a theory which, even if it cannot claim absolute confirmation, can postulate a certain extent of its validity. So, we need to make a clear distinction between statements like "all swans are white" and theoretical statements like "the genetic code of swans predisposes them to be white". The first statement, as a purely empirical and inductivist statement, has no particular theoretical value. It can be entirely invalidated by the discovery of a black swan. The second statement, on the other hand, is part of a more global theory, of which the result "all swans are white" is only a "local" consequence. If the second statement is invalidated by the discovery of a black swan, this does not mean that the theory from which the statement is derived is necessarily false. The discovery of a black swan may prompt the theorist to revise his theory locally (is the genetic predisposition of swans to be white universal? What are the conditions or genetic modifications that can lead the swan to be black?) without disqualifying it entirely (unless, of course, the theory is entirely invalid, i.e. it has no explanatory power): theories that are contradicted by experience are not necessarily entirely invalidated; on the contrary, they can be corrected in order to extend their field of validity. Nevertheless, a theory that has been corrected or patched up too often may, at some point in its evolution, be abandoned in favour of another theory with greater clarity and explanatory power. The new theory will then extend the field of validity of its statements, while at the same time proving to be more convenient to use (the simplicity of the theory coupled with its ease of use is often described, particularly by mathematicians and physicists, as "elegance").

A theory is first and foremost a general form, a kind of representative metasystem from which a certain number of empirical statements can be derived. It is these statements that can be said to be true or false, not the theory itself. This distinction between the non-empirical nature of theories — i.e. their irreducibility to the sensible given — and the empirical scope of their statements does not seem to appear explicitly in Popper's work. By favouring the demarcation between scientific and non-scientific statements, Popper essentially emphasises the critical moment of thought, which, in our perspective, constitutes only the second stage of theoretical construction: that of communication and testing, to the detriment of the initial moment of productive imagination, which is the authentically creative moment. It is this insistence on criticism that enables Popper to provide an answer to Hume's problem, but it is also what leads him to implicitly equate theories with their statements. By amalgamating the intuitive moment and the critical moment, Popper tends to consider that a theory is falsified by a single counterexample, when in reality this falsification applies only to a particular statement and not necessarily to the underlying theoretical edifice. The falsity of certain statements in a theory can certainly call into question its extension and explanatory scope, but it does not in itself constitute a criterion for global disqualification ("truth emerges more easily from error than from confusion"). However, while this assimilation of theories to their empirical statements tends, in our opinion, to reduce the complexity of the theoretical process, it does not negate Popper's fundamental contribution in his refutation of Humean scepticism. For it is by recognising that the possibility of falsifying a statement implies the possibility of a truth that we escape the impasse of simple inductivist empiricism and open the way to a more dynamic and critical conception of knowledge. We would add to Hume's criticism, however, that the error lies not only in blindly trusting in induction, but also in ignoring the true mode of constitution of theories. Explanatory theories, being neither purely analytical nor deducible from observation, are the product of an intuitive and aesthetic construction that goes beyond the simple generalisation of an empirical regularity — even though it is often this regularity that initially motivates the theoretical elaboration. This is where the distinction lies between a purely statistical inference — such as "the sun has risen every morning, so it will rise tomorrow" — which has only analytical value and virtually no scientific significance, and a deduction based on a theoretical model derived from a structured intuition and corroborated by experience (my cosmological theoretical model tells me that, barring an unforeseen event whose cause has not yet been incorporated into the theory, the sun will rise tomorrow). The inductivist approach, on the other hand, is limited to inferring empirical regularities, which are then turned into rules based on an implicit belief in the stability of nature. But these rules, having no other status than statistical, cannot form the basis of any real explanatory knowledge. Bertrand Russell illustrated the fragility of this inductive method with his famous example of the particularly logically gifted turkey, who believed that the infallible regularity with which the farmer fed it was a universal and eternal truth, until Thanksgiving Day when it ended up with its head cut off. The belief in the regularity of natural phenomena, even if corroborated by numerous examples, cannot form the basis of an explanatory theory: to explain is not to extend a curve. It is a classic error of reasoning to infer a general truth from a particular phenomenon (or even from a succession of phenomena if this succession is not supported by a concrete explanatory model). While the inductivist method, based on statistics and probabilities, can undoubtedly have predictive power — since regularities do indeed exist in nature — on the other hand it has no explanatory power.

So, for example, the statistical and stochastic models developed by stock market speculators only rarely and accidentally tell us anything about the intrinsic value of a share. These models use the same inductivist method: they infer trends from random movements created by the market itself. It is then the ability to anticipate the intrinsic logic of these movements that will enable the speculator to make money (if he has enough weight on the market, the speculator may even help to create these movements — we then return to the problem of the observer-actor). This is why mathematicians (and not economists) have acquired an increasingly important role in the financial markets. By developing algorithmic forecasting models that often have a distant relationship with the action (the 'underlying'), they act as perfect inductivist formalists. Moreover, the formal models they use are not necessarily specific and can very well be applied to fields other than financial forecasting alone (Monte-Carlo simulation methods, for example, which are commonly used in financial forecasting, are also used to simulate the trajectories of meteorological systems and estimate the uncertainties associated with forecasts). However, the success of these statistical inference models, like the success of basic forecasting models based on the belief in the eternal stability of phenomena ("the sun will rise tomorrow", "the farmer will feed me tomorrow as he always has"), should not mislead us: prediction is not the same as explanation. Although there are almost as many mathematical models of speculation as there are speculators (and although it is also fair to say that most speculative models incorporate some elements of analysis), these models generally fail to identify long-term trends or predict market reversals. In contrast to the stochastic approach to value, investment models are based on an understanding of companies' long-term business models and an analysis of their ability to develop in real markets. Analytical models (as opposed to statistical models) may well be wrong and *ultimately* prove less effective than stochastic models. Nevertheless, they are based on an attempt to analyse the "real" value of the underlying assets rather than on a statistical price forecast. It was through this analytical model, for example, that Warren Buffett, the American businessman, became the richest person in the world (and is still one of the richest people on the planet today): "value rather than price", he claimed.

With this diversions through the workings of the financial markets, we want to illustrate the fundamental difference between the statistical model, a purely formal model, which is not attached to any intuitive representation or any concrete meaning, and the analytical (intuitive) model, which attempts to determine the long-term value of a company by examining, for example, its financial solidity, the development of its market, its risk or opportunity factors — in short, by trying to derive a 'market view' of the company or portfolio under consideration. Of course, the analytical model can only be confirmed over long periods (in cycles less influenced by random short-term movements) but, like the intuitive models of physics, it is valid (relevant) in practice to a greater or lesser extent. Like the explanatory model in physics, the analytical model of the stock market, if it is locally contradicted (the share price of a portfolio may very well collapse for reasons specific to the manager of a company, for example) will not necessarily be entirely wrong: it is the long-term value of the portfolio that will demonstrate or not the relevance of the investment model, i.e. the value of the investor's theory. In stochastic models, there is nothing similar: the model is not supported by an explanation of the intrinsic value of the share (the price rather than the value). Here, form is everything, but form is not linked to meaning (or only weakly). The formal model designates nothing other than itself: it does not reproduce the complexity of mechanisms within an aesthetic model (representable and communicable by language or by an organised formal system such as mathematics) but is content to remain 'on the surface of things'. By substituting prediction for explanation, the statistical model falls back into the aporias of induction (reasoning based on a belief in regularities). This does not mean, of course, that it is devoid of effectiveness: the predictions of inductivist models, without having the force of an explanation of the value of action, may be more or less good. However, the effectiveness of the model will then be based on statistical inference and not on a general explanation of the value of the action that would 'explain' the regularity (which would allow us to integrate it into a meaningful model) rather than extend it (by inference or linear regression, for example). Here, as in modern physics, the inductivist model is used to predict the evolution of the trajectory of large masses, taking only marginal interest in the local determinants of these masses (the behaviour of the particle, the behaviour of a particular action).

48.

AGAINST THE STATISTICAL MODEL — For contemporary science, there would be great danger in mistaking a statistical rule for a law and a mathematical model for a paradigm of intuition. In *The Quark and the Jaguar*, Murray Gell-Mann, an American physicist who won the Nobel Prize in Physics in 1969 for his work on the theory of quarks, gives an interesting example of statistical regularities that have been formalised by purely observational laws (laws that in fact turn out to be conjectural rules). This is the case, for example, of Zipf's law, named after a certain George Kingsley Zipf, who taught German at Harvard in the early 1930s. Zipf's law, also known as "Zipf-Mandelbrot law" or "Zipf's distribution law", is an empirical law that describes the frequency distribution of words or events

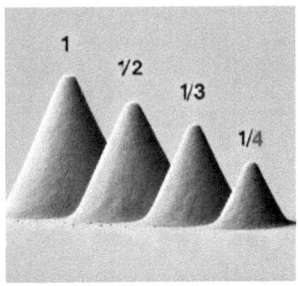

in many types of data, including natural language data, music, the size of cities within a country, etc. According to Zipf's law, if we rank elements of a set in descending order of frequency, the frequency of element k will be approximately inversely proportional to its rank k. In other words, the rank of each element is inversely proportional to its frequency. Mathematically, this can be expressed by the equation:

$$f(k) = \frac{1}{k}$$

where $f(k)$ is the frequency of the element of rank k, and k is the rank of the element under consideration.

Zipf's law was first observed in the context of word frequency in natural language. For example, in a *corpus* of text, the most frequent word (usually "the") will appear approximately twice as often as the second most frequent word, three times as often as the third most frequent word, and so on. Benoît Mandelbrot[253] has shown that a more general power law can be obtained by introducing two modifications to Zipf's initial rule. The first is to add a constant c to the denominator, which gives:

$$f(k) = \frac{1}{k + c}$$

In addition, Mandelbrot noticed a greater precision of the rule by adding a factor to the denominator, for example, a square factor to give a function of type:

$$f(k) = \frac{1}{(k + c)^2}$$

Modified and improved in this way, this probabilistic distribution model has been extrapolated to many

---

[253] Benoît Mandelbrot (1924-2010) was a Polish-born Franco-American mathematician, best known for developing fractal geometry and introducing the concept of fractals into mathematics. His work had a profound influence on many fields, from physics and economics to biology and computer science. In particular, he showed how irregular and self-similar structures (i.e. repeating on different scales) could describe natural phenomena such as seacoasts, clouds, turbulence and fluctuations in the financial markets.

fields. The Danish physicist Per Bak, for example, in collaboration with Chao Tang and Kurt Wiesenfeld, proposed an extrapolation of Zipf's power law by developing the concept of "self-organised criticality". The work of Par Bak, Chao Tang and Kurt Wiesenfeld was initially based on the observation of the formation of sand heaps on beaches or in the desert. Sand heaps are *roughly* conical, and each has a fairly well-defined slope. As a pile rises, its sides can become steeper, but only until the slope reaches a critical value, beyond which the sand pile eventually collapses, reducing the height of the pile and the angle of the slope. The heaps are therefore naturally "attracted" towards the value of the slope, without any particular external adjustment being necessary (hence the "self-organised" criticality[254]). The size of an avalanche is usually measured by the number of grains of sand involved. Observation shows that, when the slope of a pile is close to its critical value, avalanche sizes obey to a good approximation a power law (or scalar law) of the same type as Zipf's law (only, in this case, the constancy added to Zipf's power law is very large). In other words, if we assign numerical ranks to avalanches according to their size, the number of grains involved decreases very rapidly with rank. Many phenomena, natural or otherwise, follow this kind of scalar distribution law. However, simply identifying regularities and formalising them doesn't actually tell us much about the phenomena we're describing. In the case of the sand pile experiment, the scalar law does not, for

---

[254] We will briefly restate Murray Gell-Mann's review of the experiment in *The Quark and the Jaguar: Adventures in the Simple and the Complex.*

example, allow us to predict the amplitude of the next avalanche. It simply distributes avalanche sizes statistically from one end of a statistical spectrum to the other (like the famous Gauss curve). This kind of statistical law is based entirely on the identification of regularities and on the idea that these regularities will recur. All the practical and predictive power of this type of law therefore rests once again on the pure belief in the stability of the phenomena observed — but if stability is indeed to be found in phenomena (without which the world would escape all possible understanding) we cannot be satisfied with simply observing it, we must also explain it.

Statistical rules, as purely observational rules, if they are not supported by a general explanatory model, thus respond purely to the inductivist logic whose aporias David Hume noted: it is perfectly possible to find regularities that are the product of a totally random and hazardous series. If no aesthetic representation (if no representable and formalisable explanatory model) can be derived from the statistical rule, then the rule can never have the value of a law. The concept of law is, in fact, linked to the possibility of deriving from the rule (and therefore from experience of the regularities of reality) a model that fits into a global representation of the phenomena described by the law: the theory of relativity, for example, derives from rules that come from experience of reality and generates verifiable laws in reality. We must not, therefore, fall into the trap of mistaking rules for laws and regularities for theorems. The law is predictive in that it makes it possible to identify and validate new regularities predicted by the law. The pure statistical rule, as an inductive statement, has no content other than that of the empirical regularities it records, and cannot claim to be intelligible in its own right without resorting to conjectures whose explanatory scope remains uncertain. Its validity depends on the stability of the phenomenon it describes; if this stability were to falter, it would immediately be null and void. The law, on the other hand, is not simply a matter of observing regularities, but constitutes a conceptual framework capable of incorporating the irregularity of an isolated phenomenon without being immediately disqualified. This process does not consist of a simple adaptation by adding exceptions, but of a critical re-evaluation that allows the explanatory framework to be reformulated, as shown by the transition from Copernicus' circular model to Kepler's elliptical model, which was not a global refutation of the heliocentric system, but rather its deepening.

It might be objected that statistics, in order to make up for its shortcomings, can also be improved by gradually incorporating phenomena that it did not anticipate, by increasingly formalising the signals that trigger these irregularities. However, even when it has been amended and enriched by incorporating its own errors, the statistical method still lags behind the phenomena it observes, always in a position to follow them rather than anticipate them. By limiting itself to large-scale regularities, it fails to take account of the specific determinants that shape each singular phenomenon. In this respect, statistics appears less as a tool for explanation than as a categorisation device, a machine for producing classifications, whose resources have been widely exploited by modern sociology, often to the detriment of an analysis of the fundamental principles governing the phenomena studied.

The explanatory model, when it is correct and empirically corroborated, is distinguished by its genuine predictive power: it anticipates phenomena rather than giving the illusion of them by successive adjustments using statistical calculations. It is a mistake to conceive of science as a simple synthesis of isolated theories, increasingly reduced to experimental rules. Scientific unification does not proceed by aggregation or by the progressive adjustment of particular rules — the law is not a rule of rules. On the contrary, it is based on the emergence of a unitary vision, an intellectual and sensitive (aesthetic) intuition, which can certainly be formally approximated, but which can never be reduced to pure formalism. The example of Einstein is illuminating in this respect: his ambition was never to unify the sciences according to a purely analytical principle or by seeking a "theory of theories". His approach developed in the opposite direction: unification was not the product of a progressive synthesis, but of a global conceptual vision, first perceived in an abstract and intuitive form, then translated into an accessible language, before finally being formalised mathematically. For him, this mathematical formalisation was not the starting point for theoretical construction. It was with the help of his friend Marcel Grossmann, a mathematician at Zurich Polytechnic, that Einstein was able to give his theory of relativity a rigorous structure. The history of science shows that theoretical unification does not result from the juxtaposition of partial theories, but from a conceptual reformulation capable of reorganising knowledge under a new paradigm.

49.

AGAINST THE PROBABILISTIC INTERPRETATION OF QUANTUM MECHANICS — In an article entitled *Les représentations concrètes en microphysique (Concrete representations in microphysics)*, published in 1967 in an encyclopaedic volume of the Pléiade, entitled *Logique et connaissance scientifique (Logic and scientific knowledge*[255]), Louis de Broglie insisted on the statistician drifts of modern science and in particular of quantum physics. For Broglie, the appearance of probabilities in physics was initially the result of a partial ignorance of the state of the physical world. He drew an interesting semantic distinction between what he called "current probabilities" and what he called "predicted probabilities". Present probabilities, he explained, referred to a situation of which we are partially unaware, but which is "presently" realised, whereas predicted probabilities related to a situation that could be realised with a certain modification of the present situation. But, Broglie noted, this distinction was completely abolished in quantum mechanics.

In quantum mechanics, the particles of matter can never be directly examined: we can only detect their existence by observing a macroscopic phenomenon (such as the local darkening of a photographic plate, the formation of a liquid droplet in a Wilson chamber, etc.), which is *triggered* by the action of the particle. The

---

[255] Op. cit., pp. 706-725 of the French Edition

behaviour of particles is therefore *deduced*, i.e. indirectly derived from experience. At the subatomic scale, deduction replaces facts, since facts cannot be observed directly. If we look closely at the way in which probabilities come into play in the orthodox interpretation of wave mechanics (the Copenhagen interpretation), we see that the notion of probabilities no longer has the same meaning as in the theories of classical physics. In quantum mechanics, the introduction of probabilities is not the result of our partial ignorance of the behaviour of individual molecules (as in the kinetic theory of gases, for example[256]) but of a genuine "indeterminacy" of certain quantities. This concept of indeterminacy introduces modifications into the very notion of probabilities which, as Louis de Broglie points out, "seem rather obscure and on the whole unsatisfactory[257]". Broglie regretted that the form of the microphysical theories of his time had led to "a complete abandonment of concrete representations of physical reality on a very small scale[258]". In short, Broglie deplored the fact that physical science had suddenly abandoned explanations based on intuitive images in favour of a formalistic inflation that had disconnected physicists from the concrete meanings of their predictive models. The atom, Broglie wrote, had thus become "a system of equations[259]" to which no intuitive representation was attached. However, as Broglie rightly noted, if modern

---

[256] Boltzmann wrote on this subject that entropy is a lack of information about the final state of the system.
[257] Ibid., p. 715
[258] Ibid., p. 717
[259] Ibid.

science refused to rely on concrete representations to communicate its results, it was far from being as rigorous in its formal demonstrations: "we reject concrete images and constantly make use of conceptions derived from these images, such as the position of a corpuscle, the quantity of motion, etc..., We use configuration space, the very definition of which introduces the coordinates of corpuscles, while refusing to admit that corpuscles always have a location in space, etc.[260]" This ambiguous attitude towards images on the part of the theorists of modern science no doubt explains why a large number of them, refusing to think in terms of schemes (or "mental images") derived from intuition, were caught up in inextricable contradictions[261] which in turn gave rise to confused explanations: "we can see in current theory the constant use of purely verbal explanations which are equivalent to refusals to explain[262]", notes Broglie. The contradictions stemmed in fact from the absence of a structuring model, or an "overall vision", capable of supporting the theoretical edifice we were trying to describe. By over-formalising phenomena, we thought we were achieving an illusory objectivity which was in fact no more than a formal synthesis of reality with limited predictive power. In the belief that it was freeing itself from the subjectivism of mental images,

---

[260] Ibid., p. 718

[261] We believe, as we developed earlier, that it is not possible to think without schemas, and we fall back into the aporias of positivism and reductionist monism: to claim to think without schemas is to try to think outside the field of signification.

[262] Ibid.

modern science was once again subjugating itself to inductivism, which can only predict without describing: "To the preceding criticisms", wrote Broglie, "we must add a very important remark. With the exception of a few recent attempts, the usual microphysical theory [...] is based entirely on linear equations which, when several solutions have been found, make it possible to obtain a new solution by adding them together (principle of superposition): this means that the solutions of the equations can be added together without reacting in any way to each other. Since mathematicians have been able to analyse linear equations in great depth, quantum mechanics has been able to build up a body of doctrine that is formally very rigorous and very elegant. But it is not enough for a physical theory to be mathematically rigorous and elegant: it must also accurately translate physical reality[263]." It is precisely this translation of physical reality that quantum mechanics lacked. Prediction is not description. While formalism is always dependent on re-presentation, it is never a representation 'in itself' (if it is to have any meaning, it must transcribe more than itself). In other words, it is not because the theory is unified by mathematical formalism that it designates something concrete, a physical reality. This is why the mathematical unification of the body of doctrine of quantum mechanics has not always had as its corollary the unification of the physical theory itself — (which refers back to the distinction we drew earlier between unification by synthesis of statistical rules and

---

[263] Ibid., pp. 718-719

unification by an explanatory model capable of predicting more than itself).

Almost forty years after the publication of Louis de Broglie's article, Lee Smolin, a physical theorist who, along with Carlo Rovelli, is one of the founders of the theory of quantum loop gravitation (which presents itself as an alternative to string theory), made a similar observation: "The [quantum] theory," he wrote, "produces only probabilities". "A particle— an atomic electron, say— can be anywhere until we measure it; our observation in some sense determines its state. All of this suggests that quantum theory does not tell the whole story[264]." For Lee Smolin, the many difficulties raised by the challenge of unifying quantum mechanics and relativity theory (and in particular, according to Smolin, the internal difficulties of string theory) are partly due to the lack of interest shown by quantum mechanics theorists in the major epistemological questions raised by modern physics: In the approach to research in theoretical physics developed and taught by Richard Feynman, Freeman Dyson and others", notes Smolin, "reflection on fundamental problems had no place in research[265]." In fact, in line with Smolin's analysis, this lack of interest in epistemological questions is particularly marked in the case of Richard Feynman, who declared, for, in the introduction to *The Strange Theory of Light and Matter* (1985): " [Physicists]

---

[264] Lee Smolin, *The Trouble with Physics: The Rise of String Theory, the Fall of a Science, and What Comes Next*, Part I, The Unfinished Revolution, 1. The Five Great Problems in Theoretical Physics, Penguin Books, 2006
[265] Ibid., Introduction

have learned to realize that whether they like a theory or they don't like a theory is not the essential question. Rather, it is whether or not the theory gives predictions that agree with experiment. It is not a question of whether a theory is philosophically delightful, or easy to understand, or perfectly reasonable from the point of view of common sense. The theory of quantum electro-dynamics describes Nature as absurd from the point of view of common sense. And it agrees fully with experiment. So I hope you can accept Nature as She is-absurd[266]." Here we see how Feynman places the emphasis on prediction ("whether or not the theory gives predictions that agree with experiment ") to the detriment of the description and communication of the theory. The model must work, regardless of its comprehensibility. A little further on, in *The Strange Theory of Light and Matter*, Richard Feynman explicitly states that modern science must give up its pretensions and not try to understand what it describes. This renunciation marks a return to an essentially inductivist and statistical stance, where predictive efficiency takes precedence over theoretical intelligibility: "Does this mean", asks Feynman, "that physics, a science of great exactitude, has been reduced to calculating only the probability of an event, and not predicting exactly what will happen? Yes. That's a retreat, but that's the way it is: Nature permits us to calculate only probabilities[267]." Here we see an equivalence emerging between (i) the idea that in atomic physics the scientist who can no longer observe is obliged to conjecture (a state of affairs

---

[266] *The Strange Theory of Light and Matter*, original publisher: Princeton University Press; Princeton, N.J., p. 10
[267] Ibid., p. 19

on which there is broad consensus) and (ii) the idea that the behaviour of matter is *intrinsically* unpredictable: "Try as we might to invent a reasonable theory that can explain how a photon 'makes up its mind' whether to go through glass or bounce back, it is impossible to predict which way a given photon will go[268]", Feynman laments. But from this impossibility, which is profoundly linked to the problem of measurement (i.e. to our conjectural mode of inter-action with matter, interpretation at the subatomic level having replaced observation), Feynman turns it into a kind of metaphysical impossibility that almost tends to become a property of the photon itself. It is no longer the scientist who fails to predict the trajectory of the photon through a partially reflective surface; it is the photon itself that becomes "unpredictable". Feynman thus surreptitiously transforms a judgement about things into a property of the things themselves, which, for the reasons we have already mentioned, seems to us to be a serious methodological error (see *What is a thing*, § 23 — *Is there anything 'in itself'*).

Unpredictability, considered an intrinsic character of quantum phenomena, is nevertheless at the very foundation of the theory. The uncertainty (or indeterminacy) principle enunciated by Heisenberg in 1927 states that it is impossible to measure the position and velocity of a subatomic particle simultaneously and with infinite precision. From this principle onwards, the idea that this impossibility is due to the very nature of particle behaviour is asserted. But are we not confusing a limitation on our judgement of things — in

---

[268] Ibid., p. 19

this case, the fact that observation inevitably disturbs phenomena on the subatomic scale — with an *intrinsic* property of the objects themselves? In this way, uncertainty, first recognised as a limit of measurement, becomes an ontological characteristic of the quantum particles themselves — as if a particle could be, 'in itself', 'certain' or 'uncertain' of anything! This is a metaphysical question that we would like to put to Heisenberg. From this assimilation, most microphysics theorists conclude that the quantum world is intrinsically probabilistic. But how could an object be, 'in itself', predictable or unpredictable? Doesn't such a position mark an implicit return to a form of absolute objectivity, in contradiction with the great lessons of positivism and scientism at the end of the nineteenth and beginning of the twentieth centuries, which had rightly recognised the limits of any claim to a knowable in-itself?

As we have said, a thing is always a representation, an *a posteriori* construction of the subject, a construction that is certainly based on concrete reality (which *refers to* a substratum) but cannot be reduced to it. In short, the construction of what we call a "thing" or "phenomenon" is always the result of an encounter, an interaction between an "objective" substrate (a *stimulus*) and our consciousness as a sentient being which, seized by the *stimulus*, constructs a reality of its own (based on the flow it receives, decodes and organises). In other words, when microphysical theorists declare that the quantum world is intrinsically probabilistic (or probabilistic "in itself", which amounts to the same thing), they are merely qualifying our relationship with the "quantum world" (we put quantum world in inverted commas, because the idea of quantum world is already in itself a co-creation, a concept drawn from our deductive experience of this "world"). Thus, the quantum world is not probabilistic 'in itself'; it is our relationship with it, i.e. the way in which we can relate to it and represent it to ourselves, that induces a probabilistic approach. Indeed, there is nothing in the physical world that allows us to assert that the photon's trajectory is indeterminable 'in the absolute': indeterminability is linked to our mode of interaction with the photon, and the idea of 'absolute', 'intrinsic' or 'in itself' means nothing from *the point of view of the photon*. The photon is a mental construct, a scheme of the productive imagination. Let us repeat again and again that, in the perception of the phenomenon, the pattern of productive imagination is not detached from the substratum at its root: we are not absolute idealists (any more than we are materialists, and for the same reasons). The schema is indeed a co-construction of the material reality of the world and our imagination which, relying on sensitive intuition, decodes and organises the world by making it legible 'for us'. While it is undoubtedly true that the behaviour of matter at the subatomic level represents a formidable challenge to our understanding, we must somehow 'keep our nerve' and not abandon all our epistemological rigour in the face of this immense challenge. Scientific progress is certainly defined by the renewal of paradigms and representations of reality. However, there would undoubtedly be some danger in seeking, in modern science, to break with 'common sense' (a vague and ill-defined expression, which ultimately refers to our ability to understand our own formal models and to integrate them into a meaningful overall vision).

Science, as an activity of understanding (and therefore explaining) reality, probably has much to lose than to gain from this abandonment. Indeed, it has always been the greatness of science to refuse to stick to paradoxes (paradox literally meaning that which goes against common sense: *para doxa*, against the δόξα, against common opinion). Science, on the contrary, has always defined itself as an activity of resolving paradoxes (posited in and by common sense). In this respect, it rejects magical thinking: phenomena can be explained, they cannot be worshipped. Trying to rid science of common sense is like trying to pull a tree up by its roots, while hoping that it will continue to grow. We have no tools other than common sense and common language to understand the world. Any theory that claimed to do without them would inevitably sink into contradiction, as Louis de Broglie noted in 1967. This is also the point made by Lee Smolin in a passage that closely follows the one quoted above: "quantum language contains verbs, that refer to our preparations and measurements, and nouns, that refer to what is then seen. [...] Since quantum theory was first proposed, a debate has raged between those who accept this way of doing science and those who reject it. Many of the founders of quantum mechanics, including Einstein, Erwin Schrödinger and Louis de Broglie, found this approach of physics repugnant. They were realists. For them, quantum theory, no matter how well it worked, was not a complete theory, because it did not provide a picture of reality absent our interaction with it. On the other side were Nils Bohr, Werner Heisenberg, and many others. Rather than being appalled, they embraced this new way of doing

381

science[269]." Louis de Broglie was no different when he wrote, forty years before Smolin: "We thus arrive at the following very important conclusion: if the present interpretation of wave mechanics has proved incapable of representing in a clear and concrete way the duality of waves and corpuscles, it is perhaps because it has deliberately confined itself *a priori* within the too narrow framework of linearity. To conclude this paragraph, we must point out that various scientists, including such eminent minds as Einstein and Schrödinger, have raised serious objections to the current interpretation of quantum microphysics and shown that this interpretation has led in some cases to paradoxical and highly unacceptable results. Although their arguments have been contested, we personally believe, after giving them a great deal of thought, that these arguments are of great value and cast serious doubt on all the ideas currently accepted[270]."

---

[269] Ibid., Part I, The Unfinished Revolution, 1. The Five Great Problems in Theoretical Physics. It should be pointed out that, even if we subscribe to Lee Smolin's general idea, we are not entirely in phase with the idea of a reality 'in our absence' which may designate a form of absolute reality, But it is probable that reality 'in our absence' here refers more to reality as it is, independently of its interaction with the measuring instruments at our disposal, a reality that is by definition unknowable to us (undecidable in our system of interaction with reality), which does not mean, however, that it has no existence of its own.

[270] Louis de Broglie, *Les représentations concrètes en microphysique* (*Concrete Representations in Microphysics*), p. 719. Louis de Broglie probably forgets to mention Max Planck, who in

Einführung in die theoretische Physik (1934) drew a distinction between statistical laws and dynamic laws. He wrote: "Thus, for reasons drawn from both theory and practice, it is essential to establish a fundamental distinction between necessary laws and those which are merely probable. Whenever we are confronted with a law, the first thing to ask is: is this law a statistical law or a dynamic law? There is a dualism here, and even an inevitable one, from the moment that statistical considerations are given a place in physics, but many people have not been fully satisfied with it and have sought to make it disappear. To this end, they have resigned themselves to denying the existence of any absolute certainty or impossibility and to admitting only probabilities of greater or lesser magnitude. According to them, there are no longer any dynamic laws in nature, only statistical laws, and the concept of absolute necessity should be excluded from physics. Against this opinion, which is a gross and pernicious error, we can object that all reversible phenomena, without exception, are governed by dynamic laws, so there is no reason to do away with this last category of laws. But there is something even better: physics, no more than any other science, whether this science be a science of nature or a science of the human mind, cannot do without the notion of absolute law; without this notion, statistics itself would only provide results devoid of their most essential foundation". Here we come back to the idea that modern physics intends squarely to substitute statistical laws for dynamic laws (those that respond to a schema of the imagination, one might say) and to Max Planck's warning about the dangers of this substitution, which would deprive science of its most essential foundation.

50.

Out of sight, out of trouble[271].

French Proverb

THE AGE OF TECHNOLOGY OR THE RETURN OF MAGICAL THINKING — The "age of technology[272]" is characterised not so much by the transformation of our relationship with the world into a purely utilitarian one, as by the advent of a mechanical way of thinking that enshrines the Hilbertian approach to reality: the illusion that our entire relationship with the world can be formalised, provided we have sufficiently precise initial parameters. Since Gödel, we have known that this ambition is not only utopian, but also logically incoherent. Not everything is measurable, calculable or expressible in a totalising formal system: this is what the incompleteness theorems demonstrate (these theorems certainly do not prohibit formalising the world, but they do impose a structural limit on formalisation), and this is also what we have sought to establish by re-examining the concept of meaning. This concept, by its very nature dualistic, is based on the articulation between intuition and sensibility, two radically distinct dimensions of the rational analytic system. Far from being reduced to a simple complementarity, this separation in turn gives rise to a multiplicity of systematic levels, each irreducible to the others.

---

[271] Pas vu, pas pris (pris, pendu !).
[272] To use the expression used by Martin Heidegger in 1954 in *Die Frage nach der Technik*

While Alan Turing, when he wrote his doctoral thesis[273], had clearly exposed the problem of incompleteness, he intended to reduce it asymptotically by integrating it into higher-level computable systems (formal systems with recursive loops). Turing cannot be criticised for trying to reduce the problem of incompleteness: his approach was not that of a philosopher or even an epistemologist of science; his work was in fact directed towards a practical and pragmatic objective, that of the conceptual formalisation of what would become modern computer science. However, what for Turing was still a theoretical-practical orientation (the development of a theoretical basis for computer science) was subsequently transformed — particularly in the field of neuroscience, which in the 1970s and 1980s experienced a new boom thanks to the development of brain imaging — into an unthought-of epistemological paradigm: that of the mechanisation of the world, and that of the victory of the technical and inductivist approach to knowledge.

Some time ago I had a dream (or perhaps it was a dream in a half-sleep?). At the time, I was having my house built in the South-West of France. I distinctly remember this imagined conversation with my positivist architect (in my dream, the architect presented himself as a convinced positivist). The house was built in the Basque country, on sand, close to the Atlantic coast. When I asked what kind of foundations the house was going to be built on, the positivist architect replied: "All we know is that it stands on its

---

[273] *Systems of Logic Based on Ordinals*, 1938

own feet". The answer, of course, left me rather perplexed and half reassured. The modern approach to science is becoming more and more like that of the positivist architect: let's stick to the facts, the facts alone are decisive, not the representation of the facts (just know that your house stands on its own feet, the others also stand on theirs, that should be enough for you). This is what we call the "technical approach to reality", i.e. the consecration of the analytical model, the formal modelling of regularity rather than the integration of regularity within a general theory: statistics rather than explanation. In many ways, modern science has become a mechanics of predictability. In our view, this technical approach to knowledge is a resurgence of magical thinking, which David Hume was already lamenting in the eighteenth century, and which Ernst Cassirer describes in *The Philosophy of Symbolic Forms* when he identifies mythical thinking with the ability we have to make synthetic links between elements that have no particular connection with each other[274]. Magical thinking (or mythical thinking for Cassirer) is

---

[274] See in particular Ernst Cassirer, *The Philosophy of Symbolic Forms*, Volume 2, *Mythical Thought*: "Whereas theoretical thought respects the autonomy of the elements between which it makes a certain synthetic connection and separates them and keeps them at a distance by the very act of relating them, mythical thought merges the terms into a single, integrated figure, regarding them as correlative and unified by a magical link. From then on, what is most dissimilar from the point of view of immediate perception, or most heterogeneous from the point of view of our 'rational' concepts, can appear 'similar' or 'of the same nature', on the simple condition that they form an integral part of one and the same global complex", *The Emergence of the Sense of Self*

precisely the result of this method, which consists in establishing links (of a statistical nature, even if statistics are often marred by confirmatory cognitive biases) between heterogeneous elements, which may well be completely unrelated (the relationships, for example, between rain dance rituals, offerings to the gods or invocations and the occurrence of rain in primitive peoples). If there is no meaningful model, i.e. no intuitive model that can be communicated by language or by a mathematical formalisation meaningful (non-monistic) to support the prediction, then the prediction will have no value other than statistical: it will remain based on a mythical or magical belief. In the field of financial prediction, for example, it is well known that very strong statistical correlations can be established retrospectively between elements that have virtually nothing to do with each other, for example the trend in the world oil price over the last ten years and the trend in the price of quinoa on South American markets in the nineteenth century. If we derive a future correlation ("predicted probabilities") from these past correlations without any general model to support these correlations, we will certainly be wrong in our predictions. The correlation of statistical series therefore means nothing in itself without a general model to support a possible causal link. There may also be correlations involving hidden variables, as is the case, for example, in the correlation between trends in ice cream sales and the number of drownings in swimming pools. In this case, the correlation between the two statistical series does not mean that ice cream sales should be banned (magical thinking), but rather that there is a hidden variable influencing the two series (changes in temperature and sunshine levels influencing the number of swims in swimming pools — non-probabilistic critical thinking). Critical thinking, unlike magical thinking, is not content with statistical correlations. It does not take reality as a kind of undifferentiated whole but defines itself on the contrary by its ability to retroactively revisit the models proposed by the productive imagination. Beyond this "filter" function, critical thinking is always part of a desire to explain reality through a meaningful model (a model is said to be meaningful if it can be understood and communicated as a sensitive and intellectual image of reality, an image corroborated by the facts): it does not take correlations for truths. The activity of thinking is related to this exercise in the sensitive schematisation of the world: thinking means making the real signifying itself, "making an image" of the real. This close relationship between thinking and the ability to create a meaningful image no doubt explains why even the most sophisticated algorithms have long failed to compete with the best chess players[275]. As there are an infinite number of possible combinations in a game of chess, chess is, by its very nature, a game of intuition

---

[275] We know that machines are now capable of beating chess champions. Our point here is not so much to claim superiority of the human brain over machines, but rather to emphasise the efficiency of the human brain, capable of overcoming the enormous handicap it has in relation to the machine (since it is far from possessing its computing power) by something that the machine does not possess (its faculty of intellectual intuition, of productive imagination). It's worth noting that the machines capable of beating the best chess players were largely inspired by the structure of neural networks.

and visualisation, rather than a game of memorisation (even if memorising combinations undoubtedly plays a fundamental role, it should be noted that in this case we are talking about specific combinations and not undifferentiated combinations tested at random by a mechanical process). In fact, the best chess players, thanks to their ability to *visualise* the different possible (significant) combinations of a game, to contextualise the game in relation to their opponent and to adapt their way of playing to the understanding of a particular context, have been able to compete for several decades with machines possessing calculation capacities infinitely superior to their own. Chess players were only able to compensate for the enormous deficit they had in terms of calculating capacity compared with machines by differentiating combinations intuitively (the natural elimination of losing combinations by visualising possible winning combinations through the productive imagination). In this way, the activity of thinking is essentially a differentiating, "segmenting" activity. Unlike algorithms, human thought "does not put everything on the same level". It classifies and ranks reality in order to form a global image (in the same way, moreover, that our consciousness ranks information, by the *focus* effect, as in Troxler's paradox, see § 25 — *What is a phenomenon?*) This is why it is more efficient than a machine that would try to test all the combinations in the game (efficiency can be understood as the ratio between energy expended and effectiveness, i.e. the achievement of the objective we have set ourselves). Neuroscientists will quickly retort that the brain also processes information statistically: in the field of visual perception, for example, the brain integrates information from multiple sensory sources and uses statistical models to recognise objects or shapes in the environment. We do not deny this reality, but we need to make a clear distinction between the statistical processing of information that all sentient organisms must necessarily carry out if they hope to survive in a world that does not always leave them time to reflect, and the *intellectual deduction* that the brain makes on the basis of this statistical processing. The explanatory model of reality, born of the articulation between imagination and understanding, is neither statistical in nature nor strictly calculable (computable) in structure. As a model of how the world can be read, it relates above all to the sensibility through which it is viewed and according to which it is constructed. It is only through the development of a general theory (a theory necessarily born of the productive imagination) that the model can become meaningful (for a being endowed with sensibility) and thus escape the aporias of the inductivist approach to statistics (what we have called magical thinking).

Here again, it would be easy to object to the effectiveness of quantum mechanical predictions. Statistical predictions, insofar as they make it possible to predict (statistically) the behaviour of particles, are not worthless: they are effective (they make it possible to effectively predict the behaviour of large masses of particles, for example). But this effectiveness, while it testifies to the regularity of the rules drawn from nature, is not yet based on a general model (a communicable scheme) that could support it. In this respect, the predictions of quantum mechanics still come under the heading of magical thinking (the idea that the event will reproduce itself as it has always done under the conditions in which it occurred). The probabilistic approach of current mechanics, which is still the dominant paradigm of modern science, differs radically from that which consists of trying to formalise reality in a general model that would be distinguished by its ability to make predictions that would not be the result of extrapolating a statistical series: the prediction that I can make as to whether or not the sun will rise tomorrow is profoundly different from the one that led, for example, to the prediction of the existence of the Higgs boson. The Higgs boson was a prediction that derived from the Higgs field theory (a theory developed by Peter Higgs, Robert Brout and François Englert in the 1960s), according to which a field that permeates the entire universe interacts with elementary particles, giving them their mass. Higgs proposed that the existence of this field also implied the existence of an associated particle, called the Higgs boson, which in fact corresponds to the quantum of excitation of the Higgs field. The discovery of the Higgs boson at CERN's Large Hadron Collider (LHC) on 4 July 2012 confirmed the existence of the Higgs field and validated the proposed mechanism for giving particles mass. Of course, we are deliberately simplifying the current scientific paradigm. In reality, despite this paradigm, the truth is that many of the discoveries of quantum mechanics are, in fact, associated with a theoretical model supporting the discovery (a communicable, illustrable theoretical model), This is despite more than fifty years of research devoted to string theory, the very aim of which is to provide a link between the theory of relativity (based on a paradigm that is clear and formalised in *common sense*) and quantum mechanics (which is still waiting for its paradigm).

CAN WE THINK WITHOUT A PATTERN?

> There are two forms of excess: to exclude reason and to admit nothing but reason.
>
> Blaise Pascal, *Pensées*, 1669 (Posthumous)

51.

THE PROBLEM OF METHOD — In *The Character of Physical Law*, a popular work published in 1965 when he was awarded the Nobel Prize for his work in quantum electrodynamics, Richard Feynman insisted that the essential thing in the practice of science was not to find the method, but *a* method that worked. His ambition was to think without intermediate prejudices (or models[276]). It has to be said that this approach paid off for Feynman, as it enabled him to win the Nobel Prize in Physics. It should be pointed out, however, that in his popular science book, Feynman uses the term "method" in a sense that differs significantly from that used by Descartes[277]. Whereas, in the latter — as generally in common parlance — method refers to an organised and systematised set of steps or procedures used to explore, understand, analyse or solve a specific problem, in Feynman's work the word method seems to refer more to a set of scientific dogmas, assumptions and prejudices specific to an era (judging in particular

---

[276] For example, he writes: "Theoretical physicists are a notoriously pragmatic lot. They will use whichever method is the easiest. There is none of the mathematicians' petulant insistence on rigor and proof. Whatever works, man!", *The Character of Physical Law*, p. xvi (introduction).

[277] Notably, of course, in the *Discourse on Method*

by the examples Feynman gives in his chapter entitled *In Search of New Laws*). If Feynman's intention is to assert that, in science as elsewhere, we should not systematically reason according to the paradigms inherited from our predecessors, we fully subscribe to this perspective. As we have seen, it is often paradigm shifts that have led to major discoveries. However, if we focus on what Feynman says about the scientific method, putting aside what he says about scientific paradigms and prejudices, we find that Feynman is actually much closer to the traditional method of approaching science than he thinks. In *Seeking New Laws*, he states: " When you get it right, it's obvious that it's right. At least if you have any experience Because most of what happens is that more comes out than goes in, that your guess is, in fact, that something is very simple. And at the moment you guess that it's simpler than you thought, then it turns out that it's right, if it can't be immediately disproved. Doesn't sound silly. I mean, if you can't see immediately that it's wrong, and it's simpler than it was before, then it's right. [...] What we need is imagination. But imagination is a terrible straitjacket. We have to find a new view of the world that has to agree with everything that's known, but disagree in its predictions, some way. Otherwise it's not interesting.[278]" Could Feynman be any more of a traditionalist? His approach to scientific practice is almost Cartesian (methodical doubt, the search for certainty, the quest for simplicity and clarity, rational evidence, etc.). Admittedly, Feynman declares that he wants to look for new paradigms and is prepared to

---

[278] Op. cit., see for instance : https://jamesclear.com/great-speeches/seeking-new-laws-by-richard-feynman

find models that go against common sense (in this respect, is he really breaking with the scientific tradition?), but paradigm and method should not be confused here. Whereas the paradigm is a model of the productive imagination passed through the filter of critical reason, the method is much more a pragmatism of scientific research than a dogma of reason. While method is not necessarily the starting point for all scientific practice (we don't begin by testing a method, we always first test an idea that is itself deduced from the observation of facts), scientists must nevertheless be able to derive from their experiments a *way of acting*, i.e. a breadcrumb trail that enables them to avoid getting lost in the crevices of their own subjectivism: As the pragmatism of the scientific approach, the method is not a dogma; it is deduced from action (experience) rather than presiding over it. The scientist is in fact free to adopt his own method, provided that this method can be formalised and respond to critical objections. If the method that consists, to use the metaphor from the *Discourse on Method*, in "walking straight ahead", as one would do in a dark forest from which one is trying to find one's way out, has been able to provide a model of action for modern science, there is nothing to indicate that this method is the most suitable for getting out of the difficulties of microphysics. To have a method is to derive from experience any rule that would enable us to make progress in understanding our situation in relation to the world (or in relation to the phenomena we are trying to describe). We therefore fully subscribe to the idea developed by Paul Feyerabend in the opening chapters of his book *Against Method* (1975) that any methodology must be pluralistic, i.e. adapted to its object. However, on several occasions Paul Feyerabend, like Richard Feynman, seems to confuse method in the strict sense (a kind of pragmatic theory of practice, as we tried to define it earlier) with paradigm and theory. Thus, for example, he states immediately after mentioning the problem of method (at the end of the second chapter) that "the proliferation of theories is beneficial to science" (beginning of the third chapter). It is striking to see how we leap here once again from rule to paradigm and from paradigm to theory without any clear semantic distinctions. As early as the first chapter, Paul Feyerabend mixes method and theory in the same sentence: "it is clear", he states, "that the idea of a fixed method, or of a fixed theory of rationality, rests on too naive a view of man and his social surroundings [279]." It seems to us here that the implicit assimilation of "the idea of a fixed method" and a "fixed theory of rationality" is abusive, the first expression designating a systematised approach to reality that draws its rules from experience, the second designating the general paradigm that reason applies to itself in an attempt to define its field of application. For Paul Feyerabend, the fixed theory of rationality needs to be reviewed in the light of a radically critical approach that would call into question the very notion of scientific 'facts'. This idea of Feyerabend's — which in our opinion must be clearly dissociated from his concept of 'fixed method' (which does not have the same field of application) — is not without interest. As we have emphasised, facts are never simply raw data, but the result of a collaborative construction involving several levels of interaction between reality and the

---

[279] Paul Feyerabend, *Against Method* (1975)

mind. They emerge from an objective material substratum, which is given to consciousness through sensitive intuition, but this intuition is not enough to constitute a fact as such. It is extended by the physical imagination — or *productive imagination*, in Husserlian terminology — which projects a form onto the perceived object. The understanding then intervenes to organise and structure the combined data of intuition and imagination, while critical reason ensures a broader coherence: it interprets the forms by integrating them into a network of meanings and validating their general consistency. In this way, a fact is never an immediate given, but a complex articulation between these different instances of knowledge. There is no such thing as the objectivity of facts, as there might be, for example, in mathematics. Facts (phenomena) always present themselves to us in a decoded way, in other words, they are always 'already' interpreted. However, contrary to what Feyerabend pretends to believe, this organised interpretation of phenomena (or facts) is not a free dissertation of the imagination. While Paul Feyerabend is right to emphasise the "historical-physiological character of evidence, the fact that it not only describes an objective state of affairs, but also expresses subjective, mythical or long-forgotten conceptions concerning this state of affairs[280]", he exaggerates the scope of his criticism by giving it a radical and universal validity. There is certainly a "subjective" dimension to any description of the facts. But this subjective dimension is consubstantial with the very notion of signification (without duality, there is no

---

[280] Paul Feyerabend, *Against Method* (1975) Third edition published by Verso 1993, p. 18

signification). It is not, therefore, a kind of earthworm that needs to be extracted from an apple: it is consubstantial with the apple itself. As a signifying construction, the fact is always linked to a complex network of meanings. It is precisely from this network that the fact derives its own signification (without signification there is no fact). From this co-determination of the fact (the fact as a collusion between an objective substratum and a meaning that fits into a general paradigm of sensible origin) we cannot conclude that the fact is 'radically subjective', which would lead us to total relativism. The role of the scientist is precisely to shake up the existing system of paradigms in order to give the fact *a new meaning* that will fit into a general theory whose explanatory power will be greater than that of the previous theory. In the process of scientific discovery, then, it is not so much the 'fact' that is at stake, but rather *the paradigm from which it derives its meaning*. In our view, Feyerabend is wrong to say that "the evidence is contaminated[281]". Evidence (from the Latin *evidere*, meaning "to see clearly" or "to distinguish clearly") cannot be objective or vitiated in itself, but rather it is the network of meanings into which it is inserted that has a more or less extensive explanatory scope for reality. It is true, however, that our own paradigms and conceptual schemes can influence our perception of phenomena. A number of contemporary studies have shown intercultural variability in visual perceptions and interpretations of

---

[281] Ibid., p. 22

ambiguous figures[282]. However, while these studies show a variability that seems to be induced by cultural differences (and not by genetic inheritance, for example, insofar as, according to these same studies, marginal differences in perceptions of phenomena apply in the same way to immigrants who do not share the genetic inheritance of the host culture), they do not establish radical differences between cultures, capable of re-qualifying our relationship with reality. Intercultural differences in perception, no more than inter-individual differences in perception, are likely to call into question the idea of the effectivity of phenomena, i.e. the idea of the constraint that reality *ultimately* imposes on us in our relationship to phenomena (see chapter *What is a thing?*).

---

[282] See for example Kitayama, S., Duffy, S., Kawamura, T., & Larsen, J. T. (2003), *Perceiving an Object and its Context in Different Cultures: A Cultural Look at New look*. Psychological Science, 14(3), 201-206.
Masuda, T., & Nisbett, R. E. (2001). *Attending Holistically versus Analytically: Comparing the Context Sensitivity of Japanese and Americans*. Journal of Personality and Social Psychology, 81(5), 922-934.
Ji, L. J., Peng, K., & Nisbett, R. E. (2000). *Culture, Control, and Perception of Relationships in the Environment*. Journal of Personality and Social Psychology, 78(5), 943-955.
Chua, H. F., Boland, J. E., & Nisbett, R. E. (2005). *Cultural Variation in Eye Movements During Scene Perception*. Proceedings of the National Academy of Sciences, 102(35), 12629-12633.

In this respect, it seems to us inaccurate to describe facts as speculative[283], as Feyerabend does, or to assert that they "are constituted by older ideologies[284]". Such a perspective tends to reduce the construction of facts to a simple ideological projection, obscuring the objective dimension of the material substratum and the structuring effected by understanding and critical reason. While facts are not immediately accessible raw data, they are not purely arbitrary constructions, devoid of any anchorage in reality. Under the guise of novelty, and by exploiting the power of seduction inherent in any radical statement, Feyerabend is simply updating the old critique of subjectivism — the idea that our relationship with reality has a subjective origin — and, in so doing, reviving its classic consequence: relativism. By taking to extremes a criticism of facts which, while legitimate in principle, becomes excessive in scope, he tips over into a primary anti-rationalism, based on "the rejection of all universal standards[285]". This stance leads him to a naïve vision of science, where today's knowledge can become tomorrow's fairy-tale. Under the guise of questioning the authority of facts, such a perspective dissolves any possibility of a stable criterion of truth and reduces knowledge to a set of arbitrary constructions, with no anchoring or rational coherence.

---

[283] "'Facts' come from negotiations between different parties and the final product - the published report - is influenced by physical events, dataprocessors, compromises, exhaustion, lack of money, national pride and so on.", Ibid., p. xi, *Preface of the third edition* (here Feyerabend is mixing, in our opinion, facts and interpretation, science and ideology).
[284] Ibid., p. 5
[285] Ibid., p. 12

In short, science, like any exercise that consists of trying to understand the world by detaching ourselves from our first impressions, becomes, according to Feyerabend, an activity like any other, an activity that is dictatorial and from which the modern individual must try to escape in order to gain his freedom (here we find, almost intact, the anti-rationalist argumentative bloc of the 1960s and 1970s[286]). For Paul Feyerabend, this dubious origin of facts is the starting point for a long argument against critical rationalism. As is usual in this kind of charge, Feyerabend ends up developing an epistemology without a subject, where everything becomes *ego*: "with the cultivation of individuality which alone produces, or can produce, well-developed human beings[287]" writes Feyerabend, quoting John Stuart Mill (in a context that is quite foreign to the British philosopher's issues).

If we are to be honest with Paul Feyerabend's text, we must recognise that it has the merit of underlining the anti-critical (non-analytical) character of resolutive moments that are first and foremost productions of our imagination (of an intellectual intuition that originates in our sensitive mode of relation to the world). By reading Karl Popper (whom he quotes several times), Paul Feyerabend has clearly identified the problem posed by the inductivist approach to science. He therefore urges us to overcome the aporias of the inductivist method by building bridges between the so-

---

[286] On this subject, see for example Zeev Sternhell, *The Anti-Enlightenment Tradition* (2006), or Geoffroy de Clisson, *Les Anti-humanistes ou l'avènement des Contre-Lumières* (2020).
[287] Op. cit., p. 12

called exact sciences and the human sciences[288]: "this is why", he writes, "therefore, the first step in our criticism of customary concepts and customary reactions is to step outside the circle and either to invent a new conceptual system, for example a new theory, that clashes with the most carefully established observational results and confounds the most plausible theoretical principles, or to import such a system from outside science, from religion, from mythology, from the ideas of incompetents, or the ramblings of madmen[289]." We think, as Feyerabend seems to be suggesting here, that the resolutive moment of knowledge is not an analytical or critical moment. However, this idea of the pre-eminence of intuition and productive imagination in any scientific discovery (and more generally in the individual construction of our knowledge) should not lead us to neglect the critical moment of rationality. It is through analysis and criticism that the model of imagination becomes communicable, in other words, scientific. Without critical feedback, models of productive imagination cannot prove their coherence or effectiveness. Here again, Paul Feyerabend seems to be confusing method with scientific paradigms. For example, when he states in the introduction to his book that "science is an essentially anarchic enterprise[290]", he cannot be referring to science as a formalised and refutable *corpus*. Indeed, nothing could be less anarchic than the formalised whole constituted by the so-called 'exact'

---

[288] In this, Feyerabend also draws heavily on Ernst Cassirer, but in a way that Cassirer would probably have rejected.
[289] Ibid., pp. 52 ff.
[290] Ibid., p. 5

sciences. The state of formalised knowledge that constitutes science (as a coherent and more or less unified doctrinaire system) cannot be said to be 'anarchic' for the simple reason that it derives its legitimacy from its rational, universalisable and therefore communicable character: the scientist is not a guru who expresses himself in an esoteric language that only he understands. Scientific theory always postulates a certain extent of validity. In so doing, it courts the judgement of the community to which it is addressed. The scientist's effort consists precisely in trying to prove the validity of his theory in a formal language that can be understood and criticised (the theory must be capable of being understood and possibly refuted, to use Popper's vocabulary). In this sense, the scientific statement is an effort, a tension towards universality. So, it is not science as a *corpus* of knowledge that is anarchic, but science as an *activity* (and this is probably how Feyerabend understands it), and science as a dynamic activity is what we call scientific *research*.

That scientific research can progress with the help of new paradigms, through a kind of anarchic proliferation of forms, is what we are more or less convinced of, subject to two objections. Firstly, as Thomas Kuhn did, we need to separate 'normal' science, which progresses within the same paradigm, from 'revolutionary' science which, by proposing a new paradigm, radically and durably modifies the theoretical perception of reality. And yet, as Kuhn himself points out in *The Structure of Scientific Revolutions*, it is perfectly possible to develop and deepen science within a single paradigm (indeed, this is the most widespread scientific activity). On the other hand — and this is our second objection — it is highly probable that the development of a new model or a revolutionary paradigm which, by means of a new representation of the world, manages to extend the explanatory and predictive power of the phenomena it describes within a given scientific field, is not the result of a totally anarchic process. Even if the moment of discovery is often brief and sudden, as if "scales fell from our eyes" (see § 38 — *Eureka!*), the idea that this brevity is the result of a haphazard and aimless proliferation is probably not entirely accurate. In the vast majority of cases, in fact, the appearance of a new revolutionary paradigm is not the result of complete chance, but on the contrary occurs at the end of a slow process of maturation. In fact, the revolutionary idea tends to come to the mind of the theoretician who has spent a long time working on the problems he intends to solve, and less often to that of the first-year student (even if it is true, as Thomas Kuhn points out, that most of the great revolutions are the work of theorists who are relatively young or new to their discipline, probably because they are not yet fully conditioned by the dominant paradigms). Admittedly, the ability to generate such an idea probably stems from an "anarchic" background in the mind of the theorist (the famous image of the mad scientist) who neither accepts nor rejects any rule or paradigm *a priori*. However, we must be wary of adopting an over-romantic view of science, which would reduce it to the purely intuitive moment of the brilliant scientist. The emergence of a new paradigm is always the fruit of several moments, as we have already pointed out: the moment of revelation of the idea, the moment of its formalisation (formalisation that makes the idea 'testable') and the moment of testing the extent of its validity. To abolish the moment of communication and criticism, as Feyerabend does, is in fact to give no credence to the idea of scientific truth. Indeed, this is what Feyerabend himself ends up confessing in an astonishing profession of anti-rational faith: "who would have the fortitude," he writes, "or even the insight, to declare that 'truth' might be unimportant, and perhaps even undesirable[291]?" At the end of Feyerabend's book, we are plunged into an assumed relativism, made possible by the systematic disqualification of the notion of "scientific facts" undertaken at the beginning of the book. This attempt, which in our view is unsuccessful, is based on arguments which we have already examined, and which fail to justify the erasure of any distinction between scientific knowledge and arbitrary construction. It is only because Feyerabend believes that he has first removed all substance from facts and their objective reality that he can then authorise himself to turn the scientific paradigm into a model of the imagination that escapes all criticism[292] (in chapter 15, Feyerabend

---

[291] Ibid., 1970 edition, p. 73

[292] In many respects, the distinction we are making between productive imagination (derived from sensitive intuition) and analytical and critical reason is reminiscent of the distinction Friedrich Nietzsche draws between the Dionysian and the Apollonian in art, see Nietzsche, *The Birth of Tragedy*: without the formalism of the Apollonian, the anarchic Dionysian background is nothing, can be nothing. We'll come back to this in the second part of our book. We know that Nietzsche later regretted his over-simplistic dichotomy between the

makes a negative assessment of the attitude that consists in developing "ideas so that they can be criticized[293]"). Science without criticism thus becomes a form of egotistical affirmation of the scientist, of his genial and indisputable intuitive ideas.

One of Feyerabend's errors, over and above the confusion he makes between his critique of the "fixed method" and his critique of "fixed rationality", is to have believed, or to have pretended to believe, that method always had a determined content (that method was necessarily conceived as a set of dogmas that would impose themselves as prescriptions of critical reason). But any coherent theory of method necessarily starts from the opposite premise. Since method is the Ariadne's thread that links reason to facts, it cannot be conceived as an *a priori* doctrine of reason (or as an *a priori* doctrine of reason). Indeed, this is the idea that Descartes puts forward in the opening lines of his *Discourse on Method*: "But I will not be afraid to say that I think I have had a great deal of luck in having encountered from my youth certain paths that have led me to considerations and maxims from which I have formed a method, by which it seems to me that I have a means of increasing my knowledge by degrees, and of

---

Apollonian and the Dionysian (although he maintained it later in his work). He also criticised his interpretation of these forces as static and opposed, whereas he believed they were in fact dynamic and interconnected.

[293] Ibid., p. 151: "Develop your ideas so that they can be criticized; attack them relentlessly; do not try to protect them, but exhibit their weak spots; eliminate them as soon as such weak spots have become manifest - these are some of the rules put forth by our critical rationalists." (third edition).

raising it little by little to the highest point to which the mediocrity of my mind and the shortness of my life will enable it to reach[294]." It was the paths taken in Descartes' youth that led him to the considerations and maxims "from which he formed a method". For Descartes, then, method is deduced from experience; it is not, as Feyerabend suggests, a paradigm of rigid thought that the authoritarian rationalist would attempt to impose as a universal and transcendent truth. Descartes himself does not make his method an immutable paradigm of reason, but instead insists on its personal and particular character: "Thus," he writes, "my purpose here is not to teach the method that everyone must follow in order to conduct his reason properly, but only to show in what way I have tried to conduct mine[295]". Like any theory derived from experience, it remains subject to criticism, amendment and evolution. In this respect, we would like to criticise the genealogical method that Feyerabend uses in his book, a method that is curiously shared by a large number of anti-rationalists (Nietzsche, Heidegger, Foucault, Deleuze, etc.), and one of whose greatest flaws is that it encourages cognitive confirmation bias (the genealogist tends to analyse the historical facts that confirm his thesis and to neglect the arguments that might contradict or qualify it). There is, in fact, a paradox in seeking to refute the very idea of method while resorting to a tried and tested method, widely shared by thinkers whose theses converge with those we seek to defend — while, at the same time, denying that we follow any method at all. Should we see this as

---

[294] Op. cit., *Considerations concerning the sciences*
[295] Ibid.

a normative unthinking, an underlying contradiction that we find precisely in the genealogists we have mentioned? Or is it a form of cognitive schizophrenia, a dual posture that oscillates between the rejection and implicit use of methodological principles? This is a question that we will be careful not to answer, as it involves a debate that goes beyond the scope of this review. However, we must remember that here, as elsewhere, method in itself neither produces nor proves anything. It is merely a tool whose value depends on how it is used and the principles that guide it. It would therefore be wrong to consider that the genealogy of science possesses, in itself, any legitimacy in the field of the epistemology of science — just as it would be debatable to claim that the genealogy of morality can, on its own, form the basis of a relevant discourse on morality. To confuse the origin of a practice or concept with its present validity is to commit a genetic fallacy, by reducing the scope of an idea to the historical conditions of its emergence, instead of assessing its intrinsic coherence and value. While the historical or genealogical method can undoubtedly support a demonstration, it cannot replace it. In fact, in the field of knowledge, it is not enough to show, we must also demonstrate, in other words develop a model capable of predicting and explaining the facts. Feyerabend is undoubtedly aware of this difficulty. So, although he rejects the critical method of subjecting his own theory to rigorous examination by formulating all possible objections to it — in other words, testing it — he nevertheless engages in a historical comparison of scientific theories and comments on the history of their progress. Critical analysis, excluded on principle, returns by necessity. Indeed, how can theories be compared with each other without criteria for comparison? If we want to make a history of science, we have to accept that science has a history, in other words that it progresses according to a dynamic that enables phenomena to be determined more and more precisely and predictively. Without progress, there can be no scientific history, and without normative criteria, there can be no rigorous evaluation of theories. By denying these principles, Feyerabend runs the risk of an internal contradiction: claiming to analyse the evolution of the sciences while denying the very tools that make it possible to recognise and explain this evolution. To deny facts their capacity to determine formalisable and objectively valid models is tantamount to abandoning the very idea of science and giving in to relativism, which is ultimately no more than a sophisticated version of scepticism — which, as we have seen, contributes nothing to the construction of knowledge. This renunciation of objectivity, and therefore of the communicability of science as a shared *corpus*, actually conceals an excessive exaltation of the *ego*. For Feyerabend, this position manifests itself in a systematic rejection of all forms of authority, whether political, scientific or moral. Behind the criticism of an allegedly oppressive science lies a negation of the very framework that authorises the collective construction of knowledge. Feyerabend's epistemological anarchism is, so to speak, a kind of enlarged egotism that tolerates neither contradiction nor criticism: if no one is right, then no one is wrong; the point is not to be right, but to emerge victorious from the struggle[296].

52.

PARADIGMS WITHOUT A CONCEPTUAL FRAMEWORK? — Having attempted, in the previous chapter, to clarify the notion of method (and its relationship with experience and facts), we must now try to understand the role of paradigms in the formation of scientific theories. Indeed, it is only through the (apparently

---

[296] This brings to mind the title of a book by Professor Raoult, *La science est un sport de combat*. Professor Raoult made a name for himself in France by taking positions that ran counter to those of the scientific community on the role of hydroxychloroquine in the treatment of patients with Covid-19. While the proposal undoubtedly deserved to be tested (it is undeniably the role of the scientist to break away from the dominant paradigm of his or her community, and I admit that I defended Professor Raoult on this precise point), it would also undoubtedly have been necessary to recognise *in fine* that its curative power was limited or non-existent. Professor Raoult's fault was not, in our view, in proposing a treatment that was to arouse the scepticism of the scientific community, but rather in not admitting, once tested, that it was ineffective or disappointing (not to mention the problematic nature of the trials conducted by Professor Raoult, and his lack of critical objectivity in analysing their results). It is interesting to note in this respect that Didier Raoult claims the influence of Paul Feyerabend in his approach to science (just as he surprisingly claims the influence of Karl Popper, even though he is almost antagonistic to Feyerabend). The method (we would almost be tempted to say 'any method') could, in this case, have been very useful to Professor Raoult.

anarchic) emergence of new paradigms of intuition that what we call 'scientific progress' (or, at any rate, its most spectacular, revolutionary expression) can occur. We have shown that the formation of scientific paradigms does not obey a linear logic and cannot, therefore, be reduced to the criteria of calculability (if, in fact, the emergence of new paradigms obeyed a purely formal logic, scientific progress would be more or less constant and would not pass through phases of rupture). We have also established that neither the paradigm nor the pattern (the latter having here a more local scope, whereas the paradigm refers to a more general and structuring framework) should be posited a priori before the observation of phenomena and experimentation. Scientific research does not consist in the mechanical application of a pre-existing model to reality, as if the theorist could choose from a repertoire of conceptual schemes independently of the concrete problems he encounters. Like the artist of genius who, according to Kant, "gives his rules to art", the scientist of genius is not content to apply pre-established frameworks: he derives from the questions he explores new theoretical structures, new formal frameworks which, once experimentally validated, impose themselves as explanatory paradigms. Science is therefore not simply a matter of bringing reality into line with abstract schemes, but a dynamic process in which the concepts themselves emerge in response to resistance from reality. The paradigm does not derive from a pre-existing rule; on the contrary, it constitutes the structuring image — or formal schema — from which a new communicable rule can be developed. In this way, it does not simply apply a previous normative framework but enables the emergence of a new conceptual order capable of organising our understanding of the phenomenon.

The creation of new patterns or new paradigms, while free (as an active projection of the imagination) is certainly not, for all that, devoid of a conceptual framework: the researcher is never "epistemologically neutral". They are always already imbued with a framework that is, for them, a provisional tool for 'clearing' reality. What's more, he always approaches problems with the unthinking of his own language and habits. As we have already mentioned, while scientific geniuses are often relatively young or new to their discipline, they are not white geese devoid of structure. The resolving moment (the emergence of the new paradigm) always takes place within a pre-existing signifying framework, a framework that is bound to evolve and redefine itself in the light of a concrete problem that disturbs its margins. In many cases, it is the study of a concrete problem that gives rise to the idea from which the new paradigm can emerge (in Einstein's case, for example, the problem of train timetables).

If we accept the fact that it is always patterns and paradigms that make science progress (sometimes suddenly), then we also accept the idea that the form, pattern or paradigm, although derived from the experience of concrete problems, are also *ideal* abstractions that have the power to explain (integration into a signifying system) and to predict reality (a prediction which, if correct, gives the paradigm or pattern its value). It is in fact the abstract representation of the pattern (the *idea* of the pattern or even the schema of the pattern) which holds the key to the resolution of the problem (the key to the unification of problems which might at first appear to be heterogeneous). On the basis of this observation, we can make two hypotheses: that of conventionalism (Henri Poincaré's position), which sees the pattern as a practical convention used to describe concrete problems, or that of critical idealism (Kant's position), which sees the pattern as a transcendental, and therefore *a priori*, schematic production. In the field of geometry, Poincaré, drawing on the lessons of non-Euclidean geometry (developed by Lobatchevski, Bolyai and Riemann), supported the idea that the axioms of geometry are not necessarily absolute truths, but rather conventions of human convenience. In *Science and Hypothesis* (1902), for example, Poincaré wrote: "Geometrical axioms are therefore neither a priori synthetic judgements nor experimental facts. They are *conventions*; our choice, from among all the possible conventions, is *guided* by experimental facts; but it remains *free* and is limited only by the need to avoid contradiction. [In other words, *the axioms of geometry [...] are merely definitions in disguise*. So, what are we to make of the question: Is Euclidean geometry true? It makes no sense. [...] One geometry cannot be more true than another; it can only be *more convenient*[297]." Poincaré thus thinks of space not as an "*a priori* form of sensibility" but as a convention deduced from our (sensory) experience of phenomena: "None of our

---

[297] Henri Poincaré, *La science et l'hypothèse*, Flammarion, 1902 for the original edition, 2017 for the edition quoted, Paris, p. 80. Poincaré's emphasis (italics). Here we find Poincaré's idea of a duality in the freedom of the theorist, whose choice is "guided" but remains "free".

sensations, in isolation", he writes, "could have led us to the idea of space; we are led to it only by studying the laws according to which these sensations succeed one another[298]." However, Poincaré's conventionalism and the idea that geometry is an *a posteriori* construction of our senses (a construction drawn from our experience of reality) do not imply, for Poincaré, that geometry is an experimental science: "It would be a mistake", he writes, "to conclude that geometry is an experimental science, even in part[299]. If it were experimental, it would only be approximate and provisional." As a science of relations, geometry actually applies to the study of groups, Poincaré asserts: "What is the object of geometry is the study of a particular 'group'; but the general concept of group pre-exists in our minds, at least in potential. It imposes itself on us, not as a form of our sensibility (in this Poincaré is not a Kantian), but as a form of our understanding[300]." For Poincaré, then, it is not so much space and time that are *a priori* structures (or forms) of our sensibility. As these forms are in fact deduced from our experience of reality, they are, says Poincaré, "conventional", and respond only to the criterion of convenience: "Experience guides us in this choice which it does not impose on us; it makes us recognise not which is the truest geometry, but which is the most *convenient*". On the other hand, says Poincaré, "the general concept of a group pre-exists in our minds". We therefore have the innate ability to establish relations

---

[298] Ibid., p. 89, again italic by Poincaré.
[299] Ibid., p. 102
[300] Ibid., p. 103

between objects[301] — This is what Kant calls, in the *Critique of Pure Reason*, the category of relation, one of the four fundamental concepts of human understanding (along with the categories of quantity, quality and modality) which, for Kant, are *a priori* forms of thought that structure our experience of the sensible world (on this point, Poincaré does not disagree with Kant). If we return to the Kantian vocabulary, we could therefore say that Poincaré makes space and time a deduction from the categories of human understanding rather than an *a priori* form of sensibility. It is this deduced character of time and space that authorises Poincaré to think of geometric space as a pure convention and not as an *a priori* condition of our relationship to the world. Poincaré writes that we could very well imagine imaginary beings living in a non-Euclidean world, so that "beings like us, brought up in such a world, would not have the same geometry as we do[302]". This brings us back to the idea of effectivity (or efficiency): if imaginary beings live in a non-Euclidean world, there is a good chance that, by virtue of their relationship of effectivity with the world, they will develop a geometry that is different from ours (our Euclidean geometry). However, this does not imply relativism, either in terms of our relationship with the world (the relation of effectivity is preserved), or in terms of competing geometric theories. Indeed — and

---

[301] See Henri Poincaré, "Mathematicians do not study objects, but relations between objects; it is therefore indifferent to them to replace objects by others, as long as the relations do not change. Matter does not matter to them, only form", Op. cit., p. 45.
[302] Ibid., p. 100

this is a point of great importance — Poincaré clearly notes the translatable nature of the different geometries: "Let's take [...] Lobachevsky's theorems and translate them using this dictionary, just as we would translate a German text using a German-French dictionary, *In this way we will obtain theorems from ordinary geometry*[303]." If there is a way of "translating" non-Euclidean geometries into the language of Euclidean geometry, it is because the geometries share a common epistemological foundation (or a common logic, a common signifying language). This common epistemological foundation, which according to Poincaré derives from the form of our understanding, from its capacity to link objects together and thus *create* a space, is what enables geometries to understand and compare with each other. In this way, Poincaré rejects the absolute in geometry, just as he rejects the idea of absolute space (as did Kant), since space always derives from a conception of the relationships between objects, in other words from a particular geometry among a set

---

[303] Ibid., p. 70. To move from Lobachevsky's geometry to Euclidean geometry, Poincaré proposed, for example, the following 'bilingual' dictionary:
Space: portion of space above the fundamental plane.
Plane: sphere orthogonally intersecting the fundamental plane.
Line: circle intersecting the fundamental plane orthogonally.
Sphere: sphere.
Circle: circle.
Angle: angle.
Distance between two points: logarithm of the anharmonic ratio of these two points and of the intersections of the fundamental plane with a circle passing through these two points and intersecting it orthogonally, etc.

of possible geometries. The preference of one geometry over another will therefore be given according to its convenience in relation to the reality we are trying to describe. In the same way that Feynman asserted that the essential thing in science was not to find the method, but to find *a* method that worked, Poincaré advocated a plural and pragmatic approach to geometries (geometric paradigms, we should rather say). However, although we subscribe to this pragmatic approach to scientific research, based on the convenience of theoretical frameworks, it should be emphasised that this notion of convenience — particularly with regard to the choice of geometries based on their simplicity in a given context — does not completely eliminate the normative and regulatory idea of efficiency. In other words, while the choice of a geometric or theoretical framework is partly determined by practical considerations, it remains subject to a requirement of efficiency, i.e. its capacity to organise reality in an operative and predictive way. So even an approach based on the flexibility of models cannot escape a fundamental criterion: their explanatory power and their ability to structure knowledge. A more 'convenient' geometry is one that allows phenomena to be expressed more simply: the ratio between the energy it requires[304] and the result

---

[304] We understand the term "energy" here to mean the quantity of mechanical movement required to solve a complex formula (which requires x intermediate operations, for example). Think of the amount of energy needed by a computer to carry out the operations in a complex formula compared with the amount of energy needed to carry out the

obtained is the lowest. So, for example, in the theory of general relativity, geodesics, the paths followed by free particles in a curved space, will be described more efficiently by non-Euclidean geometry than by Euclidean geometry. The efficiency criterion (which is a derivative of the effectiveness criterion) plays a regulating role in the choice of theories or paradigms. To take up briefly the theories developed by Claude Shannon in his 1948 article *A Mathematical Theory of Communication*, published in the *Bell System Technical Journal*, we could say that the efficiency of the mathematical (or more generally systemic) formulation of a theory or the efficiency of the axiomatic choice of a system can be measured by the increase or decrease in the entropy of the system (in the thermodynamic sense). To put it trivially (and no doubt not entirely in the sense of Shannon's theory), the best axiomatic systems or the best theories are those that manage to "heat up the machine" the least while remaining correct.

Through this analysis of Poincaré's thought, we note that each conceptual framework needs another conceptual framework (in relation to which it is understood or translated) in order to define itself. This brings us back to the problem of incompleteness. No system is complete 'in itself'. It always needs axioms, and these axioms refer to a reality that is external to the system and cannot be integrated into it: nothing can be defined *absolutely*. The fundamental problem of reference cannot be reduced to a system that is by and

---

operations in a simple formula that would produce the same result.

in itself meaningful. The system will always be defined in relation to another system, which will itself *refer to* an external reality. Thus, for example, in spherical geometries, the concept of a straight line can be expressed as the trajectory of minimum length between two points on a sphere and be materialised as a large circle on the sphere (think, for example, of the trajectories of a long-haul aircraft, which are the shortest routes on a globe, but which appear as curved on a planisphere: from the point of view of the plane travelling in its three-dimensional space, the route is indeed straight, whereas from the point of view of the traveller observing the route on his small on-board screen, the trajectory appears curved), however, spherical geometries are well expressed by maintaining a reference link to Euclidean geometry. The initial axioms are only modified: the plane becomes a sphere intersecting orthogonally the fundamental plane (see Poincaré's definition). If spherical geometry can be expressed in Euclidean geometry, albeit in a less convenient way (by going from the globe to the sphere, it is much more complex for us to calculate the shortest trajectories), it is because it *refers to* it in its axioms. Furthermore, from the point of view of the plane, the idea of the straight line remains, and the plane does have a straight trajectory (the shortest trajectory from one point to another). But in a curved space, the shortest trajectory from one point to another is a curved trajectory.

53.

SHOULD WE ABANDON CRITICAL IDEALISM? — Since the advent of quantum mechanics, contemporary science has been marked by an unprecedented acceleration in the production of models to describe and explain the behaviour of particles at the subatomic level. The profusion of these new models was concomitant, as we have already mentioned, with the abandonment of the old theoretical re-presentations of science, which remained valid on a large scale but failed to explain quantum phenomena. With the rejection of the old theoretical representations, the entire conceptual framework of classical physics was called into question: its representations of the world, but also its paradigms, methods and epistemology. In the epistemological storm that swept through physics circles from the 1920s onwards, transcendental critical idealism (which had been the dominant paradigm at the end of the nineteenth century and the beginning of the twentieth) was, with a few exceptions (which we mentioned earlier), largely abandoned. But was it necessary to 'throw the baby out with the bathwater'? By abandoning critical idealism, theorists had thought they were getting rid of a framework which, they believed, had restricted scientific research by giving too much prominence to defining the conditions of validity of reason to the detriment of the facts themselves. But could we do without a conceptual framework? Didn't the rejection of the framework of critical idealism, which was undoubtedly too narrow at the time, go hand in hand with the advent of other frameworks, despite the supposed neutrality of the theorists of the new science?

If the theorists of quantum mechanics had, of necessity, to temporarily suspend their previous conceptions in order to account for phenomena apparently defying all established mechanical causality, it seems difficult to accept that this suspension, initially motivated by the legitimate astonishment aroused by quantum paradoxes, could have crystallised into a perennial doctrine of ἐποχή[305] understood as a definitive renunciation of all causal intelligibility. Having been unable to account for quantum phenomena within the epistemological framework of classical physics, scientists came to consider that their role was no longer to explain their causes, but only to formulate a rigorous description of them, without seeking to fit them into an explanatory scheme in the traditional sense. However, the phenomena had to be described in a language that everyone could understand. Theorising, even if it was 'purely' descriptive, meant that the theory had to be communicable. By reducing this communicability to its most formal aspects, we thought we had got rid of the problem of reference. This was to forget too quickly that formalism without reference means nothing. It was all too easy to move from the idea that new phenomena had to be thought of without predefined patterns to the idea that it was possible to represent the world without epistemology or outside

---

[305] Epochê: Greek suspension of judgement. Epoche consists of a temporary suspension of judgement on any assertion or belief, particularly those concerning metaphysical, ethical or epistemological questions.

any conceptual framework[306]. In fact, many theorists who thought themselves agnostic actually adopted the conceptual reflexes of logical positivism — we think, for example, of the influence of Rudolph Carnap and the "Vienna Circle" on some of the great theorists of quantum mechanics such as Niels Bohr, Werner Heisenberg, Wolfgang Pauli or Max Born[307] —, pragmatism (Richard Feynman in particular) or reductionist materialism.

Did the fundamental questions raised by the emerging field of microphysics require us to abandon entirely the epistemological framework inherited from classical physics, as conceived by Descartes, Newton and Kant? We do not believe that this break should be considered necessary, for two essential reasons: firstly, because of the internal logic of scientific discoveries, to use Karl Popper's terms; and secondly, because of the need for them to be communicable, an essential condition of any scientific undertaking. We emphasised in the

---

[306] With Feynman or Feyerabend, for example, it is a broad amalgam between the terms "method", "paradigm" or "epistemology" that supports this belief in a possible epistemological agnosticism. It is highly unlikely that Feynman could have been influenced by Feyerabend in his epistemological approach to science.

[307] Niels Bohr interacted with some members of the Vienna Circle, notably Rudolf Carnap. Although Bohr did not adopt logical positivism in its entirety, his ideas on the interpretation of quantum mechanics were influenced by discussions with logical empiricist philosophers. Written exchanges between Bohr, Pauli, Born and Heisenberg testify to the penetration of the ideas of the Vienna Circle in the evolution of the doctrine of quantum mechanics.

previous paragraph that the major scientific discoveries were not exclusively the result of a formalism presented as 'agnostic' and linear (we use this expression with reservation, considering that the agnosticism of formalism is merely an illusion of language), but that they found their source, more fundamentally, in moments of intuition and aesthetics, which played a decisive role in the emergence of new forms, new patterns and paradigms. And it was precisely the emergence of these imaginatively produced forms that enabled scientific progress and the unification of the sciences into meaningful wholes. The communicable nature of these signifying sets (which are first and foremost schematic productions of the mind) is what in turn made it possible to understand these sets, in other words to integrate them into our representations of the world. As soon as we eliminated these two moments (the moment of productive imagination[308], the moment of communication), the world once again became opaque and incomprehensible: magical thinking reappeared.

If, then, against this temptation of 'magical thinking', we try to broaden critical idealism beyond its strict Kantian definition, we could define it as a doctrine that takes note of the dual origin of phenomena (the phenomenon as a co-construction between the physical substratum and the subject) at the same time as it recognises in the sentient subject the faculty of creating and projecting onto phenomena ideas that are not

---

[308] Which is rooted in sensitive intuition

reduced to them: the schemas of the imagination[309]. It should be noted here that, in the dualist epistemology we are defending, schemas and categories do not necessarily have to be conceived of as transcendental in the sense that they precede all experience of the world. First and foremost, it is important to emphasise that schemas cannot be reduced to mere material phenomena, a point we have already argued at length. They can certainly be derived from experience, without constituting objects of empirical knowledge in the strict sense of the term. By abandoning the idea that imaginative schemes are strictly *a priori*, we are probably not departing fundamentally from the conceptual framework of critical idealism. However, this in no way implies that the legislative principles that derive from them — in particular geometric laws — can be deprived of their universal scope, since the law retains its binding value here (it is imposed on us as we impose it on reality[310] — this is the principle of reason that is both legislated and legislating).

---

[309] For Kant, schemas are said to be *transcendental* insofar as they are conditions of the possibility of experience and knowledge but are not themselves objects of empirical knowledge.

[310] If we can rightly maintain that the subject is at the origin of the schemas created by his imagination (from his sensibility) that enable him to apprehend and think the world, we can hardly defend the idea that the rules and properties that derive from these schemas are pure inventions of the subject. If this were the case, it would give rise, among other things, to insoluble paradoxes concerning the communicability of models and the invariability of laws

Beyond the formal debates on the *a priori* or non-*a priori* nature of the schemes and categories structuring our apprehension of the world, the main merit of Kantian idealism lay, in our view, in its insistence on the conditions of application of reason to phenomena. With critical idealism, Kant was carrying out a genuine analysis of the knowing subject, not as a mere passive entity, but as a 'measuring instrument' of reality, whose limits and conditions of operation had to be examined. This is why we consider critical idealism to be far more rigorous[311] than logical positivism, pragmatism or reductionism, since these doctrines privileged the emergent part of phenomena — their observable and measurable dimension — while neglecting the very instrument by which this reality was apprehended. In so doing, they made the subject a normative unthinkable, forgetting that all knowledge presupposes a prior structuring framework.

To be altered, a norm must first be established. It is only by establishing an ideal norm, like a gauge, that the subject can organise his perception of the real. The real does not merge with this norm, but neither can it totally free itself from it: it distinguishes itself from it while constantly referring to it, since it is through this norm that it determines and measures itself. It is by assimilation or difference that the subject succeeds in

---

within given geometric systems. Schemes are created by the subject, not their properties (this, incidentally, refers to a remark Gödel makes in his correspondence with Wang, which we quoted earlier).

[311] Which is not to say, of course, that idealism is a perfectly finished doctrine that has no vocation to evolve by criticising itself.

representing himself and making signifying the phenomenon that manifests itself to his consciousness (inserting the phenomenon into his network of significations). To put it another way, to think of a curved line, for example, the subject needs to imagine the straight line and the circle (what does a curved line mean, if not an angular deviation from a straight line, a deviation that locally adopts a curvature similar to that of a circle of a defined radius?) The line is always curved in relation to another (ideal) line which is not (a line whose curvature is zero and which serves as a reference for the line whose curvature is positive or negative). So, independently of the axioms on which a theory is based, there is always an *ideal* reference point (we do not use the term ideal here so as not to imply that we consider the idea to be an absolute, since the ideal we are referring to refers to the idea as a *gauge* of reality, i.e. as a *signifying reference* and not as an *absolute*). To take the example of spherical geometries again, there is indeed an *ideal* frame of reference which is the sphere (which replaces the plane of Euclidean geometry), a frame of reference in which, moreover, the idea of the *ideal* straight line is well preserved. If we return to the planisphere of our transatlantic flight (which here symbolises Euclidean geometry), we see that the transposition of the 'straight' line as the shortest path between two points on a globe is certainly manifested by the drawing of a curve on a plane (on the planisphere on our screen). However, the transition from one geometric system to another has not abolished the idea of the straight line (or, in general, similar regulatory ideas). The notion of ideality, which is intrinsically linked to the way in which we represent geometries (Euclidean or non-Euclidean), in fact persists in representations of spherical geometry: we still have the idea of the definition of the straight line as *the shortest* path between two points, this idea involving the quantitative category of distance (distance is an ideal notion, which, like space, is in our understanding, not in things themselves). Moreover, spherical geometries are well defined in terms of the ideality of a plane (in Euclidean terms, explains Henri Poincaré, for example, in *Science and Hypothesis*, the plane of spherical geometries is defined as a sphere orthogonally intersecting the fundamental plane) and therefore in terms of the idea of the straight line only, since these geometries are constrained by their basic axioms, they do not necessarily allow the straight line (the straight rectilinear line of the fundamental plane) as a possible projection with respect to the spherical plane (which would imply, for example, the possibility of a straight rectilinear line crossing the sphere or leaving the spherical plane, which may be forbidden by the axioms of the geometries under consideration).

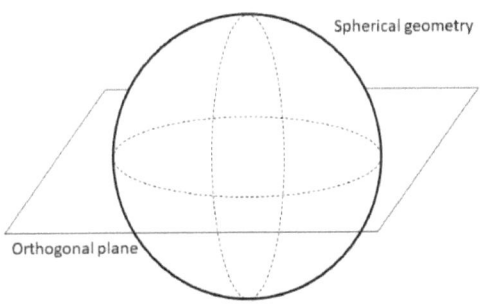

More generally, non-Euclidean geometries (like Lobatechevskian hyperbolic geometry, projective geometry, affine geometry, or even 'self-similar' fractal geometry), as geometries associated with figurative representations, always have *ideal* re-presentations as their corollaries. In other words, they are the projected concretisation of *ideal* structures that can be formulated by understanding. As *ideal* systems, geometries — and this is undoubtedly one of the important consequences of the epistemology we are defending — are meaningful, that is, they relate to abstract elements that can be apprehended and understood by the knowing subject. Their convenience thus refers not only to their simple utilitarian character, it is also the manifestation of their explanatory power within a signifying system (a system that is not merely formal, that refers to more than its mere form). This is why we profoundly disagree with the instrumental or pragmatic interpretation of quantum mechanics, according to which the theory should be treated solely as a mathematical tool for making predictions (an interpretation that is in fact close to the positions of the Copenhagen school, considered to be the guarantor of the 'orthodox' interpretation of quantum mechanics). The mathematical tool can never be reduced to its strict utility. At the same time, it must always be apprehended and understood in its referential and meaningful dimension. If the idea is a gauge, we must always bear in mind that it is a gauge that *refers*. In this respect, it should be pointed out that the critical idealism we defend is not only not in-compatible with the idea of relative reference frame, but is, on the contrary, consubstantial with it. Critical idealism, despite the objections that have been made to it — which largely stemmed from a certain reading of Kant's transcendental aesthetics — is not linked to the idea of absoluteness. On the contrary, its merit is to acknowledge the finite and sensitive nature of the subject and to emphasise its capacity to propose gauges of the real, without, however, considering these gauges as absolute realities in themselves. In this respect, critical idealism is perfectly compatible with the idea of the confrontation of reference frames, which we find in Ernst Mach and Einstein in particular, and which inspired Einstein's relativistic model (Einstein insisted on several occasions that we must not confuse relativity with relativism, at the risk of committing a serious misunderstanding). Ultimately, the problem of critical idealism once again intersects with the problem of meaning. There is no such thing as meaning 'in itself'; meaning always calls on a double level of references: the first being the network of objects in a given system of meanings (the meanings of the objects are defined in relation to each other within the same set or system), the second being the axioms on which the system is based, inevitably referring to another language, another system of references in relation to which the system in question is defined. Critical idealism cannot therefore be taken to mean that there is an absolute referential system that transcends all others. At best, referential systems will be adopted according to their convenience of use in relation to the reality we are trying to describe (this is the idea of conventionalism developed by Henri Poincaré, for example). But as soon as there is a system, there is the idea of a system. The system is ideality. To deny the existence of the ideality of systems is to deny the possibility of thinking about the world, the system being in some sense the paradigm that allows us to apprehend and organise the physical substratum of phenomena, at the same time as it is what allows us to make this substratum meaningful *to us*. The example of the circle (or the sphere) can help us to better understand what we mean by meaning *for us*. Strictly speaking, neither the circle nor the sphere has any existence in reality, other than an ideal one. The real world never presents us with a perfect or absolute circle. In the same way, the properties of the circle are never encountered by chance in nature; they are logical deductions from our ideal projection of the circle, deductions which in turn help us to think about reality. The number π, for example, although it has no objective reality (as a logical deduction from an ideality that is an *ideal* projection of our sensitive imagination), helps us to think about and predict phenomena. In fields such as structural engineering and acoustics, for example, π is used to model vibrations and oscillations[312], in classical mechanics, π is used to describe circular motion[313], and finally π appears in various

---

[312] The resonant frequency of a vibrating string is proportional to the square root of the applied tension and inversely proportional to its length. π appears in the equations describing these phenomena.

[313] When an object moves in a circle, its period (T) corresponds to the time it takes to complete one complete revolution, i.e. the circumference of the circle ($C=2\pi r$). The angular velocity (ω), measured in radians per second, directly relates the period to the movement: $\omega= T\ 2\pi$. The number π is used in these relationships because it is fundamental to defining the geometry of the circle and the angles in radians. The planets orbiting the Sun follow these principles. Their period depends on the size of their orbit and their angular velocity.

equations describing electro-magnetic phenomena, notably in Maxwell's laws and in the equations for the propagation of electro-magnetic waves. Even though the number π is and can only be the deduction of an ideal projection, it is thus found to have an effective descriptive and predictive power over real phenomena. On the other hand, while it has a certain validity in this predictive description of reality, π also has a concrete meaning *for us*. In fact, we can form a clear image of what the phenomena described and explained mean *for us* by means of idealities that are ultimately figurative (and therefore meaningful) projections. Here again, the ideality of the circle plays the role of reference or gauge of reality (we know, for example, that when it comes to planetary orbits, it is rather the elliptical movement that is observed, a movement that in turn can be defined as an *ideal* and meaningful projection *for us*, a projection that we use in our intuitive understanding of the movement of the planets). Ideality can therefore be understood as a system of gauges and references developed by the productive imagination, a system which, without having an objective reality, enables us to apprehend, describe and predict phenomena using rules which, not being contained *in* the phenomena themselves (except that the phenomenon is always the meeting of a real substratum and a sensible reality which is both that which contributes to forming the phenomenon and that from which our *ideal* projections derive) nevertheless enable us to predict their behaviour in an effective way.

54.

THE PROBLEM OF SPACE — We know that Albert Einstein on several occasions adopted pragmatic and realistic positions that could probably have tipped him over into the subjectless epistemology that was proposed in the 1920s by the new theorists of quantum mechanics. These positions should probably be analysed through the prism of the influence of the Austrian physicist and epistemologist Ernst Mach — whose ideas played a decisive role in the formation of the Vienna Circle. In terms of physical theory, Ernst Mach was best known for the "Mach Principle", which Einstein did much to popularise (he is even said to have originated the name of the principle) and which Mach intuited during his contribution to the experimental activities of Doctor Joseph Breuer, during which he came up with the idea of a sixth sense, that of orientation. The integration of the vectors of the other senses into the motor activity of postural equilibrium gave rise to Mach's idea of a more general redefinition of mass in terms of the frame of reference of inertia. This principle postulated that the laws of physics were in fact determined by masses interacting with the rest of the universe. Mass was no longer an absolute, but relative to the distribution of bodies in the universe. This idea had a major influence on Einstein, particularly in his own redefinition of the principle of gravitation, derived from the theory of general relativity, according to which gravitation is not only due to the presence of mass, but also to the curvature of space-time induced by the general distribution of bodies and energy in the universe. Einstein also credited Ernst Mach (as well as David Hume) with playing a major role in understanding the problem of simultaneity, which led him to the theory of relativity: "The type of critical reasoning required for the discovery of this central point was decisively furthered, in my case, especially by the reading of David Hume's and Ernst Mach's philosophical writings[314].", he writes, for example, in his auto-biographical notes. Nevertheless, it seems that Mach's theoretical and epistemological views had an influence above all on the young Einstein: "We must not be surprised", he wrote, "that… all physicists of the last century saw in classical mechanics a firm and final foundation for all of physics, yes, indeed, for all natural science [...] It was Ernst Mach who, in his *History of Mechanics*, shook this dogmatic faith; this book exercised a profound influence upon me in this regard while I was a student. I see Mach's greatness in his incorruptible scepticism and independence; in my younger years, however, Mach's epistemological position also influenced me very greatly, a position which today appears to be essentially untenable[315]."

We know that Ernst Mach was initially influenced by the critical idealism of Kant before returning to the conceptions of the "consistent" idealists who, for him, were Hume and Berkeley[316]. These Anglo-Saxon

---

[314] Albert Einstein, *Autobiographical Notes*, 1949
[315] Ibid., 1946
[316] "My relation s to Kant have been peculiar. His critical idealism was, as I recognize with the greatest gratitude, the starting-point of my critical thought: but it was impossible for me to retain my allegiance to it. I very soon began to gravitate again towards the views of Berkeley, which are contained, in a more or less latent form, in Kant's writings. By studying the physiology of the senses and by reading Herbert, I then arrived at views akin to those of Hume,

conceptions inspired his central thesis, according to which "bodies do not produce sensations, but complexes of elements (complexes of sensations) make up bodies[317]", a thesis that we believe to be incomplete, that seriously sidesteps the problem of reference and closely resembles the psychologistic theory that we have previously rejected (see in particular § 31 — *Against psychologism*). In *The Analysis of Sensations and the Relations between the Physical and the Psychical*, his main philosophical work, Ernst Mach attempted a clear assimilation between the psychical and the physical by rejecting any formal dualism: "After these general remarks, I may perhaps be able to explain my position with regards to the dualism of the physical and the psychical. This dualism is to my mind artificial and unnecessary[318]." Although grateful for the debt he owed to Mach's theories, Albert Einstein finally detached himself quite early from his radical epistemology, even considering his former teacher a "deplorable philosopher" as early as 1922. In the Bulletin de la Société Française de Philosophie,

---

though at that time I was still unacquainted with Hume himself. To this very day, I cannot help regarding Berkeley and Hume as far more logically consistent thinkers than Kant", Ernst Mach, *The Analysis of Sensations and the Relations of the Physical to the Psychical*, pp. 367 ff., translated from German into English by C. M. Williams, The Open Court Publishing Company, Chicago and London. First published in 1886 under the title: *Beiträge zur Analyse der Empfindungen* (Contributions to the Analysis of Sensations). Second publication in 1900 under the title: *Die Analyse der Empfindungen und das Verhältnis des Physischen zum Psychischen*.
[317] Ibid., p. 29
[318] Ibid., p. 41

Einstein declared: "Mach's system studies the relations that exist between the data of experience; the whole of these relations is, for Mach, science. In short, Mach's work is a catalogue, not a system. As good a mechanic as Mach was, he was a deplorable philosopher. This short-sighted view of science led him to reject the existence of atoms. It is likely that if Mach were alive today, he would change his mind[319]. Over the next few years, Einstein's enthusiasm for Mach's principle steadily waned and finally disappeared. In 1954, Einstein wrote to one of his colleagues: "As a matter of fact, one should no longer speak of Mach's principle at all[320]."

In any case, Einstein's reflections on inertial reference frames in the early 1900s led him to have major reservations about certain aspects of Kant's philosophy, and in particular about the transcendental aesthetics that made up the first part of the *Critique of Pure Reason*. In particular, Einstein criticised Kant for the overly aprioristic nature of his philosophy: "if one does not want to assert that relativity theory goes against reason, one cannot retain the *a priori* concepts and norms of Kant's system", he declared, for example, in the 1920s[321]. In Einstein's view, by making space and time *a priori* forms of sensibility, Kant gave them a rigidity that hindered the emergence of new non-Euclidean paradigms. If we can concede to Einstein

---

[319] Albert Einstein, *Bulletin de la société française de philosophie*, meeting of 6 April 1922, p. 249, (translated from French)
[320] Letter to F. Pirani, 2 February 1954
[321] The account appeared in a 1924 review by Einstein of a text, Alfred C. Elsbach, *Kant und Einstein*.

that Kant's epistemology was partly dependent on Newton's physics and the scientific problems of his time, it is undoubtedly unfair to see in his transcendental idealism an attempt to reify or defend the absoluteness of space — which Einstein himself later acknowledged. In the *Critique of Pure Reason*, Kant, while he did indeed designate space and time as *a priori* forms of our sensibility, never made them an objective absolute: in this he was explicitly antagonistic to the positions of Newton and other physicists who considered space to be an absolute real being (Samuel Clarke, J.C Sturm). In his pre-critical work, however, Kant fully adopted Newton's and Clarke's theses on the irreducibility of space and time to logical relations; he agreed with them in considering space and time as *receptacles* (according to the word used by Kant in his dissertation to characterise Newton's thesis: "*immensum rerum possibilium receptaculum*[322]"), prior to the things they are intended to receive. The Kantian forms of space and time played precisely this role of receptacles, in that they contained within them relations that were their own and independent of the objects that were to be inscribed in them — and not relations derived from the things we perceive in them. But this receptacle was not external to the perceiving subject, as Newton had assumed when he conceived of space as God's sensory environment; on the contrary, it belonged entirely to the subject himself, thus constituting man's sensory

---

[322] "The unlimited receptacle of possible things": Immanuel Kant, *De mundi sensibilis atque intelligibilis forma et principiis*, 1770, quoted by Martial Gueroult, *Kant's Critique of Pure Reason, Transcendental Aesthetics*.

environment[323]. In the *Critique of Pure Reason*, Kant constantly repeated that space and time have no objective existence. For transcendental philosophy, as for general relativity, space and time are neither objects, nor substantial beings, nor psychic entities; they are forms that make experience intelligible, of which they are, moreover, objectively inseparable: "space," wrote Kant, "is simply the form of external intuition, but not a real object that can be intuited externally[324]". Moreover, Kant frequently emphasised that the forms of space and time were meaningless in themselves if they were not related to the world of experience, whose very constitution as such they made possible: "if we want to put space and time outside all phenomena, the result is all sorts of determinations that are empty of external intuition, but which are not, however, possible perceptions", he wrote, for example, in the *Critique of Pure Reason*[325].

If the non-absolute and non-substantial character of space can be recognised as a fundamental contribution of Kantian philosophy, it was the determination of space and time as *a priori* forms of sensibility that

---

[323] See Martial Gueroult, *Kant's Critique of Pure Reason, Transcendental Aesthetics*, pp. 79-110 (French).
[324] "Transcendental Dialectic", *note on the antithesis of the first antinomy*, *Critique of Pure Reason*, AK III, 297; Œuvres philosophiques, t. I, p. 1089, quoted by Jean Seidengart in the presentation of Ernst Cassirer's *La théorie de la relativité d'Einstein*, (*Substance and Function & Einstein's Theory of Relativity*), Les éditions du Cerf, 2000, trans. Jean Seidengart, p. 19 (French).
[325] Op. cit., AK III 297; Œuvres philosophiques, t. 1, p. 1089, quoted by Ernst Cassirer.

provoked Einstein's criticism. If space and time were *a priori* forms, it became problematic, from the point of view of reason, to conceive of them as relating to the distribution of matter and energy. But did this idea of the a priori nature of space necessarily contradict the Einsteinian idea of understanding space (and time) in their dynamic relationship with the distribution of matter and energy? In other words, did the idea that reason was predestined to think about space as a condition and formal framework for phenomena necessarily exclude the possibility of thinking about the dynamic interaction between phenomena (the very dynamism that was to underpin our intuitive perception of space)?

We know that we have a three-dimensional perception of space that obeys our intuitive geometry, which is that of Euclid. On our own scale, we have to recognise that we live in a Euclidean world: Euclid's geometry is the most 'convenient' and *effective* for us (it corresponds best to our interpretation of the world that is immediately available to us, i.e. our environment). Here we find the idea of a reason with a double trigger: legislated, in that it is anchored in the physical world, subject to the material structures and laws of nature of which it is the product (it is the 'initial parameters' of sensibility that first determine reason), and legislating, in that it is not simply a passive transcription of reality, but a tool that actively organises and structures experience, producing conceptual frameworks that make sense of phenomena. This dual nature of reason implies a dialectical relationship with reality: it is constrained by the material structures of the world but remains autonomous in its ability to develop principles and interpretative models. If reason is adapted, it is also because it has been conditioned by our sensitive interactions with the physical world. It is precisely because of this that space and time are intuitive forms and not intellectual constructs (which would fall within the categories of understanding, for example). Before we can construct the world mathematically, we have to interact with it in a sensible way. And this sensible interaction is only possible on condition that we are always already adjusted to things (in an effective way, so that we can survive in the world). Before it can be calculated and deduced, the world always first gives itself to us in our sensibility, in our sensations.

As we have said, Kant's thought is not a thought of reification (of things or of space), but a thought that attempts to give a critical foundation to the sciences (and to understand the conditions of the relationship between things). It should also be noted that Kant never rejected the idea of non-Euclidean geometries, and even went so far as to show their possible coherence[326], but their non-intuitive nature alone should, in his view, render them inapplicable to physics (because they would have arisen from analytical judgements rather than *a priori* synthetic judgements). However, nothing seems to force us to consider non-Euclidean geometries as 'non-intuitive' (contrary to Kant's assertion). On the contrary, Riemannian space could very well be the intuitive framework for Einstein's relativistic physics (one of the formal manifestations of our general, abstract intuition of

---

[326] See Immanuel Kant, "Analytic", postulate of possibility, *Critique of Pure Reason*, AK III, 187

space). Henri Poincaré imagined a thought experiment in which creatures lived in a non-Euclidean space, such as a curved surface (a sphere or hyperbola). According to him, such beings would have perceived space differently from a being evolving in a Euclidean space, their sensibility being somehow guided by effectivity or by what he called 'convenience'. Unaware of the curvature of their space, they would have had perceptions and measurement tools perfectly adapted to their environment. In determining the initial parameters of our sensitivity, it is always the idea of effectiveness that dominates. The 'initial parameters' of our sensitivity should not therefore be seen as a kind of homogeneous absolute that confers its properties on reality. For all that, the determined initial parameters of our sensibility must not lead us towards the idea of relativism either. As we saw in the previous paragraph, we can think analytically about any space (any geometry) on the basis of the paradigm we deduce from our 'intuitive space'. Cassirer wrote on this subject: "the development of the theory of general relativity [...] has shown that what presented itself to Riemann as a geometrical hypothesis, as a mere possibility of thought, was an appropriate organ for the knowledge of actual reality[327]." Thus, if we conceive of critical philosophy not necessarily as a doctrine of the *a priori* (which could lead to a doctrine of absolute idealism that Kant has always rejected), but as a way of thinking that attempts to lead scientific theories back to their conditions of possibility, going from their positive structure to their proper meaning, it then becomes possible to consider its compatibility with all the frames

---

[327] Ernst Cassirer, *The Philosophy of Symbolic Forms*

of reference and paradigms of modern physics, provided that these frames have a *meaning* (and given that the frames of reference will never exhaust the general idea of space, an idea that is independent of its concrete or theoretical realisations). The absoluteness of a particular frame of reference should not therefore be regarded as a prerequisite of critical philosophy, this idea of absoluteness moreover giving rise, as we have already mentioned, to a paradox from the point of view of set theory[328].

Our Euclidean vision of space must therefore be understood and interpreted in the light of the idea that the form of our sensitive intuition is the result of an adaptive process which, by tailoring our sensitivity to what we need to feel about the world in order to survive in it, 'blows' the axioms of Euclidean geometry into our heads. Euclidean geometry is therefore not an *a priori* absolute given to us by our intuition, but an *ideal* gauge, drawn from our general intuition of space (from our sensitive pre-determination to think space), which allows us to apprehend and define reality by identity and difference (in the same way that our sensitivity gave us an idea of what heat is, this idea not corresponding to the physical reality of heat, but allowing us to enter into the physical question). The point here, however, is

---

[328] If an absolute frame of reference contains all frames of reference, does it also contain itself as an absolute frame of reference? If no, then it does not contain all frames of reference. If yes, then what about the status of the absolute frame of reference of level n contained by the absolute frame of reference of *level $n+1$*: can it be said to be *absolute*, i.e. to contain all sets, when it is itself contained in the set of all frames of reference?

to separate clearly the *schematic manifestation of a given spatial referential* from *the abstract and general idea of space* (which is not a whole as such but a general framework given by sensible intuition[329], rather as the concept is the general idea of a thing — we have seen that the intentional paradoxes of concepts remain an open problem, see § 43 — *Thought and reflection: thought and its mirror*). It is on the basis of our general idea of space, which is given to us by the form of our sensibility (by its natural predetermination), that we can think different spatial schemes and different geometries which in applying themselves to reality become gauges of our understanding. However, if the gauge can be considered contingent (responding to the criterion of convenience), it does not necessarily follow that it cannot have the value of an objective measure. This is why, once again, it is important not to confuse the ideas of our reason with what these same ideas attempt to measure and describe (the transition from the subjective to the objective). In Kantian philosophy (from which, admittedly, we have departed somewhat), as in Einstein's physics, we must always return to the problem of reference: if we ignore the referential dimension of critical philosophy, or if we ignore the problem of reference in Einstein, as is too often the case, then we miss the point of understanding the

---

[329] This general framework is the only one that allows us to think of things (and make them meaningful) in their heterogeneity, that is, in their non-reducibility to one another, that is, in their dynamic relationships, in their interconnections.

theory of relativity (this is, moreover, what Einstein would criticise Ernst Mach for).

In fact, critical idealism is not incompatible with the idea of referential frameworks, if we bear in mind that these frameworks are always *ideal* projections (and not external realities independent of observation) and if we consider that these *ideal* projections never exhaust the abstract and general idea of space[330]. The *a priori* determination of the forms of our sensibility does not imply the idea of a dogmatic imposition of reason aimed at fixing a reality in itself but designates the very conditions of possibility of our experience. The forms of our sensibility are *the means by which* the world manifests itself to us and becomes intelligible. We must

---

[330] In his preface to Ernst Cassirer's *The Theory of Einstein's Relativity*, Jean Seidengart wrote: "The element of general relativity that brings critical idealism to its highest expression, according to Cassirer, is its new conception of the relationship between matter and form. Of course, special relativity, despite its elimination of Newtonian absolute space and time, retained the classical idea that Minkowski's form of space-time remains *independent* of its material content. On the other hand, general relativity has shown that the space-time form has metric properties that are directly determined as a function of the distribution of its matter-energy content. Although this causal relationship is strictly of a *physico-mathematical* order, it presents a certain analogy with the *transcendental relationship* that unites the form and matter of knowledge", Op. cit., p.19 (French). In the theory of general relativity, time as an *ideal* projection (physico-mathematical says Jean Seidengart, or rather mathematico-physical if we want to better adhere to the framework of critical idealism) presents strong conceptual similarities with the views of critical idealism.

therefore be careful not to reduce what gives rise to the paradigms of reason (the forms of our sensibility that give us our sensitive intuition of reality and enable our understanding to "function") to the paradigms themselves. As rational pro-ductions, paradigms are not directly reducible to experience; strictly speaking, they are not 'experimental'. The rules that derive from geometry, for example, if they are first given to us through sensible intuition, cannot logically be reduced to it (they are not themselves "sensible": a geometric figure has general properties that are not sensible properties).

It is therefore essential to distinguish three levels in our apprehension of space, (i) the intuitive and sensitive experience of space, i.e. that by which space is 'immediately' *given to* us not as a concept, but as a general framework our perception of heterogeneous phenomena (ii) the ability to *grasp* space, i.e. to represent space in a way that is meaningful to us by projecting it, by imagining it in its forms (this aptitude does not necessarily precede any experience, but results from an interaction between our cognitive capacities and our exposure to the world), (iii) the formal and scientific expression of space, which derives from our capacity to project spatial schemas and which translates into theoretical models that make it possible to structure our understanding of reality (an expression that has more to do with understanding than with the intuition of space). When we speak of space, we are speaking indifferently of space as a form of our sensibility, as a signifying projection of phenomena and as a formal expression of this projective experience. This undifferentiation of the meanings of space leads to the difficulties and paradoxes that we find in the interpretations of the theory of relativity.

According to Einstein's first descriptions of relativity theory, as we have said, space is not an empty, conceptual container that is 'filled' with matter, but rather a dynamic entity that can be affected by the presence of matter: matter and energy alone can create, form and deform space (space has no concrete reality outside matter or the field equations; it is deduced rather than postulated). Moreover, in line with the epistemological presuppositions of modern science, and in particular through the influence that Ernst Mach[331] had on him in the years 1900 and 1910, Einstein sought to purge physics of any reference to non-measurable notions (which led him to abolish Newtonian absolute space and time in the theory of special relativity, but also towards the idea of a rapprochement between space and time, a rapprochement no doubt facilitated by the fact that the measurement of time precisely implies its spatialisation). It is thus the measurable character of the real that creates the real. But it is precisely the criterion of measurability that needs to be studied and questioned. This is what Ernst Cassirer quite rightly notes in his commentary on the theory of relativity: "Planck's brief formula concerning the physical criterion of the object, which he summarises by declaring that *only that which can be measured exists*, may seem fully sufficient from the point of view of physics;

---

[331] For whom physical laws should be reduced to empirical regularities, without recourse to hypothetical entities such as the ether or atoms.

but from the point of view of the theory of knowledge, it only contains within it a challenge to discover precisely the fundamental conditions of this very measurability and to develop them in a complete and systematic way[332]. The methodological convenience according to which, from the physicist's point of view, "*only that which can be measured exists* " should not be confused with an epistemological statement relating to the theory of knowledge. Here, as so often, the problem is transformed into a postulate[333]. In fact, Cassirer adds, "All measurement, even the simplest, must be based on certain theoretical presuppositions, on certain 'principles', on certain 'hypotheses' or 'axioms' which it cannot derive from the world of sensations, but which it must refer to this world as postulates of thought. In this sense, the physicist's reality is opposed to the reality of immediate perception as something entirely mediate; as a set, not of existing things nor of properties, but of abstract symbols of

---

[332] Ernst Cassirer, *Einstein's Theory of Relativity*, I. *Concept of Measures and Concepts of Thing*

[333] Ernst Cassirer wrote: "Goethe wrote to Zelter: 'The greatest art in worldly life and in study consists in transforming the *problem into a postulate*; that is how one achieves success.' In fact, this was the approach taken by Einstein in his first fundamental dissertation *Zur Elektrodynamik Bewegster Systeme* [*On the electrodynamics of moving bodies*] back in 1905. The principle of constancy of the speed of light appears at the top, as a postulate." *Einstein's Theory of Relativity*, p. 51, although he goes on to note that from the point of view of the theory of general relativity, the law of the constancy of the speed of light in a vacuum no longer has unlimited validity, II. *The Empirical and Conceptual Foundations of the Theory of Relativity*.

thought which serve to express determined relationships of magnitudes and measurements, of functional coordinations and determined dependencies between phenomena[334]." It is these "abstract symbols of thought" which, together with the general formal framework of these symbols, constitute, in relation to the objects they constitute and describe, what we call the "problem of reference", a problem often ignored by both empiricist and positivist philosophies. In relativity theory, as in any scientific construct, it is impossible to disregard the meaning of space and time *for us*, in other words the role they play in our experience and understanding of reality. This meaning cannot be dissociated from our sensory intuition: space and time constitute the necessary frameworks for the manifestation of phenomena (they give phenomena meaning). Far from being mere arbitrary frames of reference, space and time are first and foremost, as we have said, the forms through which we are seized phenomena, in their heterogeneity, in their irreducibility to one another, that is, in their dynamism. Space and time are thus not pure abstract concepts derived from understanding, nor entities independent of experience, but the conditions through which all phenomenal reality takes on meaning and becomes accessible to knowledge. This conception of space and time as structuring forms of our relationship to phenomena is, in our view, compatible with the theory of relativity (it in no way implies the absoluteness of space and time, but on the contrary insists on the causal interactions between phenomena that in some way set in motion this formal perception that we already had

---

[334] Ibid.

within us 'potentially'). It is in fact only because space and time are given to us by the form (the initial programming) of our sensibility that we are capable of generating meaningful images, that is, of proposing to reality figures of evaluation and correspondence (we are always testing ideas and patterns that are meaningful *to us*).

This reference to a reality that makes sense to us, i.e. that can be thought of by the mind and represented by the imagination, is clearly apparent in Einstein's explanations of his own concept of gravitation. The theory of general relativity, Einstein explains, can intuitively be represented using a stretched sheet of rubber to symbolise space-time. If we place a heavy lead ball on this sheet, the ball will create a depression, deforming the surface around it. This imaginary analogy helps us to visualise the way in which matter interacts with space-time and to understand that gravitation does not, as Newton thought, involve a force of attraction that would induce a form of action at a distance, but actually corresponds to the deformation of space-time by matter. If Einstein's representation is more conveniently expressed in Riemannian geometry (a geometry which, according to Cassirer, "may well constitute the intuitive *a priori* of Einstein's relativistic physics"), it can also be seen in relation to a Euclidean space, to which Einstein refers through the symbol of the rubber sheet. As Henri Poincaré pointed out, Riemannian geometry is not independent of Euclidean

geometry. It simply subjects it to a series of axiomatic transformations[335]. In this way, the theory of relativity remains linked to an *ideal* representation, a representation which alone enables the theory to be thought and developed. Moreover, — and this is an essential point for us — no spatial reference frame will ever exhaust the abstract and dynamic idea of space (an idea that we must not confuse with the different and contradictory idea of absolute space).

In his presentation of Ernst Cassirer's *Substance and function, and Einstein's theory of relativity*, Jean Seidengart[336]

---

[335] It should also be noted that, in formulating the principle of special relativity, for example, Einstein took the old representations (Galileo-Newton mechanics) and subjected them to a series of transformations that led to the formulation of the principles of relativity. Einstein's and Newton's mechanics are not unrelated. Einstein himself wrote: "It must not be thought that Newton's great creation can really be overthrown by this or any other theory. His clear and vast ideas will always retain their essential role as the foundations on which our conceptions of physics have been built". Albert Einstein, *What is the Theory of Relativity?* Reproduced from the original version published in the London Times, 28 November 191, in *Conceptions scientifiques*, Flammarion, Paris, 1952, reprinted in Champs Sciences, Flammarion, Paris, 1952. Champs Sciences, Flammarion, 2016, p. 18 (French).

[336] Jean Seidengart is Professor Emeritus of Philosophy at the University of Paris-Nanterre. He is also a founding and permanent member of the Internationale Ernst *Cassirer-Gesellschaft* in Heidelberg and Berlin and of *the Centro Internazionale di Studi Bruniani at the Istituto Italiano per gli studi Filosofici* in Naples. He was my professor at the University of

notes an aspect of similarity between the spatio-temporal form of the metric properties of Einstein's general relativity and Kant's theory of space: Although this causal relationship [the relationship between space and the distribution of its matter-energy content]," he writes, "is strictly of a *physico-mathematical* order [in the theory of general relativity], it presents a certain analogy with the *transcendental relationship* that unites the form and matter of knowledge [in the Kantian theory of space]. In transcendental aesthetics, as in the theory of general relativity, we find the same matter-form pair. Form," says Jean Seidengart, "is, in short, what allows us to think about matter (the articulation of matter through this interpretative fiction that the subject calls 'space'). The rise of the modern sciences has rendered obsolete what Kant borrowed from the sciences of his time, but the synthesising and unifying function of his philosophy, the dimension of which has been widely emphasised by Ernst Cassirer, remains. It is precisely through this synthetic and unifying dimension of our reason that we are able not only to conceive and found geometries, but also to understand the world by restoring it in a system of meaningful references (derived from sensitive intuition). *Ideal* representation (which is itself a two-stage process: (i) representation of the abstract general idea of space that derives from the form of our sensitive intuition, but which is not, for all that, a formalisation of this sensitive intuition, and (ii) formalisation of concrete spatial schemas derived from this intuitive understanding of space) is thus the

---

Paris-Nanterre in 2003. I would like to thank him for introducing me to the philosophy of Ernst Cassirer just over 20 years ago!

articulated link that binds our understanding to reality. Understanding the real is only possible through this articulation, which we call *synthetic* insofar as it is a signifying bridge between our understanding and the substratum we are trying to think (i.e. to make signifying for ourselves). Synthesis is this effort at cohabitation between the intuitive forms conceptualised by our understanding and the substratum of reality which, for us, comes together, i.e. takes on its form and meaning in what we have called the "phenomenon[337]".

In Einstein's case, it is well known that the idea for the theory of relativity did not come to him directly from the analytical theory of mathematics, but rather from a general intuition that was initially non-formal. It is true, however — contrary perhaps to what we have some-

---

[337] If our relationship with reality is primarily aesthetic and synthetic (synthetic in the way we attempt to express reality), it can nevertheless happen that a theorem or a law can be demonstrated analytically before being understood or formalised synthetically. As we pointed out earlier, Gauss, Riemann and Christoffel founded differential geometries on strictly mathematical considerations before these geometries later found their meaningful and synthetic formulation. This apparent porosity between the synthetic and the analytical can in fact be explained by the synthetic foundation of most formal systems (especially formal systems that are in fact derived from geometry). It is because of this synthetic foundation that certain formal systems manage to be *ahead of* their geometrical implications and, consequently, of their physical application. Far from calling into question the intuitive basis of our knowledge, the predictive nature of these formal systems confirms it

times suggested a little too much in this book about scientific discovery — that the theory of general relativity did not suddenly appear to Einstein as an illumination or revealed truth. In fact, the formulation of the theory of general relativity in 1915 had been preceded, ten years before its publication, by the theory of special relativity. Back in 1905, Einstein had already developed the fundamental ideas that would inspire the theory of general relativity a few years later: firstly, the principle of relativity, according to which the laws of physics are the same in all inertial frames of reference (the frames of reference of observers moving at constant speed relative to each other), the principle of constancy of the speed of light (which has the role of a frame of reference for Einstein, This is because the speed of light is not affected by the relative motion of the light source or the observer), as well as the implications of these principles for time dilation, length contraction, mass-energy equivalence ($E=mc^2$) and the invariance of space-time (space-time is invariant under Lorentz transformations, which means that the laws of physics are the same for all inertial observers). It was from this model of special relativity that Einstein intuited the model of general relativity, which included a description of gravity derived from the new understanding of space-time (gravitation not as an action at a distance, but as the consequence of the deformation of space-time) and the principle of equivalence according to which the acceleration due to gravity is equivalent to the acceleration due to a force. By drawing on his first intuition (that of the theory of special relativity), Einstein arrived at a general representation that gave rise to the formalisation of a more complete theory of the universe. However, this representation, which was in fact a sequential construction over ten years (from 1905 to 1915), involved *ideal* representations (projections of the imagination) at each stage of its generalisation. Both special relativity and general relativity are theories supported by concrete representations. In this respect, it is interesting to note the extent to which Einstein's language is imagery-based, using representations that are commonplace and taken from everyday life (the image of a station and moving trains for special relativity, the image of a lift or a rubber plane for general relativity). The idea that scientific discoveries are first and foremost projections of the imagination, in other words referential and meaningful representations, seems to be deeply rooted in Einstein's thinking. In an article published in 1940, reacting to recent developments in quantum theory, Einstein wrote on this subject: "Some physicists, among them myself, cannot believe that we must abandon, actually and forever, the idea of direct representation of physical reality in space and time; or that we must accept the view that events in nature are analogous to a game of chance[338]". In a 1934 article entitled *In Memory of Paul Ehrenfest*, Einstein also praised the spirit of clarity, implicitly referring to the problem of imagination (which stems from sensitive intuition) and reference. As he wrote about the Austrian theorist and physicist Paul Ehrenfest following his tragic death[339], Ehrenfest's had extraordinary ability "to grasp

---

[338] Albert Einstein, *on Quantum Physics*, 1954

[339] From correspondence with close friends, it appears that from May 1931 Paul Ehrenfest was suffering from a severe depression. In August 1932, Albert Einstein was so worried

the essence of a theoretical notion, to strip a theory of its mathematical accoutrements until the simple basic idea emerged with clarity[340]" that made him "a peerless teacher". From the 1930s onwards, Einstein made more and more statements that seemed to be along the lines of critical idealism (or at least a dualist doctrine of scientific practice). For example, in a letter to Karl Popper dated 11 September 1935, he wrote: "Altogether I really do not at all like the now fashionable "positivistic" tendency of clinging to what is observable ... and I think (like you, by the way) that theory cannot be fabricated out of the results of observation, but that it can only be invented.[341]" In 1938, in a book entitled *The Evolution of Physics* presenting a series of lectures given by Einstein at Princeton in 1936, he wrote: "Physical concepts are free creations of the human mind, and are not, however it may seem, uniquely determined by the external world. In our endeavour to understand reality we are somewhat like a man trying to understand the mechanism of a closed watch. He sees the face and the moving hands, even hears its ticking, but he has no way of opening the case. If he is ingenious, he may form

---

that he wrote to the board of Leiden University, expressing deep concern and suggesting ways of reducing Ehrenfest's workload. On 25 September 1933, Paul Ehrenfest went to the Waterink Institute for handicapped children in Amsterdam with a pistol and shot his fifteen-year-old son Wassik, who had Down's Syndrome, in the head before immediately turning the gun on himself.

[340] Op. cit., in *Conceptions scientifiques*, Flammarion, Paris, 1952, republished in Champs Sciences, Flammarion, 2016, p. 168.
[341] Letter on the *Theoretical Status of Mechanics*

some picture of a mechanism which could be responsible for all the things he observes, but he may never be quite sure his picture is the only one which could explain his observations. He will never be able to compare his picture with the real mechanism and he cannot even imagine the possibility or the meaning of such a comparison. But he certainly believes that, as his knowledge increases, his picture of reality will become simpler and simpler and will explain a wider and wider range of his sensuous impressions. He may also believe in the existence of the ideal limit of knowledge and that it is approached by the human mind. He may call this ideal limit the objective truth[342]." One of the constants in these statements is the systematic association of scientific discoveries with the activity of the imagination, which gives us an idea, i.e. a representation of the reality we are trying to explain ("compare its image with the real mechanism", wrote Einstein). However, Einstein was aware that this comparison of the image with reality cannot be understood as an objective correspondence (the watch is closed and the phenomenon is a construction). We therefore need to rely on the effectiveness of our mental representations and try to extend these representations to "ever more extensive domains". Was this influenced by Kurt Gödel, whom Einstein met at Princeton University at the time, and with whom he regularly exchanged ideas on long walks? In any case, in the 1930s, Einstein seemed to be moving more and more towards a form of critical idealism that acknowledged the dual nature of the world and the non-reducibility of the mind's

---

[342] Op. Cit., Cambridge University Press, The scientific Book club, p. 33

creations to their external *stimuli* ("physical concepts are free creations of the human mind and are not, as one might think, determined solely by the external world"), while at the same time insisting on the scientist's theoretical activity as the production of schemas and intuitive images ("to form some image of the mechanism") that must first be expressed and communicated clearly without their "mathematical garb". In the 1940s, Einstein became an outspoken anti-positivist. In a letter to Max Born dated 18 March 1948, for example, he said: "I would love to tear your positivist philosophy apart myself, but that is unlikely to happen in our lives[343]." Reading these regular statements in favour of a form of critical idealism and increasingly against radical empiricism or the positivist positions of the Vienna Circle and the Copenhagen School, one wonders why Einstein continued to resist Cassirer's interpretation of relativity, for example. As Françoise Balibar, a French physicist and historian of science, wrote in an article devoted to Cassirer's book on relativity: "I have no answer to this question, other than the stubborn refusal to fall under any philosophical banner. 'In philosophy I am an opportunist[344]', said Einstein."

---

[343] Einstein to Max Born 18 March 1948 The Born-Einstein Letters

[344] We don't have the exact quote from Einstein but we do have writings supporting this vision: "[The scientist] therefore must appear to the systematic epistemologist as a type of unscrupulous opportunist: he appears as *realist* insofar as he seeks to describe a world independent of the acts of perception; as *idealist* insofar as he looks upon

55.

THE PROBLEM OF TIME — To fully understand the scope of the problem of time, we need to resituate it within our general problematic, which is that of reference and meaning. In the light of Albert Einstein's work on relativity and its implications for time in modern physics, we need to ask ourselves the following questions: (i) what is time from the physicist's point of view? (ii) what is time from the point of view of consciousness? (iii) what, finally, is the meaning of time for us (physicists and philosophers)?

(i) *What is time from a physicist's point of view?* Einstein approached the question of time

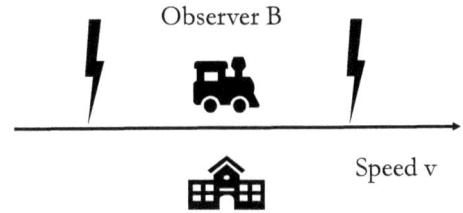

through that of simultaneity, which he

---

the concepts and theories as free inventions of the human spirit (not logically derivable from what is empirically given); as *positivist* insofar as he considers his concepts and theories justified *only* to the extent to which they furnish a logical representation of relations among sensory experiences. He may even appear as *Platonist* or *Pythagorean* insofar as he considers the viewpoint of logical simplicity as an indispensable and effective tool of his research.", (Einstein 1949, 683–684).

showed to be relative to an observer's frame of reference. According to special relativity, two events perceived as simultaneous in a given inertial frame of reference may not be so in another frame of reference in relative motion. This relativity of simultaneity follows directly from the Lorentz transformations, which link space and time into a single framework. As a result, there is no such thing as absolute simultaneity, independent of the frame of reference adopted. To illustrate this phenomenon, Einstein proposed the following example: suppose an observer A, standing still on a station platform, sees two flashes of lightning strike the front and rear of a moving train simultaneously. How-ever, an observer B inside the train would not perceive the flashes as simultaneous.

The reason for this is that, in the train's frame of reference, the front and rear of the train (the points of impact of the flashes) are in motion relative to the platform, whereas in the platform's frame of reference, these points remain fixed. Observer A, positioned at the centre of the platform, sees the light from the two flashes propagating at equal speed and reaching a median point (the centre of the train) at the same time. However, for observer B, who is travelling with the train, this mid-point is not static: it moves towards the light coming from the front of the train and away from the light coming from the rear. Since the speed c of light is the same for all observers[345], it follows that B will first perceive the light coming from the front of the train, then that coming from the back. For him, the flashes did not occur simultaneously. So, each frame of reference has its own time frame, and an indication of simultaneity only makes sense in relation to a given frame of reference. Since no frame of reference can be considered absolute, there is no universal framework for defining simultaneity that is independent of the observer. As Einstein asserted, simultaneity is therefore a property relative to inertial reference frames and cannot be universally defined.

---

[345] The invariance of the speed of light is based on experimental observations, in particular the Michelson-Morley experiment (1887), which showed that the speed of light does not depend on the movement of the Earth. In special relativity, this constancy derives from the fact that space and time are transformed in such a way as to preserve c for all observers. Unlike material objects, whose speed is added according to classical mechanics, light always travels at a constant speed in a vacuum, regardless of the motion of the source or the observer. This property is confirmed by all modern experiments in particle physics and astrophysics.

Now imagine two observers, A and B, in relative motion at high speed. Observer A is on a beach, while observer B is on board

a boat travelling at constant speed. At the top of the boat's mast, a beam of light is emitted towards the ground. In the frame of reference of sailor B, who considers his boat to be stationary, the light travels in a straight line down to the foot of the mast. The path of the light therefore simply corresponds to the height of the mast. For observer A on the beach, on the other hand, the boat moves forward at the same time as the light descends. So instead of following a strictly vertical trajectory, the light beam follows a diagonal: it has to travel not only the height of the mast, but also a horizontal distance due to the movement of the boat. Since the speed of light is the same in all frames of reference, why does light seem to travel a greater distance in the frame of reference of the beach?

According to the theory of special relativity, there is only one possible conclusion: time does not elapse in the same way in the two reference frames. In other words, if light takes a certain time to travel downwards in the boat's frame of reference, it takes a longer time to travel a greater distance as seen from the beach. Each observer measures a different time for the same physical phenomenon. The shortest duration, called the proper duration, is that measured in the frame of reference where the two events (emission and reception of the light beam) occur at the same point, i.e. the boat. In the frame of reference of the observer on the beach, the duration measured is longer: this is time dilation. This effect, which derives from the Lorentz transformations, was reformulated by Hermann Minkowski in 1908 as part of the theory of space-time.

Special relativity is based on two fundamental postulates: firstly, the principle of relativity, according to which the laws of physics are identical in all inertial reference frames, what-ever their motion at constant speed (which means that it is impossible to distinguish a state of rest from uniform rectilinear motion by internal experience[346]), secondly, the principle of the

---

[346] The principle of relativity stems from the idea that no inertial frame of reference is privileged in the universe. It was

invariance of the speed of light c, which states that the speed of light in a vacuum is the same for all observers, regardless of their relative motion (note that the invariance of the speed of light is based on experimental observations, in particular the Michelson-Morley experiment mentioned in the previous footnote). One of the major consequences of these principles is time dilation: the faster an object moves relative to an observer, the slower its own time becomes. This phenomenon, which stems from the Lorentz trans-formations, has been confirmed experimentally on several times, notably by comparing atomic clocks on board aircraft or satellites with clocks on the ground[347].

---

formulated by Galileo and then generalised by Einstein to include electromagnetism. Experimentally, no physical phenomenon (mechanical, electromagnetic, etc.) can distinguish uniform rectilinear motion from a state of absolute rest. For example, in a train moving at constant speed, a dropped marble will fall vertically for a passenger, as if the train were stationary. This principle has been confirmed by all experiments, including quantum mechanics and particle physics.

[347] A famous experiment in this field is the Hafele-Keating experiment, carried out in 1971. Atomic clocks were placed on board commercial aircraft that flew at different altitudes and directions around the world. The results confirmed the prediction of special relativity that time measured by clocks in motion would slow down relative to that measured by

While special relativity has shown that time and space are not absolute, but depend on the relative motion of observers, it only applies to inertial reference frames, i.e. in the absence of acceleration or gravity. The presence of mass in the universe introduces a curvature into space-time that modifies not only the trajectories of objects, but also the flow of time itself. It was to take account of this interaction between gravity and time that Einstein developed the theory of general relativity, an extension of the theory of special relativity that encompasses accelerated reference frames and gravitational fields. Einstein's general relativity establishes that gravity is not a force, as Newton explained it, but a consequence of the curvature of space-time caused by the presence of mass and energy. This deformation affects not only the trajectories of objects, but also the flow of time. One of the fundamental principles of the theory of general relativity is the principle of equivalence: an observer in free fall in an intense gravitational field feels no gravity, while an observer standing still in this field

---

clocks at rest, due to time dilation. Many other similar experiments have been carried out since then, with greater precision thanks to technological advances, and they continue to confirm the predictions of Einstein's special relativity on time dilation and other aspects of the theory.

experiences acceleration. This means that the effects of a gravitational field are locally in-distinguishable from those of an accelerated frame of reference. Since acceleration influences the passage of time, an object subject to strong acceleration (such as a stationary observer near a black hole) will see its time pass more slowly than an observer at a distance from the gravitational field. In an intense gravitational field, space-time is bent in such a way that the trajectories of objects are altered, giving rise to the apparent effect of the gravitational 'force'. Clocks in a weaker gravitational potential beat faster than those in a stronger potential. The closer an object is to a massive object, the more it is 'accelerated' towards it, even if it remains stationary in its own frame of reference. This acceleration, which reflects the force of gravity in a relativistic framework, leads to time dilation: the object closer to the mass sees its time slow down compared to an observer further away.

(ii) *What is time from the point of view of consciousness?* To ask what time means from the point of view of consciousness is to ask what time is *for us*, insofar as we experience its duration. It might be tempting to define time in the same way as we previously defined space, i.e. by distinguishing between three levels of apprehension of time: the intuitive and sensitive experience of time (by which time is 'immediately' *given to* us as the general framework of our perception of heterogeneous phenomena), the ability to *grasp* time (to represent it to us 'meaningfully' by imagining it in its forms) and the formal and scientific expression of time that would derive from this ability to represent time to us. However, unlike space, time cannot be formalised mediately by concrete projections from the imagination. If I draw a closed geometric figure, for example, my figure defines an interior space (the space contained in the figure) at the same time as I delimit a space outside the figure. But there's nothing like this with time: I can't give myself a meaningful image of time unless I spatialise it. So how can we make time meaningful to ourselves (in other words, what does time mean *to us*)? Whereas space is perceived through objects that are given to us by sensitive intuition, time is not given to us by any external object. This is why Kant makes it a condition of all internal experience, an *a priori* form of sensibility. It is precisely this apriorism, as we have said, that bothers Einstein. This idea of the apriority of time is indeed embarrassing if we consider that its corollary is an absolute and fixist vision of time. We know that Kant sees time as the structure in which we are aware of our successive thoughts (which is why he speaks of internal intuition, even though we prefer, for the reasons we explained earlier, to reserve the term intuition for an "external" grasp). However, Kant does not insist so much on the homogeneity of time, but on the grasp of time as a form of succession. In other words, Kant emphasises the binding nature of time, seeing it as the framework that structures the relationships between phenomena. In this way, time could be defined as the general framework that allows the subject to establish synthetic links between objects (in other words, it is the framework through which objects become meaningful *to us*). As the general framework of connections between objects, time is intimately linked to space. The perception of figures and forms, that is, the identification of their spatial connections, always takes place *in time*. It is within the structuring framework of time that the subject has the intuition of space (straight lines, angles, shapes, etc.). It is therefore problematic for us to reduce the question of time to that of space (or to claim to spatialise time) insofar as it is precisely time that gives substance to space by enabling it to be apprehended globally in the succession of forms that make it up.

We know that Hermann Cohen, who along with Paul Natorp was one of the founders of the neo-Kantian school in Marburg, amended Kant's philosophy by making time and space categories of understanding. Thus, whereas Kant distinguished four categories of understanding (categories of quantity, quality, relation and modality) that were secondary to space and time[348], Hermann Cohen turned space and time into mathematical categories, derived from the category of quantity (which in Kant's case included unity, plurality and totality). For Cohen, plurality thus became the foundation of time (time as a succession of units), while space was placed on the side of totality in the idea of simultaneity. According to Hermann Cohen, moving from time to space was tantamount to moving from succession to simultaneity. For us, this view is problematic in that it overlooks the special status of space and time in the constitution of the signifying world (we think of space and time as the structuring framework of our experience of phenomena, not as a pure construct of understanding). Moreover, Cohen's idea that space is that which is given in totality and simultaneity can, in our view, lead to confusion. While space can be seen as a

---

[348] Categories do not create phenomena; they merely give them an intelligible unity. This is why they are secondary to the forms of sensibility: they can only function if intuitions are already given to them in space and time.

structuring framework of its own, the way in which it is given in determined forms and figures (in nature or geometry) is, in our view, always sequenced (it takes place in time). To perceive a square, a straight line or a circle, we have to mentally go through its elements. Although we have a sort of illusion of immediacy, the journey that determines the shape of an object is successive and takes place over time (we always apprehend various elements that we bring together to form a meaningful whole). So we must not confuse the act of grasping through the intuition of forms, which always implies successiveness (an act that takes place over time), with the act of gathering and synthesising (the act of understanding), which implies a form of simultaneity (we gather diverse elements into a synthetic unity, and this gathering implies the coexistence of diverse elements over time, a coexistence that is necessary for the signifying grasp, i.e. for the act of gathering).

By insisting on the functional and binding character of the signifying frameworks of space and time, we avoid the idea that space and time are *a priori* rigid frameworks that would prohibit the theory of relativity. For us, time and space are in fact frameworks within which the binding functions of the mind operate, functions that authorise relativistic conceptions.

(iii) *What is the meaning of time for us (physicists and philosophers)?* Is there a difference in nature between the "time of philosophers", the "time of physicists" and "psychological time" (the time perceived by consciousness)? In response to a lengthy comment made by Henri Bergson at the meeting of the Société Française de Philosophie on 6 April 1922, Albert Einstein replied: "The question is this: Is the philosopher's time the same as the physicist's? The philosopher's time, I believe, is both psychological and physical time, and physical time can be derived from the time of consciousness. Initially, individuals had the notion of the simultaneity of perception; they could then agree among themselves and agree on something about what they perceived; this was a first step towards objective reality. But there are objective events that are independent of individuals, and we have moved on from the simultaneity of perceptions to the simultaneity of the events them-selves. And, in fact, for a long time, this simultaneity did not lead to any contradiction because of the great speed at which light propagates. The concept of simultaneity could therefore be transferred from perceptions to objects. It was only a short step from there to deducing a temporal order in events, and instinct did just that. But there is nothing in our consciousness that allows us to conclude that events are simultaneous, because they are merely mental constructs, logical beings. So, there is no philosopher's time; there is only psychological time, different from the physicist's time[349]". It is interesting to note here that Albert Einstein identified psychological time and physical time separately. For Einstein, psychological time is an *a posteriori* reconstruction of consciousness, which is why he distinguishes between the "simultaneity of perceptions" and that of "events themselves". The mistake made by the pre-relativistic physicist was, in Einstein's view, to move from the simultaneity of perception to the simultaneity of objects (i.e. objective signals).

It should be noted, however, that although Einstein revealed that simultaneity is a non-absolute notion in relativistic physics, the fact remains that this question had already arisen, in a different form, in classical physics. Indeed, even in a Newtonian framework, the simultaneity of distant events could only be defined in relation to a given observer and the means available to him to perceive them. Let's imagine, for example, that lightning strikes simultaneously, according to a single Galilean reference frame at rest, three kilometres to the east and three kilometres

---

[349] Albert Einstein, *Bulletin de la société française de philosophie*, meeting of 6 April 1922, translated from French

to the west of observer A. For him, these events appear simultaneous. For him, these events appear simultaneous because the sound of the lightning strikes reaches him at the same instant. However, if an observer B is closer to one of the points of impact, he will hear the thunder of the nearest flash before that of the farthest one, because of the limited speed of sound (around 344 m/s).

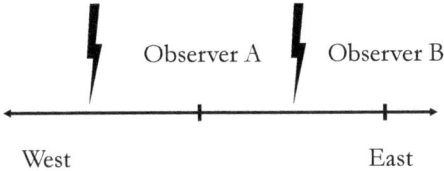

He will then be able to conclude that the two events, which are simultaneous in his frame of reference, are out of sync. This effect does not call into question simultaneity in classical physics, since, given the speed of sound and the distances involved, an observer could always correct this apparent desynchronisation to reconstruct the absolute simultaneity of the flashes. However, he shows that the simultaneity of distant events can only be defined as a function of the means of perception and the position of the observer. This problem is even more obvious in the field of acoustics. In a large concert hall, a spectator on the left of the stage may perceive a slight shift in sound compared with a spectator on the right. This phenomenon is well known to sound engineers and has led to the development of sound synchronisation systems in concert halls and stadiums. What's more, on a finer scale, our own ears never receive a sound at exactly the same moment, unless we are perfectly centred between two synchronous sound sources. So even before special relativity, the idea of simultaneity was already problematic: it depended on the position and mode of perception of the observer. Although classical physics always made it possible to correct these discrepancies by reconstructing an "absolute" framework (from the point of view of classical physics), it showed that simultaneity was never an immediate given of reality, but always a construction based on observations that depended on the observer's point of view. This raised a more fundamental question: is simultaneity a good basis for defining the nature of time? If, even in classical physics, simultaneity seems problematic within a single frame of reference, how could it be sufficient to characterise time itself?

The difficulty arises above all from the fact that simultaneity, as we have examined it, is always based on a perceptual construction or an intellectual reconstitution supported by measuring instruments, which extend our sensory faculties without revealing to us an essence of time. It is also inseparable, in modern physics, from the occurrence of events in space, which leads to a spatialisation of time and further complicates any attempt to apprehend it other than through quantifiable reference points. The problem of simultaneity is really just a special case of the question of time, which requires an understanding not just of what a reference point in time is (which refers back to the measurability of time, and therefore to the possibility of determining whether or not two events can be synchronous), but also of what time is insofar as it flows and passes (time 'for us', or time as a synthetic construct of our consciousness). But one difficulty remains: how can we deduce time from the movement of matter if we do not already have some intuition of time? In other words, if we reject the idea that time is an intrinsic property of things, must we not recognise that a conception of time pre-exists any attempt to measure it? This question brings us back to the fundamental problem of apriorism: can we think about time without possessing a prior capacity to apprehend it?

We propose the following response to this problem: (i) as material beings born of evolution, we have an innate disposition to perceive and organise reality (our "initial programming"). This disposition is the mode by which the world manifests itself to us in its intelligibility. Einstein might agree with this observation, who credited Kant with showing "the postulation of a real external world would be senseless without this comprehensibility[350]". We have attempted to describe this problem of the intelligibility of the world through the dual notion of reason as legislated (since it is constituted by matter) and as legislating (insofar as it has the intuition of the rules of matter). We admit, however, that we have not resolved the question of "the first cause" of the intelligibility of the world (if this question can have any meaning for us). We have confined ourselves to establishing its reality — in particular by introducing the concept of the effectivity of ideas, i.e. by proving their validity or invalidity in relation to the reality given to us, as well as by the logical rejection of monistic theories. However, the question of the cause of the intelligibility of the world does not directly concern our demonstration, and we limit ourselves to noting that (ii) this innate disposition to perceive and organise reality is linked both to our capacity to be affected by reality and to form a certain idea (a pattern) of reality. We do not simply react to *stimuli*. As sentient

---

[350] Albert Einstein, Albert Einstein, *Physics and Reality*, 1936, p. 292, from the Journal of the Franklin Institute, Vol. 221, No. 3, 3 March 1936

organisms become more autonomous, they form a more and more precise (i.e. more and more *effective* from the point of view of science) idea of reality (see in particular § 18 and § 19 — *Degrees of freedom*). As far as the specific problem of time is concerned, this idea of reality depends on our habits of perception, our history and our culture (as Ernst Cassirer points out in *The Philosophy of Symbolic Forms*), but is not reducible to experience (since it would be contradictory to make time an intrinsic characteristic of things, which would lead us back to the monistic systems we have rejected). To understand this paradox of the non-reducibility of time to the experience of time, we need to separate, as we did for space, two distinct ideas of time which, although grouped under the same term, in fact designate different realities. Firstly, there is the idea of time as the concrete synthesis of our daily experience of duration, which leads me to say that time 'passes' more or less quickly, whereas in reality, as Bergson rightly points out, it is *I* who am passing, it is my subjective experience that is at stake. Then there is the idea of time as an abstract form of my experience of reality: I know that time exists outside my subjective experience of duration, it's the idea of time in general (time as the general framework of phenomena). This is the idea of time in general (time as the general framework of phenomena). It is this idea of time that is at stake when I assert, for example, that phenomena unfold "in time". To take up the thesis we developed in relation to space (and geometry), we can say that from this abstract idea of time derive all the forms of *ideal* structures that allow us to grasp the question of change. The idea of change is certainly nothing without the experience of change, but neither can it be contained in things themselves (even if we know that in relativity, time is intrinsically linked to the physical state of the world). It is always the subject who derives from things the idea of change, and therefore the idea of duration. Without the experience of things, this idea remains an empty shell, but the idea itself cannot be contained in things; since things have no 'in-itself', they can have no intrinsic characteristics either (see § 23 — *Is there anything 'in-itself'?*). In this way, time is the signifying form of the heterogeneity of reality, of its non-reducibility to unity, a unity that is given to us *a contrario* by the intuition of space. Time is, in a way, the signifying framework of the relation, of the articulation of the heterogeneous real. When, for example, we perceive a simple figure like a square, we see a sequencing in time of a figure (com-posed of lines and angles) and at the same time grasp its spatial unity, which is given to us by the intuition of space (which proceeds from a unitary gathering and not a sequencing).

But what exactly is the nature of the space-time that Einstein introduced in his theory of special relativity? In his famous controversy with Bergson, Einstein made a clear distinction between psychological time, which is our subjective experience of duration and change, and the physicist's time, which is the time of measurable relationships between events in space-time. However, he rejects the idea of a "philosopher's time" distinct from the physicist's time, saying: "So there is no such thing as a philosopher's time; there is only a psychological time that is different from the physicist's time. This rejection deserves to be questioned. The physicist's time does not emerge *ex nihilo*; it is structured by conceptual frameworks that derive first and foremost from our sensitive intuitions. By too hastily assimilating (philosophical) time, as a condition authorising the structuring of phenomenal relations, to time conceived as an objective physical reality, we run the risk of reintroducing, in another form, a problematic metaphysical realism. If we were to make time a purely extrinsic entity, detached from the knowing subject, we would once again be locked into the impasses of naive realism, which would lead us to postulate an absolute time[351] existing independently of all consciousness. This perspective, close to that defended by Newton in the *Principia Mathematica* — where he defines time as a continuous and autonomous flow, "absolute, true and mathematical, flowing uniformly without relation to anything external" — brings us back precisely to the difficulties we were trying to overcome.

This is why, before measuring and understanding time, we need to think about the subjective conditions that make this measurement and understanding possible. But precisely to define time as the condition of our sensible experience of succession (and therefore of causality) is not to assume its absoluteness. Let's take an image from the analysis of concepts: our concept of "dog" corresponds neither to an ideal and absolute image of a dog, serving as an immutable reference for all the others, nor to the exhaustive set of all existing or possible dogs. Such a set would necessarily be evolving, making any attempt at totalisation illusory. In reality, the concept of a dog is above all an

---

[351] It should be noted that by positing absolute time, we would in fact be led back to the paradoxes of totalising sets: a set that claims to encompass all its parts is logically problematic, just as a theory of time that denied all relativity while postulating an underlying universal structure would be contradictory.

analytical and logical construction, formed from the concrete experience of a particular dog. It is therefore neither a fixed essence nor a totalising abstraction, but a conceptual scheme that is defined by relations to perceptual elements distinct from the concept itself: for example, recognising a dog involves taking into account characteristics such as its eyes, its teeth, its silhouette — elements which, in themselves, are not "the dog" but which, by being integrated into a network of meanings, enable the immediate identifycation of the concept of dog. Similarly, time and space share a relational structure with concepts but differ from them in their fundamental role in our way of organising reality. They are not simply objects of knowledge like any others; they are the frameworks within which all possible experience unfolds (even if these frameworks are deduced from experience or, as it were, 'activated' by experience). They are consubstantial with the possibility of external intuition, that is, with our capacity to organise and structure sensible experience. However, in the same way that the concept of 'dog' is neither an absolute referential nor a fixed totality, the structuring frameworks of space and time cannot be assimilated to absolute reference frame or fixed totalities. They are subjective frameworks within which phenomena unfold and acquire meaning for us, according to our own frame of reference of observation. Consequently, in the same way that the concept of 'dog' does not bark[352], the formal frameworks of time and space do not expand or contract under the effect of gravitational mass. These frameworks, while allowing the emergence of paradigms that define the physicist's time, cannot be totally identified with these paradigms, which is why we believe that we must maintain the distinction between what Einstein called "the time of philosophers" and the time of physicists (even if his controversy with Bergson concerns aspects of time other than those we have just directly mentioned).

---

[352] We use the example of the concept as an abstract idea to illustrate the distinction between the general abstract idea of time (which arises from intuition) and the reference frames of time (which are mathematical or geometrical ideas) that give rise to Einstein's idea of the "deformation" of time. Kant makes it clear in his *Critique of Pure Reason* that time is not a concept: "Time is not a discursive or, as we say, universal concept, but a pure form of sensible intuition. Different times are only parts of the same time. Now the representation that can only be given by a single object is an intuition."

"The whole representation does not have to be given by concepts (for these contain only partial representations), but an immediate intuition must serve as their foundation", Op. cit., *A 32, B 48*.

If we return to the question of the meaning of time for us, we can now distinguish at least three dimensions of time, each corresponding to a distinct mode of understanding and experience, (i) psychological time: this is time as it is subjectively perceived, that which gives us the impression of duration and in which we observe change. It results from the synthesis of our temporal experiences and varies according to our inner state, (ii) time as the general framework of our intuition of phenomena which allows us to apprehend in particular the relationship between phenomena independently of the way in which we measure them; this is the time we might call "philosopher's time", (iii) time as a concrete physical figure understood itself through the paradigms of our understanding: this is time as it is quantified, spatialised and modelled in modern physics[353]. It is this time that we are referring to when we say that "time dilates when approaching a mass", in reference to the effects of relativity. This physical time, as formalised in our scientific theories, is not immediately given as a raw datum of experience, but is the result of a rational construction, the result of an articulation of *ideal* schemes elaborated by thought. Even before time dilation was confirmed empirically by experience (for example, through the desynchronisation of clocks in general relativity), this idea already existed in the form of a theoretical projection, as a necessary consequence of rational principles applied to

---

[353] Aristotle already said that "time is the number of motion", underlining its intrinsic link with the measurement of change. From Kepler onwards, kinematic models made it possible to spatialise time, making it a quantity defined by its relationship with space and motion.

the dynamics of space and time. However, this construction cannot be totally autonomous from experience: it is through our intuition of time, which is given to us in the experience of phenomena (without being reducible to phenomena), that we are able to conceptualise theories and models of physical time. Without this fundamental intuition of temporal succession, we would not be able to develop spatialised schematic representations of time, which are nonetheless essential to the formulation and understanding of modern physical theories.

56.

SHOULD WE ABANDON THE PRINCIPLE OF CAUSALITY? — In paragraph 49, entitled *Against the probabilistic interpretation of quantum mechanics*, we have already indicated the epistemological impasses of the probabilistic and statistical interpretation of quantum mechanics, referring in particular to the problematic conception of knowledge that would take as its sole foundation the inductivist principle, a problem that had already been highlighted by David Hume, but which had not found a concrete resolution in his philosophy. With the advent of quantum mechanics came the development of a new paradigm, dominant among microphysicists, according to which the quantum world is not deterministic and can only be described using probabilities. Once again, we need to ask ourselves what this description of the quantum world means. Is the probabilistic nature of quantum mechanics an intrinsic characteristic of the phenomena we are trying to describe — which amounts to saying that the phenomenon, as a co-construction of our sensitive intuition, our projective (productive) imagination and the material substrate through which it is expressed, would be "non-deterministic" in nature? Or is it a property of things in themselves? We have already pointed out on several occasions the aporias of reasoning about things in themselves: as sentient beings, we never have access to things as they are in themselves, but always to things as they are manifested through our sensitive intuition and as they are shaped by our imagination and our understanding. To ask about the non-deterministic nature of things is therefore to ask about the non-deterministic nature of the phenomena we observe, phenomena that are always mental constructs for us. But what is causality, from the point of view of phenomena, if not the physical manifestation of a principle that we have established logically: *radical* dualism (the heterogeneity of reality, its non-reducibility to unity)?

For us, the first moment of causality is the relationship that is established between the material substratum (the "thing-in-itself" but which is not yet anything really defined for us) and the phenomenon (the "thing-in-itself" which becomes a thing for us). This relationship between the phenomenon and its substrate presupposes (i) the existence of a world that is external to us (an existence we tried to establish by relying on the Gödelian problem of incompleteness, which led us to Putnam's problem of reference) and (ii) the idea that this external world is indeed at the origin of our sensations (which we also tried to establish with Putnam's example of the "brain in a vat"). If we have established (i) and (ii) then, we have also established that there exists between the substratum and its phenomenon a link of influence, a relation that we call causality, intelligible relation, or "intelligible reason". This link is not situated in space and time (by construction, it escapes our sensibility, not our reason[354]) but can be logically posited as a relation of influence between heterogeneous, but not independent, realities. It relates the structure of the duality between the organism and the objects by which it is affected. The second moment of causality (which is often posited as the first moment) is that of the relationship *between* phenomena. It is this moment that David Hume emphasises in his *Enquiry into Human Understanding*. David Hume rightly asserts that when we see an event A closely followed in time by an event B, we tend to assume that A is the cause of B. However, according to Hume, we can never perceive this relationship of cause and effect itself. All we perceive are the two events occurring in succession, not a necessary connection between them. David Hume is right to point out that this empirical approach to causality is based on habit and the association of ideas, and in no way constitutes a rational foundation. It is precisely here that we see the main difficulty with the principle of causality. If we make the principle of causality into an experimental deduction (a relationship between phenomena), then we expose ourselves to the legitimate criticism that a temporal sequence (a succession in time) between two phenomena, i.e. between two representations, is not necessarily a causal sequence. On the contrary, if we make the principle of causality into a purely intelligible

---

[354] The real is never given to us except through our senses, so we can only assume the link between the real and our senses, which is by construction 'extrasensory'.

and *a priori* principle, i.e. a formal principle (a principle that would be at work in arithmetic, for example), we fail to claim a causal link between this formal principle and the phenomena we experience in space and time (even if this formal principle, derived from our intuition of time and space, can claim this validity link for itself within its formal system, it cannot use this link to apply it to objects). This difficulty disappears, however, if we make the principle of causality the logico-empirical articulation relation of *radical* dualism. For us, the founding principle of causality is to be found neither in phenomena, nor in an intelligible *a priori*, nor even in things "in themselves", but rather in the dynamic articulation between heterogeneous, but not independent, systems. Indeed, to demonstrate the founding and legitimate role of the principle of causality, we need to focus on the idea that underpins it: that of the articulation, that is, the 'non-identity' of heterogeneous realities, which, by virtue of their heterogeneity, have the possibility of interacting, that is, of modifying and changing. If we were to conceive of the world in general and phenomena in particular as unitary and perfectly homogeneous, it would then be possible to deny the principle of causality. Phenomena would then rest within themselves in a kind of imperturbable and eternal stability. In this conception, however, we would be led to admit that no dynamics or change would be possible or comprehensible. In fact, change is precisely the form of heterogeneity, that is, of *radical* dualism (of non-identity). What is dynamics if not the modification of the phenomenon in time and space? And how can we explain this modification if not by introducing a duality (a 'non-unity') into the world, a duality that contradicts precisely the thesis that seeks to deny the principle of causality? If the phenomenon changes (and it doesn't matter whether this change is only in my perception or in the phenomenal object of my perception), it's because *something* related to this phenomenon changes. This "something" is, and can only be, the intelligible manifestation *in the sensible* of the heterogeneity of the phenomenon with what acts on it, that is, of *radical* dualism (of the heterogeneity of the real, if you prefer). If we were to assume, as Hume did, that the principle of causality is only inferred from empirical observation, it would become impossible for us to understand change, that is, to make it *meaningful to* us. In other words, causality is, for us, the "signifiance" of change. This does not mean that causality is a mere signifying convention, but rather that it is *the only way in which* we can imagine change, that is, make it signifying and comprehensible to us. With the principle of causality thus established as the articulatory structure of *radical* dualism (the articulation between phenomena and their substratum, *and the* articulation between phenomena insofar as they are not 'pure representations' but elements of a system open to a material reality), we must now ask ourselves about the notion of determinism and the way in which the principle of determinism has been used and understood in modern science. If causality is the signifying form of change, which characterises the relationship in time and space between two heterogeneous entities that cannot be reduced to one another (even if this relationship, although taking place in time and space, is not of phenomenal origin), determinism is the idea that the same causes *always and necessarily* produce the same effects. The idea of determinism is therefore linked not only to the principle of causality, but also to the idea of identity and permanence of the causal link (identity in the sense that, all other things being equal, the same cause always produces the same result). However, once we have posited a heterogeneity and its resolution in the idea of relation which induces the idea of causal influence, it seems artificial to make a *distinction* (a little too convenient) between causality and determinism. At the most fundamental level, we would find it very difficult to envisage the idea that the homogeneity of the causes and conditions of an experience could be translated into a heterogeneity of its consequences without thinking that *something* of the experience has escaped us (whether in the characterisation of the link between the phenomenon and its substratum or in the characterisation of the link between the phenomena themselves). Indeed, since the causal link is not material in itself (since it is rather the form of change), it would be difficult to imagine that it could be such as to bring about indeterminate changes. It is true that the introduction of the notion of indeterminacy at the level of quantum particles within a macroscopic universe that remained deterministic caused great perplexity and even a certain amount of disarray in the scientific community of the 1920s. However, this discomfort quickly dissolved in the formal non-deterministic paradigm of Heisenberg and Bohr. If, however, we take seriously the deterministic epistemology — that underpinned the whole of science until the beginning of the twentieth century, and which is based on the idea of a dual opposition between inside and outside, which alone makes it possible to support the possibility of dynamism and change — then we are left with only two possibilities for interpreting quantum phenomena: either (i) there is no indeterminism insofar as quantum experiments simultaneously realise all their options — in this case, the same causes do indeed produce the same effects, even if these effects are multiple and contradictory, or (ii) if quantum events seem to us to be of a non-deterministic nature it is because other causal links have not been identified (that the phenomenon has not reached its most fundamental expression), and that determination subsists at a more fundamental level. The first branch of the alternative, that which induces the multiple realisation of quantum events in reality, has been the subject of debate in modern physics, the best-known of these having crystallised around the famous thought experiment of Schrödinger's cat[355] and the idea of the superposition

---

[355] Schrödinger's cat experiment is a quantum physics thought experiment proposed by Schrödinger in 1935 to illustrate the paradoxes of quantum theory. In this experiment, a cat is placed in a box with a device containing a radioactive atom, a radioactivity detector, a vial of poison and a mechanism for releasing the poison. According to quantum theory, the radioactive atom has a certain probability of decaying in a given time. If the atom decays, the radioactivity detector is activated, triggering the poison release mechanism and killing the cat. According to quantum theory, before the box is opened to observe the cat, it is in a superimposed state, both alive and dead, until the state of the system is measured (here we return to the problematic identity between measurability and reality). This is what we call quantum superposition: before any measurement, the system can be in a linear combination of its own states, each with a certain probability amplitude. For example, a quantum particle can be in both a "high" and a "low" spin state simultaneously, with respective probabilities. When the

of quantum states that could only be resolved at the moment of measurement and by the collapse of the wave function. In this idea of quantum superposition, we find the idea of multi-realisation, conveniently reduced to an instant of reason before the event of measurement, which alone triggers the reality of the world (our reality), which remains unitary (except in Hugh Everett's theory of parallel worlds, in which all the quantum states are realised unitarily, but in distinct parallel worlds). The other branch of the alternative is

system is measured or observed, it 'collapses' into one of its eigenstates, with a probability determined by the probability amplitudes associated with each state in the superposition. This collapse is often referred to as 'wave packet reduction'. Erwin Schrödinger devised this thought experiment to highlight the apparent problems with the Copenhagen interpretation of quantum mechanics, developed by Niels Bohr and Werner Heisenberg. Schrödinger was critical of the Copenhagen interpretation, which suggested that quantum particles could exist in a state of superposition until they were measured, at which point their state would be determined probabilistically. For Schrödinger, this interpretation seemed to imply that macroscopic objects, such as a cat, could also be in a state of superposition, which seemed absurd.

the one that opens the debate on the incompleteness of quantum theory. In both cases, it is the problem of measurement that crystallises and aggregates the reasons for questioning causal determinism. This problem is, in our opinion, a direct consequence of the contradictions of positivist epistemology and its influence on modern science, an influence which was reflected in modern science by the *credo* that only that which is measurable has an existence (a *credo* which in fact stems from the transformation of a methodological hypothesis into a metaphysical postulate, the co-

implication relationship between measurability and existence never having been established). So, just as we must not confuse existence and measurability, we must not confuse the notions of unpredictability and indeterminability. Brownian motion, for example (illustration opposite), while undoubtedly impossible to predict (unpredictability), cannot be said to be 'indeterministic', insofar as it responds to locally determining factors (collisions with other particles, thermal fluctuations, etc.), although these factors introduce too much randomness to be the subject of a predictive model. In the same way, it seems to us that Heisenberg's uncertainty principle is wrongly called the indeterminacy principle: while the principle's unpredictability has been established, its indeterminacy has not. In quantum theory, since changes of state are only indirectly observable (unlike in the world of classical physics), indeterminacy is postulated rather than demonstrated. In fact, the world of microphysics, unlike the world of classical physics, does not directly observe phenomena, but, as it approaches the unobservable unity of matter (assuming that such a unity exists and can ever be discovered), it manipulates signs and logical-mathematical objects: it thus leaves the world of observation to enter the world of signs, i.e. of signification[356]. The paradoxes of modern science arise, however, when signification is cut off from the signifier. This is why, even more than for classical physics, the epistemology of microphysics is essential to understanding the objects we set out to study. In *The Large, the Small and the Human Mind*, Roger Penrose, future Nobel Prize winner in physics[357] in 2020 for his theoretical work on black holes,

---

[356] Niels Bohr himself made this very clear when he said, for example: "There is no quantum world. There is only an abstract quantum physical description. It is wrong to think that the task of physics is to find out how nature is. Physics concerns what we can say about nature." Quoted by Aage Petersen, Bulletin of the Atomic Scientists. Sep 1963, Vol. 19 Issue 7, p.12

[357] With Reinhard Genzel and Andrea Ghez

established this separation between classical physics (which he called "C") and quantum physics (which he called "U" for "*undetermined*"), writing: "It is only in going from the U to the C level that you introduce non-determinism. This non-determinism comes with R (the reduction of the wave function). Everything at the U level is deterministic - quantum mechanics only becomes non-deterministic when we do this thing we call 'measurement'[358]." The problem of measurement lies at the heart of the epistemological problem of microphysics. Where, in classical physics, we were dealing with phenomena, that is to say with mental constructs based on the real and effective affectation of our senses, in microphysics we are always confronted with logical deductions that are made through a measurement that is itself already a causal interaction with the object we are trying to describe. We must therefore interpret the results and theories of quantum mechanics while remaining aware of its fundamental conditions: we are never directly affected by the phenomena we are describing. In other words, quantum phenomena are never observed: they are inferred. Following on from the passage quoted above, Roger Penrose draws a distinction between the Z mysteries (for '*puzzling*') and the X mysteries, which are the problems associated with measurement in quantum mechanics. The Z mysteries are those that can be said to be disturbing, such as wave-particle duality, spin or non-local effects. All this is undoubtedly disturbing," says Penrose, "but few people dispute its reality; it's part of nature. As for the X problems, those relating to

---

[358] Roger Penrose, *The Large, The Small and the Human Mind*, Cambridge University Press, 1997,1999, p. 59

measurement, Penrose writes: "My view is that we must learn to snooze happily with the Z-mysteries but the-X mysteries should be crossed off when we have a better theory[359]." In fact, although the purely indeterministic interpretation of quantum mechanics undoubtedly represents a majority view among microphysicists, it is not the only possible interpretation. A purely causal and deterministic interpretation had in fact been proposed by Louis de Broglie before 1927 in his theory of the pilot wave. In 1927, crushed by the Heisenberg-Pauli-Bohr axis at the Solvay Congress in 1927, Louis de Broglie abandoned his theory and rallied to the supporters of complementarity. It was not until the early 1950s that Louis de Broglie returned to his old ideas, thanks to a memoir sent to him in the summer of 1951 by the young American physicist David Bohm. Bohm, Vigier and Broglie joined forces, before expanding their collaboration to include Takabayashi and Terletskii, as well as young physicists[360]. Bohm's work, which essentially took up Broglie's 1927 ideas and his "double solution theory" and provided him with a more extensive conceptual framework, was in turn largely neglected, until an exploration of Bohm's developments by John Stewart Bell led him to his famous inequality, which — contrary to popular belief — constitutes a proof of the pilot wave theory, and not its refutation[361]. At the end of the 1980s, John Stewart

---

[359] Ibid., p. 64

[360] These include Fer, Lochak, Andrade e Silva, Hillion, Thiounn, Halbwachs and Leruste.

[361] "Amazingly, we will see that as early as 1924 (before the discovery of the matrix mechanics and Schrodinger theory)

Bell himself wondered about the silence of physicists with regard to the de Broglie-Bohm theory: "But why, wrote Bell, then had Born not told me of this 'pilot wave?' If only to point out what was wrong with it? Why did von Neumann not consider it? More extraordinarily, why did people go on producing 'impossibility' proofs after 1952, and as recently as 1978? When even Pauli, Rosenfeld, and Heisenberg, could produce no more devastating criticism of Bohm's version than to brand it as 'metaphysical' and 'ideological?' Why is the pilot wave picture ignored in text books? Should it not be taught, not as the only way, but as an antidote to the prevailing complacency? To show that vagueness, subjectivity, and indeterminism, are not forced on us by experimental facts, but by deliberate theoretical choice[362]?" Even before the demonstration

---

Louis de Broglie had the essence of the idea, and in fact he subsequently presented the more-or-less complete mathematical theory at the famous Solvay conference in 1927. How he ended up being beaten into the ground by the Heisenberg/Pauli/Bohr axis, abandoning his theory until Bohm took it up again the 1950s, is a fascinating story which we shall explore. As is the fact that Bohm was in his turn ignored and misinterpreted until an exploration of his work led Bell to his famous inequality which contrary to popular belief- can be taken as evidence for the pilot-wave theory, rather than as a disproof of it. Even today, relatively few people have even heard of the theory.", Mike Towler, *Pilot-wave Theory Bohmian metaphysics and the Foundations of Quantum Mechanics, A Graduate Lecture Course by Mike Towler* (University of Cambridge, Lent term 2009), 10 December 2008.
[362] J.S.Bell, *On the Impossible Pilot Wave,* April 13, 1982, Reprinted from Foundations of Physics, Vol 12, No 10, October 1982, p. 149

of the violation of Bell's inequalities by Alain Aspect's experiments, whose conclusions prohibited local theories with hidden variables, this interpretation not only assumed non-locality (Bell in fact showed that quantum mechanics was by nature non-local), but made it explicit: "It is a merit of the de Broglie-Bohm version to bring this [nonlocality] out so explicitly that it cannot be ignored[363].", declared Bell in 1987 in a book compiling a collection of his lectures, articles and essays. In fact, Louis de Broglie himself was already stressing the non-local nature of quantum mechanics in his 1924 thesis. After the initial hesitations of the 1920s, the deterministic theory of the pilot wave was not seriously challenged or invalidated by the community of microphysicists. Bell's work, which was inspired by the pilot wave theory, even provided a solid theoretical basis for non-locality and decisive arguments for Alain Aspect's experimental confirmations. However, the deterministic de Broglie-Bohm theory was largely set aside, as the majority of physicists remained attached to the hypothesis of indeterminism. The principle of indeterminacy, in fact, was confirmed by the de Broglie-Bohm theory, not, it is true, in the sense in which it is generally understood (we cannot know the speed and position of a particle because there is no particle and no trajectory as such, but a dual entity, described by antinomic notions, the wave-corpuscle duality) but in the sense that any 'measurement', any

---

[363] J.S. Bell, *Speakable and Unspeakable in Quantum Mechanics*, p. 115

experiment, is part of an undetermined universe of particles with deterministic trajectories[364].

Much more recently, in 2011, the experiment *by Steinberg et al*, described as the Physics Breakthrough of the Year in 2011[365], reproduced the trajectories predicted by the de Broglie-Bohm theory[366]. It was also commented on positively in several articles, which confirmed that the particles in Steinberg's experiment

---

[364] See S. Goldstein, D. Dürr, N. Zanghì, *A Global Equilibrium as the Foundation of Quantum Randomness*, Foundations of Physics 23, 721-738 (1993) "Therefore in a universe governed by Bohmian mechanics there is *a priori* only one wave function, namely that of the universe, as there is *a priori* only one system governed by Bohmian mechanics, namely the universe itself. (...) We cannot perform the very same experiment more than once. We can perform only many similar experiments, differing, however, at the very least, by location or time. In other words, insofar as the use of probability in physics is concerned, what is relevant is not sampling across an ensemble of universes, but sampling across space and time within a single universe. What is relevant is empirical distributions-actual relative frequencies for an ensemble of actual events. (...) In other words, we establish the remarkable fact that the observed quantum randomness, as expressed by Born's statistical law, is a simple manifestation of universal quantum equilibrium, in the sense of typicality."

[365] "Physics World reveals its top 10 breakthroughs for 2011", physicsworld.com

[366] See Kocsis, Sacha, Boris Braverman, Sylvain Ravets, Martin J. Stevens, Richard P. Mirin, L. Krister Shalm, and Aephraim M. Steinberg, *Observing the Average Trajectories of Single Photons in a Two-Slit Interferometer*, Science, 332, n° 6034, 2011, pp. 1179-1173.

seemed to be guided by a pilot wave (or quantum potential)[367]. We will not enter into the debate, internal to modern physics, about the coherence or scope of these deterministic interpretations (even if it seems fairly widely established that the de Broglie-Bohm interpretation is formally coherent and acceptable). What we are simply trying to show here is (i) the problematic character of the orthodox approach to quantum mechanics, which seems to renounce the possibility of understanding physics, i.e. of giving meaning to its formal productions, (ii) the possibility of a causal and deterministic approach, (ii) the possibility of a causal and deterministic approach, albeit within a

---

[367] "However, these results show us that deBB particle trajectories are much more than a part of a controversial interpretation of QM. They are a part of QM itself, irrespective of the interpretation. However, what different interpretations disagree on is what these trajectories really are. In this sense, trajectories play a role in QM similar to the role of the wave function. All interpretations involve the wave function, but different interpretations disagree on what this wave function really 'is'." Mike Towler, *A Brief Discussion about Weak Measurements*, Electronic Structure Discussion Group, TCM Group, Cavendish Laboratory, University of Cambridge, February 2012.

Braverman, Boris, and Christoph Simon, *Proposal to Observe the Nonlocality of Bohmian Trajectories with Entangled Photons*, Physical Review Letters 110, n° 6 (February 7, 2013): 060406. doi:10.1103/PhysRevLett.110.060406.

Schleich, W. P., M. Freyberger, and M. S. Zubairy, *Reconstruction of Bohm Trajectories and Wave Functions from Interferometric Measurements*, Physical Review A 87, n° 1 (January 16, 2013): 014102.
doi:10.1103/PhysRevA.87.014102.

non-local framework, and consequently (iii) the need to re-examine the epistemological foundations of modern science, a need that seems to be reinforced by the as yet unresolved problems of compatibility between quantum mechanics and the theory of relativity. It should also be noted that, contrary to what might have been expected, the Broglie-Bohm interpretation did not really meet with Einstein's approval, as he found it too 'easy'. In particular, Einstein criticised Broglie-Bohm for remaining within the general theoretical framework of quantum mechanics instead of recasting it in a more general theory (yet to be invented). In a letter that Einstein wrote to Aron Kupperman in 1953, for example, he wrote on this subject: "I think that it is not possible to get rid of the statistical character of the present quantum theory by simply adding something to it without changing the fundamental concepts relating to the whole structure. The principle of superposition and the statistical interpretation are inseparably linked. If we think that we should avoid the statistical interpretation and replace it, it seems that we cannot keep a linear Schrödinger equation, which implies, by its linearity, the principle of superposition of the "states"." This remark applies just as well, says Einstein, to all theoretical models of this kind. Ever since the Solvay Congress, Einstein had constantly criticised the orthodox approach to quantum mechanics, which he saw as both dogmatic and incomplete. In a 1928 letter to Erwin Schrödinger, for example, he wrote: "The tranquillising philosophy of Heisenberg and Bohr — or is it a religion? — is so skilfully constructed that it allows true believers to rest on a pillow so soft that it is not easy to wake them up". In 1950, in a speech he gave to the International Congress of Surgeons, Einstein seemed to have varied little from his positions, declaring for example: "Quantum in-determinacy, is this credo definitive? I think a smile is better than an answer". What Einstein was denouncing here, and what we are also taking up, is the resurgence of a form of obscurantism or 'magical thinking' within the community of quantum physicists, who, for the most part, accept the disconnection between the models used to describe reality and the meaning of these models. This divorce between the model and its meaning is, in our view, all the more problematic in that these models, in order to claim the consistency of what they describe, should logically lead us to seek a meaning that is external to them (which is deduced in particular from Gödel's second incompleteness theorem), yet in the orthodox interpretation of quantum mechanics, it is precisely this connection to an external meaning that is lacking.

Paradoxically, modern science, which had begun by massively embracing materialism and the idea of an integral determinism of matter, ended up rejecting determinism, in the name of the same principles. It was because "we must not postulate more than matter" that we were finally able to dispense with determinism, which was not, strictly speaking, a *principle of matter* (a principle that would be contained in matter or that would be an intrinsic property of it). In this respect, the modern *doxa* of science was consistent with its founding principles (empiricism, positivism, reductionism, etc.): since determinism was not a physical principle, it seemed legitimate to abandon it along the way, like abandoning a pair of shoes that had been worn out to the bone. But this abandonment was problematic: although determinism, like all other principles, models and ideas, might seem entirely contingent in the eyes of the materialist scientist who attaches no importance to the idea of truth outside the experience of things, it had nonetheless proved its constant effectiveness throughout the ages of science. So, what could be done with this effectiveness? Bohr proposed confining it to the world of classical physics, thus creating a gaping hole between two worlds, one of which was supposed to be the foundation of the other. What followed was a long period of epistemological wandering, which eventually dis-solved, for the majority of quantum physicists, into a kind of epistemological agnosticism (still imbued with a few materialist and pragmatic vestiges), while the life sciences clung desperately to integral determinism (more convenient for the scale of work of the life sciences and chemistry).

Among American and French neuroscientists in particular, psychologistic theories once again enjoyed great success (thanks in particular to the influence of cybernetics, as we have already mentioned), the ambition of the neural sciences having long been to reduce the abstract ideas and principles of reason to concrete (observable) mental processes which, from then on, were to mean nothing more than what they induced (as behaviours, beliefs or actions). On the one hand, the advocates of an integral materialism applied to the brain sciences continued to defend unfailing determinism (the brain being understood as a complex and totally deterministic machine, a kind of super-computer, a Turing machine[368]); on the other hand, the advocates of a more pragmatic materialism (even an agnosticism that could go as far as anti-materialism) thought they were entitled to abandon determinism while retaining some of the principles of materialism. Some curious intermediate positions were also proposed, notably by Roger Penrose himself, who thought he had found in quantum superposition an argument against the determinism of our ideas and behaviour and who tried to identify in the brain the locus of this superposition (the systems of microtubes in a neuron), while remaining within the "Plato-Gödel[369]" conceptual framework. The reductionism

---

[368] Psychologists thought they had proof of their success when they established that our thoughts were linked to electrical activity in the brain, activity that is visible on medical imaging. But who could have seriously doubted this? Who could have denied that mental processes, ideation processes, were not based on physically observable mental activity? In fact, much of philosophy had anticipated these results. By establishing the fact that mental processes were based on observable physical activity, reductionism did not in fact provide any additional foundation for the materialist doctrine it thought it was supporting. It merely led straight to psychologism, the limits and inconsistencies of which we have already shown (see § 31 - *Against psychologism*).

[369] The attempt to locate the site of quantum superposition in the brain strikes us as a curious approach to the overall problem of the opposition between determinism and freedom. As we have already mentioned, we can only understand freedom in close opposition to determinism. In a way, freedom is based on determinism, since an entirely indeterministic universe cannot be conducive to the exercise

and psychologism — which is basically nothing other than the epistemological deduction of materialist reductionism — by denying the specific character of subjectivity, i.e. by reducing it to an objective fragmentation (the subject as an *ad hoc* and illusory synthesis of objective processes that go beyond it), also necessarily missed the subjective problematic of time and permanence. This is one of the reasons why these doctrines invariably led to insoluble paradoxes within their conceptual framework. If, in fact, we consider with coherent reductionism and psychologism that the world is reduced to matter, then we cannot assert any rule that would persist outside the 'matter' of the rule, i.e. outside the *material moment* in which the rule is thought (this prohibition would, moreover, be valid for

---

of my freedom (if only because of the problem of the chain of command between my intention and my action: how can I be free if my actions are not determined by my intentions?) In our view, freedom should not be understood in opposition to determinism, just as ideas should not be understood in opposition to matter. On the other hand, we find the problem of quantum indeterminacy particularly interesting in that it actually reflects the structure of our relationship with reality. Quantum indeterminacy is linked to the problem of measurement, i.e. the problem of interference between the measurable and the measured. In a way, this circular structure is reminiscent of the structure of the acting individual, who modifies his behaviour and actions as he becomes aware of himself and his intentions, in an upward spiral (I commit an action or have a thought, I see myself committing an action or having a thought through self-reflexivity, I see myself seeing myself, etc.). In short, indeterminism here is sequenced in time and is based on my internal division and my ability to represent myself).

psychologism itself: would it only be 'true' each time I think it as such?) In our brains and in our consciousnesses, this material moment manifests itself in a certain chemical combination (a material assembly) that gives us the impression of grasping the rule or the idea — it's the moment of comprehension — an ephemeral impression that only remains within consciousness for a few moments (although we would have to identify this moment precisely, which is impossible in psychologism insofar as the problem of the subject's temporality remains unthought of). Now, if we follow the psychologist thesis, this impression only has validity (insofar as it can claim any validity) at the moment when it manifests itself to consciousness, i.e. at the moment when the idea is truly thought. However, this — conception, which Putnam criticised when he said "*meanings just ain't in the head*" — apart from the fact that it seriously neglected the temporal sequencing of ideas[370], led to the extreme idea that the world only has an "attestable" existence in the permanence of my thought (I can only formally attest to its existence and permanence as long as I think of it as an existing and permanent world). According to

---

[370] Ideas are not just ephemeral impressions; they can also be constructed or deduced in a temporal causal sequence. How do we deal with the problem of sequencing when we only give credence to what the subject is thinking at the time he is thinking it? In the case of sequenced reasoning, can the stage (n-1) of the reasoning which no longer has any validity (insofar as it is no longer thought by the subject who has progressed in the sequence of his reasoning) nevertheless continue to constitute the basis of the reasoning and the idea? Here we have a contradiction.

psychologist theories, I should therefore not be led to claim permanence 'outside my head' since, by definition, I could only experience this permanence concretely in my head and, what's more, in a transitory way — each time I happened to think about it. This is how the tautological circle of integral materialism closed[371]. It was by starting from radically anti-

---

[371] Critical idealism, on the other hand, recognises the logical foundations of materialism, and claims and defends them. But it also defends the idea that our mental processes, although necessarily based on material processes, cannot be reduced to them either (at the risk of missing the fundamental problem of meaning). These processes must, in other words, necessarily have a validity *outside the moment in which they take place*. It is this "timeless" or "non-temporal" validity that we have called "effectivity", when we spoke, for example, of the "effectivity of the rule". This validity presupposes both (i) that judgements or ideas about things can be valid even outside the moments when they are formulated (in Euclidean geometry, for example, the sum of the angles of a triangle is equal to 180 degrees, even when I'm not thinking about a triangle) and (ii) that things (and therefore the world) can have persistence outside the moment when I'm thinking about them. In fact, it is precisely this persistence that makes it possible to think about their coherence (in other words, to think about them "at all", since we cannot think about the concrete existence of incoherence*). Our experience of things therefore leads us to postulate their permanence, or at any rate their independence from our perception. This hypothesis is corroborated both by its efficiency (i.e. by the simplicity of its expression compared with the complexity of demonstrating the opposite hypothesis) and by its effectiveness (its experimental confirmations, which lead us

subjectivist positions (the subject as a pure atomistic material reduction) that we arrived at extreme solipsistic subjectivist positions (nothing exists outside my immediate experience of the material world). Once again, it was these same positions that led materialists to abandon the principle of causality that had founded their doctrine: without a subject, there is no temporality; without temporality, there is no duality; without duality, there is no causality. The tautological circle was transformed into a spiral of negation. It was probably similar ideas that crossed Einstein's mind when, during an evening walk with Abraham Pais on his way back from Princeton University, he asked the latter: "Do you really believe that the Moon is not there when you are not looking at it?

---

to postulate more than ourselves through the experience of others— it is the possibility of intersubjectivity to which we shall return — and through our experience of the world).

*We can, of course, think that something is incoherent, but we cannot concretely imagine the incoherent thing, i.e. fit it into our network of (comprehensible) meanings.

SUBJECTIVE AND OBJECTIVE

57.

OBJECTIVE SUBJECTIVITY — There is a semantic misunderstanding, fairly widespread in modern philosophy and science, which consists in treating the concept of subjectivity as a quasi-equivalent of the concept of relativism. Thus, what is 'subjective' today in common parlance designates what is 'relative to each person' and therefore cannot be the subject of a discussion that could take place within a common framework. The pairing of subjectivity and objectivity thus constitutes a radically antagonistic pair, with the term subjectivity generally reserved for personal experiences that are supposed to be, as such, incommunicable (experience of art, feelings, the relationship with mysticism or religion), while the term objectivity is reserved for scientific language and discourses on knowledge. If we conceive of objectivity and subjectivity as radically and definitively opposed, it becomes impossible for us to think about reality, since our experience of the world is always manifested through what constitutes our subjectivity: our intuition, our senses, our understanding and, to a certain extent, our culture. Yet subjectivity, far from being a weapon that massively disqualifies knowledge, is on the contrary its necessary and unsurpassable foundation.

In *Wege zur Physikalischen Erkenntnis*, Max Planck notes that scientific knowledge is the result of a process of de-anthropomorphising reality. In the field of thermodynamics, for example, we first think that heat spreads by 'mixing' with cold, just as we would mix liquids together. This is a metaphorical, anthropomorphic mode of reasoning: we are tempted to reduce the unknown to the known by means of comparative comparisons (intuitive application of a pattern drawn from our common experience). However, with the work of Sadi Carnot, Clausius and later Maxwell and Boltzmann, we discovered that heat actually depends on the statistical distribution of particles and their agitation in a given space. If a hot body gives up heat to a cold body, this is only an enormous probability, not an absolute necessity," wrote Planck[372]. It is the atomic theory of matter that actually makes the paradigm shift possible. Here we see how, starting from common sense (intuitive perception of heat — what is heat for a being devoid of sensitivity? — application of erroneous anthropomorphic patterns) we arrive at a theory of heat which, while not confirming what we mistakenly took for self-evident, remains explicable in the language of common sense. For Planck, the fact that science starts from subjectivity (i.e. our sensitive capacity to perceive reality) is not an argument against the objectivity of scientific discoveries. However, in the process of validating any theory (scientific or otherwise), critical, retroactive and formalised analysis is of decisive importance. This dialogue between the production of new schemas and critical feedback is what defines our rationality, i.e. our progress towards objectivity. In this progression, it is subjective

---

[372] "On the other hand, if a hot body gives up heat to a colder one, this is only an enormous probability and not an absolute necessity. It is perfectly possible to conceive of a special arrangement of atoms with speeds such that exactly the opposite would result."

prejudices that are overcome, not subjectivity itself. Subjectivity, as the foundation of the objective moment, is never entirely melted or overcome in the objectivity of science. It remains there as a foundation and as a signifying connection to the real. In *Against Method*, Paul Feyerabend rightly insists on the subjective character of our perceptions, and then goes on to emphasise the relative and relativistic character of science: "Questionable views on cognition, such as the view that our senses, used in normal circumstances, give reliable information about the world, may invade the observation language itself, constituting the observational terms as well as the distinction between veridical and illusory appearance. As a result, observation languages may become tied to older layers of speculation which affect, in this roundabout fashion, even the most progressive methodology. (Example: the absolute space-time frame of classical physics which was codified and consecrated by Kant.) The sensory impression, however simple, contains a component that expresses the physiological reaction of the perceiving organism and has no objective correlate. This 'subjective' component often merges with the rest and forms an unstructured whole which must be subdivided from the outside with the help of counter inductive procedures. (An example is the appearance of a fixed star to the naked eye, which contains the effects of irradiation diffraction, diffusion, restricted by the lateral inhibition of adjacent elements of the retina and is further modified in the brain[373].)" We quote this passage *in extenso* because it seems to us to be interesting and representative of Feyerabend's thought

---

[373] Op. cit., V, p. 51

in several respects. Firstly, the denunciation of the naïve idea that our senses, "in normal circumstances", would provide us with solid data about the world, an idea that is in fact largely rejected by critical idealism and analytic philosophy; secondly, the idea that observation can be polluted by ancient cultural or scientific conceptions that are not directly linked to our senses, This is a more original idea, but one that had already been widely developed by post-Kantians in the 1920s (in particular in Cassirer's work, which we have already cited several times). Finally, there is the classic amalgam between the subjective and the objective (the subjective component mixing with the rest to form an "unstructured" whole, according to Feyerabend). It is worth noting in passing that Feyerabend attempts to undermine Kant's philosophy by making the latter a defender of the idea of absolute space and time, an idea that Kant did not in fact defend (see § 54 and 55 on the problems of time and space). Unlike Newton's epistemology, Kant's critical philosophy remained within a subjectivist framework, the question of space and time being approached through the prism of sensibility (space and time as *a priori* forms sensibility). For Kant, the subjectivist framework did not preclude the objective transcendence of scientific knowledge and morality: on the contrary, it gave this transcendence a foundation. Interestingly, however, the passage we are quoting concludes with an example which, although it is supposed to support Feyerabend's position, can in fact oppose it. When Feyerabend talks about the subjective effects of the irradiation, diffraction and scattering of light from a star on the naked eye, he is certainly highlighting the relative (subjective, non-absolute) nature of all perception, but he is also showing how this relative nature not only rests on objective facts (the objective and scientifically established facts that are precisely the effects of the irradiation, diffraction and scattering of light on the retina) but also allows them to be founded. In fact, it is by going back and forth between the ideas suggested to us by our senses (the appearance of a star to the naked eye: the star has "branches" and twinkles) and the logical-systemic deductions that we make from these ideas to give the world an overall coherence, that our knowledge progresses towards greater and greater objectivity (we could say that this is a tension between the forms spontaneously produced by our understanding, which it derives from a natural and utilitarian intuition of reality, and the forms constructed by this same understanding against its initial impulses). It is precisely in this way that science can be understood, as Max Planck put it, as a process of deanthropomorphisation of reality, not in the sense that reality loses its subjective character (we cannot adopt a Sirius point of view on the world, or attempt to do so), but rather in the sense that it is a process of de-anthropomorphisation of reality, as Baron Munchhausen did, to pull ourselves by the hair out of the quicksand in which our mount has become entangled), but insofar as reality would no longer be a game of immediate appearance or given anthropomorphic evidence. In other words, for the caveman (and for the children we once were), the star is white and twinkles on its branches. For the scientist, the star is a celestial object composed mainly of gas that shines with its own light thanks to the nuclear reactions that take place at its core. However, it remains a white star with several branches that twinkles in the dark.

Subjective phenomena, as the basis (or first approach) to our relationship with reality, are reinterpreted objectively in scientific discourse. The subjective distortion of our perception of the star is reduced, in scientific discourse, to objective determinants (irradiation, diffraction, diffusion). In Feyerabend's discourse, on the other hand, this process of objectifying subjective perceptions is an example of the relativisation of successive discourses on truth: as one theory contradicts another, we conclude that all theories are relativistic. However, this overlooks the fact that, on the one hand, not all theories are equal (some are false or have zero validity) and that, on the other hand, some theories can have a greater explanatory power than previous theories without contradicting them (as we have said on several occasions, general relativity does not contradict all of Newton's physics; on the contrary, it gives it a broader conceptual framework). So we can't really talk about the "historico-physiological character of evidence[374]" as Feyerabend does, without at the same time pointing out that what we call "evidence" can also constitute the basis of an objective overcoming of evidence, an overcoming that is precisely the object of all attempts to model the world, i.e. attempts to explain reality by means of a representative and meaningful theory. Our sensitive organisms subjectively perceive the sensation of heat. Although this sensation is undeniably subjective (what would the notion of warm water mean objectively, for example?), it can nevertheless constitute a perfectly valid objective foundation. The perception of heat can certainly be said to be

---

[374] Ibid., p. 52

'subjective' insofar as it is linked to our senses and the adaptation of our organisms to the surrounding world — it is therefore impossible to take sides *objectively* in the debate between those who wish to open the window in a car and those who wish to keep it closed, but it cannot be denied that this sensation relates in a more or less precise and distended way to concrete and objectifiable measures, in this case measurable. If we fail to settle the debate about the ideal interior temperature of a vehicle or an enclosed space, we will have much less of a debate about the objectivity of temperature measurement. This is a banal but no less valid example of the transition from subjectivity to objectivity. In the objective measurement of temperature, subjectivity is not denied (it remains the foundation, the first question linked to this phenomenon that we feel and that we call "heat"); on the contrary, it is integrated into a more global theory whose anthropomorphic character gradually disappears. In the example of heat, de-anthropomorphisation corresponds to progressive objectivation, objectivation itself being a long scientific process that culminates in a statistical theory of particles (atomic theory of matter). In the movement towards knowledge, the subjective root persists but is modified by a back-and-forth between subjective perception (evidence, phenomena as they reach our consciousness, mental representations associated with phenomena, etc.) and the objective and measurable theorisation of this perception. In this respect, objectivity appears more as the signifying systematisation of subjectivity than as its antithesis. This systemisation, starting from evidence, can lead to evidence being radically called into question without, however, disqualifying it as a subjective signal (this is the movement of de-anthropomorphisation). Indeed, although evidence is the manifestation of our first relationship with the world (although this relationship is never really first and never really immediate), it is neither the ultimate foundation nor the culmination of objective knowledge: the process of knowledge, although having evidence as its starting point, very often ends up deconstructing it. The coherence of our general perception of the world is, and can only be, achieved at the cost of this deconstruction. Evidence, as the product of our adaptation to things, is an effective reduction of the world (see § 25 — *What is a phenomenon?*). This utilitarian and statistical reduction of our relationship to the world, which is what constitutes evidence for us, is what enables us to live and survive in a world that can be hostile to us. Nietzsche was right to write, in *Human, All too Human* about the metaphysical world: "Even if the existence of such a world could be best proved, it would still be established that knowledge of it is the most in-different of all knowledge: even more indifferent than knowledge of the chemical analysis of water should be to a sailor in a storm[375]. As inhabitants of the world, we must analyse it, understand it and react quickly: our survival depends on it. So, it doesn't matter to us what the chemical composition of the water is when the wave breaks over us: we just have to understand that it threatens our lives, dive in, swim fast or set sail. Our relationship to the world is first and foremost constituted by a relationship of effectivity to things, that's an established fact, but while effectivity allows us to confirm and

---

[375] Op. cit., Section One, *Of first and last things*, § 9 - *Metaphysical World*

establish our knowledge within the world we inhabit, it is not the only criterion of truth. As the observation of our positive action on the world, the criterion of effectivity is already the moment of the return of the loop of knowledge, the moment of informed experience of the world. We know we have to dive under the wave, because we've probably already caught the first wave in the face. We deduced from this that diving could protect us from the surge of water (effectiveness of knowledge: diving under the wave protects me from the wave). When we dive under the wave, we are indifferent to the composition of the water: we have no particular *interest in* it. Our relationship with the water is then one of defence, a mode of relationship that alone guides our perception (in the face of danger, the field of perception is reduced to concentrate on the danger, a process known as 'tunnel effect'). Of course, Nietzsche could argue that the composition of water will become much more interesting to us the day we have to drink it (it could, for example, be of vital interest to us to know whether the water is contaminated by a deadly bacterium). All we need to remember here is that the obvious is linked to our position in the world, our position in relation to things and our relationship of interest with them (in this respect, the 'obvious' reality of the water in the wave will no doubt seem very different to us from the 'obvious' reality of the water in the lake, which we will have to drink or not drink). However, the fact that we take an interest in things, and that this interest is constitutive of what we call 'evidence', is not for us a valid criticism of knowledge. The process of knowledge certainly always starts from this relationship of interest in things, in other words from what we call "evidence", but evidence does not constitute the ultimate foundation of knowledge: on the contrary, it initiates the movement that leads to its overcoming. This is why the evident (from the Latin *videre*, meaning 'to see') may differ over time or between cultures (which is an argument against the objectivity of knowledge in Feyerabend's work, for example): the obvious, as co-constructions of the senses, understanding and reason, are always linked to a state of knowledge, that is to say to a state of the system of meanings (personal, cultural, etc.): the obvious differs from one culture to another, and also from one age to another. What is obvious to an adult is not necessarily obvious to a child[376]. Far from constituting an argument against the objectivity of knowledge, these changes in evidence over the ages reveal the structure of our relationship to the world. In the passage from one evidence to another, we should not necessarily see the manifestation of a process of a relativistic nature, but on the contrary understand that the modification of our perception and understanding of things is linked to the general state of our knowledge. Progress towards objectivity is not, for us, the negation of subjectivity, but the integration of subjectivity into explanatory models of the world (models of signifying coherence).

---

[376] See, in particular, Jean Piaget's work on the stages in the development of intelligence in children and on learning theory.

58.

THE OBJECTIVE CONSTANCY OF RELATIONSHIPS —
We have seen that subjectivity can constitute not a foundation, but a valid starting point for objective knowledge. The subjective origin of science does not disqualify its objective scope. Science is a process towards objectivity, i.e. a coherent and representable systematisation of our subjective perceptions. This is what Planck emphasises in *Wege zur Physikalischen Erkenntnis*: "There is nothing more disappointing than the hollow phrase 'everything is relative'. In physics, it is already inaccurate: all the universal constants, such as the mass and charge of the electron or proton, and the value of the quantum of action, are absolute quantities[377]." By emphasising the objective constancy of relationships in the physical world, Max Planck is indirectly attempting to deconstruct the idea that the subjective origin of our relationship to the world implies relativism. In the same way that relativity should not be confused with relativism, we believe that it is wrong to think that the absence of an absolute point of view on things (i.e. the absence of a stable and definitive formal framework *applied to the world of physics*) implies a fundamental questioning of the possibility of knowing them. Planck's constant (h), for which Max Planck was awarded the Nobel Prize in Physics in 1918, refers to the minimum amount of energy that a physical system can possess on a quantum scale. It is interesting to note that its numerical value (approximately $6.62607015 \times 10^{-34}$ J-s) remains identical in all contexts

---

[377] Max Planck, *Wege zur Physikalischen Erkenntnis*, 1934

of physics. In other words, whatever the situation or physical system being studied, the value of Planck's constant remains unchanged. In the theory of relativity, we find a similar result: the relativity of inertial systems does not imply the relativity of physical laws, which remain the same in different inertial systems. The relativity of inertial systems does not therefore imply the relativism of physical laws. Paradoxically, progress in science and in the general theory of knowledge, by overtaking the previous state of knowledge that it implies, provides easy arguments against the very idea of progress. However, we must be wary of over-hasty analogies and unproven implications: relativity does not imply relativism, and subjectivity does not preclude the objective process that lies at the root of science and progress.

Reconciling the world: Truth is a humanism

What does science mean — How can science be linked to mankind?

59.

SCIENCE AND MEANING — In our previous comments, we stressed that science should not be separated from meaning. If, in fact, we decouple science from the meaning it has "for us", i.e. if we give up on inserting scientific statements and theories into our systems of representations, then we run the risk of turning science into a mere πρᾶξις, a technique (in the sense of τέχνη in ancient Greek, i.e. production, manufacture or even effective action). Yet science cannot be reduced to the simple activity of modelling reality; it is always at the same time an exercise in understanding the world. Technique, on the other hand, can certainly do without what we call "science". The technician is first and foremost someone who has a relationship with things, who tries to understand them by iterating and repeating what he experiences. For him, technique is first and foremost a πρᾶξις, a practice of things. Like Newton, the technician is one who affirms "*hypotheses non fingo*": he first lets himself be seized by things, tries to understand how they work and the regularities (which are not yet rules). It is by repeating the same thing that the technician acquires practical knowledge about things. So, for example, the technique of fire (the acquisition by humans of the knowledge needed to create and control fire) precedes the science of fire by several millennia (the understanding of the process that leads to ignition, its theorisation and modelling, which no longer proceeds from an inductivist method as we showed earlier). Technique, as an iterative practice, remains *at the level of things*. It may well give rise to technology (the science of technology), but technology is never really anything other than a theorisation (a modelling) of practical knowledge. This familiarity with things is essential to the scientist. A good scientist is undoubtedly also a good technician: he knows how to observe, understand and reproduce. However, the scientist's activity is not limited to a purely technical one. The practice of science is above all a practice of meaning. Scientists do not seek to acquire or develop operating rules; they seek to explain phenomena, to decode their invisible mechanisms. They are like "the man who tries to understand the mechanism of a closed watch", as Einstein wrote. In this respect, the scientist is at the crossroads between the technician and the "ordinary man": he always links his observations to a systemic network of existing meanings. It is this link that enables them to understand reality, predict it and explain its mechanisms. If, however, the scientist gives up the idea of giving an account of his observations in a meaningful language (which makes sense to him as it does to us), then he inevitably falls back to the level of technique (and is confronted with its aporias). In short, the autonomous activity of formalisation, when it is not directly linked to an intuitive representation and when it does not find an expressible correspondence in the metasystem of concrete meanings, is also an autonomous activity that can be described as "technical" (it is an "efficient" action that we can delegate to machines). So, for example, most mathematical operations (the set of operations that can be formalised), as operations that are part of an autonomous activity (which has its own internal rules), can be described as "technical". In our practice of mathematics, we have no doubt all noticed that a large number of operations can be carried out, so to speak, "without our thinking about it" (the activities of reducing or developing formulas, for example, to name but a few). There is no doubt that, for the high-flying mathematician who has practised mathematics for a very long time, these natural operations (which he can carry out "without thinking about it") are even more frequent than for ordinary mathematicians. We could certainly point out here that the operations that we carry out 'without thinking about it' are first and foremost operations that we have thought about, that we have integrated and understood. However, it has to be said that as we progress in our practice of mathematics (as in that of all formal systems in general, including language, even though language, as we have said, admits the entanglement and cohabitation of different formal levels and is an open system that differs from classical formal systems), the underlying signifiers appear to us less and less clearly. It is precisely at this moment when the 'signifying underpinnings' fade and disappear that mathematics (like all logical operations that use signs defined in a given axiomatic system) becomes an autonomous practice, in other words, a 'technique'. In short, in mathematics, as sometimes in language, signs end up being 'demonetised': they represent no more than a link in a formal system, with no obvious relationship to what they designate *in concreto*. This relationship nevertheless persists, but is simply lost sight of by the mathematician in the (technical) manipulation of signs. By persevering in the technical action and by perfecting the autonomous operations that preside over it, the technician may well imagine that he is "doing science" when in reality he is merely following an autonomous (formal) mechanism. Moreover, genuine discoveries can emerge from this autonomous mechanism. But these discoveries only become 'scientific' insofar as they are integrated into a system of signifying representations (or insofar as they result from a general intuition that integrates the discovery into a new system of signifying re-presentations). For us, then, science without meaning is a contradiction in terms: pure formalism can never produce knowledge if it is uncoupled from reality, and therefore from the productive imagination (which itself is only possible through intuition, the way in which we make things meaningful to us). In this sense, Kant was right to link mathematical axioms to pure intuition and to assert that we could see or perceive their truth, in a 'non-sensible' sense of 'seeing' or 'perceiving' (i.e. in the sense of figuration by the imagination, of non-sensible representation). It also seems to us that he was right to assert that pure intuition "was included in every step of every demonstration of geometry" (we do not agree with Karl Popper on this point). However, since mathematics (and algebra in particular) is based on logical articulations, i.e. on logical rules that define its practice and application, it cannot be denied at the same time, as Popper pointed out, that it uses discursive arguments (or discursive 'mechanics'). Consequently, while pure intuition underpins the different stages of mathematical demonstrations (in arithmetic — by reference to axioms and theorems —

and in geometry for more obvious reasons), the articulations between the stages are indeed of a 'mechanico-logical' order (the strict application of rules and theorems does not require the intervention of intuition). In this sense, mathematical demonstration is a sequential construction, a construction of constru-- ctions. Here we are at the heart of the ambivalence of mathematics and of all formal systems: both intuitive and analytical, they are characterised by this double reality, that of the meaningful representation of their statements and that of the mechanical articulation of their development. However, most formal systems are victims of their dissymmetry: their autonomous complexification (responding to the logical rules on which they are based) is exponential and inflationary, while our capacity for representation *in concreto* is synthetic and limited.

60.

TECHNIQUE AND MEANING — The general problem of technique is linked to the problems we have just mentioned, which concern the relationship between science and meaning. In the same way that science divorced from the question of foundation and meaning becomes a blind practice, technology divorced from the question of meaning (for human beings) is an anomic practice, albeit a normalised one. If technology is indeed a normalised practice in the sense that it obeys internal rules that constitute its 'mechanics', it does not in fact have a defined direction. However, like any practice, it cannot claim to be neutral with regard to these developments. Technology, as an effective action on things, is at the same time an action on the world, our world. As such, it carries with it a principle of responsibility (responsibility towards the things on which it acts, but also and above all responsibility towards other sentient beings).

In the great ideological struggle of the 1930s and 1940s, Martin Heidegger and his successors succeeded in the tour de force of disqualifying, through a violent attack on Cartesian metaphysics, modern science and technology, which together were held solely responsible for the industrialisation, mechanisation and, finally, alienation of the world and of mankind. By making himself "master and possessor of nature", Cartesian man heralded, in Heideggerian gloss, the great mechanisation of the world, the reification of the sensible and of human beings, which was ultimately to lead to the catastrophe of the gas chambers. From the writing of *Being and Time* (1927) and even more so in his 1940s lectures on Nietzsche[378], Heidegger denounced Descartes' "calculating" and mathematised reason and made his philosophy into a thought of dominating subjectivity, the culmination of which was, in Nietzsche, the will to power. In volume II of *Nietzsche*, from which Hannah Arendt situates Heidegger's famous *khere*, Nietzsche was thus presented by Heidegger as the last metaphysician of modern times, the one who completed the domination of the dominating metaphysical subject to which Descartes had paved the way: "In the sense of Nietzsche's

---

[378] The lectures are collected in two books entitled *Nietzsche I* and *Nietzsche II*, based on the seminars of 1939-1940 for Nietzsche I (*The Will to Power as Knowledge*) and those of 1941-1942 for Nietzsche II (*The Metaphysics of the Eternal Return*).

metaphysics", writes Heidegger, "only the superman conforms to the absolute 'machine economy' [...]. The door to the essential district of this metaphysically understood sovereignty was opened by Descartes with his proposition: *cogito sum*[379]." Although this connection between Descartes and Nietzsche may not seem very obvious, it was nevertheless enshrined by the post-Heideggerians, to such an extent that the idea that Descartes was the ancestor of all the ills of modern man became a commonplace in philosophy from the 1950s onwards. In 1951, six years after the end of the war, at the Zurich Seminar, Heidegger continued to point to Descartes as the person responsible for man's subjective domination of nature. What's more, he made the extermination of millions of Jews a historical event to which our subjectivist Western thought had supposedly led Europe, thus absolving himself of his active (and early) support for the Third Reich[380].

Taken out of context, Descartes' call for man to become "master and possessor of nature" can be interpreted as an incitement to the over-exploitation of nature for man's benefit. However, this highly ideological reading does not do justice to Descartes'

---

[379] Heidegger, *Nietzsche II*

[380] See on this subject the works of Emmanuel Faye, in particular *La pensée métaphysique de Descartes et son 'interprétation' par Heidegger* in *Y a-t-il une histoire de la métaphysique ? (coll.)*, [Descartes' Metaphysical Thought and Its 'Interpretation' by Heidegger in Is There a History of Metaphysics?] Paris, P.U.F., 2005 and *Heidegger, l'introduction du nazisme dans la philosophie : autour des séminaires inédits de 1933-1935.* [Heidegger, the Introduction of Nazism into Philosophy: On the Unpublished Seminars of 1933-1935.]

thinking. In this famous passage, taken from the sixth part of the *Discourse on Method*, Descartes is in fact praising the neighbourhood and practical knowledge of things, a knowledge that he also contrasts with "the speculative philosophy taught in schools". This desire to master nature is not an aspiration to domination (the term domination does not appear in the *Discourse on Method*), but rather a desire to tame things rather than suffer them. Thus, the main purpose of technology is "to preserve health, which is undoubtedly the first good and the foundation of all other goods[381]". It is interesting to note that, in this passage, Descartes evokes a specific aim for technology. Practical knowledge is not understood as an autonomous activity to be developed without a compass. On the contrary, technique is immediately linked to a humanist objective (that of preserving health). Better still, for Descartes, this objective of care and conservation should make it possible to make men more skilful and wiser: "for even the mind depends so strongly on temperament and the disposition of the body's organs, that if it is possible to find some means that will commonly make men wiser and more skilful than they have been hitherto, I believe that it is in medicine that it should be sought[382]." We are therefore a long way from the intentions of domination and subjugation of nature that Heidegger attributes to Descartes. For Descartes, progress is neither reduced to unlimited accumulation nor to a desire for absolute mastery of nature and beings, but is, on the contrary, part of an ideal of wisdom and

---

[381] René Descartes, *Discourse on Method*, Part Six, *Things Needed to Go Further in the Search for Nature*.
[382] Ibid.

preservation, particularly of health. What's more, his thinking reveals no explicit ambition to mathematise or totally mechanise our relationship with the world. On the contrary, it seems to us that Descartes, as the dynamiter of sclerotic thought, the "speculative philosophy taught in schools", is the herald of the philosophy of the Enlightenment, the philosophy of the autonomy of thought, the philosophy of the passage from the state of minority and submission to the state of majority, the philosophy that Heidegger despises and intends, in his own words, to "liquidate[383]".

If it is dangerous to consider technology as a totally autonomous and independent activity, it would be just as reductive to see science as a simple deployment of abstract mechanisms. As a practice rooted in a direct relationship with things and the world, technology is always a bearer of meaning and, consequently, engages the responsibility of the technician. They cannot act "without thinking about it", like mathematicians

---

[383] As early as 1925, at the end of the *Cassel Lectures*, Heidegger, quoting Count Yorck von Wartenburg at length from his correspondence with Dilthey, writes:

"The waves called forth by the eccentric principle that brought forth a new epoch more than four hundred years ago seem to me to have become extremely distant and insensitive, knowledge to have progressed to the point of suppressing itself, and man to have become so far removed from himself that he has disappeared from his field of vision. Modern man", in other words man since the Renaissance, is fit to be buried.

Earl of York, *Letter to Dilthey, 21 August 1889*, quoted by Heidegger in *Les conférences de Cassel*

making abstract calculations that have no direct impact on the world. This responsibility is also enshrined in the great Greek myths of technology, those of Prometheus and Icarus, which illustrate both the creative power and the inherent danger of technology. In the myth of Prometheus, it is the terrible punishment[384] inflicted on Prometheus for having stolen the sacred fire from the gods and taught mankind the art of technology that highlights the importance of his crime. The myth of Icarus sheds an interesting light on the nature of technology insofar as it establishes a separation between the technician, represented by the figure of the ingenious Daedalus, and the user of the technology, the unfortunate Icarus. While it is Icarus alone who melts the wax on his wings by getting too close to the Sun, despite his father's warnings, it is also in a sense Daedalus, the technician, who is responsible for his son's death, having failed to anticipate the recklessness and drunkenness of young Icarus. As well as being the myth of the separation between the technician and the user of the product of technology, the myth of Icarus is also the myth of the detachment of technology from its objective purpose (its meaning). Daedalus only conceived of wings as a means of escaping from the labyrinth of the Minotaur, in which he and his son were held captive by King Minos. It was Icarus' inappropriate use of wings that condemned him. In the myth of Icarus, the technique,

---

[384] According to the famous myth, Zeus ordered Prometheus to be chained to a rock on Mount Caucasus. Every day, an eagle comes and devours his liver, which then grows back every night, perpetuating a cycle of eternal pain and suffering.

initially conceived as a means of freeing himself from the labyrinth, finds itself diverted from its original purpose in response to the reckless impulses of its user. This story illustrates the danger of technology being emancipated from any purpose, perceived as a purely autonomous and "innocent" activity, with responsibility resting solely with those who use it. In the same way, we should be wary of any theory of knowledge that dissociates the analytical moment from the intuitive (and imaginative) moment, because in both cases the question of meaning is evacuated. In the technical field, this loss of meaning is manifested in the absence of reflection on the purpose of technical production: what are its implications? How do they fit into the wider question of meaning? Do they simply change our environment, or do they also transform our relationship with the world? Do they really help to improve the condition of living beings? In the field of knowledge, this same loss of meaning occurs when cognitive activity becomes fragmented to the point of losing sight of its place in a global network of meanings, where intuition and analysis cannot be dissociated without altering our understanding of reality. So, in both cases, it is by refusing to question the purpose and integration of knowledge or technology within a wider framework that we condemn ourselves to indiscriminate and potentially destructive use.

By reducing thought to an organised system of formal processes — which is the underlying assumption of every monistic theory — we come to obliterate what underpins our humanity and our relationship with the world. This reduction, which assimilates thought to a set of mechanisable procedures, is precisely what we call the 'technicisation of thought'. It is based on the denial of the duality that is constitutive of things, and on the desire to extract things from the network of meanings to which they belong. Herein lies the real danger of dehumanisation, a trend that has run through the various branches of knowledge since the beginning of the nineteenth century and which, in many respects, structures the modern approach to technology. This dehumanisation (which we must be careful not to confuse with the very different concept of de-anthropomorphisation found in Max Planck) is originally based on an illusion of the scientific mind, which seeks to unify the diverse through a codified formal synthesis, while refusing to see the conditions and limits of this unification. It was the (thwarted) ambition of Hilbert's programme to make mathematics a unified, complete and coherent system. While in terms of practical ('mechanical') developments, Hilbert's ideas were undeniably fruitful (particularly through the later developments of Turing and Church, who steered humanity towards cybernetics and computer science), his theoretical programme failed. Hilbert's practical successes should not obscure the fact that his overall theoretical ambition not only failed, but also led to the demonstration of its impossibility (incompleteness theorems). Pushed to the limit of their logical consequences, formal systems always point to their heteronomy, i.e. their fundamental openness: the system (always) needs a master!

61.

IS MAN THE FOUNDATION OF KNOWLEDGE? — To ask whether man is the foundation of knowledge, i.e. whether he is, as Protagoras put it, "the measure of all things", is to ask a question that both contains a truism and introduces a problematic reduction; a truism, because since man is the one who thinks reality, it seems difficult to imagine that he is not the starting point of all knowledge; a reduction, because this formulation suggests that the problem of knowledge could be limited to man and his finiteness, thus obscuring the possibility of structuring principles independent of the knowing individual. We have shown that knowledge, while it finds its starting point in man's relationship to the world, in other words in his capacity to grasp things through sensitive intuition, to represent them in an abstract way through projective imagination or to grasp them through intellectual intuition, is not necessarily marked by the indelible stamp of sensibility and man's finitude, in other words by his material determination. As we have seen, this finitary conception of knowledge has led to support for the positions of integral materialism, the logical outcome of which is psychologism — which is itself nothing other than a systematised form of scepticism. By denying the possibility of attesting to the permanence of things, psychologism deprived us of the possibility of knowing and communicating the world. If the problems raised by psychologism were genuine epistemological questions, the answers to them came up against contradictions that had to do, in particular, with the tautological basis of the theory. The proof of the apriority of the rule over its concrete application (of which science has provided us with numerous examples), the problem of reference, which Putnam illustrated in his experience of the Twin Lands (see § 31 — *Against psychologism*), and the incompleteness theorems were all objections which, for us, led psychologistic positions to a theoretical impasse. It is certainly impossible for us to deny that man (or any rational sentient being) is at the foundation of all knowledge (we can only know the world through our experience of it), but if we do not make the assumption that knowledge goes beyond our experience of things, then we cannot break the tautological circle — which is in reality a regressive and contradictory spiral — of radical scepticism. It is precisely because the possible domain of knowledge goes beyond our experience of reality that the world, otherness and intersubjectivity are possible. Knowledge is, in this sense, the acceptance of otherness, the recognition that *there is something outside myself*, that I am not everything[385].

---

[385] Let us point out in passing, by way of difference, the "bulimia" of Heidegger's *Dasein*. In most of *Being and Time*, Heidegger describes a hegemonic Dasein: it does not undergo history, it is itself historical, it appropriates its own death and makes it an existential determination. In the same way, it is time, without which the world cannot exist. It even appropriates the existence of others in the realisation of *Gemeinschaft*. In this way, Dasein has an omnivorous disposition to appropriate everything. In a highly critical book entitled *On the Pseudo-Concreteness of Heidegger's Philosophy*, Günther Anders ends with the following sentence: "Nietzsche's words: 'If a God existed, how could I bear not to be God?' seem to be transformed into 'If history exists,

It is the very structure of this otherness that Gödel's theorems reflect. The incompleteness theorems are also theorems of limitation: on the one hand, the true exceeds the demonstrable (limitation of the scope of formalism induced by the first theorem: "there is no reason why 'truth' should not be a wider concept than 'knowledge'," Bertrand Russell rightly noted on this subject in 1940 in *An Inquiry Into Meaning And Truth*), on the other the demonstrability of the system's consistency can only be made outside the system (introduction of a form of limiting otherness). In short, Gödel's theorems attest to the fact that mathematics does indeed have a content, i.e. that, like language, it refers to something external to itself. In fact, we always need certain indefinite terms (in the system) and certain axioms, in other words unprovable assertions. These axioms only have a rational basis if their truth can be directly perceived (through the external meaning of the terms or through an intuition of the objects that fall under them) or if we accept these foundations on the

---

how could I bear not to be history? For Heidegger, *Dasein* is an almost self-sufficient *ipseity*. This illusion is based on the fact that Heidegger systematically recasts every characteristic of the world as an existential determination of *Dasein*. Thus, the world is historical because *Dasein* itself is historical, it is spatial because Dasein is spatial and, ultimately, the world owes its very existence to that of *Dasein*. Everything that grounds *Dasein*'s possibility of being-in-the-world becomes an existential determination.

basis of inductive arguments, i.e. through their effectiveness (the success of their applications) [386].

For us, then, man is the foundation of knowledge, not insofar as he could constitute a knowing absolute (which would lead us one step closer to total relativism) but rather because, through his sensitivity, he is the embodiment of openness, that is, of what we can call "signifying duality". It is precisely man's limitation (his incomplete, non-hegemonic nature) that makes knowledge possible. Indeed, it is only in duality, in the conscious confrontation between two heterogeneous realities, that we find the possibility of meaning (which is why we have taken the view that artificial intelligence can only become natural or authentic at the price of recognising this duality, which implies self-consciousness as an integral and separate sentient entity[387], an entity that must be preserved and protected from everything that threatens it). At the root of our understanding of the world, there is always a sensitive intuition (intuition as the articulation between the interior and the exterior). This intuition is both the foundation of our relationship with things and the

---

[386] On this subject, see Jacqueline Boniface, *Gödel : des théorèmes d'incomplétude à la théorie des concepts*, in *Sciences du vivant et phénoménologie de la vie, II. Problèmes logiques et logiques du vivant*, pp. 131-147, [Gödel: From the Incompleteness Theorems to the Theory of Concepts, in Life Sciences and Phenomenology of Life, II. Logical Problems and Logics of the Living] some of whose developments are repeated here.
[387] This awareness can be individual or extended, the essential thing being that it is differentiating (it contrasts an organic or organisational unity with a diversity that is heterogeneous and non-reducible).

medium through which we ensure that our knowledge is effective. Here we come back to Gödel's idea: truth is either directly perceived (by intuition, which is the vector of union between two limited realities) or ascertained by the successful application of our theoretical idea of truth (effectivity).

In an essay entitled *Is mathematics a syntax of language?* Gödel asserted against Carnap, whose positions he criticised: "to eliminate mathematical intuition or empirical induction by positing the mathematical axioms to be true by convention is not possible[388]." Gödel's proof of this statement was again based on his limitation theorems. A demonstration of the consistency of a system requires the addition of axioms of at least equal strength, and these new axioms can only be justified by a new demonstration of consistency, without which these axioms are subject to refutation. Gödel summed this up by saying that " if mathematical intuition is accepted as a source of knowledge, the existence of a content of mathematics evidently is admitted. If it is rejected, mathematics becomes open to disproof and for this reason has content.[389]" In Gödel's view, reducing mathematics to logic, and thus conceiving of its content as being exclusively logical in essence, inevitably led to a dead end. For him, mathematical content could be neither strictly logical nor purely syntactic; it was based on the

---

[388] Kurt Gödel, Op. cit., *Is Mathematics Syntax of Language?* written between 1953 and 1955, published in 1963

[389] Kurt Gödel, *Is Mathematics Syntax of Language?* II, 32, in Kurt Gödel Unpublished Philosophical Essays, Springe Basel AG, 1995, p. 182

existence of mathematical facts, which had to be clearly differentiated from empirical facts (in which respect he agreed with the thesis of critical idealism, the separation between the idea and the fact to which it was trying to be applied): "It can be shown", he writes, "that the reasoning which leads to the conclusion that no mathematical facts exist is nothing but a *petitio principii*, i.e. 'fact' from the beginning is identified with 'empirical fact', i.e. 'fact in the world of sense perception'[390]."

Turing, taking note of Gödel's contributions, had clearly separated formalisable mathematics from intuitive mathematics in his 1937 thesis. For Turing, a function was in fact calculable if, for each of its arguments, its value could be determined in a finite number of steps. For Turing, computability thus became synonymous with what was "achievable by a machine[391]". However, in the same work, Turing asserted (despite his recognition of the validity of Gödel's theorems) that mental procedures did not go beyond mechanical procedures (a hypothesis he was never able to prove, of course). By reducing the development of mathematics to a simple series of stages leading to increasingly complex formal systems, Turing was suggesting that the mind of the mathematician (and the human mind in general) could

---

[390] Ibid., § 35 (development of the idea in § 37), p. 184

[391] In fact, Gödel admits that calculability can be equated with the idea of a potential that can be realised by a machine: he writes in a note: "in my opinion, the terms 'formal system' or 'formalism' should only be used for this concept [...]. The characteristic property [of these formal systems] is that in them, and in principle, reasoning can be entirely replaced by mechanical rules".

be modelled by a machine, in other words reduced to finite processes. In so doing, he largely ignored the problem of intuition, regarding it as a sort of 'residual factor' that mathematics would eventually formalise or reduce to the point of making it negligible (we find a similar line of reasoning among neuroscientists, Stanislas Dehaene, who believes, for example, that neuroscience will eventually 'explain everything', including the residual problem of the emergence of consciousness — a problem which, far from being a marginal issue, is in fact for us the central problem of the philosophy of knowledge). In contrast to Turing and Church, Gödel's position was to recognise that the human mind goes formal modelling and, unlike a machine, is capable of genuine intuition. It was this intuitive capacity that, in his view, gave access to mathematical content, and more particularly to the content of non-finitary mathematics. For Gödel, understanding concepts and recognising the truth of axioms exceeded definitional and demonstrative (mechanistic) capacities. Without going back to Kantianism, Gödel revalued forms of justification that were not strictly logical (or logical formalism). Jacqueline Boniface, in her article *Gödel: des théorèmes d'incomplétude à la théorie des concepts (Gödel: From the Incompleteness Theorems to the Theory of Concepts)*, distinguishes four modes of justification in Gödel. The first is metamathematical justification, based on a semantic conception of truth. This is the case with the undecidable but true proposition used by Gödel in the proof of his incompleteness theorem: a proposition asserting its own non-provability is necessarily true since it cannot be proved within the system. The second mode is justification by external demonstration, which relies on a proof outside the system concerned. This is particularly the case for demonstrations of consistency, which require more powerful means than those available within the system itself. Here, the truth demonstrated (like the consistency of the system) is syntactic. The third mode is justification by consequences, based on the evaluation of the implications of a proposition. The continuum hypothesis is an example: according to Gödel, it must be considered false, unlike Cantor's conjecture, because it leads to consequences that are implausible in topology. This type of justification gives truth a pragmatic status, which remains only probable. Finally, justification by pure intuition, according to Gödel, provides access to an understanding of mathematical concepts, but its validity is ultimately based on a form of belief. In the different modes of justification given by Gödel, we always find the structure of the inside-outside duality[392] as well as the idea of a dynamic overcoming of logical formalism (this overcoming being the fundamental condition of the judgement of true and false).

As a systemic expression of duality, formalism can give the illusion of independence. Without a relationship with what is external to it (another formal system which itself will always be based on syntactic concepts that will require a theory of concepts, i.e. a new formalisation of our relationship to things), however, the formal system does not enter into its signifying

---

[392] Except possibly for the fourth mode of justification, but we could show that pure intuition presupposes sensibility; it is given by sensible intuition, which is the articulated pin between the interior and the exterior.

dimension: it expresses nothing other than itself and cannot reach the level of coherence and consistency. We therefore support the idea that man (or the sentient and rational being) constitutes the only possible foundation of know-ledge, not, as in Hans Albert's reformulation of Fries's trilemma[393], in the sense of introducing a rupture that would be the apodictic foundation of all knowledge, a rupture that would appeal to a principle of final justification such as evidence, experience or intuition, but in the sense that man's sensitive and rational character, together with his awareness of being an entity separate from the world, constitutes, strictly speaking, the only possibility of knowledge (knowledge as the "tuning" of our signifying systems to one another, as the dynamic organisation of our sensations and representations to one another, the only organisation capable of establishing a link between the external world and phenomenal constructions, while at the same time ensuring the systematised coherence of our understanding of phenomena in relation to one another). If, therefore, machines were one day to rise to an 'authentic' form of intelligence (an authenticity which, in our view, requires a unitary, and

---

[393] Hans Albert develops his criticisms and reformulations of Fries' trilemma in a book entitled *Traktat über kritische Vernunft* (*Treatise on critical reason*) published in 1968 (1975 for the French translation). In this book, Albert explores the limits of rationality and justification, drawing on the ideas of Karl Popper and proposing a critical approach to reason. It is in this context that he addresses Fries' trilemma, detailing the three possible outcomes of all reasoning (regression to infinity, logical circularity, and rupture) and categorising them as forms of dogma.

therefore limitative, awareness), this conscious rise would undoubtedly not be the result of a progressive refinement of their formalism (of their formal algorithms) but would, on the contrary, respond to a process of an 'emergent' type comparable to the process of emergence of consciousness in living organisms. In other words, access to consciousness would take place according to a process that would escape, at least in part, its creators (like Dr. Frankenstein's creature).

62.

AGAINST LOGICAL ATOMISM — In our view, the idea — supported in particular by Bertrand Russell in *The Principles of Mathematics* (1903) and by Ludwig Wittgenstein in The *Tractatus Logico-Philosophicus* (1921) — that the logical structures of language and thought can be analysed in terms of simple fundamental elements, is based on a reductive vision of thought that gives too great a place to formalism. Logical atomism, which maintains that any complex proposition can be analysed in terms of simple atomic propositions (in much the same way as the atom in physics once represented the simplest unitary element of matter), is based on the idea of a correspondence between an atomic proposition and an atomic fact in the real world (an elementary fact of reality), which could be defined by a syntactic convention. The atomistic vision, while preserving the distinction between the phenomenon and the material world, which in our view is necessary and unsurpassable, as well as the distinction between syntax and its object, nevertheless points paradoxically in the direction of logical reductionism. The idea that there are simple atoms of truths, reflected in formal systems, implies the possibility, for Russell, of thinking of reality as a set of data (essentially *sense data*, which Russell particularly emphasised in the 1910s and 1920s before modifying his views) that can be entirely formalised. Logical atomism therefore *ultimately* relates to the idea of the calculability and predictability of thought, which Russell defines as a process governed by fixed rules. In *The Analysis of Mind* (1921), Bertrand Russell adopted a behaviourist approach to the philosophy of mind, following on from his early atomist theses, in which mental states and processes had to be explained in terms of observable behaviour and causal relations (Russell did, in fact, gradually detach himself from behaviourist theses from the mid-1920s, and even more so from 1940 onwards with the publication of *An Inquiry Into Meaning And Truth*[394]). While logical atomism supported the idea that there is a relation of correspondence between a simple atomic proposition and an atomic fact, thus confirming a dual vision of the world which runs counter to Hilbertian

---

[394] In *An Inquiry into Meaning and Truth,* Russell writes: "The observer, when he seems to himself to be observing a stone, is really, if physics is to be believed, observing the effects of the stone upon himself. Thus, science seems to be at war with itself: when it most means to be objective, it finds itself plunged into subjectivity against its will. Naive realism leads to physics, and physics, if true, shows that naive realism is false. Therefore, naive realism, if true, is false; therefore, it is false., And therefore the behaviourist, when he thinks he is recording observations about the outer world, is really recording observations about what is happening in him.", London George Allen and Unwin Ltd. Fifth impression, 1956, p. 15

formalism (and which, in our view, comes very close to idealist positions), Russell was paradoxically led to adopt, In the 1920s, Russell would paradoxically be led to adopt positions similar to those adopted by Turing and Church on the reduction of all mental processes to formalisable rules, i.e. rules that can be calculated ('computable') or mechanised (theses that can be found in part in Von Neumann and most modern computer theorists). This similarity with some of the theses of the behaviourists (the first 'behaviourists', such as William James and John Broadus Watson) is, in our opinion, to be analysed and understood in the continuity of Russell's early developments on atomism which, by emphasising organised systems, led him to neglect the fundamental problem of their creation and to obscure the general problem of creativity. This static approach to formal systems (considering formal systems always as a constituted *whole* and not in the creative dimension of the mind that produced them) is explicitly criticised by Gödel in an article entitled *Some Remarks on the Undecidability Results*, in which he comments on Turing's 1937 thesis: "What Turing disregards completely", he writes, "is the fact that mind, in its use, is not static, but constantly developing, i.e., that we understand abstract terms more and more precisely as we go on using them, and that more and more abstract terms enter the sphere of our understanding[395]." In Gödel's view, Turing's computational reductionism (which is

---

[395] Gödel, K. *Some Remarks on the Undecidability Results*. In Kurt Gödel. Collected Works. Volume II: Publications 1938–1974; Feferman, S., Dawson, J., Kleene, S.C., Moore, G.H., Solovay, R.M., van Heijenoort, J., Eds.; Oxford University Press: Oxford, UK, 1972; pp. 305–307

clearly related to the ideas of early Russell and Carnap) underestimates the human mind's capacity for abstraction, i.e. its ability to integrate abstract concepts into interdependent networks of meaning and thus to create meaningful systems. In short, logical atomism (like computational reductionism, which is a logical-practical extension of it), in attempting to focus its attention on islands of meaning, struggles to link these islands to the overall system from which they derive their meaning (this concealment of the holistic dimension of language from the outset is also characteristic of the approach Carnap develops in *The Logical Structure of the World*, which comes close to Russell's early atomistic positions, particularly through the notions of "immediate sensory data" or "primitive data", which are supposed to form the basis of the logical structure of the world). Like mass, which, according to Mach's principle, is not an absolute given but is relative to its distribution in the universe, we could consider that the atoms of meaning cannot be analysed by isolating one part of the system, but must be understood in their relationship with the other "signifying masses". We can certainly envisage very simple systems in which a single word, say for example the word "dog", corresponds to a single concrete reality, i.e. our experience of the visual, auditory or olfactory sensation corresponding to the concept of "dog". However, even in this extremely simple system, which seems atomic and unitary, there will be an implied relationship, which is that of differentiation between the dog and the speaker. In any descriptive statement, I always really understand myself as a separate entity. When I refer to a dog (or even a human), I never just say "there is a dog", but also "I identify a dog", or "I observe what the perception of an object I identify as a dog produces in me". The subject (even if unthought of) is always assumed, the 'there is' is a logical fiction. In fact, when I say, "there is a dog", I'm not just making the word "dog" correspond to the concrete atomic reality "dog", I'm positing myself as an integral entity separate from the dog. The statement "there is a dog" is indeed, according to Russell's theory, an atomic statement insofar as it cannot be broken down into smaller propositions, but we cannot directly analyse this statement in terms of a correspondence between a statement and a fact (the statement "there is a dog" is true if, in reality, there is actually a dog in front of me). In fact, the statement "there is a dog" is not a simple statement of binomial nature (which would imply the possibility of a direct comparison between the statement and the fact) but already a complex statement involving the tripartite structure between the statement, the raw fact (if we use the terminology of atomism) and the speaker, i.e. the one who states and interprets the fact and who understands himself as separate from what he designates. In fact, the simplest statement is not atomic (a lexical atom can correspond to a non-lexical reality) but already systemic and global. If we analyse statements not as static, established structures, but as dynamic productions, we are led to recognise that descriptive statements induce and presuppose the "*I*". Formalism attempts precisely to reduce this *I*, to drown it in the formal system, but this attempt amounts to trying to jump over its shadow. In *The Logical Structure of the World* (1928), Rudolf Carnap's attempt, following on from Russell's early theses, to base knowledge not on simple entities and atomic facts, as in Russell's case, but on what he calls 'elementary experiences', logically leads him to adopt the same formalism that leads him to the negation of dualism. From the very first pages of *The Logical Structure of the World*, he declares that the general problem of the correspondence between a concept and its object is a useless quarrel: "We can actually go even further" Carnap writes, "and say that the concept and its object are the same thing. and state boldly that the object and its concept are one and the same. This identification does not amount to a reification of the concept, but, on the contrary, is a 'functionalization' of the object.[396]" If Carnap does not substantialise the concept, it is because he wants to avoid falling into the trap of realism, which would place him back in the old debate between realism and idealism that he intends to overcome. The functional status of the object thus directs Carnap towards a systemic formalism on which he bases his "logical construction". This logical construction, however, is clearly based on a solipsistic methodology (which assumes that the thesis of monistic formalism is accepted and verified): "Since the choice of an autopsychological basis amounts merely to an application of the form and method of solipsism, but not to an acknowledgment of its central thesis, we may describe our position as *methodological solipsism*[397]." If, for Carnap, solipsism is "methodological", it nevertheless indicates an order of precedence, precedence not of the subject, but of its statements and the system derived from them. In fact, Carnap's

---

[396] Rudolf Carnap, *The Logical Structure of the World*, Concept and Object, translated by Rolf A. George, University of California Press, Berkeley and Los Angeles, p. 10
[397] Ibid., p. 102

methodical solipsism should not be understood as radical subjectivism, but rather as the axiomatic foundation of logical formalism, as Carnap himself makes clear. In the third part of *The Logical Structure of the World*, entitled *The Formal Problems of the Construction System*, Carnap writes as follows: "The Given Does Not Have a Subject: The expressions 'autopsychological basis' and 'methodological solipsism' are not to be interpreted as if we wanted to separate, to begin with, the 'ipse', or the 'self', from the other subjects, or as if we wanted to single out one of the empirical subjects and declare it to be the epistemological subject. At the outset, we can speak neither of other[398]." In short, it is the formal systems that are posited by Carnap before the *ipseity* of the *I*. As soon as formal systems are established in this way (outside any problematic of the "subject"), logical construction becomes possible. For Carnap, the *I* is not primary; it is in fact a late logical constitution that Carnap seems to equate with the logical consciousness of the *self*. It is precisely this assimilation of the problematic of the *self* to the *logical conscientization of the self* that poses, in our opinion, a fundamental problem in Carnap's thesis. It is not because the logical construction of the *self* is late ("The existence of the *self* is not an originally given fact. […] The self does not belong to the expression of the basic experience at all, but is constructed only latter, essentially for the purpose of delineation against the 'others'; that is, only on a high constitution level, after the construction of the heteropsychological[399]." Carnap writes, for example), that the *self* does not pre-exist as

---

[398] Ibid., p. 103
[399] Ibid., p. 261

an evaluator unthought of in any statement it makes about the world. Carnap, by expelling the *self* from "the expression of the basic experience" thought he had got rid of the problem of the foundations of formal systems. However, it seems contradictory to us to make the self "the class of elementary experiences[400]" and then to consider that the self, not being consciously (or logically) constituted, would no longer intervene in the elaboration of formal systems and would only become a passive spectator. Thus, while Carnap notes that "the 'given' never exists in consciousness in the state of pure, unprocessed material, but always within more or less complex combinations and configurations[401]" and that he also points out that there is a "cognitive synthesis" and a "processing of the given to form and represent things", at the same time, he points out that this processing is most often done "without intention, or according to a conscious procedure[402]", which must no doubt lend credence to the idea that cognitive synthesis is a formalism (a mechanic). However, while we can subscribe to the idea that the mechanisms of cognitive synthesis and "data processing" may be subject to a certain formalism, the same cannot be said of the formation (and, to a certain extent, the use) of concepts. When a child (or primitive man) points at a dog and formally designates it with the word 'dog', we don't think it can be seriously argued that this designation is devoid of intentionality. If the synthetic

---

[400] Ibid., by making me a "class", it seems to us that Carnap too quickly evacuates the ontological question linked to this class.
[401] Ibid., p. 104
[402] Ibid.

mechanism is not intentional (although it would be a matter of substantiating this thesis, since the loss of intentionality of the synthetic mechanism itself could very well be due to habits of association), the same cannot be said of the conceptual designation, which cannot fail to have a subjective intentionality[403]. At the root of "elementary experiences" there is always something living: experience cannot take place in the absence of the living. This "subjective intentionality" (in the sense that it involves the "subject" or *at least* an *ipseity* that cannot logically be reduced to the formal system that derives from it) does not imply, however, that any statement is necessarily tainted by an indescribable subjectivity (on the contrary, we have shown how we can move from the subjective to the objective, particularly in the scientific approach), only that no coherent formalism can conceal the dual and dynamic origin of systems. Even if the general idea of dualism (and therefore, in a sense, of the correspondence or tuning of systems to what they are supposed to express) must, in our view, be retained, we believe that, in the continuity, for example, of the work of

---

[403] On this subject, see also Husserl's well-known work on intentionality as a fundamental characteristic of consciousness, which refers to its capacity to be directed towards something (all consciousness is always consciousness of something). Husserl also insists on the fundamental distinction, absent in Carnap, between the act of thinking, the way in which consciousness apprehends the object (the noesis), and the object as it is perceived or represented in the act of consciousness (the noeme, which is not the object in itself, but the object as it is experienced or intended by consciousness).

W.V.O. Quine (see in particular *The Two Dogmas of Empiricism*, 1951), that empirical confirmations of signifying systems do not apply to isolated individual statements, but to our knowledge system as a whole: our statements about the world are not verified individually, but as part of an interconnected network of beliefs and hypo-theses[404]. Thus, my conception of the word 'dog' (or my individual experience of the concept of dog, if we adopt a psychologist's perspective) will not be exactly the same if, for example, I am aware of the concept of 'cat' or if I know nothing about it. In one case, the word 'dog' will refer to an entity separate from me that goes 'woof woof'; in the other case, the word 'dog' will refer to a separate entity that goes 'woof woof' and doesn't like cats (which go 'meow meow'). As the system becomes more complex, the colouration and general meaning of words changes. The fact that meaning is, so to speak, "non-local" means that we need to revise the idea of "correspondence" truth (truth as the adequacy of discourse with facts) in favour of a more general conception of formal systems or a general theory of concepts (which has yet to be established, but which Gödel tried to tackle), the same fact can be expressed within different formal systems (or several different

---

[404] Rudolf Carnap probably had an intuition of this kind when he stated, in *The Logical Structure of the World*, commenting on Cassirer's work that "it is relation extensions which must initially be posited" (p. 122), but Carnap still analyses relations as fundamental entities without a subject, and not as an act that is precisely posited intentionally by the knowing subject.

axiomatic systems[405]) and, conversely, the same sign can have different meanings in heterogeneous systems (in heterogeneous languages, or even within the same language with meanings that are themselves heterogeneous[406] — in which case, as Bourdieu said at, understanding may well be a "special case", or even a borderline case of misunderstanding[407]). Carnap's

---

[405] By dint of clarifying their foundations and correcting each other, some apparently contradictory philosophies end up converging on the essentials (we have cited the example of absolute idealism and integral materialism, but there are many examples in the history of thought of seemingly opposing philosophies converging).

[406] In *Word and Object* (1960), Quine gives this example: " Different persons growing up in the same language are like different bushes trimmed and trained to take the shape of identical elephants. The anatomical details of twigs and branches will fulfil the elephantine form differently from bush to bush, but the overall outward results are alike.", Op. cit., new edition, the MIT Press, Cambridge, Massachusetts, 1960, 2013, Ch. 1, p.8. Individuals brought up in the same language have the ability to understand each other, even if the meaningful resonance of the words within them is not totally identical.

[407] Quine rightly points out that the same concept can have different definitions, which raises the question of its communicability, and therefore of understanding: "Picture two physicists discussing whether neutrinos have mass. Are they discussing the same objects? They agree that the physical theory which they initially share, the preneutrino theory, needs emendation in the light of an experimental result now confronting them. The one physicist is urging an emendation which involves positing a new category of particles, without mass. The other is urging an alternative

material thesis, according to which "the basic elements are experiences as unanalyzable units[408]", seems to us to be ill-founded insofar as (i) these experiences are essentially heterogeneous, which calls into question their fundamental character (how can we explain, according to Carnap's theory, that two fundamental experiences, for example, the perception of a patch of colour or a sound, if they are indivisible units, can be manifested logically, physically and psychologically in different ways from one individual to another, since the patch of colour and the sound can relate to a network of meanings that differ from one sentient being to another or from one context to another[409]?) and where (ii) the concept of isolated experiences is itself problematic, since the experience always relates to the existing structure of the *living* (of the one who lives), that is to say, to that of signification and dualism. In *The*

---

emendation which involves positing a new category of particles with mass. The fact that both physicists use the word 'neutrino' is not significant. To discern two phases here, the first an agreement as to what the objects are (viz. neutrinos) and the second a disagreement as to how they are (massless or massive), is absurd. " Ibid., p. 15.

[408] Rudolf Carnap, *The Logical Structure of the World*, p. 239

[409] For example, the perception of the colour red will be different if it is isolated or associated with other colours (taken from a network of colours that becomes meaningful). The same applies to the perception of the note "C" which, depending on the context, can be pleasant (in a harmony) or unpleasant (a false note in a melody). The colour red or the sound "C" may even elicit different physical reactions from one individual to another (everyone has their "favourite colour", although it's true that there are very few individuals who, for example, dislike the note "C" or prefer "F" to it).

Logical Structure of the World, Carnap explicitly argues in favour of monism, ignoring the problem of the original differentiation between the living and the lived, and reducing dualism to a simple difference between the two categories of objects he considers to be physical objects and psychic objects (which, as we know, can be equated with each other in the reductionist doctrine): Carnap writes: "Thus, in the final, analysis, in turns out that is an arbitrary reduction to two important, but not fundamentally preeminent object domain. As a thesis concerning the fundamental constitution of the world, it is certainly not tenable but has to give way to pluralism which recognizes in the world an unlimited number of aspects or substances[410]." By reducing the problem of dualism to the categorical distinction between the psychic and the physical (and not to the fundamental and logical dimension of the separation between speaker and utterance), Carnap obscures the whole problem of the foundation of meaning. While Carnap asserts that "objects are constituted from those that precede them, in the cognitive order[411]", he never considers the object as a construction of the *self* on the convenient grounds that, since the logical *self* is not constituted, it does not yet exist to construct the object. But this is a petition of principle: if we postulate that the *self* is not primary, we can only reach the opposite conclusion by being confronted, at the heart of his theory, with indescribable paradoxes. But it is precisely these paradoxes that Carnap ignores by referring the whole problem of identity to the logical construction of the *self*. On the contrary, we defend the idea that

---

[410] Ibid., p. 260
[411] Ibid.

pluralism (the plural categorical distinctions that Carnap proposes) is only possible on the condition that we admit a *radical* dualism that is at the origin of all dynamic processes. We therefore need to consider the idea of truth not just in terms of a static correspondence, but as the product of a dual dynamic process that includes the effort of synthesis that the subject makes in relation to the external world (assimilation and designation of the world) and the effort of analysis and synthesis that the subject makes within the formal systems that it develops. What we call 'truth' thus depends as much on the internal coherence of the formal systems (let's say the mechanical or 'analytical' part of the systems, which must not be tainted by mechanical errors of reasoning) as on the consistency of the re-presentations supported by these systems in relation to what we perceive (and construct) as the 'real' (the applicative or 'synthetic' part of the systems). We know that Quine, in *The Two Dogmas of Empiricism* (1951), denounces this distinction between synthetic and analytic on the grounds that, in his view, there is no clear, non-circular criterion that would allow us to distinguish analytic from synthetic propositions. This ambiguity and, shall we say, interconnection between analytic and synthetic propositions had been perceived by Kant, when he noted, for example, that pure intuition "is included in every stage of every demonstration of geometry". It is true that analytic propositions always rest on synthetic foundations, for the simple reason that analytic propositions require the use of language (of syntax) which is, and can only be, of synthetic origin (as we have seen, language is first and foremost the expression of otherness and therefore of duality, the understanding of the organised separate unity that we form against or alongside the world). It seems to us, however, that we need to maintain the distinction between the analytic and the synthetic, with analytic processes being defined as those that conform to pre-existing rules (in this sense, the analytic is akin to computability) and synthetic processes being those that bring two heterogeneous realities together in a meaningful way (a synthesis), either within the same system (through the development of a new rule or a new theorem, for example) or between a formal system and an 'external' physical reality. In this respect, the analytic is closer to the formal (i.e. 'static' systems, already formed, with existing rules that are, according to Turing's thesis, computable), while the synthetic is closer to intuition: sensitive intuition in the case of the practical application of a theory to reality, intellectual intuition in the case of meaningful projections that come from internal experience. In other words, the analytic is what "plays by the rules", while the synthetic is an extension of the rules, i.e. an increase in knowledge (this is why we can say that the analytic always derives from the synthetic, it is a kind of "fossilised synthesis"). There is, however, an ambiguity in this distinction: a sum of analytical judgements can produce synthetic propositions. Artificial intelligence systems, for example, can identify complex patterns by analysing large quantities of data. When trained on varied sets of data, they can make predictions or generate propositions that go beyond the initial data of their programming (which are not directly deduced from the rules or algorithms they obey). For example, an artificial intelligence model could analyse weather data and predict the weather for the week, which would be a synthetic judgement in a pragmatic (applicative) sense. Natural language processing models can also produce texts that contain new ideas or novel associations that we might consider "synthetic" in the sense that they could be understood as a progression of knowledge (the effort of synthesis as a dynamic overcoming movement — the predicate adds something to the subject that is not already contained in the subject). However, the dynamic of knowledge, the dynamic at work in synthetic judgements, can only be properly "dynamic" if it refers to a global network of meaning (and thus to the possibility of understanding "for us"). In the *Critique of Pure Reason*, Kant asserts that the proposition "5 + 7 = 12" is synthetic insofar as the predicate "12" is not contained in the subject "5 + 7". However, for this proposition to be truly synthetic, it is not enough, in our opinion, to posit that the synthesis "12" is not directly contained in the predicate "5 + 7": the subject must also perform a mental act that leads it to declare that 5 + 7 is equal to 12. This is why Kant, in the *Critique of Pure Reason*, speaks of synthetic judgements rather than synthetic propositions. It is the mental act that produces the synthesis, not the proposition itself, and we produce this synthesis each time (i) we produce this mental act and (ii) this mental act means *something* to us, that it relates to our system of understanding the world (for example, the fact that a child can count to 12 on his fingers). In short, we have a concrete image of what 5 + 7 is (two hands plus two fingers, for example), just as we have an abstract and approximate mental image of what 500 + 700 is. So it is the signifying act that is really synthetic, not the dead proposition "5 + 7 = 12" (which, by analytic extension, can generate an infinite number of logical propositions that are, in a way, analytic computations of originally synthetic acts). This is also what still separates human functioning from that of the "intelligent" machine. For a human being, five plus seven equals twelve, whereas for a machine, the proposition "5 + 7 = 12" is simply a meaningless writing game, derived from formal rules that the machine applies. As such, it is not authentically synthetic, since any act of synthesis requires a form of duality, i.e. an emerging ability to think for itself. Thus, when the machine predicts the weather or when it makes connections between ideas that are not directly derived from its algorithmic rules, it is not the propositions themselves that are synthetic, but the mental operations that we, sentient beings, perform to make them meaningful to us. Indeed, we could say that the judgement "5 + 7 = 12" is synthetic only insofar as it means something to us "every time". The mathematician (or any other sentient being in full possession of his abilities and over the age of seven[412]), when he performs these elementary operations, does not always invest them with a meaning other than purely formal (he does not count on his fingers). Most of the time, we perform these operations mechanically (and therefore non-synthetically), like machines. What we call "dynamism" (in other words, the drive towards knowledge, the concrete effort to synthesise) is not, therefore, the permanent work of our mind; it is merely characterised by the effort of the *ego* to make the world

---

[412] We set this age limit somewhat arbitrarily, considering that from around the age of seven (and even earlier), children stop performing simple operations on their fingers.

meaningful (comprehensible) by trying to increase the domain of the known.

In short, formalism, like atomism or logical empiricism, although based on different logics, raises the same contradictions and the same paradoxes: by concentrating on established (static) systems, they miss the central issue of creativity, and also that of synthetic dynamism which, as we have already pointed out, is of an aesthetic (intuitive) nature before being systemic. Thus, it is always man (or any sentient and rational being who might be endowed with the same cognitive and creative capacities) who is at the foundation of all formal and syntactic systems, man and not the 'atoms of truth' or formal systems that pre-exist him. Of course, any formal system, once it has been defined axiomatically, is subject to a network of constraints that make it internally coherent. The rules that derive from the axioms or hypotheses of the system then impose themselves on those who have perceived and formalised them, but it is always a relationship of synthesis that the system expresses, and this relationship is only possible (dynamically) if we accept a force of creation and recognition that is specific to man (or to any sensitive and rational creature capable of representing itself as an integrated organism which, although belonging to the world, conceives of itself as distinct from it). Man must therefore be understood in terms of his threefold creative dimension, i.e. firstly in terms of his ability to recognise and represent himself (to create himself, in short) as a separate organism, and secondly in terms of his ability to designate and name otherness (conventionally naming the objects he perceives within or outside himself), and finally, in its ability to develop organised systems that signify and are doubly interconnected, firstly with all the things they designate 'individually' (synthetic connections with the objects of reality) and secondly within them, in the linking of things together (synthetic connections within the system, made possible by the ability to generate meaning by levels[413]).

---

[413] On this subject, Russell, in *Signification and Truth* (1940), clearly emphasises the hierarchisation of languages, a hierarchisation that is essential to our understanding of language, and which makes it possible to resolve certain paradoxes (in particular self-reference paradoxes). On this subject, see Ch. 4 on Object-Language, in which Russell draws on Tarski's *The Concept of Truth in Formalised Languages*, published in 1936, in which Tarski defends the idea that the words "true" and "false", when applied to sentences in a given language, always require another higher-order language: "The conception of a hierarchy of languages," writes Russell, "is involved in the theory of types, which in some form, is necessary for the solutions of paradoxes; it plays an important part Carnap's work as well as in Tarski's. I suggested it in my introduction to Wittgenstein's *Tractatus*, as an escape from his theory that syntax can only be 'shown', not expressed in words. The arguments for the necessity of a hierarchy of languages are overwhelming, and I shall henceforth assume their validity ", Op. cit., p. 62

The Possibility of intersubjectivity

63.

WHAT IS INTERSUBJECTIVITY? — We have just mentioned the paradoxes raised by theories such as logical atomism and empirical atomism, which attempted to understand the entities and primitive relations that structure formal systems without questioning the fundamental relationship between these formalised systems and the sentient beings that give rise to them. In Russell's early writings, as in Carnap's theory, the attention paid to already constituted systems led to thinking of the world as an entanglement of systems and to understanding man as the result of these structured systems. In short, by attempting to provide a solid basis for knowledge, atomism led to an epistemology without a subject ("the given is without a subject", Carnap asserted), and therefore without an *episteme*. If, *zur Physikalischen Erkenntnis*, Max Planck spoke of scientific knowledge as a process of de-anthropomorphisation of reality, it is striking to observe that Carnap used the term "desubjectivation". As he wrote in *The Logical Structure of the World*: "One can easily see that physics is almost altogether desubjectivized, since almost all physical concepts have been transformed into purely structural concepts[414]." Contrary to Carnap's idea, subjectivity was not denied in the process of increasing knowledge, but only codified, criticised and made coherent with observation. So, in any scientific process, subjectivity is "tuned in" to the formal systems it creates and is

---

[414] Op. cit., p. 29

expressed in an objective language (a *logos*, which is the same for everyone). If we can regard science as a process of de-anthropomorphisation, it is not because objective knowledge is opposed to all forms of subjectivity, but because the codification and systematisation of subjective impressions enables these impressions to be objectively criticised, a criticism that can *ultimately* lead to common sense and first impressions being called into question. We cited earlier the example of the construction of the theory of heat (see § 57, *Objective subjectivity*): the very idea of heat arises first of all from a subjective impression (heat is first of all a sensible impression, like radiation and everything to do with energy in general) but can be objectified in the concept of temperature. If, in the name of the objectivity of scientific knowledge, we pretend to erase the subject from science, then the notion of intersubjectivity (that is, in short, of objective intersubjective communicability) will become problematic. How can we think of intersubjectivity without a subject, language without a speaker, and the class of relations without an *episteme*? The attempt to replace the heterogeneity of sensible impressions by the objectivity of relations based on fundamental sensible data, although it seems to correspond to the scientific approach — which aims to objectify and systematise subjective impressions — cannot be reduced to a simple substitution of sensible impressions by a codification supposed to be equivalent to them. In Carnap's philosophy, this equivalence is postulated but never demonstrated. The first stage of Carnap's logical construction consists in ejecting the subject from the question of knowledge, and the second stage consists in establishing that it is no longer there. Thus, for

Carnap, intersubjectivity is only possible on the condition of an *a posteriori* reconstruction: the other as another body and as another psyche only appears at "a higher level" of the logical construction of the subject (after "physical objects", according to the plan of *The Logical Structure of the World*). The other is not, therefore, a 'given'; it is (like the *self*, incidentally) a late construction. In fact, communication with the other can only take place at the cost of a twofold reduction: firstly, the reduction of experiences to fundamental unitary experiences (the problematic nature of which we have noted), and secondly the reductive formalisation of these fundamental experiences into communicable signs. With Carnap, intersubjectivity is achieved through the coordination of protocol statements (the formalised statements that describe perceptions). In this, Carnap is close to our theory, which consists of describing science as a process of objectification of subjectivity: we start with subjective experience to arrive at an objective formal language that allows us to systematise our sensitive impressions and make them coherent with each other. For Carnap, it is language, and even more so logical systems, that support objective knowledge. Scientific language (logic) serves to transcend subjective differences, providing a common basis for scientific communication. For Carnap, the use of this language makes it possible to translate individual experiences into a coherent intersubjective framework. However, it seems to us that Carnap forgets to close the loop that he himself opened: if language and, more generally still, any *logos* is an objective formalisation, its use must produce in us the subjective reaction that we call 'understanding'. Where we see a process of iterative adjustment between the subjectivity of our impressions and the objectivity of our *logos*, Carnap sees only a linear progression from subjectivity to objectivity. But in the physical sciences, as elsewhere, the theoretical formalisation of reality is not the end of the knowledge process. At the end of the loop of objective knowledge, there has to be experimental verification (it works, it is 'effective'), and this verification again involves the subjectivity of the observer. So, while intersubjectivity does indeed involve, in the case of scientific knowledge, an objectification (a formalisation) of subjective impressions, it is also an iterative (and progressive, i.e. not static) loop that points in the direction of the subject(s). However, we must bear in mind that knowledge cannot be reduced to formal knowledge or scientific (objective) knowledge. Communication is always partial and incomplete, and the formalisation of experiences has the limits we have already mentioned (understanding as a "borderline case" of communication).

64.

THE SUBSTRATUM OF REALITY AND THE INTELLIGIBILITY OF THE WORLD — Carnap, as we have seen, bases the possibility of intersubjectivity on the objectification of our fundamental experiences (which is what we subscribe to in the context of objective knowledge, although we would point out here that intersubjectivity is not limited to the communication of objective knowledge). However, by devoting his attention essentially to formal systems and systemic communication (which is one of the characteristics of the positivist method to which he adheres), Rudolf Carnap rejects the problem of duality, i.e. the question concerning the 'designation' of signs and the meaning of systems. In our opinion, this is the reason why his theory remains in the air and, so to speak, does not 'land on its feet'. Against Carnap, we maintain that intersubjectivity is made possible not only because we are able to divide up our sensible impressions unitarily, formalise them and insert them, as primitive entities, into a formal system that is the basis of our communication, but also because the world, the things we designate, have an existence of their own outside our own (see § 56 — *Should we abandon the principle of causality?*). This existence is just as fundamental a given as what Carnap calls 'fundamental experiences'. It is precisely this tripartition (I, others, the external world) that is lacking in Carnap's work. Communicability exists only because there is *something* to communicate, and this something cannot be merely a formalism without content. For Carnap, " the object and its concept are one and the same[415] ". How, then, can we initiate a communication that is not a pure game of the mind (without mind)? On the contrary, we maintain that intersubjectivity can only exist insofar as we have a common world, which we can express verbally (and systematised) or non-verbally. Intersubjectivity is only possible through the logical permanence of the explanatory structures of the world (structures produced by the subject in an objective way, as Carnap maintains) on condition that these explanatory structures are logically founded and express an external reference. Without this external reference, the methodological solipsism defended by Carnap is doomed to remain an ontological solipsism. This is one

---

[415] Op. cit., p. 10

of the lessons of the *Cogito* and Putnam's modern reformulation of it: not just the "I think, therefore I am" of the *Discourse on Method*, but perhaps above all the "I am, I exist" of the *Metaphysical Meditations*, that proposition that is necessarily true, according to Descartes, "whenever I utter it or conceive it in my mind[416]". In "I am, I exist", it is both my own existence and the recognition of the identity of the *self* as an autonomous and separate organisation that is logically and epistemologically posited: "I find here that thought is an attribute that belongs to me[417]" writes Descartes. For Descartes, it is not a question of reducing the *self* to "a thing that thinks" (Descartes goes on to specify that I am also a thing that feels, that heats up and that doubts), but rather of linking, as we have done, the problem of thought to that of *the* thinker, that is, to *the thing that thinks* and that we are (for Descartes, thought does not take place outside the *self* or in its absence). It is on the basis of the existence of the *self* that Descartes can posit the existence of the world, not by appealing to the ontological argument of the existence of God in the Fifth Meditation, as has often been written, but by noting that the multiple possible transformations of the piece of wax cannot be contained in my imagination before my experience of this reality: "Do I not imagine", writes Descartes, "that this wax, being round, is capable of becoming square, and of changing from square to triangular? No, of course not, since I conceive it capable of receiving an infinite number of similar changes, and yet I cannot go through this infinity by my imagination, and consequently this conception that I

---

[416] René Descartes, *Second Meditation*
[417] Ibid.

have of wax is not achieved by the faculty of imagining[418]." If the many possible forms of the piece of wax are not contained in my imagination, it is because, according to Descartes, it is my understanding that is confronted with the external reality of the piece of wax. There are therefore two essential moments in the Second Meditation: the first consists in establishing the existence of the *self*, the second in setting its limits (which has the consequence of establishing the existence of a reality external to the *self*). It is, in fact, through the limitation of the faculties of the imagination (the imagination cannot conceive or represent everything to the subject[419]) that the *self* attests to itself from a world that is external to it. The Cartesian *self*, in short, is not bulimic: it is aware of its own limitations, and therefore of the existence of the world. For Descartes, the ontological argument of the existence of God serves not so much to attest to the reality of the external world, but rather to assure me of its 'corporeal' nature. Thus, if my understanding is grasped (Descartes does not use the term intuition in the sense that Kant would later use it, for example), Descartes does not imagine that this could be by anything other than a physical, i.e. material, substratum,

---

[418] Ibid.

[419] For example, Descartes says that I can easily imagine a triangle, but not a chiliogone (a thousand-sided polygon). If I can represent a thousand-sided figure in a confused way, my imagination will not be able to distinguish it from a 900-sided figure. If I encounter this kind of figure in nature, it is because, as Descartes says, I am not imagining it, but my understanding is confronted with it as if it were something external.

because, he writes: "I do not see how [God] could be excused for deception, if in effect these ideas originated or were produced by causes other than by corporeal things[420]." So, the question here is not so much about the existence of an external reality (which Descartes established in the Second Meditation), but about the very different problem of the permanence of things, i.e. my capacity to know them.

To claim to settle the question of the homogeneity of the causal relationship between the phenomenon and its substrate would lead us to make metaphysical conjectures (the causal relationship between the phenomenon and its substrate being necessarily situated beyond or below what is possible for us to know, see in particular § 33 — *Are our representations independent of their substrate?*) We can only postulate the homogeneity of this relationship and consider it sufficiently corroborated to envisage it as a 'valid' working hypothesis (see in particular the arguments we give on this subject in § 13 — *Can we imagine a world without laws?* and especially in § 56 — *Should we abandon the principle of causality?* The main arguments are (i) the possibility of an anomic world, incoherent 'in itself' and which would not collapse in on itself, and (ii) the efficiency of the hypothesis of the permanence of things: We would spend a lot more energy modelling a world in which, for example, the Moon would only exist each time we looked at it and noticed its existence (iii) corroboration of reality: we lack a concrete counter-example to the inconsistency of the world). We must, however, separate the question of the 'derived'

---

[420] Ibid., *Sixth Meditation*

truth of formal systems (or mechanical truth, if you prefer), which is the central question of truth for the first Russell, for Carnap and then again (albeit from a different perspective) for Turing, Church and, in a sense, Von Neumann, from that of synthetic truth, i.e. the truth of our discourse on the world. The question of the homogeneity of the causal relationship between the phenomenon and its substrate (which is a properly meta-physical question, i.e. one that goes beyond the physical world as it appears to us and as we construct it) is not of the same 'nature' as that of formal systems. Formal systems, in other words, if they derive their axiomatic origin from our synthetic relationship to the world, have their own internal, binding logic. As such, they do not need empirical (synthetic) confirmation to attest to their internal truth: the truth derived from the theoretical sciences is already a truth. The question of the synthetic value of systems, on the other hand, is fundamentally linked to the question of the permanence and coherence of the world. If we cannot prove this permanence (although we questioned the possibility of the existence of an anomic world, i.e. one that is incoherent and inconsistent, in § 13, we could rigorously envisage, for example, that the rules, while continuing to exist and support the consistency of the world, change regularly), we can establish that his hypothesis (the hypothesis of the permanence of the causal link between the phenomenon and its substrate, but also of the homogeneity of this link between the phenomena) is at the origin of the possibility of knowing the world and communicating this knowledge by means of formal systems. While the internal truth of formal systems does not depend directly on the permanence of the causal link between the phenomenon and the material thing, the external truth of these same systems (the signifying, synthetic truth) does depend indirectly on it. When we theorise the world using formal systems, we postulate the permanence of this link, in the same way, in a sense, that we postulate the permanence of the validity of operations internal to formal systems (the proposition "5 + 7 = 12" is true even if my mind is not thinking that five plus seven equals twelve. We must not confuse here the synthetic meaning of the statement, which is an active synthesis of the mind each time the mind consciously performs the signifying act — like Descartes, moreover, who affirms the validity of the statement "I am, I exist" each time I conceive it in my mind — and the validity of a statement that can be postulated outside the moment when I think it. The machine will thus invariably return the result "12" to the operation "5 + 7", regardless of whether I'm there to check the result or not). This external validity, or 'fossilised validity' of the systems, presupposes that our *ego* is clearly separated from the world, in other words that we move away from the unsubstantiated hypothesis of solipsism (unsubstantiated either by 'reality' or by the systems of thought themselves, as we have tried to show throughout this book devoted to knowledge). We have seen that while we can show that solipsism is a logical contradiction, the permanence of the world and its rules outside *me* (i.e. outside the moment when I think them or conceive them) is for us an effective hypothesis insofar as it finds numerous empirical confirmations (nobody has been able, for example, How can we theorise and understand a world in which the Moon would disappear in our absence, or in which the operation '5 + 7 = 12' would cease to be correct if no one were there to count on their fingers? How can we also understand the permanence of the world without the permanence of the rules that support it?). Perhaps, moreover, there is a certain narcissism of the *ego* in making the hypothesis that nothing concrete can happen outside it. Throughout our demonstration, we have made the opposite hypothesis: the *self* is not alone, it is immediately surrounded by a world made up of similar beings (alter egos, others than myself who are also other *selves*). He defines himself in his partition with reality (reality is not entirely contained within him), this partition manifesting itself in the understanding of a double exteriority, exteriority, first of all, of the world that is not the *self*, exteriority also of the rules of my mind that are also the rules of the external world (my mind also being, albeit in a different way, the external world, made up of the same matter as the world and yet, as we have shown, non-reducible to that matter). This is undoubtedly the main difficulty of any theory of knowledge: understanding that the world and its rules are external to me and that, at the same time, I myself have the capacity to grasp and understand them within my own interiority (which is both internal and external to me, the *self* grasping itself as *me* also being obliged, at the same time, to observe itself as *me*, i.e. to come out of itself, to divide itself in two in order to observe and understand itself as *me*, as we shall see later: the *self* is at once, rather like time, a primitive experience, an abstract idea and an empirical synthesis). It is only on the condition of admitting this double exteriority (since it arises both from a logical construction and from the everyday experience of the *self* and the world) that we can found a coherent doctrine of intersubjectivity. Intersubjectivity presupposes recognition by the subject of other subjectivities, but also the identification of a *space* between subjectivities (inter-), a common space which is that of the external world, which, although we undoubtedly receive it differently (in the manner specific to our modes of perception, our culture, our personal history, the natural disposition of our senses), is always given to us (until there is proof, so far unproven, to the contrary) in a similar manner. The fact that things may be perceived and expressed differently according to species, individuals or cultures is therefore not an argument against the reality of the world and against the idea that this world is given to everyone in the same way. It is precisely on this condition (the condition of the objectivity of the world, assumed on a methodological basis and corroborated logically and experimentally) that intersubjectivity, i.e. the translation of our impressions and judgements about the world, is possible (translation as formalisation in language, but also as transposition from one language to another).

65.

OPERATIVE LANGUAGE — Up to now, as part of our general problematic on knowledge, we have been mainly interested in the descriptive dimension of language. Our aim has been to examine monistic theories of knowledge (integral materialism, absolute idealism, physicalism, reductionism, psychologism, etc.), to point out their paradoxes and to show their contradictions (contradictions which we have shown to be insoluble within monistic or reductionist systems). Our approach to language then consisted in showing how our innate logical structures could provide proof of the duality of the world, a duality that we did not envisage through the prism of the great classical oppositions between body and soul, sensible and intelligible, material and divine, but rather as a complementarity between raw matter and its legality (its rule) that we are trying to express through the structures of language (and more generally through all the systems based on the designation and symbolisation of external objects). This approach naturally directed us towards the descriptive aspects of language, our problem then being to identify the conditions under which a discourse on reality could claim to be "true". This led us, on the one hand, to consider only part of the problem of description (for us, the problem related to the description of real or legal objects) and, on the other hand, to largely neglect the other dimensions of language (performative, expressive, imperative, commissive, declarative language, etc.). However, as part of our reflection on intersubjectivity, we feel it would be appropriate to focus on what the British philosopher John Langshaw Austin has called the 'performativity' of language. In *How to do Things with Words* (1962), Austin distinguishes three types of speech act: (i) locutionary acts which concern the simple act of producing sounds, words and sentences by following grammatical rules (what we have called the internal formalism of the system), these locutionary acts include the phonetic act, the phatic act (organisation of sounds into words and phrases) and the rhetorical act (use of words and phrases in a given sense), (ii) the illocutionary acts, which concern the intention behind the utterance, what we are doing when we say something (promising, ordering, questioning, declaring, etc.), the illocutionary forces at work in the utterance, (iii) the illocutionary acts, which concern the intention behind the utterance, what we are doing when we say something (promising, ordering, questioning, declaring, etc.).); illocutionary forces give a performative dimension to the utterance ("I promise to come", for example, is not just a sentence, but an act of promise); and (iii) perlocutionary acts, which concern the effects produced by the utterance on the listener (convincing, persuading, frightening, etc.): saying "watch out for the dog" can have the effect of frightening someone or making them move away (see § 21 — *The active idea: Morality as a possibility*). For Austin, unlike descriptive or constative statements (which describe a state of affairs that may or may not be true), performative statements are neither true nor false, but succeed or fail. For a performative speech act to succeed, certain conditions must be met. First, the context must be appropriate to the act. For example, for 'I now pronounce you man and wife' to be valid, it must be uttered by an authorised person and in the context of a marriage ceremony. Secondly, Austin explains, the intention must be sincere (see § 40 — *What does it mean to think?* Notably our passage on the intentionality of the liar in the resolution of the liar's paradox): a promise, for example, must be made with the intention of keeping it. Finally, the success of a performative speech act depends on adherence to pre-established norms: there must be conventions that determine how the act is to be performed. Over the course of the twelve lectures (given at Harvard in 1955) that make up his text *How to do Things with Words*, Austin gives increasing importance to performative utterances, arguing in particular that almost any utterance can have a performative dimension, and that the importance lies in the illocutionary act performed by the utterance (the proposition "it's cold here" can mean "it's cold here"), as we pointed out earlier in our presentation, "I want you to close the window", while the apparently totally descriptive proposition "the roses are red" can be interpreted as an illocutionary intention to confirm, clarify or teach the listener something). By pointing out the importance of intention, context and the conventions of language, Austin shows the reductive aspect of the behaviourist approach to language. Language is not a game of back and forth between external *stimuli* and observable responses; on the contrary, it must be understood as a complex and intentional means of carrying out acts in a social (or intersubjective) context. In the absence of the other, language loses all its substance, the aim of language being to express thought for the other within me (who is also me) and for the other outside me (who is another *me*). The theory of speech acts shows that utterances are not just "observable behaviours", but actions with specific meanings in particular contexts. To understand language, we need to consider what speakers *do* when they speak, and not just the words they use or the reactions they provoke. The problem of intentionality (i.e. the speaker's action) is only accessible, however, if we accept the possibility of the existence of an acting being (which behaviourism vigorously rejects, as behaviourist theory is based on the idea that language speaks for us, that people *are spoken* rather than they speak). By emphasising the role of intention in language, John L. Austin is simply reaffirming the fundamentally tripartite structure of language: the speaker (acting), the object of language (real or non-real objects) and the interlocutor (the person or persons for whom the utterance is intended). For Austin, as for Chomsky (whom Austin met in the 1950s at the Aristotelian Society), the speaker must always be understood as an active (intentional) subject and not as the passive result of logical structures that determine him materially. It is only by understanding this intrinsic duality of language that we can resolve questions relating to the deep syntactic structures of language (the underlying structure of sentences, independent of surface form, which Chomsky showed to be part of what he called generative capacity[421]). Language must be analysed not just as a formal system, but as a human creation. It is only on this condition that we can escape the contradictions of behaviourism and understand performative utterances in their signifying dimension (utterances that also echo the internal network of meanings of the individuals who receive them). In fact, as we pointed out earlier, statements should not only be understood in their 'fossilised', i.e. purely formal, dimension, but first and foremost in their dynamic, i.e. intentional and signifying, aspect. From the speaker's point of view, then, the statement "there is a dog" already means, as we pointed out earlier, "I, an entity separate from the dog, identify there an object that I call a dog" (tripartite structure of the affirmation, i — the enunciator, ii — me, iii — the dog), but also, as Austin points out, "I commit myself in all sincerity (or not) to saying that I see there, in front of me, a dog". So, when I say "there's a dog", I'm already implicitly inviting my interlocutor (or myself, if I'm alone) to react to this statement (for example, to reply "he looks mean, let's go away" — an illocutionary act of request, or else

---

[421] See, for example, Noam Chomsky, *Syntaxic Structures*, 1957

"no, it's not a dog, it's a cat"). It is only by integrating this problem of intentionality into language (which brings with it the problem of signification and levels of signification) that we can resolve paradoxes of the structure of the liar, for example. In short, intersubjectivity is the profound and presupposed structure of every speech act. On the contrary, it is a fundamental disposition of language, which must first be understood in terms of its objective of communication, of relating to the other in the world we share. In this sense, language is not just a formal instrument for describing the world; it is also, and above all, a tool for acting on the world.

BOOK I – WHAT DO WE MEAN BY KNOWLEDGE

WHY MATERIALISM IS A LOGICAL DEAD END	**31**
THE IMPASSES OF REDUCTIONIST PHYSICALISM AND NEO-DARWINISM	31
WHAT IS DARWINISM?	31
IS PHYSICALIST MONISM LOGICALLY TENABLE?	34
MATERIALISM IS BASED ON A PETITION OF PRINCIPLES	44
PHYSICALIST TAUTOLOGIES	44
"MY BRAIN SAID THAT"	46
THE QUESTION OF THE EMERGENCE OF CONSCIOUSNESS	47
HOW DOES MATTER THINK?	47
AN INTELLECTUALLY FERTILISED UNIVERSE? **ERREUR ! SIGNET NON DEFINI.**	
THE PROBLEM OF THE EMERGENCE OF CONSCIOUS-NESS WITHIN THE FRAMEWORK OF A MONISTIC EPISTEMOLOGY	58
THE SCHEMATIC DUALITY OF THE WORLD: THE SEPARATE WORLD	**60**
WHAT IS DUALISM? THE STORY OF A MISUNDERSTANDING	60
DUALISM FROM A NEUROSCIENTIFIC POINT OF VIEW	60
CONFUSION BETWEEN INFORMATION AND ITS MEDIUM	61
DEGREES OF EMERGENCE – DEGREES OF FREEDOM – MORALITY	62
THE MACHINE AS A CONCRETE FIGURE OF DUALISM	62
CAN WE IMAGINE A WORLD WITHOUT LAWS?	65
WHAT IS AN ORGANISM?	85
THE DUALISMS OF LANGUAGE	86
RADICAL DUALISM IN MATHEMATICS	88
THE STATUS OF FORMAL COHERENCE	90
WHAT IS FREEDOM?	92
DEGREES OF FREEDOM	98
THE IDEA AS NON-MATTER ACTING ON MATTER	104
THE ACTIVE IDEA: MORALITY AS A POSSIBILITY	119
THE IDEA OF MAN AS THE FOUNDATION OF MORAL-ITY	130

THE FORM, THE THING, THE PHENOMENON, THE CONCEPT	**135**
WHAT IS A THING?	135
IS THERE ANYTHING 'IN ITSELF'?	135
THE PRODUCTION OF FORMS	140
WHAT IS A PHENOMENON?	146
PATHOLOGICAL SITUATIONS	160
WHAT ARE CONCEPTS?	163
THE STRAITJACKET OF THE CONCEPT, THE STRAIT-JACKET OF FORM	165
FREEDOM AS THE CREATION OF NEW FORMS	165
WHAT IS INTUITION?	167
AGAINST PSYCHOLOGISM	178
THE AUTONOMY OF LANGUAGE	194
OUR REPRESENTATIONS INDEPENDENT OF THEIR SUBSTRATUM?	200
WHAT DOES IT MEAN TO THINK?	**208**
FORMALISM VS. INTUITIONISM	208
INTUITIONISM AS A RESPONSE TO THE LOGICAL APORIAS OF FORMALISM	208
DIALECTIC BETWEEN INTUITION AND FORMALISM	237
EFFECTIVENESS OF MATHEMATICS	239
IS TRUTH A VALUE?	245
THE AESTHETIC MOMENT OF KNOWLEDGE	249
EUREKA!	249
TO WHAT EXTENT CAN INTELLIGENCE BE MECHA-NISED?	260
THOUGHT AS CIRCULATION BETWEEN LEVELS OF MEANING	290
WHAT DOES IT MEAN TO THINK?	290
WHO THINKS? THE PROBLEM OF IDENTITY AND SELF-REFERENCE	302
WHAT IS COMPREHENSION?	311
THOUGHT AND REFLECTION: THOUGHT AND ITS MIRROR	323
LEVELS OF UNDERSTANDING AND LEVELS OF MEANING	331
OVERCOMING THE SUBJECTIVE MOMENT	**336**
THE SHAPE OF THEORIES	336
WHAT IS A THEORY? THEIR INTUITIVE ORIGINS	336
ARE THEORIES FORMS OF FORMS?	349
MOVING BEYOND THE INDUCTIVIST VIEW	354
AGAINST THE STATISTICAL MODEL	365
AGAINST THE PROBABILISTIC INTERPRETATION OF QUANTUM MECHANICS	371
THE AGE OF TECHNOLOGY OR THE RETURN OF MAGICAL THINKING	383

CAN WE THINK WITHOUT A PATTERN?	391
THE PROBLEM OF METHOD	391
PARADIGMS WITHOUT A CONCEPTUAL FRAMEWORK?	408
SHOULD WE ABANDON CRITICAL IDEALISM?	418
THE PROBLEM OF SPACE	430
THE PROBLEM OF TIME	455
SHOULD WE ABANDON THE PRINCIPLE OF CAUSALITY?	480
SUBJECTIVE AND OBJECTIVE	504
OBJECTIVE SUBJECTIVITY	504
THE OBJECTIVE CONSTANCY OF RELATIONSHIPS	514
RECONCILING THE WORLD: TRUTH IS A HUMANISM	**516**
WHAT DOES SCIENCE MEAN	516
SCIENCE AND MEANING	516
TECHNIQUE AND MEANING	520
IS MAN THE FOUNDATION OF KNOWLEDGE?	528
AGAINST LOGICAL ATOMISM	537
THE POSSIBILITY OF INTERSUBJECTIVITY	556
WHAT IS INTERSUBJECTIVITY?	556
THE SUBSTRATUM OF REALITY - THE INTELLIGIBILITY OF THE WORLD	559
OPERATIVE LANGUAGE	567

© 2025 Geoffroy de Clisson
Édition : BoD · Books on Demand,
31 avenue Saint-Rémy,
57600 Forbach
bod@bod.fr
Impression : Libri Plureos GmbH
Friedensallee 273
22763 Hamburg (Allemagne)
Impression à la demande
ISBN: 978-2-3225-7168-0
Dépôt légal : Avril 2025